Advance Praise for

The Future that Brought Her Here

"The sensual-mystic poet Deborah DeNicola has given us a lovely, thoughtful memoir of her long extraordinary, painful and enlightening journey. She begins in Jung and ends in a deeper understanding of herself and of life, along the way floating us downstream through the ages of esoteric understanding, to arrive finally in the vast ocean of collective realization. This is an important book for our time, embodying in one brave woman's course in life, our culture's story of the past thirty years, as we, like DeNicola, stand on the verge of the New Paradigm."

—THOMAS KAPLAN-MAXFIELD,
AUTHOR OF *MEMOIRS OF A SHAPE-SHIFTER*

"A magical and mysterious memoir, *The Future that Brought Her Here* explores the emerging archetype of Mary Magdalene as an image of the desperation and hope for spiritual regeneration we all feel in politically and spiritually uncertain times. In an era of academic dryness and almost illiterate new age enthusiasm, DeNicola is that rarest of writers, a true visionary, whose lucid prose both startles and informs, frequently bursting into the lyrical intensity of finely crafted poems. Her words are as sensuous and soothing to the inner eye and ear as the ideas she presents are titillating to the spirit."

—KURT LELAND,
AUTHOR OF *THE MULTIDIM!*
ASTRAL PROJECTION AS A SP!

D1472512

THE **FUTURE** THAT
BROUGHT HER HERE

A MEMOIR OF A CALL TO AWAKEN

❧ ❧

DEBORAH DeNICOLA

IBIS PRESS
Lake Worth, FL

16.95

for Deborah Rose

Published in 2009 by
IBIS PRESS
an imprint of Nicolas-Hays, Inc.
P. O. Box 540206 • Lake Worth, FL 33454-0206
www.nicolashays.com
Distributed to the trade by Red Wheel/Weiser, LLC
65 Parker St., Unit 7 • Newburyport, MA 01950-4600
www.redwheelweiser.com

Library of Congress Cataloging-in-Publication Data
DeNicola, Deborah, 1947-
The future that brought her here : a memoir of a call to awaken / Deborah DeNicola.
p. cm.
Includes bibliographical references.
ISBN 978-0-89254-148-5 (alk. paper)
1. DeNicola, Deborah, 1947- 2. Spiritual biography.
3. Parapsychology--Biography. I. Title.
BF1997.D46A3 2009
299'.93--dc22
[B]   2009018600
VG
Cover and text design by Kathryn Sky-Peck

Cover art by Nicholas Roerich: "Mother of the World," 1930s
Tempera on canvas mounted on cardboard. 98 x 65.5 cm.
Nicholas Roerich Museum, New York. Used by permission.

Printed in the United States of America
12 11 10 09 08 07 06
7 6 5 4 3 2 1

CONTENTS

ACKNOWLEDGMENTS

There are many people I wish to thank for their support. Yvonne Paglia for her encouragement and talent, my first reader, Camilla Jenkins for her editing and careful reading of an earlier version. Robert Bosnak for his teaching and mentorship or my dream work. Kathryn Sky-Peck for her editorial advice, enthusiasm and patience. Gerry Bowman for channeling John. The Rosemont women, Jeanette Clonan, Barbara Connolly, Camilla Jenkins, Kathy Trainor, Ludi Papas, Betsy Kenedy and Michele Massaglia for their long lasting friendship and financial support. Paula Connors for her financial support. Barbara Helfgott Hyett for her advice on some of my poems, Kurt Leland for his close reading of "The World's Veil," The National Endowment of the Arts, which awarded me a poetry fellowship for excerpts from "The World's Veil." All my poetry publishers, a special thank you to my mother for the roof over my head, and my sister Deena for her emotional support and encouragement.

298

Alone, I cannot be—
For Hosts—do visit me—
Recordless Company—
Who baffle Key—
They have no Robes, nor Names—
No Almanacs—nor Climes—
But general Homes
Like Gnomes—
Their Coming, may be known
By Couriers within—
Their going—is not—
For they've never gone—

EMILY DICKINSON

INTRODUCTION

This is a story of a depressed skeptic's spiritual awakening. As a poet, I have always nurtured an inner life. I was raised and educated a Catholic and had an innate belief in numinous events, although I had little proof that they occurred in the modern world of 20th-century American life. Most of my life, unconsciously, I searched for a deeper meaning behind what appeared to be the random events of the world.

I cherished the stories of saints and miracles. My favorite was always the story of three children in Fatima, Portugal who saw an apparition of Mother Mary in a grotto in 1917. For several months, Mary appeared on the 13th day and told the children that the world needed more prayers, warning of more wars. I wrote a poem in the voice of the eldest child, twelve-year-old Lucia, whose own mother did not believe her. This always struck me as tragic—that one could witness a "miracle" and be called a liar. Perhaps that is the reason I've taken many years to write this book. Although communities of spirituality and miraculous healing have grown throughout the world, in 2007, the intellectual cynics and non-believers of the secular world continue to dominate politics, allowing business-as-usual to create and perpetuate inequities in the global population.

In mid-life, I suffered a broken heart. Out of desperation, I began consciously seeking "wholeness." My quest began with Jungian psychotherapy and archetypal dreams. As I wavered on the verge of dysfunction and longed for emotional relief from hopelessness and an agitated depression, I began to ask for help from invisible forces. And in spite of the news media and the despairing attitude of many that the world is barely holding on to a functional reality, I became sentiently aware of the evolutionary process our planet is undergoing. For forty-seven years, I had experienced the world, like most, through my five senses. Quite unexpectedly, however, I developed clair-sentience and an aspect of clairvoyance. I found that I, like many other people on this planet at this time in history, could gradually see and feel other dimensions.

I had been practicing transcendental meditation for over twenty-one years when unexpectedly, through my "third eye" (the "anja" chakra in Indian tradition), I began to see into alternative worlds, where figures I call "spirits" and what appear to be angels made physical contact with me. I had also become interested in the tales of Mary Magdalen as a result of my study of *The Nag Hammadi Library*, the hidden third-century Gnostic gospels found buried in a jar in Egypt in 1945. These experiences took many forms and this book is an account of the development of my visions and awakening consciousness. I will also tell you of newer experiences I went through during three meaningful and rewarding journeys—to Israel in 1997, to Colorado in 1998, and to France in 2000.

This last voyage, taken with five other women, was led by Deborah Rose, an acupuncturist from Somerville, Massachusetts, who had been researching and following the Black Madonna legends for two decades. In the winter of 2000, I had a call from my friend Joanie Sullivan, who had been in a dream group I facilitated a few years before. Joanie called to tell me her acupuncturist was putting together a small group of women to travel through France to view and meditate with some of France's 200 Black Madonnas. Joanie also mentioned that Deborah's intention was to experience the journey as a pilgrimage to regain a lost feminine heritage. Through my own independent study, I had been making connections between the heretical legends of Mary Magdalen and the mystery of the Black Madonna. At the time, I knew of only one Black Madonna, Our Lady of Czestochowa, whose poster-size framed image hung in my Polish grandmother's farmhouse until she died in the mid Sixties. My mother inherited the image and has had it hanging over her bed for thirty years.

As soon as I hung up with Joanie, I remembered a dream I had worked on in 1988 in a dream group with my mentor, Robert Bosnak. We met weekly in a small room above the barn next to his house in Sudbury, Massachusetts. During this period of my life, I was recovering from the loss of my lover. My dream placed me in an underground tunnel with mud walls. As the group moved me imaginatively, taking the dream further, someone suggested I examine the walls of the passage. I began to see the outline of a woman covered in mud. With our eyes closed, the group followed me deeper into the cave. The feeling was overwhelmingly claustrophobic, but I crept along the mud floor until I knew instinctively a spot in the wall where I must begin digging. To my surprise—for this was long before my interest in the Black Madonnas—my active imagination uncovered a black African woman, very proud and strong. She was an object, yet she felt alive. Though she seemed thoroughly *other*, my emotional attachment to her was immediate. I remember ending the session with the statement that I knew she had been walled in for a very, very long time.

At that time, I had been teaching a short story from the turn of the century—"The Yellow Wallpaper" by Margaret Perkins Gilman, a "found" feminist, or feminist before her time. She was a writer who suffered a breakdown as part of a post-partum depression. A Freudian doctor prescribed bedrest and inactivity, but, like the woman in her short story, she kept a diary despite the prescription to quiet her mind. In the story, the woman furtively writes an account of her breakdown and how she was subsequently silenced by her physician husband. Slowly, by staring at the ugly wallpaper of the room where she is isolated, she begins to see a woman trapped beneath the pattern. By the end of the story, the woman has gone mad, crawling and ripping the wallpaper off to free the woman inside.

While I hadn't had a breakdown, I did suffer a post-partum depression in the early years of my marriage. As for the dream, the only association I could identify was to that short story. Yet I couldn't understand why, in my unconscious imagination, the woman was black. Now, all these years later, I can finally put this dream into a larger context. Despite the fact that it came years before I developed an interest in Mary Magdalen and the heresies of the 12th and 13th centuries in France, I know that it presaged my fascination with the mysteries of the Black Madonnas.

I've discovered over the years that there is no "time" in the unconscious. I have had a number of dreams and experiences whose significance only revealed itself later beyond any possibilities of my conscious knowledge. You could say these dreams were prescient, and that my inner Black Madonna was unearthed and would transform through the alchemical process of dream work.

My personal memoir of France is but one piece in a longer spiritual journey—one that I will especially treasure, however, because of my friendship with Deborah Rose, who passed on from breast cancer six years after our trip. I will always remember her as a vibrant being and a beautiful guide who stimulated me to make more effort to live in harmony with a conscious universe and the multidimensional aspects of myself.

This book is a personal account of my literal travels, as well as travels through dreams, synchronicities, and visions that connected me to a larger view of my own particular soul and its speculative parallel and past lives. I have seen, and I am still seeing, various images through my third eye during my regular twenty-minute meditations. These visions became clearer and more focused after I took a workshop in psychologist Stanislav Grof's holotropic breath work, which uses music and specific breathing techniques to reach an altered state of consciousness similar to that induced by taking the drug LSD. Because the visions are integral to my story, I begin with my initial conscious awareness of invisible presences. Although I was not previously interested in paranormal phenomena, my studies of the 13th-century Sufi poet, Rumi, awakened my awareness of their power. Many years of archetypal dream work and Jungian therapy contributed to and deepened my changing beliefs about the unconscious mind and the spiritual world.

Then I discovered Gnosticism, a loose blend of early Christian and Jewish sects that includes influences from Neoplatonism and ancient mystery schools. Gnosticism proposed beliefs in direct conflict with both religious and secular life as we know it on this planet, its most revolutionary implication being that human beings themselves are part of the Godhead that creates our reality.

The Gnostic texts were condemned as heresy by churchmen struggling to establish an institutionalized dogma.[1] The Dead Sea Scrolls, discovered only two years later, have some affinity with the Gnostic texts. They too tell mythological tales of apocryphal war between powers of darkness and light. They have been associated with the Essene Jews, whose community was wiped out by the Romans in the great raid of 70 A.D., an event that Christ foresaw; his vision is recorded in the traditional gospels.

One basic tenet of all these belief systems is that our world is a perfect world of light, corrupted only by ignorance and darkness. This is the equivalent of a belief in sin and evil. The authors of these texts believed that, by transcending humanity's misinterpretation of the world, the original unfallen state of creation could be restored. The Essenes and both Jewish and Christian Gnostics found that they could only practice their beliefs by withdrawing from the secular world. In his introduction to *The Nag Hammadi Library*, James Robinson surmises,

---

1. James Robinson, The *Nag Hammadi Library* (San Francisco: HarperCollins, 1981), p. 2.

Thus Gnosticism seems not to have been in its essence just an alternate form of Christianity. Rather it was a radical trend of release from the dominion of evil or of inner transcendence that swept through late antiquity and emerged within Christianity, Judaism, Neoplatonism, the mystery religions, and the like.[2]

These same beliefs have withstood the test of time, and have arisen again periodically throughout history. They exemplify truths alluded to by both ancient and modern mystic poets, and they are found in a wide range of traditions as far back as the Egyptian mystery schools. You could even say they have led to what we now call the "New Age," an often misunderstood term that denotes, ironically, a *return* to esoteric knowledge. Mayan prophecies mark the official date for the beginning of this Age of Return as 2012.

Harvard scholar Elaine Pagels identifies a mystery tradition in some Gnostic manuscripts as knowledge passed "from Jesus through James and through Mary Magdalen."[3] Concepts found in *The Nag Hammadi Library* have only recently moved into mass consciousness and the question of Mary Magdalen's relationship to Jesus Christ and his apostles is under exploration by many scholars. Dan Brown's best-selling novel and mystery "thriller," *The Da Vinci Code*, has brought the medieval French mysteries and the question of ancient texts and secrets into the mainstream.

In sharing my images, I speak only for myself. I have little doubt, however, that the spiritual paradigm is changing on this Earth, transforming more quickly every day as we integrate the new energies available to us. Regardless of how the shift affects each of us, all of us have the opportunity to make some deliberate choices in how we live our lives for the greatest benefit of everyone. Like many others, I now believe the planet herself is conscious and evolving with us (or without us!). As we are forced through the Earth changes and tapped to awaken, we can choose to move with her into a higher dimension. We have free will either to resist or to help with this huge transition. Depending on the level of resistance we offer, we may be in for a bumpy ride. We entered the Aquarian Age at the millennium, and Aquarian energy is concerned with new systems, technology, community, and the higher mind. The Piscean Age of duality has ended, as we witness its last battles between "good" and "evil" being played out in the confusing wars scattered about the planet. Each of us will take our own route into the understanding of this new era.

---

2. Robinson, *Nag Hammadi*, p. 10.
3. Elaine Pagels, *The Gnostic Gospels* (New York: Vintage Books, 1981), p. 59.

I believe that the hour has come to restore feminine power and wisdom. The mystery of the Black Madonnas provides a different understanding of the figure of Mary Magdalen as an apostle of Christ's original teachings, many of which were compromised, edited, and misunderstood by the institution of the Catholic Church. The feminine way of knowing is one of many direct routes into wholeness. With its emphasis on faith, intuition, and inner vision, it is now gaining respect over the dominating rational mind and patriarchal logos we have experienced and expanded for five millennia.

Our ancient birthright, or esoteric potential, has atrophied through lack of use, although it has remained alive through the occult traditions. As humanity is reintroduced to these talents, the integration of mind and heart will provide all who choose it with greater psychic abilities, greater compassion for one another, greater advancements in physical healing, and an absolute understanding that we are all interrelated as *One*.

In the present transition to a new aeon, and as a consequence of our growing understanding of our powers, a new Earth is manifesting within the old and dying one. My personal story is interwoven within the collective story. The story of Mary Magdalen and her association with the mysterious Black Madonnas is also interwoven with the symbolic woman in Saint John's Revelation. The grave state of the world in our new century is none other than her labor to birth the imagined world many have dreamed of and prayed for—a world for which most people have long given up hope. A world without polarization or victimization. A world without separation, without rival religions, without economic hardships. A conscious, consensus-minded and resource-rich world. The difficult birth of this divine child represents all of humanity reclaiming its divine heritage. The symbolic power of the Black Madonnas continues its synchronistic significance in different areas of my life. My journey is but one glimpse into this universal pilgrimage, one example of the alchemical, human shift whose time has come.

Chapter One

THE WRINKLE IN TIME

In Spiritual Emergencies non-ordinary states of consciousness develop spontaneously for unknown reasons in the middle of everyday life . . .
STANISLAV GROF, *THE COSMIC GAME*

All heartbreak stories are more or less the same and mine was not exceptional. One morning in the fall of 1984, a period I refer to as "the heartbreak initiation," I woke up crying. It usually took me a few minutes to realize I was awake and then to remember my heavy sorrow. The man I loved and had been happy with for the last several years, I'll call him C., had fallen in love with someone else. I handled the revelation without much dignity—crying, arguing, raging like a Medusa—but many months into the separation, I was still suffering acutely. I wasn't particularly young. I already had one divorce behind me. My life had already been a series of heights and abysses, but I was in mid life now and, although I didn't know it, this was to be my most important crisis.

Maybe I had a dream bad enough that I forgot it immediately, but my face and pillow were wet from crying. I wiped my eyes, sat up, and looked around my bedroom astonished. It was as if I had gone to bed in one room of the house and awakened in another. I imagined I was hallucinating. But why?

Three years earlier, I had moved upstairs to a small in-law apartment in the New England Victorian house my ex and I had renovated when we were married. When my ex moved out, I moved upstairs and rented out the first two floors and main part of the house. My present bedroom was directly above the master bedroom on the second floor, which had been our bedroom when we were married. Both bedrooms were about the same size. The bedroom I had shared with my husband had red flowered wallpaper and a fireplace. My present bedroom was painted light green. In both rooms, the beds were on the east wall facing the same way. Instead of a fireplace, however, I now had a bureau and a television. In the master bedroom, there had been a night table with a phone next to the bed and a built-in bookcase on the north wall. In my present bedroom, I also had a night table with a phone next to the bed, but there was a dressing table on the north wall.

As I slowly awakened, the strangest phenomenon occurred. I literally couldn't believe my eyes. It was as if I had moved back in time and my bedroom had strangely become the master bedroom downstairs. I kept turning my head right and left, expecting to snap out of a dream. But I knew one reality from another and this was no dream. The wall that had been green was now papered red. Instead of the television, the fireplace from the old bedroom was there, as was the built-in bookcase. I felt panicky. Although I had been known to suffer anxiety attacks, I sat there very calmly and quietly for a few more minutes, continuously blinking my eyes, waiting for the room to return to normal.

In retrospect, I don't know why I didn't walk over and touch the fireplace or run my hand along the bright rose fleur-de-lis-patterned paper. But I finally did get up and tiptoe into my kitchen to make some mint tea. Small, quiet steps. It was as if I were afraid of falling through a hole, sliding down a tunnel into some subterranean complex complete with its physical correlative—the historic rooms of my emotions, so to speak. Something like Alice's experience in Wonderland.

I purposely didn't look back into the bedroom until the tea was ready. I sat at the table and looked at the trees outside the window. They were as they should be, waving a little in the morning breeze. It was mid autumn and patches of frost freeze-dried the back yard. Attached to his cement fountain, the cherub who presided there seemed to be holding his breath.

When the kettle began to sing, I lifted it and poured myself a cup, which I took to the threshold of the bedroom. The vision was still clearly there, like a scrim across my retinas in the full regalia of everyday three-dimensional reality: the red bedroom, *not* the green one I supposedly lived in now. I stood quietly in the doorway, straddling two worlds. Like Alice, or maybe Dorothy in Oz, I stepped into my Wonderland, climbed back into bed, and dialed C's number.

I guess in situations like this, you call your best friend. I was used to calling him, as we'd been so close for so long. I knew he'd be home. C spent his mornings writing before heading to the restaurant where he worked in the afternoon. When he answered, I explained in a low voice what was happening. I just wanted to tell him about it. I couldn't figure it out. My young son was at his father's and, since I was alone, I just needed to know the rest of the world was out there doing its regular thing. That there hadn't been a nuclear explosion. That I wasn't blown into some Star Trekking seventh dimension. Yet, as far as I knew, it was a twilight zone. To my surprise C, a master of pragmatism, said "I'll be right over."

In fifteen minutes or so, he came in. He still had a key, so I didn't even need to get up. I heard him climbing the stairs and wondered if his presence would shatter the spell. Coming into the room, he sat on the lower edge of the messy bed. I looked at him and looked around.

"It's still there" I said. He had a take-out coffee with him and we sat there and drank our coffee and tea in a palpable, though not uncomfortable, silence. He looked around.

"I don't see it," he said finally.

"I didn't think you would. But I'm not making this up," I responded sincerely.

"I know," he answered.

This was several months into our breakup and I hoped he wasn't thinking I had manipulated him into coming over to share another of those "breaking-up" conversations. That whole awful opera. But he had volunteered to come. He was concerned. Probably he didn't want to feel responsible for me losing my mind. Yet I felt perfectly normal. That is, normal for the heartbreak mode. I didn't think I had lost my mind; I was, quite simply, amazed! I felt more secure with his company and, in the past, he had always trusted my intuition. He knew me; I wasn't crazy. We continued to sit. We didn't analyze it. And we actually held a superficial conversation about other irrelevant topics I can't recall. I remember talking, while continually glancing at the walls between words and sentences.

After about twenty minutes, red, green, purple—whatever!—I thanked him for coming and told him he could leave; I had to take a shower and get to work at my bookstore. Somehow, I was able to accept this irrational detail in what was, most likely, a rational world. I think I accepted it as my hallucination and was willing to write it off and continue my daily life. What else was there to do? C offered to wait while I took a long hot shower with the door ajar, as there was no fan in the old bathroom and it steamed up, which in turn caused the ceiling to crack. When I turned off the shower, C was in the bathroom and handed me a towel through the curtain.

When I stepped out of the tub wrapped in the towel, C took another and began to dry me. It was not erotic. It was as if he were a parent (I hesitate to say father) and I, the child. It was a caring gesture, a loving kind of concern. I felt sad, but didn't resist. He dried me off with gentle taps of the towel on my shoulders and back. A few minutes later, snug in my bathrobe, I walked down the short hallway into my room and stood in the doorway again.

"It's gone," I said, not knowing if that was good or bad. "It's back to normal." He looked at me very seriously. I smiled weakly. And it *was* back to normal, just like that. Of course, I wondered what had happened. I wondered how it had happened. I had never had such an experience. Though, as a child of the Sixties, I had smoked marijuana and hash in my time, I had never taken LSD or mushrooms or other hallucinogenics, so it couldn't have been a drug flashback. C said he would wait till I got dressed and we would walk out together. We did and I thanked him again, patting his arm, afraid to communicate too much. The cold air was sobering. He looked at me hard. I shrugged, as if to say "I'm back in the real world." Surprisingly, I didn't feel foolish.

When we'd first met, C and I discovered we had the same car, *Le Car*, the little French Renault. (Mine died a few weeks after the relationship ended completely.) But that day, C and I left my haunted house, got into our small cars, waved goodbye, and went about our usual business. Though I would never forget that strange incident and the synchronous movement of our twin cars turning in their different directions, mostly I remember how kind he was in those moments.

Over the next several years, as I developed an interest in dream work and came to know several Jungian psychologists, I asked many times if anyone had ever heard of the phenomenon I had experienced. No one gave me an explanation until I read Stanislav Grof on spiritual emergencies. It was then that I knew I had simply hallucinated a previous room where I had felt deep emotional pain. There had certainly been days during the end of my marriage when I was overcome with the inertia of unhappiness. I recall lying exhausted on my bed in the afternoon, unable to quiet my mind long enough to rest, while our child napped in the next room. I recall looking at that room, the red print wallpaper of the previous owner, the sheer curtains, the candlesticks on the fireplace mantle. For some reason, on that strange morning, my mind showed me an emotional correspondence, how deep emotions create unusual states of consciousness. It seems that, when we lower our regular guards, we are more porous; our assumptions are more permeable, more susceptible to seeing through what we think of as "reality." This makes it possible to penetrate the firewall between time dimensions.

A few years later, while reading a book of poems by Ann Lauterbach appropriately entitled *Before Recollection,* I came across a line I found so compelling it triggered me to write my own poem about the uncanny incident in my bedroom.

When I told a few close poetry friends about the actual incident behind the poem, they said they didn't need to know it in order to appreciate the surreal leaps the poem made—which is, after all, the business of poems. I had to write the poem in the third person. I truly felt compassion for the person I was at that time, but I didn't want to return to that mind-set completely by writing in the first person. Standing outside myself and watching the incident felt safer. Still, the poem has always been precious to me, as it does express some of the pain I felt at that moment in the coming together of three different experiences of loss in my life: my breakup with C and my divorce, which both brought up my father's death.

I wanted to capture, however discreetly, the marvel of that bizarre descent into sorrow, the magical aspects of the abyss that, unbeknownst to me at that time, began an exploration that I've yet to finish. I've come to treasure the poem as well because it reminds me of how generous C was to me that morning. There will always be some bittersweet beauty in that memory, despite the real anguish of the situation at the time. The epigram I chose to introduce the poem really defines the experience itself:

The Future that Brought Her Here

. . . the invisible pressure of some other time on time.
—ANN LAUTERBACH

> She's still discovering injury.
> The childhood doll
> with its cobalt eyes struck open,
> ginger lashes greasy with years,
> a death in her retina
> where only an absence appears.
> The woman blinks
> into the dawning, violet
> light of her bedroom
> rinsed in hallucination—
> Wrapped in the quilt
> of her flowering sorrow,
> she arranges the cumulative rain.
> Birds swoop and crop her terrain

in a scree of time
and the room slides through its layered history:
bookcase into fireplace,
latex into lacy paper,
the same hydrangeas bluing the air.
And she is years back, masked
to an earlier sensation, married
to memory that blunts her senses
the way hunter's headlights stun
deer. And she falls
through the future
that brought her here.

TIME IS FLEXIBLE

During the next twenty or so years, I had many more what I hesitate only slightly to call "mystical" moments. In retrospect, that situation doesn't seem quite as frightening as it did then. As Einstein posited, and the quantum physicists have now proved indisputably, time is flexible. In fact, time, as an absolute, does not exist. Time is a structure we impose on our experience. Everything—past, present and future—is happening together in the "Eternal Now" and our consciousness can go anywhere, anytime. Twenty-seven years of practicing meditation have shown me that truth and opened me to psychic phenomena. Most of us live our lives shackled to patterns we created in the past without realizing that every moment is new and an opportunity to change ingrained emotional patterns. We are such creatures of habit that we often don't realize we have become stuck in our limiting beliefs. We create our reality personally and collectively. Until we can consciously control how we do so, however, we will continue to be trapped in our creation.

We can also change our perceptions—those of the present as well as those of the past. That is, we can change how we hold what is happening or has happened and free ourselves from automated psychological frameworks. I think the universe—or God/Goddess, or Source, or Force, or whatever you choose to call it—showed me that morning how we can fall prey to tricks of the mind. By some agreement we don't recall, we have all tuned in to the same station—what we call present time and a three-dimensional spatial reality. But it's feasible that, if we learn how to manage our awareness, we can "channel-surf" to make better choices. Collectively, we can change reality for the better. As every mystic, no matter his or her culture, tells us, the world is a mirror of our own projections. It seems we have disowned both our responsibility for that world and our power to create it.

Over the years, I've come to see this principle in action. We each need to understand as much as we can of our own personal unconscious mind and that of the collective. Mass consciousness doesn't see the cause-and-effect relationship between unconscious fear, worry, and anger that creates the energy field that attracts disaster. Carl Jung said that each person can only change him or herself—that particular personal growth is the first step toward changing the world. I didn't know for many years how my heartbreak initiated me into a new life, a deeper inquiry into poetic time, dream time, and emotional states. I didn't know for many years that there were others out there whose hard work on themselves could help the world. I simply wanted to heal my own pain. I say there is beauty in the memory of my overlaid bedrooms, because it literally showed the underlying pattern I had created unconsciously. Although I was unable to learn the lesson in that moment, I gained a respect for the magical world.

I remember learning in grammar school that the dense matter we experience as solid is really made up of spinning atoms. This surface world we know with our five senses is deceiving. We leap through time and space routinely when we write poems, creating illusions. Is it really so odd what the mystics tell us—that what we call reality is an illusion? This idea reminds me of a quote I've always liked by Andre Breton, who wrote a manifesto on surrealism: "Can dreams not be used to solve the fundamental problems of life? I believe that the apparent antagonism between dream and reality will be resolved in a kind of absolute reality—in surreality."[1] Or perhaps in what I, in reference to my own story, might call "a waking dream."

When the disillusionment of the Great War shattered an era and the aftermath provoked a psychological change in the European art world, artists ushered in an age of irreverence and experimentation in a movement known as Dadaism. New visions broke through from the collective unconscious and modern art was born. Surrealism soon eclipsed Dadaism and began to reinvent the way the eye sees reality. The foundations of the known world

---

1 Andre Breton, quoted in Carl Jung, *Man and His Symbols* (New York: Dell Publishing Co., 1968), p. 297.

expanded and displayed their depths. As more people observed surreality, due perhaps to its familiarity from the dream world, it eventually gained acceptance in the artistic mainstream. The surreality we now take for granted in videos and computer imaging was threatening back then, but here, in the first years of the 21st century, we have grown accustomed to the juxtaposition of visual worlds. And the channel-surfing we do is a good metaphor for our visionary possibilities. I think my emotional state elevated my access to those liminal areas, thresholds where the construct of time gives way to the universes behind it. I didn't question my sanity that morning. I somehow realized I had seen through a wrinkle in time.

Chapter 2

BLACK TRUCK

When all the characters are carefully imagined, the images are put under pressure,
emotions heat up, and the dream is cooked.
ROBERT BOSNAK, *A LITTLE COURSE IN DREAMS*

I was driving toward Boston, past the dismal commercial strip of Route I to RB's weekly Alchemical Dream Workshop. I had had a dream of a black truck that morning, in that liminal state we inhabit just before rising. Now that I was cruising along in my Toyota, my mind drifted up to the colorless overcast sky, then down to the road and the slithering snake of tail lights moving through the light rain, and finally back to the black truck. I realized, despite my fears of the somewhat "public" forum, I felt an itching need to work on my dream that night in the class. It was a fairly short dream, but extremely vivid. I did feel the "talking cure" in my sessions with my regular therapist was helping me cope with my breakup with C, but I had witnessed a new kind of healing in RB's powerful dream method—one that went through the images straight to the emotions, bypassing the mind, so to speak.

The dream haunted me all day and, though I understood it intellectually, I wondered how it would feel to "cook it." I've found over the years, although sometimes punctuated with an illuminating *Ah Ha!* moment of clear vision, that strictly intellectual work on a dream doesn't necessarily integrate the unconscious feelings into the gut. I had understood for a long time that my heartache and my reaction to my breakup with C was bigger than the relationship itself. I *understood* that I had projected onto him all my fantasies for the perfect partner, the male who would love me unconditionally, and that this dynamic was related to losing my father in adolescence. Yada, yada, yada. "Yes I know all that," I told myself. But it didn't *feel* as if that knowing helped me to feel any better.

This particular night, when I got to the unremarkable but ceremonious classroom and smiled shyly at a few faces in the *not*-overtly friendly crowd, my nerve began to flag. There was always this breathtaking moment when RB finished his hour-long alchemical lecture and turned to scan the class in anticipation of the second hour of the evening, when he would "work" a subject's dream. The energy in the room rose, as if crackling from the radiators. Of the thirty or so participants in the class, there were always at least three brave souls who volunteered. I gingerly raised my hand to the level of my chest in a kind of awkward wave and RB's big Paul McCartneyish eyes locked on mine. He took a swig of spring water and put the bottle down, leaning forward in his charismatic way, looking directly at me, although I was five or six rows back. "Good," he said, nodding affirmatively.

He couldn't know, of course, about the dream I had a year ago, the night I first attended his class—the dream in which he led me through a dark underground tunnel by the light of a small candle. Now I wanted to be led by him through the dark spots in this particular dream about the black truck. People settled back into their chairs and took the few minutes he always allocated to attune themselves to their bodies so they could take notice of their somatic reactions. Then he nodded at me again and, in a dispassionate but jittery voice, speaking in the present tense as RB always suggested, I closed my eyes and shared the dream I had memorized:

I'M RIDING IN A CAR WITH MY FAMILY. *My mother is driving and there are three of us in the back. My brother is teasing me and I'm ignoring him, looking out the window at the neighborhood, which seems to be urban. For some reason, I think it is Brooklyn. There are dirty garbage cans on the sidewalk and dirty snow is piled, making the road narrow as we drive along. Everything is gray. It's almost in black and white, like TV before color. But I look up into the sky and see a beautiful sunset. The sky is rose and mauve and orange and the clouds seem silver. I'm very content to gaze at the sky, whose colors remind me of Joel Meyerowitz's photographs.*

I ignore my brother's teasing, my sister's whining, the irritating conversation in the car. Then I see a black truck that appears to be out of control. It veers crazily and comes up behind us, ramming our car with a huge bang. We are jolted, but keep going until the truck approaches again and bangs us, unbelievably, a second time. The car stops and we jump out. We are not hurt, but I run to check on the passengers in the black truck. I look in the window and see an elderly Asian man stuttering and sputtering; he's almost unconscious. He's saying something about the stock market. Then I see a young girl, maybe twelve, also Asian. I figure she is his granddaughter. Her face, all covered with blood, is pressed against the cracked windshield. I pick her up in my arms and lift her out of the truck.

It seems I am alone now. I'm screaming for someone to call an ambulance, but I know there is a hospital over the big hill in front of me and I start to walk uphill with her in my arms. She is whimpering and conscious. I look at the colors of the sky again and keep walking up the hill toward them, toward the hospital. I'm carrying her. . . Then I wake up. 🙠

The class was eerily quiet as I spoke. I realized it is always this way when a dream is told but, nonetheless, I felt conspicuous. Just telling the dream aloud brought it closer to my consciousness, the film version flashing on my inner screen. In the silence that followed, I heard my voice in my mind, "I'm carrying her, I'm carrying her," as if this were the refrain to the dream's theme song, replaying as the credits rolled.

And as if he could read my mind, RB shook his head, mumbling aloud: "I'm carrying her . . . uphill . . ." At once, I thought to myself, "This is the whole meaning of the dream," and I saw it was a stupid, transparent dream and thought I was foolish to tell it to these overly intellectual, analytical strangers. Thank God, the process is such that one sits there with closed eyes. I felt safer, more comfortable, without seeing the faces of my classmates and made a quick decision not to open my eyes until the evening was done.

Of course, I was "carrying her," had been carrying her since I was about twelve. I knew she was a part of me, just as everything in the dream—figures, objects, landscape—were representative aspects of my unconscious complexes. I happened to discern the part of me that this girl represented, but the old man, for instance, was more ego-alien, less recognizably a part of my psychic make-up. I thought for a moment that I was wrong when I said she was twelve; upon closer examination, I realized she could be older, say thirteen or fourteen, more in line with my age at the time of my family crisis. Perhaps I thought she was younger because my image of young Asian women is that they are petite.

She *is* my wounded girl, I told myself. Already, I had intellectually played out the symbols in my mind, even as RB urged the group to share their reactions. Like some kind of dream program in a computer, I was downloading the reductive interpretations. I had to remind myself that RB's class was about discovery, more like following a wild goose search on the Internet, wading from one tangential Web site to another.

Someone behind me said she'd cringed when the black truck was approaching at high speed, out of control, and reported that she had felt a sharp pain in her left arm. She added that left-arm pain is sometimes related to heart attacks. In my mind, the dream screen immediately flashed "heart attack" and I saw the image of Christ's Sacred Heart surrounded by orange-and-purple flames, an image I had lived with in my Catholic childhood—the five-by-seven-inch print my mother framed for my brother's bureau. "Right," I thought, "Heart attack and then heart*break*. So how does this dream concern my breakup with C?" An astute participant who often spoke in class said she was suspicious of the dreamy sky and got very bored when I described it, and the voice of a middle-aged man to my left said he envisioned the old man in the truck as drunk. I had to keep telling myself that this was a process not a test. I tried to stop my zooming mind from thinking and vowed to stay in the moment, shifting my position on the straight-backed chair, recrossing my legs, swinging my knee-high boots the other way. But the altered state of my mind was already in motion and, as I said, I dared not open my eyes.

After a few more responses from the class, as is the procedure, I was asked to report the dream a second time. The class then noted a few distinctions in my second telling. Items skipped over or forgotten often indicate a resistance on the dreamer's part—places where the analyst should tread slowly and softly to avoid allowing the resistance to block the rise of feelings deep in the unconscious. As it turned out, in the second recitation, I forgot to mention that there were two collisions. A significant omission. I wondered myself if I forgot the second collision because I was still stuck in the distant past from the loss of my father, or if I was so stage-frightened in this room that I felt I had already overburdened the class with my big black truck. More likely, I was stuck in the recent past from the wound from C. Had I really been broad-sided *twice* in my life?

RB shared his own concerns about the truck, stressing its ominous appearance on the scene, and then he asked a few informational questions that I understood could be distracting from the depth of the work if we were to "go there" during the process. First, he wanted to know if I was an artist, perhaps because, when I described the colors in the sky, I mentioned the photographer Joel Meyerowitz. I think that Meyerowitz alters the colors in his photographs in a way that gives them their surreal beauty. I was only familiar with his work because I especially loved his book *Cape Light*, which I knew from my work in the bookstore. The book had sold very well, and I had often looked at it, admiring the unusual colors in the prints as if they were the hue of memory. I answered that I was not an artist but a poet, although I knew a good bit about art.

"And the stock market?" he asked. "Did the crash on October 13th affect you?" This was 1987 and Black Friday, as the media called it, had occurred the previous week. I thought carefully before answering: "Not directly," I finally replied. I knew my mother lived off the blue-chip portfolio my father had left her when he died back in the Sixties. He had a great intuitive gift when it came to the market and accumulated quite a bit of net worth in his short life. My mother had never had to work and hoped to eventually leave her children money, but this was not something that had been on my mind. I had recently sold my bookstore, thinking I would live off some of the proceeds for a few months—just take a break from working and pursue my poetry. But I had some guilt about not knowing just what I would do next. On one level, I had already decided I wanted to stay home for a few months while my son was still young, just entering junior high. This all went through my head very quickly and I decided the stock market dive had affected me indirectly, in that I was unconsciously worried about the money I would inherit. I did not have to give the class a full accounting of why this was so, but RB pointed out to them that, if this were private therapy, he would have asked what "indirectly" entailed. I felt him turn back to me to continue.

The one other question RB found relevant to ask before we entered the conscious dream state was about Asia. Had I been there or did I have close Asian friends? "No" and "No," I answered. But my best friend from college had spent two years in Cambodia during the war when I was newly married. We exchanged letters over those years and I often had a secret longing to be there too. Recently, I had unearthed her letters, which spoke of the view from her room in the Hotel Phnom Penh, of building shelters, of driving jeeps with foreign journalists, of speaking French daily at diplomatic parties, and even of her visits to opium dens. She sent pictures of orphans in soup kitchens. Her life seemed exotic and so *significant* compared to mine. In the past several years, I had read many of the novels and poems written by veterans. I told the class that I was, like most baby-boomers, emotionally involved in the Vietnam and Cambodian wars.

RB repeated the words "emotionally involved" aloud for the class as he had repeated "carrying her." He had a way of picking out an ordinary expression that you use every day and resonating it back to you so that you heard it vibrate across a different octave. It doesn't seem like a particularly difficult technique to master, but I think it shows what an acute listener he is and why he teaches us to listen especially closely when it comes to dreams, because, in his work, every detail counts.

He asked if anyone else in class had an expository type of question for the dreamer before we entered the alchemical container and relived the dream together. A young woman to my right did ask appropriately: "What's your relationship to Brooklyn? Did you ever live there ?"

"No, but my father grew up there," I answered. That startled me for a moment and, as I began thinking again, someone else popped in with: "Is your father in the car?"

At this point, RB put up his finger: "Wait on that, we will address it when we are in the car."

"Oh," I caught myself thinking, "Come to think of it, he is not in the car. My mother is driving and the passenger seat is empty."

This became the entryway into the work.

THE ALCHEMICAL CONTAINER

Everyone sighed and shifted again, and I fluttered my eyes to see others squinting at me. Then RB began slowly, asking in a low voice: "So you're in the car with your family. Who does that include?" I had mentioned my sister and my brother and myself, but I had not mentioned the adults. Soon it was established that my mother was driving and that my father was not in the car. In fact, the passenger seat was suspiciously vacant; we kids were in the back. Yet it was my father's car—the small Mercedes sports sedan he used to pile us into when my little brother was just a baby. A car, like a house, generally indicates the overall condition of the psyche and, more specifically, how psyche moves. "But my mother sold that car many years ago," I added. Nevertheless, there we were in the dream, seated within the literal framework of the father. This car belonged to my dead father just as surely as the planet Saturn, whose mythological referent is the father, was the ruler, the dominant planet, in my Capricorn chart.

"What about when you were twelve, did you have the car then?" someone asked.

"Yes" I answered. RB always said that the dreamer was free not to explain, but could simply give a yes or no answer and then attest to the feelings it raised, again with a yes or no. Again, what is uncanny about this method of dream work is that the dreamer who may feel too unsafe to share associative details can hold them privately and still be moved to feel the full impact of the images. RB is especially skilled in pointing out just how that works. After all, you're in a room with thirty strangers and may not want to reveal the secret significance of an embarrassing symbol about which you had no clue when you so gallantly offered up your dream for scrutiny—for example, your lily-white umbrella suddenly opening as an obvious sexual reference.

"Did something significant happen in your life when you were twelve?" A distant voice probed closer.

"Well, yes, I guess you could say that," I said, thinking how life had been good until I was thirteen and fourteen, but that, even earlier, my anxiety had intuited the trouble to come. I decided to go on with a bit more information to avoid getting too pinned down. "My father became ill and died when I was fifteen." There. That explained the absence of the driver and, of course, the death of any parent is a trauma. Let them have that much, I thought defensively. I seemed to forget I had volunteered for this, and yet I was also compelled to move deeper into it as the short scene in the car loomed larger.

We spent a few more minutes on the movement of the car, the view out the window, the season (obviously winter due to the piles of snow), and the dirty snow itself—a weight in the dream, which brought to my memory a poem I had written years before on my father's mid-December funeral.

"How did your father die?" someone asked.

I was silent for a minute, thinking what to say, when RB interrupted, "Feel free not to answer that."

The word "Suddenly" was all I could muster. There was a long pause. I figured the class sensed that I had something to hide.

"And your brother is teasing you?" RB went on.

"Yes," I said. "And he is teasing my sister too. Actually when I think about it, it feels as if he is teasing her more and I'm just peacefully looking at the sky." I could feel myself wanting to get to the sky. But RB wasn't going to move that fast. The work had to be meticulously slow so that, when the unconscious issues came up, the dreamer would inhabit them naturally without throwing up a wall.

"What is it like for your sister to be teased so intensely?" he asked.

"It's awful but she's a fighter and will throw it back at him, something I never had the energy for." I found myself answering quite openly then.

"What's she feeling as he's making fun of her?" RB went on.

"She's angry because his teasing is always witty and sometimes makes the rest of us laugh. I felt myself enter this scene as if it were happening right then. "They're beginning to fight and my mother is getting annoyed

fortable place in the dream and I knew he wouldn't let me dwell there for too long. Still, it surprised me to see that sky itself as a place with tension, and to see C slipping away. Was the sky a self-indulgent escape I couldn't get to while locked in the car? The "complex" world of the father's car?

"What time of day is it?" said a voice sitting close by.

"Somewhere between late afternoon and twilight."

"And where is the light?"

"The light is not on the street. The street is in gray shadows. The light is in the sky."

"And how does it feel to be somewhere between late afternoon and twilight, on the dirty streets, locked in your father's car with your brother's teasing, unable to get to the light of the colorful sky?" RB again. His summation startled me.

My ego perception in the dream didn't really include a literal destination, but when I felt the question symbolically, I suddenly saw that it was getting late in my life and I had no idea how to get where I wanted to go. I was more than halfway through my thirties, single again, without a specific career. My resume was interesting; I had patched together a lot of part-time work, from radio reviewer to bookstore owner to poet-in-the-schools , but I had no 401K, no retirement plan, no IRA, and no benefits. All my life I seemed to move against any system of security and yet existed on some vague inherent trust in the rightness of my decisions without practical considerations. I cared for the inner life, and was interested in the processes of creative imagination as a healing instrument. I had "followed my bliss" defiantly, but not without rattling nerves.

After what seemed like a long two or three minutes, RB saw that I was able to hold the feeling rather than escape into a digression, which some dreamers do at this point—telling an anecdote from their childhood, free-associating themselves out of the moment. This must have been what Jung meant by keeping the image central. If you are allowed to free-associate away from the tension of the feeling then, unpleasant as the moment may be, the chance of bringing it fully to consciousness is lost. The way to process it, to get past it, is to make it conscious and really feel it rather than run from it or let it sink into the body where, eventually, it becomes a habitual symptom. This was the heart of RB's teaching and this may have been my first direct understanding of the important relationship between consciousness and the body.

We all continued to sit in discomfort with the dark moment until RB asked how this experience felt compared to that of feeling the sky. At once, my body released my breath and I sighed wistfully, "The sky is expansive and spacious. *This* is tight, pressurized, frozen." He asked me to go back and forth between the two feelings, which I did until I burst out: "It's making me crazy!" The point was clearly established that these were the opposite poles of the dream and it was essential to feel both if I could.

We then moved on to the important scene. "Now what happens when you first see the truck?" I was back in the car and could see the truck clearly in the rear view mirror. I was sitting directly behind the driver—an interesting detail as well. Something about my relationship to my mother. "My inner mother is driving," I thought, but there would not be time in this session to explore that. With what aspect of my mother's personality had I identified and why? And how was that aspect running my life? Something inside whispered "Widow," but I tucked the idea away as a mental note for later. For now, I had to answer the question.

"The truck just comes out of nowhere, barrels down the street, and smacks into us."

"And what is that impact like?"

"It's immediate and terrifying, a huge jolt. A 'We're all gonna die!!' moment. We're all thrown around. There are no seat belts."

"And what's that like?"

"It's horrifying; I think we scream. There's screaming coming from somewhere, I hear it as if from inside my head."

"And how does it feel to be hit out of nowhere by the side of a black truck?" I wanted to scream a little more each time he drove the feeling home.

When I was silent, someone else piped in. "Didn't you say it hits you *twice?*"

"Yes, yes, I did say that and then forgot it, but it does. It rams us again and the second time—which seems more dangerous—the second time, the moment before I realize it's going to happen again, is unbearable—more maddening, more destructive." My responses were coming in a rush, I was getting anxious myself to protect the girl. The class then led me into that suspended moment of impact with the truck that I found difficult to hold.

"It's harrowing, literally your basic nightmare." I tried to speak normally, without emotion, and then we all laughed at the irony of the cliché. This broke the tension so completely that RB goodheartedly pointed out how we had surfaced en masse from the depths. How everyone wanted release. So I had deployed my resistance after all.

Before we could get to the scene with the girl, there were the questions about the old man who remained somewhat mysterious to me. Over the years that I've thought about this dream, I've been unable to discern exactly why he is also Asian. Yet now, I see the obvious had eluded my resistance. I never consciously think of my father as pathetic. He was one of the most, if not *the* most, lively, fun, intelligent, exuberant human being I've ever known. But the vision that my unconscious sticks to is the one of him in a helpless mode, the way I saw him several times when I was an adolescent. Since his death, all my life, in one form or another, I've dreamt of him looking as helpless as a homeless refugee.

This image clearly defied my idea of who he was in life. But I suppose my unconscious drew on its bank of images from the Vietnam War. I think specifically of the famous photo of the adolescent Vietnamese girl screaming and running from American napalm and my associations between Vietnam and victimization. It's "the father within" that has, to some extent, kept me powerless. Why that image and not other, more centered, more powerful ones? Not my father at his desk writing a poem, or at his easel painting. Not my father singing or piling us all into the big king-size bed with homemade ice-cream sundaes. Maybe the negative image was shocked into memory by the vulnerability of my own porous psyche at the time I was coming of age, seeing my father so troubled and utterly mortal.

The lesson for me in decoding the inner father has been to feel this helplessness consciously and let it go. Ten or twelve years ago, I actually thought I could get over this complex—the days I describe here—in therapy. Now I know better. You don't ever get over it and, occasionally, when I am down on myself, I still have those dreams. But as the image lives there, triggered by circumstances, and does its thing in my heart and mind, I am now more aware *in the moment* when I see it of a need to connect it to the place of fear in my present life that is calling it up. If I bring it into consciousness, I can see it for what it is—a feeling from the past that I've allowed to cripple me. It is a habitual response I can deactivate by remembering I am no longer that terrified adolescent.

"And so, after the second collision, you get out of the car? Do the others get out with you?" RB moved the discussion forward again.

"No, they don't seem to be around. It's almost a totally different place. I climb into the truck and see the old man mumbling. He's wearing a funny hat. He looks pitiful. But I don't seem to be concerned with him the way I am with the girl—all that blood. Also, her face is squashed against the cracked windshield."

"What's a cracked windshield?" another voice asked.

"A windshield that may cave in, one that could harm rather than protect."

"Can you feel the crack in your body?"

"Yes, it's . . . fragile, . . . like glass, like eggshells." I searched for the right connection. I understood the crack intellectually as a symbol of my father's split, his *crackup*, his two extremes that inhabited me, but I hadn't thought about it being inside me, in my own body. I tried to sigh, but noticed I was holding my breath.

"What does the girl's face look like against the cracked windshield?" I knew more about the depth of that crack than I was willing to reveal and tried to get back to the literal image of the girl.

"It's a still frame, one eye glaring, her nose flattened. Like a frozen scream, frozen . . . emotion." I found myself getting very precise and seeing the picture vividly.

"Frozen emotion," RB repeated. "Can you feel it?"

A few years ago, preparing to teach the play *Oedipus Rex*, I remember reading an essay by James Hillman that mentioned that Sophocles locates fate, the place where the soul is bound to fate, as literally in the lungs, liver, and deep muscle.[1] Sophocles also said this is the place from which speech issues forth. If the breath cannot reach deep enough to speak the concerns of the soul, then healing will not occur.

When I first read this, I saw it as an *apologia*, or "explanation," for tragedy. Tragedy began as a religious rite. Those who witnessed it participated vicariously in the emotions of the actors, and were psychologically cleansed. I was struck by the argument for speaking our worst grief aloud, or writing it out as poets often do. Obviously, there is something about containing our secret fears that keeps us ill. Freud, of course, realized this when he first called his method "the talking cure." To paraphrase Sophocles: When you run from your fate, you suffer *in the flesh*. Here, perhaps, is the link between disease and the mind.

It seemed like a very long time passed while I navigated my body and felt how I had to work around that scream. I found that heavy sighing (breathing deeply) helped. Finally, I answered simply, "Yes, I can feel it."

I hesitated. I had to focus and see where it was inside me. Then I felt the enormity of it, like a glacier sliding over my chest. I have never been a

---

1. James Hillman, "Athene, Ananke, and Abnormal Psychology," in *Mythic Figures, Uniform Edition of the Writings of James Hillman*, Vol. 6.1 (Putnam, CT: Spring Publications, 2007), pp. 52–53.

deep breather, and have only recently discovered through yoga the power of breath. At that moment, I felt my breathing high in my throat and saw how I habitually kept it shallow as I unconsciously resisted dislodging the scream from inside the iceberg, the tissues of my skin, the organs of my body.

The hour was coming to a close and RB again indicated to the class that, while he would have dwelt longer on this moment in a regular therapy session, time was scarce and he wanted to move on. He then had me lift and carry the injured Asian girl out of the car and up the hill imaginatively, just as I did in the dream. He spent some time on how *I* felt (that is, my dream-ego), and it was easy to say "panicky, but determined," or "scared and concerned, but steady." I realized my determination to get this girl to safety, this poor young Vietnamese girl, a war casualty herself.

I want to state here that, like most people, I have no conscious control over my dreams. I am not a "lucid dreamer" and dreams have no interest in political correctness. My unconscious chose to extrapolate from images I had stored of the Vietnam War and the emotional traumas in my own life. And I have no wish to say that I, in any way, endured the hell that ravaged the lives of the Vietnamese. However, I have found that dreams tend to exaggerate visually through metaphor to get our attention long enough to make their psychological point. (You can see why they would do so; in their natural state, so few people pay them any attention at all!)

The elderly man was also helpless. I did not have an archetypal "Wise Old Man" in this strange grandfather who was almost beyond saving, but more of a distortion of the internalized wounded father. Both grandfather and granddaughter reflected each other. But my young, feminine, feeling side was more important to me, closer to my ego's identification and I was going to save her at all costs. I felt confident I could get her to the hospital on time. After all, in my "real" day-world, wasn't I committed to long-term expensive therapy, (unsupported by insurance) where the cost alone attested to my intention to feel better? I was indeed "carrying her."

"And the sky? Is the beautiful sky still within view?" asked RB, taking over the final questions.

"Yes," I said. "It gives me hope. I am encouraged by it."

"And how do you feel now about the late afternoon, the dying light?" my new friend, the Buddhist trainee whispered.

"They're not as important; it's not so gloomy now. I know I can get her to the hospital on time. I *know* we will make it," I added.

I was asked to feel the girl in my arms, her weight, the extent of her damage. After several long minutes, RB closed the work on that image, emphasizing my confidence and stressing my own power to save her. My arms and legs felt strong as I took long strides up the hill with her in my arms. When someone asked how my feet felt climbing uphill, I answered that it seemed I had on combat boots. "I'm wearing my mother's army boots," I laughed, understanding now why and *how* she was driving my father's car; my mother was nothing if not a survivor.

The lovely sky receded, but for the moment, it was not the crucial image. Beneath the dying light, I turned my attention to the bleeding girl. First things first. I knew I could save her and, once she recovered, I would have the colors of that sky to move toward.

Chapter 3

WATER: DECISION-MAKING
THROUGH A DREAM

*One dives into water in order to be
reborn and changed.*
GASTON BACHELARD, *WATER AND DREAMS*

*Water is the sad element—Why?
Because it weeps for everyone.*
LAMARTINE, (QUOTED IN) *WATER AND DREAMS* BY GASTON BACHELARD

On my worst winter days, I looked at the dishrag sky, the anorexic trees, and felt my life was crippled along with the landscape. Years ago, I had agreed to joint custody of my son with my ex-husband; I knew I didn't want him to grow up without a father. But our settlement wasn't laid out in print and my son went back and forth with some confusion over the years. There were always those cases of the forgotten books or lunch box. To make things worse, my ex-husband moved farther away and my son began to spend time at his grandmother's as well, shuttling between the three homes, dragging his paraphernalia behind him. It occurred to me that he was now in high school, pulling away from the ministrations of a mother. The two years he had left to finish school seemed another eon to me—an eon during which I would have to put my life on hold. I wanted desperately to leave, to get to a bigger city, to be anonymous, to start fresh.

I was spending more and more time in Boston, attending classes at the Jung Institute. The memories in my small Maine town were heavy with associations of either my ex-husband or C, the man who broke my heart, and of the group of friends we had made when we were a couple. But several of my best friends lived in Boston, including one of the women from my college group. In fact, one of my oldest friends had recently left Maine to get an advanced degree at Boston University.

My son was an athlete and, as much as I enjoyed watching him play, as much as I screamed my head off when his team won a regional championship, I felt I had put in my time. His father was a coach and I was constantly in communication with him over details. I often felt manipulated. Then I inadvertently discovered some information about my marriage that infuriated me. What could I do? I was already divorced. This frustrating situation only fueled my desire to move. My son seemed to understand my need to move on and, though he was upset at losing his mother, he was often on his own—at school, with friends, playing sports, dating girls, and staying with his Dad. The truth is he was not losing his mother. I was always available and could continue to be there when needed, as I would be only two hours away. He also knew my interests and trusted me. He realized I had been commuting continually for a number of years, that I couldn't get a full-time teaching job locally, and that my opportunities increased enormously just two hours south in Boston.

I made the decision to leave in 1990, when the bottom had fallen out of the real estate boom of the early Eighties. Despite the fact that my condo was small and affordable and less than a block from the beach, I could not sell it. The Gulf War was on and I felt more emotional than ever. I was sick about the fact that, once again, young American men were being sent to die by old political hacks—sick about the fact that a supposedly civilized society could find no alternative to conflict resolution other than war. I was a true product of the Sixties—as pacifistic in my position on war as I was in standing up for myself in a divorce.

I had weekly sessions with my analyst RB, and continued to fall under the spell of his charismatic personality, his brown eyes, and his amazing work. One week, we discussed a dream about which I was clueless. But the work on this dream proved to be so synchronistically resonant that I realized my unconscious was not only giving me permission to leave my son in the care of his father, but reassuring me that all would be well even if I were to relocate without him.

The dream revisited the first home that my ex-husband and I had when we moved to Maine from Boston back in the mid Seventies. We rented a small place on a lake in the woods, thoroughly rural and peaceful. It was during the time that we lived there that I began to take my writing seriously and I later became pregnant in that house, before we bought a home in town.

IN THE DREAM, THE HOUSE BELONGS to my college friend, Maryanne, and her husband, William. They have a baby, under a year old, whom they keep in a wicker basket *floating on the lake. The basket is tied to the dock and I am surprised when they suggest we walk the quarter mile back to the house and leave the baby floating on the water. When we get to the house, I am increasingly concerned about leaving the baby alone. "Oh, he'll be fine," they say nonchalantly and go about their business. At the end of the dream, I am pleading with them to go get the baby or to allow me to go. I am afraid that the baby is wet and cold and at the mercy of insects, bees, and (god forbid) snakes. "No, no," they insist. "He's okay; we'll get him later." I wake feeling furious and fearful for the child.* ❧

RB squinted in his usual manner, rubbing his hand on his forehead. He had me enter the dream and feel the panic of my ego identity. I was unwilling even to try to feel the casual attitude of my child-abusing friends; resistance was steaming out my ears. Eventually, RB took the dream into an active imagination mode and asked me to leave the house and go down and check on the child.

Behind my closed eyes, I could clearly see the old path that we followed to the lake when I had lived there with my ex so many years ago. I left the old paneled house and trotted down to the dock. RB slowed me down just before I reached the basket and asked if I could see the baby. I said no, that the basket was afloat at the end of a rope about six feet long. He asked me to pull very slowly on the rope until I could peer into the basket. I imagined myself pulling hand over hand, evenly drawing the rope in so as not to wake the baby if it was asleep. When I could finally see the child, I was surprised to see it surrounded by snakes—standing snakes, so to speak, as if they'd been charmed by a turban-clad dervish.

RB asked me if the snakes were attacking the baby. Immediately frightened, I was almost afraid to look. But as I did, I was surprised to find that they were dancing in a circle around the child and that he was awake, cooing and gooing at them as if they comprised an entertaining mobile poised above his crib. This image knocked me out. It was nothing I could have conjured or expected.

RB then asked me to put my hand in the basket and feel if the baby was cold. I saw that he was lying in a small pool of shallow water. RB suggested I put my hand in the water. I did. I touched the baby's knee and then plunged my hand into the water in the basket. The water was warm. The baby's skin was warm. I was utterly surprised to see the baby having a grand time, both amused and protected by the snakes who danced in a magic circle around him. I sat there quietly with my eyes closed and finally had to smile at the pretty picture.

"Looks like the baby's going to be fine," RB spoke quietly. I opened my eyes.

"Yeah," I said finally. "But what does the dream have to do with me?" In dreams, babies usually refer to projects or ideas—in my case, sometimes new poems. The Divine Child archetype shows up universally in a positive way if a baby appears healthy and happy.

"Maybe it's your idea to move to Boston," RB commented, though, in retrospect, I'm sure he was purposely misleading me. And then his simple observation unlocked the puzzle. Again, I was astounded at how clever the unconscious can be, and at how blind we are to the obvious when we are so literally involved in our own images.

"Isn't your ex named Bill?" he pondered. "And what's his woman's name? Is it Maryanne?"

"Anne-Marie," I said, then quickly went on, "but this is Maryanne, my friend from college. Maryanne and her husband William." I was stuck in the visual images and couldn't see the way the dream was punning on the names.

"Maryanne, Ann-Marie. William, Bill. Pretty close," he added. The dream had actually taken the faces of my college friend, Maryanne, and her husband, William, but played on the names of my son's father and step-mother. Furthermore, I had listed my condo for sale exactly six months before, the approximate age of the baby boy in the dream. RB certainly knew about the guilt I felt at my decision to leave my son in the care of my ex-husband during his last two years of high school. He repeated, "Looks like your baby's going to be fine."

When I had my "Ah ha!" moment of revelation, I was, of course, over-joyed that I had been given the ticket to move. RB brought me back to the scene at the lake. We looked at the snakes again. I knew they were sacred guardians, ancient symbols of transformation and change. I left RB's office that day with another idea from out of the blue—that I would rent my condo and move as soon as I lined up some adjunct teaching in Boston. It would be another several months before I pulled the move together—and both my son and I needed time to get used to the idea. But the question had been settled and I trusted the unconscious, which knows no past or future, to assure me I could leave without damaging my son.

THEORY VS. REALITY

Despite the reassurance of my unconscious, it was harder parting from my son than I had ever imagined. The movers came earlier than I anticipated on a hot Monday in August. And they immediately began hauling one piece of my life after another out of our tiny living room into the deep recesses of the truck, while my son J and I stood gaping at each other. I had planned that he would drive down to Boston with me for my first night in my new home. I was pushing my budget, but had decided on a two-bedroom apartment, hoping that he might want to spend more time there after he got used to it. I wanted him to feel from day one that it was his home too. Yet at the moment, I saw the huge moving truck as a threatening whale, too rapidly swallowing us both into its black belly.

Over the past year or so, my son had made a collage on his bedroom wall, meticulously cutting up old issues of his *Sports Illustrated* magazines. He and his best friend, another J (we called him J-Two) whom I also adored, spent hours on the floor of his room arranging and rearranging the pieces before they went up on the wall. My J and J-Two, were fifteen—the age of giggling and discovery. They had first met in Little League in the fourth grade, but it wasn't until they attended the same middle school when they discovered they had the same birthday that they became pals—"twins separated at birth." At eleven, twelve, and thirteen, they had been delightful to observe. They lip-synched rap songs all done up in hip-hop costumes and made movies with J-Two's father's video camera. I don't know how many times during their sleep-overs they watched the video of the original *Airplane* and laughed until they cried. In the previous two years, I must have made a hundred pans of brownies for them, and driven them to the mall and baseball practice a hundred times. Though the quality time was brief and getting briefer, I relished all these moments and argued with myself about giving them up. Did J really still need me? After all, he wasn't a grown man yet. (J's room had never been off limits to me, so I knew that a few of my Victoria's Secrets catalogues with Cindy Crawford and company in their gossamer underwear had been, now and again, stashed under the bed.)

The sports collage had grown along with the boys. It webbed across one wall, then climbed higher, sprawling over the closet and around the corner above the bed.

It was an expression of artistry as much as idolatry. Reaching over and under each other were the various shapes of Bo Jackson, Michael Jordan, Larry Bird, Mario Lemieux, all of the 1986 Pennant-winning Red Sox, and so many other sports heroes—running, leaping, dribbling and skating across the teal-blue walls. The collage was still hanging when the last stick of furniture had been carried out to the moving van. It would be the last piece of our life there to be dismantled.

I asked J to take the collage down, casually instructing him to fold it, assuring him we could reassemble it in the new apartment in Boston. When I returned to the room, I found J slumped on the floor crying. When I saw him stricken with grief in the empty room, collapsed on the carpet, his elbows on his knees, his fists in his eyes, I realized my mistake and stood as if smacked by a plank, knowing that, if I apologized for the move one more time, I would not be able to hold back my own tears. I slumped to the floor next to him and he threw himself into my arms, holding his breath until we were both openly sobbing. I couldn't believe I was hurting him this way. It had been bad enough that his father and I split up when he was only five. Now, ten years later, he was losing his mother.

J had been supportive of the idea of my moving when we discussed it, as we did many times before I started taking real steps to relocate. But, in my self-preserving denial, my persevering determination to move on in my life, I couldn't afford to notice the brave front he was putting up. J's astrological chart is flooded with water energy. He is a Scorpio with Pisces rising and a Pisces Moon. He has no earth in his chart at all, but a few oceans of water. He is here to experience emotion and to release attachments. Astrologers have told me he is extremely sensitive and will develop psychic abilities later on in his life. But none of that crossed my mind as I held onto him there on the floor of his bedroom in the empty condo.

We cried together, looking up at the collage, and I tried to point out how easily it could be reassembled. He kept shaking his head through his tears. "No, Mom, it's over. I don't want to see it in Boston." I knew there was a certain wisdom in his words. The collage exemplified a chapter in his life that was closing, had perhaps already closed. He was an older teenager now, looking back nostalgically at his adolescent self. We were both weeping as I held him close and ran my hand through his wavy blonde hair, kissing his freckled nose and forehead. Instead of my telling him he'd be all right—"it will be all right, everything will be all right"—he told *me*, as he pulled away from my babying embrace, "I'll be okay, Mom, I'm just sad. I know you have to go." Sniffling bravely, he said, "But you're gonna have to take the collage down by yourself."

One of the movers stepped into the room and then pulled back at the sight of us both crying and clinging to each other. I told the mover I would meet them down in Boston in a few hours. It occurred to me that, by the time we got to Boston and unloaded the truck, it would be late; J would be bored with unpacking, not to mention emotional. It was going to be a very long day. As much as I hated to, I suggested a change of plans—that he spend the night at his Dad's. I promised I would come back for the weekend and assured him I would visit often. I had friends I could stay with for as long as I wanted. Then we called his Dad to come pick him up.

A half hour later, as the two of them drove away, I could scarcely speak. My ex hadn't thought I'd really go through with the move and, although he tried not to disapprove overtly, I could read his scolding thoughts from the expression on his face. J was hanging on me despite his new chauvinism. And he only began to smile when his father joked about something private between them. Then the horrendous moment passed. I stood there looking down the driveway, following the station wagon around the corner until it became a tiny dot on Beach street, erasing for a moment the aperture between houses through which I could view the water.

I went back inside and walked through the empty condo. My tenant was moving in the following week and I needed to leave the place clean and tidy. I worked on automatic pilot, unable to block the memory of the day when we'd moved in six years earlier. Still crying, I unplugged the refrigerator, opened the door, and wiped down the shelves. For ten minutes straight, I stabbed with a dull knife at a clot of frozen chocolate ice cream grafted onto the freezer wall. As hopeless as Lady Macbeth, I scrubbed at the stain of my guilt as hard as I could. Finally, I rinsed the sponge and placed it in the plastic dish. Then I dragged myself upstairs to J's room and stood facing the wall where his bed had been.

I thought for only a brief moment of one of many stories I had read him under the lamp light next to his bed, Madeleine L'Engle's *A Wrinkle in Time*. I felt fluid myself, fluid enough to pass through the walls into my next life. In a half-assed ritual, I prayed to the Great Mother for forgiveness and strength. Then, hardly discerning which figure was which, through a veil of new tears, I undid the collage myself, folding each fragile figure into the one remaining box.

A SHAKY START

My third night in my new apartment, I awoke with this dream:

> *J IS LYING UNCONSCIOUS AT THE BOTTOM of a boat. It's a small dingy and he is small—four or five years old. I am frantically reaching down to lift him out, but each time I bend into the boat, another huge wave washes over us both and it takes several interminable moments before I can lift my own head above the water and try again to reach him. I notice that the water has slowly accumulated in the dingy and that if I do not get him out, he will sink with the boat. I am fighting against invisible pressures that render me inept, uncoordinated, and clumsy. I reach and reach, but each time a wave comes, the boat rocks away from me. Finally, I see that I cannot get to him, that if he is not dead already, he will surely drown. I am beside myself, thinking this can't be happening, this can't be happening, this can't be happening . . . and yet there is no one else there, no one to hear my screams, no one to help.* 🐚

I had worked all alone for three days unpacking, hanging pictures and curtains, placing plants, filling drawers, moving furniture, vacuuming, cleaning, greeting the men from the phone company, the gas and cable companies, unpiling my thirty-two boxes of books. I was so relieved to wake that morning and realize that I had "only" been dreaming. But I wondered about the unconscious advice I had received that "the baby would be fine" in the basket on the lake. If that were so, why was J now sinking into the sea?

I had such a difficult time trying to shake off the image of the swamped dingy that I couldn't get up. I put the pillow over my head and let all my emotions drop. I sobbed and sobbed. I hadn't realized how much energy it had taken to suppress my own horror at leaving my son. Although I'd spoken to him several times a day since I left, I was plagued by a terrible, superstitious anxiety. I tried to think rationally. I supposed it was good that the dream finally provided a scenario in which I could *feel* my sorrow. If I had had the dream a week earlier, I never could have moved at all. I lay in my bed without even the strength to make coffee. I spent the whole day there, weeping in a kind of penance, sleeping and praying alternately. I had never felt so lonely. In my reptilian brain, terror and guilt hissed and snarled. Yet there was a center in my chest, to the right of my ragged heart, that held itself calmly. A little yogi sat there in lotus posture. He understood the passage for what it was—another sea journey, a necessary crossing. J and I were two separate souls in separate vessels.

I had been in the grip of the many-tentacled monster of the deep several times before in my life. My destiny was to weather a series of dramatic changes. I knew that. I knew the element of water. In this incarnation, I was leaving the land where emotion ruled. I must have done water over and over in other lives. I have no water in my chart, but many planets in water houses, which shows I have both experience and interest in emotional depths. My life lessons suggest that I find the right balance within my own emotional attachments and that I meet others at their crossings.

Later that evening, another synchronicity reassured me. I finally roused myself to wander the rooms of my new home and floated toward a box on one of the book cases marked "Jungian books." I reached through the piles on the floor, choosing randomly among them, my eye catching one title. I lay in bed that whole day with Gaston Bachelard's book *Water and Dreams: An Essay on the Imagination of Matter.* "Matter . . . Mother . . . Water . . . ," I thought as I read.

> Death is a journey, and a journey is a death. To leave is to die a little. To die is truly to leave, and no one leaves well, courageously, cleanly, except by following the current, the flow of the wide river. All rivers join the River of the Dead. This is the only mythical death, the only departure that is an adventure.[1]

Bachelard's wisdom wrapped my body like the quilt I had wrapped around my shoulders as I curled back beneath the sheets.

> One entire facet of our nocturnal soul can be explained by the myth of death conceived as a departure over water. For the dreamer, there is a continuing transposition between this departure and death. For some dreamers, water is the new movement that beckons us toward a journey never made.[2]

My journey-never-made was ongoing, each new phase a deeper penetration into self-actualization. "Matter, Mother, Water." If I had stayed, I would have made my son more and more my whole life. And when he left me, *not if,* when—only a matter of a few years down the road—*when* he left me, I might not have had the energy of the anger I utilized then to find myself a new life. It wasn't just that I had chosen the journey. I had chosen the journey because

---

1. Gaston Bachelard, *Water and Dreams: An Essay on the Imagination of Matter* (Dallas: The Pegasus Foundation. The Dallas Institute of Humanities and Culture, 1983), p. 74.
2. Bachelard, *Water and Dreams; An Essay on the Imagination of Matter,* p. 75.

it was the one that came to meet me, one that I was ready to undertake. If I hadn't moved forward, I felt as if I would have backed up on myself, become embittered, and died. An unhappy mother, perhaps more dangerous than one who visits from a distance. I won't ever know how it might have been otherwise. I consoled myself with the knowledge that J's soul had chosen me as his mother and that this experience was part of our mutual growth.

And both J and I did survive emotionally intact. "The call of water demands, as it were, a total offering, an inner offering. Water needs an inhabitant."[3] I felt for my lost voice, cleared my throat, and called J to find him safe on dry land, watching television and reading *Sports Illustrated.*

Jung used the word "animus" to define a woman's internalized masculine energy. My own young animus in J's image, the one who lay in the sinking boat, was the newest representation for my latest psychic death. On the third day, I was entombed in the womb of "mother," *(mere/mer)*, immersed in her own element, surrendering my most treasured attachment.

---

3. Bachelard, *Water and Dreams; An Essay on the Imagination of Matter,* p. 164.

Chapter 4

IN THE LAKE OF THE BED

*It costs so much to be a full human being . . . One has to abandon altogether
the search for security, reach out to the risk of living with both arms . . .
one has to court doubt and darkness as the cost of knowing.*
MORRIS WEST, *IN THE SHOES OF THE FISHERMAN*

The years vanished and my life went on in Boston as J graduated from high
school and moved on to college. I had long forgotten the manner in which
I arrived in my new life. Likewise, I had written off the incident with the
bedrooms as some freak glitch in the matrix of three-dimensional life. But I
kept searching for more inner knowledge to conquer my sorrows, believing I
was indeed a "normal" person—albeit a normal person with a biochemical
propensity for depression. From the ads for anti-depressant and anti-anxiety
medications that I saw on television, I imagined there were many of us. I
was hungry and thirsty, but food didn't satisfy. Even the mediocre bottle of
wine I sometimes turned to when alone at night was too-soon empty, leaving
me still sober and not even fatigued enough to sleep. I had had eight years
of Jungian analysis—four with a woman, four with a man—and despite all
the help I had received in dream work from my two Jungian mentors, all the
progress I'd made in processing unconscious material, I knew that never-end-
ing therapy was a luxury I couldn't afford.

I remembered Carl Jung's comments to Bill Wilson, the founder of
Alcoholics Anonymous. Jung told him his problem was not psychological; it
was spiritual. His thirst was for *spiritual fulfillment*. I recalled that, in the 19th
century, alcoholic drinks were referred to as "spirits" and realized that the
huge population of drug and alcohol abusers on the planet were not just
suffering from what might be genetic tendencies, but also from a thirst for
what the fast-paced, materialistic, superficial culture had practically eradicated—deep connections to spirit and soul. I too wanted to get out of my
own skin, to get out of this world, to go *outside* of my mind.

I remembered words of Meister Eckhart: "God is home; we are the far country." I believe that we can be closer to God, Goddess, or whatever you want to call the creative life force. As a poet, I pursued the elusive higher truths of my existence. I believe that spiritual help is there if we can only cross the wilderness of strip malls and cement lots where humanity appears to be permanently parked. I studied books about the Gnostics, the Druids, the Greeks, the Egyptians, and other indigenous cultures. I knew there were ages when the human species lived surrounded by a metaphysical consciousness, a world where objects and rituals and natural events were imbued with transcendent value. Modern consciousness, if it has a spiritual component at all, considers it to be *within* and, like many pilgrims, I searched for the simple spirit of godliness inside myself. Was I avoiding relationship? Maybe, but heartbreak had made me hypersensitive, and I found that solitude and meditation had become a satisfying part of my existence.

With my male analyst, the Dutch Jungian Robert Bosnak, I learned how to enter the alternative reality of a dreamscape. I knew that inner changes can happen by holding and sustaining an intended image consistently and faithfully, until it is a stable new field of reality that I can then step into and inhabit. There is a tremendous challenge, however, when the field you create and recreate both unconsciously and through habitual thinking is defeated and limiting. When you feel that the inner life is like an underdeveloped country with a shaky infrastructure—primitive, disadvantaged, and depressed. When the world gives back an image of success that is predominantly materialistic. Or when you undermine your conscious wishes with your own unconscious beliefs. *Success is happiness.* A psychic named Angel Gail once told me that. And happiness is a psychic state within that does not necessarily translate into material comforts, but rather into spiritual wholeness, love for others, and self-acceptance.

Despite continuing proclivities toward depression, I had to recreate myself *by myself,* and the one hour a week I couldn't afford with my analyst RB would have to be replaced with another practice. I promised myself I would not only meditate, but set time aside to visualize the changes I wanted in my energy field. So I reluctantly terminated my personal analysis with RB. As an international teacher, he still facilitated intensive dream work weekends, and I planned to keep in touch with his work through his workshops. I was still attending weekend classes at Boston's Jung Institute and developed an interest in archetypal studies. I joined a year-long monthly group led by Thomas Moore, the (now renowned) author, ex-monk, and psychologist who had many affinities with the work of Jung and the post-Jungian founder of archetypal psychology, James Hillman.

One Sunday each month, this group of twelve to fifteen people met for a day of study. I had not relinquished my interest in the underside of culture and was fascinated by Moore's book *Dark Eros*, a study of the Marquis de Sade. Imagine my surprise a few years later when my reputable psychic, David Hall, told me I had known the Marquis in a past life in France. Through an experiment in past-life regression, I experienced the life of an Abbesse in an earlier century. ("From the nun's veil to the Marquis de Sade!" I thought. "I've certainly been around.") But what surprised me was that this side of my personality, my interest in darkness and intensity, in the horrors of violence, persisted, as did my reading of literature on the Holocaust, Vietnam, and war in general. I think I chose to penetrate these regions so as not to be terrified and conquered by the thought of them.

Alone in my apartment one Sunday, I lay on my bed, deep into Tim O'Brien's novel *In the Lake of the Woods*. The book's narrator, a veteran of the Vietnam War, revisits in memory the massacre at My Lai. I remember reading the haunting prose, visualizing the images of flying chicken feathers, sand, and dust exploding into the atmosphere as the young American soldiers with orders from Lt. Calley rounded up civilians from the small village and fired their rounds into women, children, and old men. It was a horrific scene I remembered from actual photos in *Life* magazine, made all the more creepy by O'Brien's surreal and immaculate prose. As I read, I became frightened by the distinct sensation of a ghost in the room—a feeling I had never known before, but that I seemed to recognize immediately.

I felt a soft but particular pressure on the mattress of the bed, as if someone had just sat down beside me. Marking the book with my finger, I closed it and stared at the comforter. It was covered in a red satin duvet and lay flat with a few graceful folds. But something felt unusual, if not impossible. I was floating—floating as if on a raft over water. I closed my eyes. Small but obvious waves rocked beneath me. It was a calm sea, but clearly in motion. I registered the feeling as objectively as I could: "Okay . . . I am most definitely afloat."

As I sat there, more astonished than anything else, I felt a gentle, ever-so-slight tapping on the tops of my feet. First a tapping and then a magnetic-like pulling away of the air above my feet. I don't know how I knew, but I knew there were hands there, working the air around my feet, magnifying it, stretching it like taffy or putty. I had a sense of their movement, an almost audible rustle in the air around me.

I focused my senses so that my attention was precise. There was no doubt about what I was feeling and little doubt that the invisible hands were moving intently in the vicinity of my socks. It was as if I had developed another sense. This is still very difficult to describe. It was as if I could hear or see hands moving, and yet it was more than a feeling; it was a *knowing.*

My legs were straight out in front of me, crossed at the ankles. Book in one hand, I leapt off the bed and stood gaping back at it. I yanked the covers off quickly, then shook them out, one at a time. It was a cold day in September and I had an extra quilt on top of the comforter, then two blankets, then sheets. I systematically tore the bedding apart until only the thin quilted mattress pad covered the bed. Then I propped up the pillows against the spindles of painted brass, and crawled to the middle of the bed again, my back to the brass headboard and the wall behind it.

This time, as I set myself back up with my book, pillows propping my back, I examined the white mattress pad beneath me, pulling my knees up and pressing my feet flat on the firm mattress to stabilize my position. I sat and waited. Not long. Not long at all—until the floating sensation arrived again, followed by the taps on my feet and the stretched pull of the air.

I stared at the area around my feet and thought I saw it shimmer. Shimmer, that is, as in *quiver.* Thin little tremors in the air. Almost silver? No, transparent tremors; yes, transparent but perceptible, like heat above a fire, or a mirage on the highway—the way the expelled exhaust of cars affects your vision. I was dumbfounded. I got up and looked under the bed, then patted with both hands all over the top of it. Furious, I jumped up again and tore off the mattress pad. I don't know what I expected to find there. Everything looked perfectly normal. Still, I felt fear and decided then and there to move into the second bedroom—the one I had set up for my son right across the hall. I knew it was colder in that room and I dragged some of the bedding with me, throwing it carelessly on his slim single bed, pulling the quilt across my shoulders like a cloak. I remember having the odd thought that a mouse might have chewed into my mattress.

Years ago, in my house in Maine, mice had somehow managed to transport pieces of dry dog food from our pantry, through the walls, and into the drawers of the hutch in the dining room where I kept the cloth napkins, tablecloths, and place mats. Although it made no sense, for some reason I thought something similar was occurring now. It was not such a wild theory, and one I frankly preferred to that of invisible guests. And the sensation that *hands* were rustling through the air? Well, I just couldn't explain anything at all about that. Finally, in denial, I dismissed it, attributing it to my imagination. I was at an important place in my book, after all. It was Sunday; I was relaxing; I just wanted to continue reading.

Convincing myself of the mice theory, I decided not to tend to it at the moment.

So, once ensconced on my son's bed, I forgot about my disturbance and returned to O'Brien's Vietnam. I preferred the gory details of the My Lai massacre to the prospect of ghosts in my bedroom. Then again, I stopped reading and thought, perhaps there was a relationship between my reading material and what I was sensing around me. Maybe I was evoking mysterious presences by reading this dark story. I closed the book again, deciding it was time for my afternoon meditation.

OF MICE AND MEDITATION

I began practicing Transcendental Meditation (TM) in 1973, when I was twenty-five. I have stuck with it religiously, because it always gives me an energy lift and I feel that my health in general has improved because of it. I no longer have as many colds, flu, or sore throats, from which I had suffered all too regularly throughout my life.

The first few minutes of my meditations usually require the most discipline. I move around a little, trying to get more comfortable, scratching the itch that inevitably starts somewhere on my body, moving my shoulders up or down to find the perfect posture. The standard TM position is simply to sit with your neck and head unsupported. On my bed, I always rest my back against the headboard, my legs sometimes out straight, but more often folded Indian style. After five minutes or so of watching my thoughts battle for attention, I begin to feel settled and become aware of a slight buzz in my ears. Most of the time, after five to eight minutes, I disappear into the sleep that is not sleep—a restful *Theta* state in which there is no time or space at all. I think I may have been on the threshold of that restful entry state when I felt the taps begin again. Quiet taps. Tap. Pause. Tap. Right on the tops of my feet. I froze and opened as many senses as I could. Yes, I was floating once more and there were not just hands but *fingers*—fingers moving in a sewing motion, pulling magnetic threads through the outlines of my feet.

Distracted but determined, I ignored the imaginary fingers, imagined a ring of protective light around myself, and returned to my mantra. I must have let go, because I went deeply into meditation after another ten minutes. Sometimes when I meditate, my head drops forward a little, although I am not usually aware of it until I come out of the meditative state. But this time, I gradually "awoke" to a very gentle hand lifting my chin. I will go as far as to say a "beautiful" hand, despite its invisibility. I felt the touch was the most tender feeling I had ever palpably known. But suddenly, I realized the implications of this experience. *Egads!!* It was just too much—too much to believe. I jumped up again. Close to tears, I fled the room.

I don't remember how I dealt with my invisible guest for the rest of that day and night. I think I prayed. I know I got on the phone and told two close friends about the experience. Neither of them dismissed it as a figment of my imagination. One suggested it could be hormonal changes in my skin. Another told me a tale about a mouse inside a coffee table. And my mouse theory—though a theory without evidence, no holes, no dog food, no tiny turds, no munch marks—still lingered in the back of my head. I knew, of course, that mice did not have gentle, tender hands, but I decided not to look at *that*. I did call and make an appointment with David Hall, the trustworthy psychic whom I had seen once a year for the past several years.

David had encouraged my dream work and continued to say I was a "light worker," a healer for the coming changes in human evolution. He was not specific about these changes, however, except to say that they had to do with intuitive powers. He usually offered a good overview of my spiritual life, suggested places to focus my creativity, gave me warnings about wrong decisions, and consoled me for my sorrows. All in all, I found his readings heartening and sincere. He had been accurate about my decision to move to Boston from northern New England and about some questions pertaining to my family. Years later, he predicted the sudden death of "an old friend" who, it later turned out, tragically died in the TWA 800 airline disaster of 1996. And he reassured me, well before it was diagnosed, that another friend's potentially cancerous growth was benign. I had faith in David, not because he could "see" the future, but because he explained to me how most psychic knowledge worked in probabilities that were always open to change, given the fact that human free will is an important factor in how "reality" plays out.

Unfortunately, however, I had to wait two weeks for my appointment. And when I talked to David on the phone, I have to say that, despite my past trust in him, he just about scared me to death. He had once been a Protestant minister and I think it was this Puritan influence or a belief in black magic that first started him worrying. He promptly told me to rearrange my bedroom furniture, and if I had one, to place a crucifix in the room. I joked with him that this was Brookline, not Salem, and that I was not Goode Deborah. He didn't laugh. Instead, he suggested that, until we met, I read Psalm 91 aloud once a day. David had never seemed particularly religious in any traditional way, and I was surprised as well as suspicious of his reaction. Yet I trusted that he knew about spirit possession and other darker matters of the occult world.

I had a small tattered Bible from college and I looked up the psalm, only to discover it was all about protection against Satan! This fueled my fear, but also my fury. Although I'd been raised Catholic, I never believed in any traditional idea about hell or Satan, though I did know there were confused spirits between the worlds who could, by their own confusion and fear, haunt the Earth. It would be an understatement to say I was uncomfortable with the idea that invisible entities, as tender and sweet as their touch seemed to be, were putting their hands on me.

Although I respected David's ability to download information from his "guides," I knew he'd had religious issues and I wasn't going to blow his Satanic protection advice out of proportion. True, my ingrained Catholic chemistry may have made me more inclined to superstition than others, but mostly I felt blessed and surrounded by grace. It wasn't that my life was overflowing with abundance. But through dream therapy and inner work, I had created a soulful perspective and felt my rich inner life was valuable. I felt protected, in general, because I had survived my father's breakdown and death. I had summoned the courage to divorce, to endure deep depression and heartbreak, and to significantly relocate my home. My past inability to contain my dark emotions had brought me a good deal of psychological suffering, but I was still a functioning being. Although lonely and struggling financially, I didn't want for much. When I counted my blessings, there were many.

And I had learned to pray again. I certainly felt closer to "God" than I had for many many years. I didn't think I was being "tested," or "called," or seeing into other dimensions. Yes, in the past I had heard a disembodied voice, encountered synchronicities, and had both prescient and teaching dreams. But I wasn't putting all my experiences in some psychic basket and drawing any conclusions. I knew atoms were spinning, but I subscribed to a belief that the world I knew was made of concrete matter and my senses were circumscribed. Still, I taught in my composition classes a favorite essay by Annie Dilliard about experiencing a spontaneous altered state and I had read Whitley Striber's *Communion* and the late Harvard psychiatrist John Mack's books on working with victims of alien abduction. I believed aliens existed, but I had never seen them. If what I was experiencing was an alien, then I insisted it was not one of the so-called "Grays," but one of the good kind, like E.T.

All in all, I had no argument with the existence of an invisible world. I'd played with the idea ever since I had imaginary friends in childhood. John Mack's clients spoke of information from aliens that parallels many of the discoveries I had been making—that fields of energy have power, that there is a new light frequency on Earth, that the air we breathe is infused with a new vibration intending to awaken humanity. I recognized that the planet is in danger from the exploitation and poor distribution of resources, as well as the problems of overpopulation and pollution. And I was more intensely concerned about all these issues now that my immediate environment had a new intensity—a literal vibration around my body. In fact, I was only slightly worried that my dark side might have produced some kind of Spielberg gremlin.

Admittedly, I *did* read the 91st psalm aloud: "My refuge and my fortress . . . no evil will befall . . . no scourge will come near . . . ." I very much liked both the poetic content and form of "A thousand may fall at your side, ten thousand at your right hand, but it will not come near you . . . ." Yes, I even went as far as following all of David's advice, changing the position of the furniture in my bedroom and making sure the crucifix at the end of my childhood rosary was dangling from the frame of the famous Black Madonna of Czestochowa. I laughed at myself as I went about my rituals, recalling how, in childhood, my brother and I had done everything but hang garlic cloves in the windows after reading Bram Stoker's *Count Dracula*. I did take similar precautions, but something other than fear of Satan motivated me. My incentive was to invoke protection and invite loving spirits into my home.

Most of the time, what I felt was energetic pressure on various parts of my body. But occasionally, I awoke in the morning feeling hands working *inside* me. I recall awakening one morning with the feeling that I was pinned down as Gulliver had been by the Lilliputians. It felt exactly as if I were tied into position by many thin strings. Still somewhat asleep, I took a moment to tune into the feeling further. Then it was as if there were several arms lying right across my chest. I lay there frozen for a few moments. Yet these spirits were also mind readers. They suddenly seemed to know I was awake and they lifted their arms and backed off immediately. Sometimes, if I was alone when the tapping sensations began around my feet, I hollered out loud: "Stop it!" I tried to remember how loving the hand had felt that had lifted my chin in meditation that day, but I definitely did not want to encounter an alien force.

I phoned my analyst RB as well, who suggested that I come in for an appointment so we could try to communicate with the spirit. Something in me held back, however. I felt he would interpret all of this psychologically. I did believe that people could develop psychosomatic anomalies or illnesses, but I did not consider myself prone to unconscious imaginings. I knew from my dreams, of course, that there are feelings I repress. But I make my dreams as conscious as possible, and I was feeling more "normal" than I had in a long time—content, if not happy, with my life. I was without a partner, but I had an agenda that was going strong. My third collection of poetry, *Where Divinity Begins,* had just come out from a reputable poetry press and I had readings scheduled. But the irony of the simultaneous arrival of my book (especially the suggestion of the title) with the arrival of my invisible friends was lost on me at the time.

I had also been participating for several years in a peer poetry workshop that met every week at my house. I was making friends and had adjunct teaching posts at several colleges, which expanded my exposure. I had hopes that eventually I'd find a full-time teaching position. I never even thought about the previous psychic episode, my vision of the old bedroom that sad morning in my home in Maine when I was breaking up with my lover. All I could think of was that I had *never* experienced anything quite like this in my life. These hands were as real as human hands. This new energy around my body created an atmosphere I had never felt in the air before. This was something entirely new, and it felt entirely *other*.

THE SOUL WHENCE AND WHITHER

I can't say I remember getting used to the sensations, but as days passed, I went about my life as usual, only feeling more fearful at night when I was alone. I left the bottom of my hurricane lamp glowing as a night light in my bedroom. Although I put in a pale pink light bulb, it still kept me from falling asleep easily. But it felt better than being left in the dark with the strange fingers. I had some alarming thoughts about the dead clinging to the living, and even thought someone might have sent me some kind of whammy—or perhaps that my preoccupation with intense reading had summoned some black thought-forms to hover about, like one of the dark "elementals" that Carlos Casteneda refers to in his books. And since I am a reader, I ran out to the spiritual bookstores and spent all sorts of money on books about spirit contact.

Then I found a title in my own bookcase, which, prompted by nothing more than instinct, I had taken home one day just before I sold the small bookstore I owned in Maine. I had ordered it impulsively, interested by the description in the catalog and the title, *The Soul Whence and Whither*. The book, first published in 1918, contained material edited from lectures given at Suresnes, France by a certain Hazrat Inayat Khan. Its cover sported a sepia photograph of an early 20th-century Eastern guru. I recall how a friend and I were amused by the intense stare this swami shot out from the cover. In one chapter, "Spiritualism," Khan explained the concept that the dead hear and feel the thoughts of the living when the living focus upon them. This worried me. Sometimes in my depression, I spoke to my father, who died unexpectedly when I was fifteen. The book also gave a straightforward description of an apparitional presence in the third dimension. Suffice it to say that I found it appallingly similar to the sensations I was having. The book described almost exactly the faint buzzing noise and the magnetism of the pull in the air as signs of the presence of spirits. I was eerily wary, but something inside me accepted the idea as natural.

After a week or so, although I was still frightened at night, I became convinced that whatever it was would not harm me. And during the agonizing wait for my appointment with David Hall, I suddenly recalled a similar experience I had had the previous year when I spent the month of January at the MacDowell Colony in New Hampshire, where I was awarded a month-long fellowship to write.

It was the winter of 1993 and there had been an incredible ice storm. Winds blew, snow swirled, temperatures plummeted. I was living in a little cabin that served as my studio. Actually, it was not so small; it housed a grand piano and a fireplace, a bed and a few chairs, including a rocker—suitable studio space for living and working all in one room. But it was one of the more distant cabins, a good ten-minute walk to the main lodge for meals. This night, I didn't think I could make it to the lodge. The electricity was out due to wires weighted down with ice, no doubt. I was fortunate to have a big pile of wood on my porch and my days of living by the heat of Norwegian wood stoves in Maine had trained me in the making of fires. This was well before cell phones and, although I was curious about the outside world, I also found the whole experience adventurous and cozy. I had some candles with me and I made myself as comfortable as possible. I knew the snow would stop eventually, probably by morning, and I had a supply of munchies too. I remember falling asleep late that night and then awakening slowly, sensing a low pressure of weight on the bed.

I awoke immediately, but felt no fear. As I sat up in bed, I felt I was pulled into a sitting position by an invisible force and kissed on the mouth! For some reason, I had a flash that there were angels in the room. The weight on the bed had been palpable, but it was gentle too, and the force was almost magnetic. In the morning, I thought I might have dreamt it, but I remembered it distinctly and made some notes for a poem. It was such a pleasant dream that I tried to write about it, but the unfinished poem never captured my sense of comfort and exhilaration. Not long after, my friend John sent me a postcard from a museum in Amsterdam with the blown-up detail of a painting by Carvaggio of an angel kissing a woman on the mouth. It was one of those lovely synchronicities that was followed almost immediately by another when I came across a contemporary black-and-white photograph on a postcard by New York photographer Duane Michaels. This was a more comic, but also erotic, image of a man wearing little more than a jock strap and wings, leaning forward to kiss a woman in the middle of her bed in a big Manhattan loft. This image prompted me to write a more successful, playful poem that I called "Fallen Angel," after the photo's title. Both these incidents happened in the early Nineties, after a so-called "photon light belt" had been ushered in by the claims of the New Agers, who fixed its arrival on the date of the Harmonic Convergence in August, 1987, when an extraordinary alignment of planets occurred. In the ensuing years angel-mania took hold around the world.

The Fallen Angel

after the photograph by Duane Michaels

She's leaning up in the island of her bed,
knees flung open through her French cut teddy
as if she had expected his arrival

through the huge room's starry window
where the radiator glows,
awakened, like her throat

with the sudden host of his tongue in her mouth.
Naked, he's climbed astride her, pulpy wings
strapped to his back and belted round his belly—

If that's a drawback, well,
that's how he got here, winged it—
through a down draft in the alley

and you take what you get sometimes.
She's up for it anyways, up on her elbows,
her many fingers, gasping fish, replenished

by new waters, *and God, I'd take him*
whoever he is—Zeus, Apollo, Hermes—
gold ringletted hair, maple tree of a torso,

left hand, a wand, casting a spell across her nipple—
But what do I know from sex? It's been a while.
Are angels safe?

Can that plaid woolen blanket maintain
room temperature beneath their weight?
Or will it steam and hydroplane like a magic carpet

launching—Watch those falling pillows
tilt the floor
as if some prime mover

ordained a radiant resurrection,
sun coming up, white-out backdrop,
already the eight foot windows burning.

Her soul is sold,
though dressed in down-home wings, she thinks
he may be an imposter—Still,

Manhattan slumbers there
suspended like heaven
And his webbed fingers probe

the dimple in her chin,
propping her sweet face eternally under his
so this moment might never end

though if it does—
she'll have this sky-scraping simian
in the loft of her memory. This horny dream,

this shifty apparition, luciferous
spectre in diaphanous flesh—and yes,
God yes, I'm jealous.

Chapter 5

AWAKENING TO ASCENSION

We are a species that can explore and study its world; a species that looks for meaning. We are a species with self-consciousness; a species that knows that it knows.
PETER RUSSELL, *WAKING UP IN TIME*

By the time my appointment with David Hall arrived, I was a lot more calm. I had been living with the energies for two weeks and, aside from annoying me with a slight disturbance in the immediate field of my body, as far as I could tell, my "spirits" weren't causing me any harm. David greeted me anxiously at the door and we sat down on high stools in the kitchen. David is a scryer. He uses a placemat-size piece of black glass to connect with his guides, who give him images, phrases, and words when he focuses on the name of a client. The first time I saw him at work, I was astonished that he asked for nothing in advance but my name. When I arrived, he already had a sheaf of notes about me. By the time of this meeting, he knew my issues: money, my writing, more stable job possibilities, the hope of relationship, my spiritual growth, advice for my son.

"I saw a lion stroll by," he said. "It stopped and it turned and smiled at you."

"Lion, Leo, creativity," I said, thinking aloud.

"Hmmm, maybe. It was an especially strong message about your own power. I understood that you are going to be healed, deeply, at the *cellular level*," he said, looking up from his notes into my eyes. "And then, eventually, you're going to heal others."

I just sat there. He had not said this before, but certainly all my therapy with my analysts Noni and RB had affected my own healing and I did work with other people's dreams.

"I think these new energies you feel around you are emissaries. I got the sense of some angelic presence, but there are also soul extensions."

"Soul extensions?" I echoed. "What exactly are they?"

David smiled. "I'm not sure exactly. Don't know if anyone is. But it is known that we are multi-dimensional beings. That the past lives we refer to are actually on-going because of the nature of the Eternal Now. You understand that concept, don't you?" Yes, we had spoken of this before and I did understand that time itself is only a construct to which we collectively subscribe, that everything is actually going on in the same eternal moment.

"So my past lives are here to meet me?" I chuckled at the idea.

"And your future lives," David added, just above a whisper. We stared at each other. "The Future That Brought Her Here," I thought silently, the name of the poem I'd written about my first otherworldly experience, the long-forgotten flashback years ago during that period of extreme grief. When I wrote the poem, I didn't know where it came from or how it was that this phrase became the last line as well as the title of my poem.

David leaned back on the stool and said seriously, "Actually, you may be an adept." Strangely, I reminded him that I had told him, during another reading a few years back when he mentioned I had a profound future in "water issues," that I have no planets in water (the emotional realm) in my astrological chart. At that time, he pulled a book off a shelf and read to me a passage about how an adept whose soul has completed the knowledge of water, or the world of raw emotion, usually presents with a chart in which none of the planets appear in water signs, but many in water houses. This is the case with my chart. So why do I have such sensitivities? "Because," David answered, in past lives you have had very deep fluid experiences that usually sensitize an individual to emotional suffering. These moments of profound feeling help you to become a psychopomp for others in their suffering." That was vague enough to mean *anything* to me, but I tried to follow David's description.

"This has something to do with your father," he said." Tell me that story again."

I sighed. "Here's the short version: He was wonderful; he was a doctor, an artist and a poet. He got hooked on medical drugs in the early Sixties when they were very strong; he died from an overdose when I was an adolescent. I'm exactly his age now, the age when he died," I said abruptly. We looked at each other. "Forty-seven," I added, in numerology an eleven, a vibration that demands more from an individual, but delivers more as well.

"What's the legacy?" he asked.

I had to think a few moments. "Well, he wanted to leave medicine, to be an artist, a writer too. He became a doctor for his own father. He wrote poems; I write poems. My father had a dark side; I have a dark side . . . I don't know!" I said, throwing up my hands. "There were times I smoked pot and drank a lot. Maybe that's the legacy? "

"Well, that was the Sixties," David mumbled, distracted by his own thinking.

" . . . And the Seventies," I winked at him. But he didn't even smile.

"He was a doctor, a healer. And you are going to be a healer," he looked at me hard.

I scoffed. "Ha! Not any time soon. I can't afford any more schooling. I have all I can do to support myself now."

David waved his hand. "It's not about those things. This is deeper, and further down the road. I stand by what I said. These energies are here to heal you. They have to align the meridians in our bodies, those of us who will be healed. The species is changing, opening to more senses that we dumbed down through our creation of dense materialism."

"You mean, like, some people are *chosen?*" I asked, showing a little sarcasm at what seemed to be an old religious idea. He was getting a little too Christian again.

"Those of us who have asked. *You must ask* to be healed. It's a spiritual law."

Okay, I thought. I had asked. I had asked several times—the first time as far back as 1985 when the man I loved left me. In fact, I begged for help and I offered to serve humanity in whatever way necessary in exchange for more personal strength.

But I wasn't satisfied that David could tell me anything about the energy I had been perceiving. Just as I was stewing in my frustration, he continued.

"This is a time of awakening for the planet. Many people will experience this psychologically. You are to experience it *physically.* I got that you are afraid you won't make it and so, your soul arranged for this before you came in. You will feel the adjustments physically, in and around your body. The alignments are along the acupuncture meridians. You have several bodies besides your dense physical self."

He stopped and made some motions with his hands in the air outlining my body, then continued speaking . "There are emotional bodies and mental bodies and others that all make up a field around you. Those who awaken will have greater awareness of their light body, which will enable them to heal as well as intuit and manifest more clearly. I saw a spirit standing over your body as it was lying in bed. He had his hand on your throat and a great light was coming from his hand." David was now peering at me intensely over his reading glasses, his light-blue eyes very studious.

"Well, I guess that sounds good," I muttered.

"It's not a matter of good or bad," he laughed for the first time. "There are no judgments in the universe. We simply bear the consequences of our acts. In past lives, you lost an ability you once had. You lost it through persecution and fear, as well as through abuse when you were in a male body. You were executed for it."

"Typical!" I scoffed again. "There's my karma with men again. All the men I meet are the women I cast love spells on and then dumped in other lives!"

David laughed again in spite of himself. "You can't think about that. What is *is*, and it's not all for us to know. But you had esoteric power; you were persecuted for using it and, in subsequent lifetimes, never regained it. And now, in *this* body, you are going to get it back. You were blocked in the throat chakra for many subsequent lives. In effect, you have lost your voice. In this life, you will speak your truth."

"The truth will set me free," I smiled, quoting Jesus (or Saint John quoting Jesus).

But David was serious again. "It's a process—a long process—eight, ten, fifteen years, maybe more!" he said. "Many will be healed. They will heal the rest of the population as the civilization comes into greater and greater crisis." I had heard this doomsday talk from him before without giving it much credence, but I listened politely this time. Certainly the world was in bad shape in 1994 and is in worse shape now.

David went on. "We are approaching the end of a huge epoch in the history of humankind, three cycles ending at once. The millennial change, of course, from Pisces to Aquarius, but also the end of an "equinoctial cycle" that occurs approximately every 26,000 years, when the tilt in the Earth's axis has come full circle so that the pole has pointed through each sign of the zodiac. Thus, there is an end to what we call 'The Great Cosmic Year.' Then the Mayan calendar announces the dawn of a Great Mother cycle, beginning on the solstice of the year 2012. The sky on December 21, 2012 A.D.. will show an unusual astronomical alignment, with the winter solstice Sun placement right in the "dark rift" of the Milky Way.

I had heard this event foretold before. In mythological terms, the event is about the union of First Father with First Mother, symbolic of a new 26,000 year equinoctial cycle beginning.

David went on. "And it will not be an easy transition back to a spiritu-ally based culture. Systems will break down. Fear will be rampant. Many souls will leave the planet. The powers of good and evil will be polarized and, in addition to the clash and the upheaval of wars, there will be massive Earth shifts. The planet will also undergo a cleansing process."

"But what has all that to do with my dead father?" I interrupted, unable to take in all he was saying.

"I don't know exactly. But I think it's about some writing. I was told it wasn't yet time. But there will be a time in the future when you will make yourself available to write and it will come. It's about setting you free, about your own healing. And your writing and speaking in the future. Maybe you can't heal until you come to terms with your legacy. Maybe your ability to heal will not be launched until 2012."

THE "FATHER THING"

There was more to that reading than the above conversation, but that is the gist of what was significant. I have all David's readings on tape and, over the years, it still surprises me how accurate some of the little disparate details he gave me turned out to be. David himself left the planet quickly and unex-pectedly a few years later. He was in his early sixties. His lady friend said he knew he was going and was hurriedly putting his papers in order before he went in for routine prostate surgery, from which he suffered mysterious complications and never awoke. He helped many people. Several friends of mine and I like to think he had finished all he had to do here and was called to be reborn anew as one of those who have the powers to heal.

On the day of our meeting, I didn't have a context for what David was telling me. I had no intention to write about my father. Who could do the "father thing" better than the poet Sylvia Plath, who had eventually taken her own life? I had read every word she wrote. I knew the sense of abandon-ment, and I had known my father longer than she'd known hers. I had seen my father at his best—a huge, substantial energetic presence. I had known his singing, his painting, his poetry. All that raw talent came to him freely, probably, I think now, from our other lives. He was untrained, but he played the piano by ear. And he was a doctor, a surgeon, a healer himself, in awe of his own power and the responsibility it entailed. One of his paintings was the backdrop to his poem *Admonition to a Physician*, about practicing medicine as both a science and an art.

In the last two years of his life, however, I had also seen him at his worst, at the mercy of migraines and too many pills. I did not want to write about my father. It was a soap opera. I would belittle the reality. I did not think I had enough talent to transform the material. All my life, I had avoided the subject. I didn't want any legacy. I felt haunted. Much of my therapy addressed my father's breakdown and my own failed relationships with men. I had become his melodrama and it did not make me happy.

On the other hand, I liked the idea that his spirit had survived death and that he'd sent angels to me. It wasn't something I needed to consider miraculous. But I was confused. I noticed that the floating sensation continued and that the streams of air around my body had quickened. And if I looked hard against a white wall, I could see a sort of outline of a body hovering above me, arms open or over my head. And I could feel the vibes zapping me—a sensation very hard to explain, as I had never had it before. There was a sense of air, wind-like, buzzing around me. But very softly, very subtly. Occasionally, I would be touched by a hand or I would feel a sudden ache in a certain part of my body. I could brush my hand into the spot and wave the energy away. It would then stop for a while.

At home, I finished Tim O'Brien's novel, frustrated by the enigmatic ending. The question of whether the protagonist, a Vietnam veteran/politician who liked to practice magic, killed his wife or not was purposely left hanging. I didn't appreciate, at the time, the multiple possibilities of reality that O'Brien presented. I was uncomfortable living with my own mysterious magic and the thought of my multiple lives coming to me in this one. And like O'Brien's story, I had raised more questions than I had answered. I wanted clarity; I wanted answers.

It so happened I taught an overload that semester. As the term drew to a close, near Christmas, my birthday December 26th, and another anniversary of my father's death, I decided to spend some money to find my way out of the woods, to get to the bottom of my own lake, my floating bed.

Chapter 6

WELCOME TO THE LIGHT BODY

Those who cling tenaciously to a world as it once was will face increasing difficulty . . .
you may choose to cling . . . or you may dare to recognize what is undeniable
to your own senses and what is irrefutable as your own experience.
RASHA, ONENESS

Even though I intuited my new experiences as positive, it was still difficult learning to trust. I decided to see another psychic person, Jason, to find out what was going on with my head. He was recommended to me as a "spirit cleanser," a graduate of the Barbara Brennan School of Healing. Brennan is one of the most renowned energy workers in the country, indeed the world. I bought one of her books, *Hands of Light*, and saw how the drawings showed the techniques of channeled healing and the layers of the subtle bodies—etheric, mental, emotional, etc. Different colors indicate different energies. Brennan's renowned school teaches the development of psychic seeing and how to cleanse these energy fields. Although the touch of the hands I occasionally felt were extremely tender, I needed to be sure these entities were loving.

Not knowing what to expect when I arrived, I saw Jason's office as similar to that of any massage therapist. He had a table, a disc player trilling South American flutes, Santa Fe colors on the walls, and various spiritual crystals and icons placed around the room. I told him my situation and he had me lie down on the table. Closing his eyes and raising his hands about four or five inches from my body, he scanned my energy. As he walked around the table, he suddenly spoke out in a different voice, a very strong voice: "Why do you feel unworthy?" He bellowed this several times as I lay there absurdly thinking to myself of Robert DeNiro's line in the film *Taxi*, "Hey! You talkin' to *me?*" Could things get any stranger?

"Why do you feel unworthy?" he bellowed again, hands over his head in the air, eyes closed.

"Do you want *me* to answer you?" I meekly asked.

He stopped and opened his eyes. Returning to his soft-spoken voice, he said "I was just given those words. There are several beings here, most of them angelic. But there are also two masters familiar to your soul energy. They have been your teachers between lives. They are asking the question. It is something you can think about, but I, personally, don't need an answer." Jason then reassured me that these were positive presences and spoke to me about something called the ascension process.

The ascension process corresponds to what David Hall referred to as "awakening." Jason said an ascension is the transformation of a human being into a higher frequency and lighter form. This is the destiny of the human species. Like David, he told me that many people on the planet are undergoing this process consciously at this time. This is the beginning of the purification of the planet. Earth herself is ascending. The Earth has consciousness and is moving into the fifth dimension. This planet will no longer be a place of duality, good and evil, dark and light. As the process continues, much of the dark will be highlighted by crisis in our individual lives, as well as in the collective population on a massive level.

Jason spoke of how the Earth is changing. The floods and storms and quakes in recent years throughout the planet are part of the cleansing process. A consequence of these crises is that people see what is really important in their lives, simply living, and reach out to each other in their community, asking for help. No doubt many move more consciously onto a spiritual path. You do not enter into "ascension" at this point in time without asking for help. But the process can take many many years and, while it unfolds, much of humanity's collective shadow will be heightened. The abuse of the Earth will no longer be tolerated.

"By whom?" I asked naively.

Jason smiled. "By the Brotherhood of Light, the Master Avatars, guardians of this planet.

The decision has been made. There is no undoing it."

Jason suggested I do some breath work to complete the hour. I took deep breaths from my solar plexus for twenty minutes or so. As I was doing so, he worked above my body with his hands. I had no idea what he was doing, but I could feel the energies intensifying around me. Finally, he told me to stop and breathe normally. He said he had tried to work on cleansing different pockets of negative energy around my body. The solar plexus region, where we keep our fears and urges to power, was, in my case, an especially messy area. Like many in the population, I have stomach issues.

Suddenly, my entire body began to tremble. The only experience I can compare with this shaking is an episode that occurred immediately after I gave birth to my son. I went into a full body tremor. As I lay on Jason's table, shaking from head to foot, I managed to ask what was happening.

"That's fear leaving your body," he said. "We all carry deep cellular memories and you are a very shallow breather. The fear can't be released unless you breathe into your third chakra, which is quite weak." He asked me if I suffered from any digestive problems. I laughed out loud. Since my adolescence, I have had a spastic colon that acts up horribly more and more often. I also have memories of holding my breath a lot during the time of my father's illness. I was scared all throughout my adolescence. During my late teens and early twenties, I discovered that alcohol helped allay my fears and I used and abused it to feel better.

In my marriage, I had been scared as well—insecure and fearful of the future, afraid of my husband's disapproval of my ideas, worried about money. I had always held my breath. Then again, ever since the spirits had arrived, I found myself in tears during and after each meditation. I told this to Jason, who said they were releasing my fear and sorrow, and would be aligning my meridians. David's prediction exactly. In the meantime, he recommended I do some breath work and allow the sorrow to "come up."

I went back to Jason for several sessions to work on my breathing. Each time, I ended up shaking from head to foot and weeping. I only stopped the sessions because I couldn't afford any more, but I practiced the breathing at home and discovered my own body workers were right there in the air around me. With or without Jason's help, I was going to release the fear I had held so carefully as a child, a teenager, a young adult. Fear layered over fear, block after block, an inner wall of fear.

JUNG, THE GNOSTICS, AND MYSTICAL EXPERIENCE

Though I found this kind of talk suspiciously like science fiction, this information was very reassuring for me, as it confirmed some of what David had said and much of what I had been reading. There was also a place deep within me that recognized and connected with these ideas, as if I had always known that transformation was part of my reason for living. Humanity is awakening from its collective dream, its specific definition of reality, what it has created through a shared belief system. This idea wasn't entirely new to me. Through my Jungian studies, I had read of the Gnostics and felt a kinship with them.

In 1952, the Jung Institute in Zurich had acquired Codex I, known afterwards as the Jung Codex, a section of the documents dug up by accident in Nag Hammadi. Jung was fascinated with them and I read several books on his studies. Jung took alchemy as his metaphor for the individuation process, or wholeness. In the Gnostics, he found mythological material, as well as the piece that is missing in Christianity—the dark matter of the feminine body. Jung's father was a minister, fixed in his beliefs, but Jung's own thoughts about religion and Christianity were instinctively critical.

Most of us accept evil as part of the package on Earth. The idea that evil can be dispelled by a shift in collective belief was optimistically overwhelming to me. Like most people, I couldn't imagine a world without evil. I adopted a "wait and see" attitude for many years. Since then, however, I've seen that all evil begins in fear. If fear can be transformed by trust and love and the help of our higher selves, perhaps that far-off Utopian goal is possible. I can say that, at this writing, as the second war in Iraq rages and outrages, the world is still ruled by the assertion of power in fear-based individuals. As the dual poles of light and dark are heightened here in the start of a new millennium, the world will seem to many to be even more desperate and dangerous than ever.

Philosophers like Hobbes and psychologists like Freud have put the instinct of aggression at the top of the list of human characteristics, so it is difficult to believe it can be not only tamed, but eradicated. And, I might add, I have argued tirelessly with friends and relatives and anyone who will listen that the violence that is perpetuated on Earth is nothing but a response to fear. Still, I am met constantly with cynical beliefs that "basic human nature" will never change. That day in Jason's office, I again found someone who belonged to the quiet, but growing, community of those dedicated to changing their beliefs engendered by fear. I also learned *it is not necessary to try and convince others.* Each will come aboard in his or her own time.

I slowly stopped trying to convince people that this transformational time is here. I stopped telling them to look around themselves at the angel mania, to visit some of the bookstores I went to. Why should they believe me? We were approaching the millennium and many said it was just pre-millennial poppycock. Even as the human potential movement grows, the term "New Age" is still either ignored or denigrated by the cultural literati as well as the mass proletariat. It did not feel to me like a popular perspective in the society writ large.

Both friends and family thought I'd been taken advantage of by the psychics. I laughed, quoting from the Gnostic Gospels: "As Christ said: Let those who will see, see and those who have ears, hear." They joked that I had been born again. "Liberal Northeastern American poets and college professors do not suddenly become fundamentalists!" I would counter. "I can't be born again until I learn how to die to this illusion." I spoke out of conviction, but still had nagging doubts that I could do such a thing. I've since learned that living my own beliefs is all that is required. A challenge, but one I am willing to undertake. Still, I get caught up rather unconsciously in arguments and I only recently learned to back off. I am a teacher, after all, so it is hard for me to keep quiet. Not long ago, I had an Email war with my book review newspaper editor for the better part of a week. We threw quotes back and forth like shuttlecocks. He repeatedly told me I was too smart to believe in "all that crap."

My mother and sister were concerned that I was having some kind of a breakdown. I learned later that they reassured each other many times that, except for my insistence that something new was happening, I seemed perfectly normal. Yet I had my own evidence, and even the astrologer I consulted for a solar return reading that year saw a strange new aspect in my chart—something called a septile. She said that it was rare and supposedly had to do with "destiny," but that most astrologers paid little attention to it and there was very little written about it.

Although, outwardly, much was the same as it had been, my inner life changed irrevocably. I read William Blake's biography. Here was a man who saw and spoke to spirits most of his life. He visited his wife once a week after he died and told her which paintings to sell and to whom. I read about Emmanuel Swedenborg, who classified angels and experienced such intense visions that he had enough of a following to create a foundation and his own church. I became familiar with an entire tradition of visionary poets—my two favorites, Rainer Maria Rilke from the last century and Rumi, the ecstatic Sufi dancer who recited to his followers, never writing a word. Rumi is currently the best-selling poet in the United States. "Isn't this significant?" I wondered. William Butler Yeats created a whole occult system of spiritualism. And in our own times, the popular and sophisticated New York poet, James Merrill, a son of the Merrill-Lynch financier, won the Pulitzer Prize for his three-volume masterpiece *The Changing Light at Sandover,* which conveys, in verse, conversations with a Ouija board!

I confided in only one academic colleague—another woman whose spiritual life was her priority. And I worked some of the mystic poets into my syllabi. Their messages were clear. This reality is not the only reality. This reality is an illusion. I taught these ideas as theory. I was not yet ready to come out of the academic closet.

I dreamt several times of awakening from a long sleep in a huge room with hundreds of other people, as if we were waking from another life. I dreamt I was climbing mountains with teams of people, going to work for "Doctors Without Borders." I dreamt I was undergoing an operation with a team of physicians reaching into me and rearranging my nerves. I dreamt I was being initiated into a primitive tribe and had to perform various tasks. Over and over, I dreamt I was flying. I often woke up with a sudden start, as if I had slammed back into my body.

Once, I dreamt I had to have my "brakes fixed." Within a few days, I literally went to the brake shop, unconvinced when the workman told me I had at least 7000 more miles before I needed to come back. It occurred to me later that this dream was a pun. My "breaks" were being fixed—sewn together, if you will. Or something was being snipped, rerouted, and sewn.

This sensation I had was a new sense, a new way of knowing. I *knew* these beings were sewing something together just outside the periphery of my body. I don't know how I knew this, but I sensed it very particularly. I could hear the snips of something like scissors, could sense a presence there pulling a thread through me. I never thought I was crazy. I have a dim memory, like déjà vu, that I had known this would happen, that I almost remembered signing up for it. I read some of Edgar Cayce's voluminous works. Cayce contends that, somewhere along the way—perhaps at the time of the last days of Atlantis—the human species broke its connections, its access to higher states of being. With the secularization of civilization, we simply lost touch and let atrophy these networks of light and electromagnetism in the body, developing the left brain over the right. Whatever is true, I was aware that this was and is and will continue to be the new century in which we will restore those broken wires.

Later, I read about "light bodies," the spongy net-like layers of energy just outside our material bodies. There were several of these, as Jason had suggested: mental, emotional, etheric, and subtle. These are the fields that psychic healers work in and try to cleanse before the negative disturbances manifest as illness in the material body itself. I assumed my awareness of the sewing and the net-like air that I sensed around me was somehow related to these fields.

And I continued to have a frustrating repetitive dream: I had the key, but I couldn't find my car. Later, I read in a book about out-of-body (OOB) travel during the dream state, that mine was a dream common to those who had OOB experiences. Cars in your dreams represent your modes of movement. A car from your past sometimes shows you are in the same emotional realm you were in at the time you owned that particular car.

I continued to have dreams, however, that were unlike dreams I had had all my life. One in particular was very real—so real that, within the dream itself, I began to realize this wasn't a dream at all. It was real. I have had the dream many times since. In it, I am jumping on a trampoline in a summery backyard, not too different from the one I grew up in in suburban New York. As I jump, I realize that I can stay up in the air and fly. I am amazed at the sense of flying, of actually feeling stable in the air. I awoke suddenly from this dream many times with the sense of an abrupt fall into bed. I think it was this actual physical sensation of floating that permeated my dreams when the spirits were working around me.

I thought about the huge movement toward physical fitness that began in the Seventies. Gyms and clubs are everywhere now. Compared to our parents' generation, people seem to be compulsive about body work—perhaps unconsciously beginning to tune up for opening chakras and aligning meridians. And the popularization of bottled water has accompanied this movement. We need more water, not just because exercise increases thirst, but even when not exercising. Drinking water sparks electrolytes in our bodies. Everything David and Jason said made sense in this context.

SETTLING INTO SPIRIT

Over time, I got used to the sensations that invaded my reality. But at the beginning, I often had headaches. As accepting as I was that these were loving beings, sometimes when I was meditating, I got small static-like shocks that caused me to jerk. My limbs twitched and I saw explosions of white light behind my closed eyes, as if I'd just looked straight into a flashbulb. I noticed deeper colors there as well, and could feel the intensification of my electromagnetic field when I was "being worked." The sheer miracle of it was beautiful, but the sensations were unusual, if not disturbing. The whole experience was isolating and I was impatient. I now see the flashes of light in my peripheral vision several times a day.

I ordered the spirits to stop the electrical zaps. My mind wanted communication. I prowled around the spiritual bookstores and flipped through magazines like *Earth Star* and *Spirit of Change* and, later, *Natural Awakenings*—publications with short articles that described various types of physical and psychological healing. Interviews with New Age gurus punctuated information on astrology, Reiki, polarity, hypnosis, massage, and other types of body-healing work. The people who wrote for, and those who advertised in, these publications appeared to be clued into the coming changes. The words "ascension" and "awakening" appeared often, along with "transformation" and phrases like "the coming light," "fifth-dimensional frequency," and, of course, "The New Age."

At home, alone with my guides, I asked them quite forcefully to stop, to let up on their magnetic work at night so that I could fall asleep. I was never an easy sleeper and now, as a woman approaching the change of life, I had even more trouble. I lay awake, especially sensitive to the presence of these beings, for hours, longing for sleep. I saw sparks of light like static electricity literally shooting around the room when I sometimes awoke during bouts of insomnia. I got out of bed and waved my arms frantically at the cloudy outlines of figures, doing my own clearing. This came out of desperation. What could I do but believe what I'd been told? It wasn't as if I could go to a respectable doctor and state my complaints! But I found, by trial and error, techniques that worked. The energies were very eager, very persistent. David had used the word "intense." "Your healing will be *intense*." On some mornings, I awoke feeling almost drugged, my body buzzing like a motor.

I was able to go about my normal daily life—teaching, socializing, writing my poetry. But I was overwhelmed with the twist my life had taken and couldn't help sharing with a variety of friends what was happening. And I soon learned that most people were not as receptive as I was to these experiences. Some of the people I told withdrew and stopped being my friends completely. No doubt they thought I was crazy or making this up to call attention to myself. I was hurt, but I had always been a very open person and didn't want to hide the most important experience of my life from people I thought were my friends. Yet after that, I only told my oldest friends, and even reminded them how I had originally called them to talk about my "mice theory." They believed something had changed for me. Yet they could also see I was still myself. Others, those who were more consciously on a spiritual path, wondered why they didn't have these sensations too. I didn't have an answer for that, although it seemed obvious that the Global Consciousness Movement continued to grow.

Chapter 7

GOOD NEWƒ

Nothing real can be threatened.
Nothing unreal exists.
Herein lies the peace of God.
A COURSE IN MIRACLES

ƒeven Stars is the best spiritual bookstore in the Boston area. The Cambridge store's inventory is massive, shelf after shelf heavy with transpersonal psychology and esoteric philosophy. Obviously, the store has a following. I began to drop in whenever I was in Harvard Square. I am a book buyer and Harvard Square is loaded with good bookstores, including The Grolier, a favorite shop devoted entirely to poetry. Before the arrival of my "spirits," however, I had ignored the handful of occult bookshops in the vicinity.

One day when I was browsing through the Seven Stars, bookshop, I saw an inconspicuous sign that read: "Gerry Channels John, Thursday Nights." I asked the cashier who John was; he answered "John, the Apostle to Christ." I stared at him blankly.

"John, the Beloved? The disciple whom Jesus loved?" I asked incredulously. The clerk seemed like an intelligent guy, about my age, bearded, wiry thin with glasses. I asked if he attended these sessions, and if he thought it was "real."

"I take John's sessions very seriously," he answered. He didn't encourage me to come or not to come, but I was curious and decided to sit in on the next Thursday night session to hear what the author of the Book of Revelation had to say. Later, I got to know Stuart (the cashier whom I had questioned) much better. He was one of the owners of the store, intellectual and Jewish. Yvonne, a native of Sweden and an astrologer as well as his partner in the business, also became a close friend. It only occurred to me later that the store's very name was associated with John's book.

The following Thursday, I went to Seven Stars. Gerry Bowman (the Gerry of the sign) proved to be a forty-something, nice-looking "average" middle-class guy who chatted with Stuart and a few other people as they set up a microphone and recording device in a room above the shop. For $10.00, you could attend the two-hour session and afterward receive a tape of it. Gerry settled into a chair facing the several rows that made up the audience. When he sat down to go into trance, the room of about twenty-five typical Cambridge-looking people—aging and neo-hippies, birkenstocked, long-haired, batik-backed adults of all ethnicities ranging from their mid-twenties to seventy or so—quieted down completely. Some closed their eyes, and positioned their hands palms-up on their knees, quietly meditating. I looked around suspiciously.

Gerry let out a huge sigh and, after a few minutes, began to shake. He winced as if in pain, breathed deeply, and, after about five minutes of various contorting postures and facial expressions, shifted and settled his body. Opening his eyes as wide as possible, he scanned the room very slowly. His face was softer, but his body sat strangely rigid in the chair.

"What's he doing?" I whispered to the person next to me as Gerry scanned our faces slowly, looking straight through each person. Some people smiled at him and nodded their heads as if to say hello.

"He's reading the energy," the guy sitting next to me said. When Gerry looked at me, I found myself uncomfortable, not knowing what to do with my eyes. I looked back, but his stare was impenetrable, as if he could see into every aspect of me. And, was it possible? He never blinked! When he finished looking at everyone, he relaxed his body, sighed, smiled, and said in a loud voice, "Good evening. How can we be of service?"

His voice was somehow different. It rang with some kind of an accent—not English, not Irish, not Indian—the voice of someone who spoke English formally, as if it were a second language. I figured he could be faking, attempting any one of those accents and missing it. But as the night went on in a question-and-answer discussion format, I heard such powerful wisdom, such encouraging, compassionate advice along with laws of science, mathematics, and physics—some of which went over my head—that I thought to myself: "I don't care if this guy is John the Apostle or Johnny Appleseed. What he has to say has enormous value and I can see why he has a following." But was I really in an upstairs room of a bookstore in Cambridge, Massachusetts in the presence of John the Apostle? The notion was absurd.

For two hours, Gerry/John spoke to us about our various problems. Often, what he said to one person was just a different version of his last response, for we all shared the same suffering. We were all addicted to an illusion of reality. And all that he said had to do with changing the way we looked at the world, changing the way we "held" a negative experience, transcending the fears and projections of our egos.

He spoke about communication in marriage and on the job, problems with money, problems with acceptance and self-acceptance, courage and wisdom, political issues at stake in the world, about wars and accidents and the transformation of the Earth. He said there is no sin, only ignorance, and that we must cultivate acceptance, tolerance, and patience—not to mention love. And most of all, that *we must not judge,* for we are all part of one God. As we judge others, we judge ourselves, thus preventing self-acceptance and limiting our powers to create and manifest the New Reality that will arrive, nonetheless, in our lifetimes. Time is not real, he explained, echoing Jason. The New Reality is already a "done deal." Christ will not return in the flesh, but his spirit, *Christ Consciousness*, is returning within us. This is the so-called "Second Coming," happening here and now.

About halfway through the evening, I raised my hand and asked about the energies around my body. He went silent for a minute, staring into space as if listening to some invisible mentor himself. He does this occasionally when people ask him about the health of a friend or the state of a distant relative. I understood later that he was reading into the Akashic Records, the term coined by Edgar Cayce for a huge body of knowledge, a metaphorical computer in the etheric atmosphere that records every deed, every situation, every thought ever thought by everyone who ever was or will be on the planet. Then he turned back to me and smiled, raising his eyebrows in a kind of surprised gesture. "Wonderful journey!" he responded.

Gerry told me to relax and accept my disincarnate visitors. "Your soul made a very unique arrangement before coming into your body. You are getting what you asked for. Relax and allow it to unfold without having to know."

I wasn't satisfied with this answer and interrupted, "But is this my father?"

"It's not your father; it's *you.* Some of these spirits are you, come from the future, come back to help you so that people will not take advantage of you as they have in the past, as you have let them do. But it also has to do somewhat with your father. You will see. You feel you are inadequate, unworthy; but, in time, this will change. You have faith. You have always had faith. You have perished for your faith several times. Eventually, in this life, you will be healed. This is a process. You have signed a contract with yourself;

you just don't remember. Ask to remember. You will have help. You will see. You will *write*."

I wanted him to go on, but he dismissed my urgency, my sputtering, and turned to someone else as a few people smiled at me. I felt the strength from him. He was more powerful than the psychics. His words had more impact. I listened hard all evening, often laughing at his jokes. He teased us all about our lack of faith, our fears, the tricks of our egos. He could be mocking and taunting, boisterous and bombastic one minute, and then quickly shift into a grave wisdom. He taught that there is nothing real but love. That we think we are separated from the source of love, but we are like children who have run away from home, playing a game of good versus evil. Forgetting that we are playing, "doing a dance," "making a movie" (his metaphorical phrases), we become stuck in the illusion we have made. I thought about the name Christ gave to John and his brother James, *the sons of thunder.* It was appropriate to this spirit who sometimes bellowed.

Over time, as I listened to John, I realized he did not congratulate us on our faith very often. More often, he bellowed about how little faith we had. I didn't remember having faith or dying for it. But something about it felt uncannily familiar. I was searching. I had spent money on my search, on books and costly therapy that was not covered by insurance, not on my house or car or clothes. The faith seemed familiar. It mattered more than anything. I knew that much.

During that first evening, and others afterward, John referred now and then to *A Course in Miracles.* I first heard about the course when I had my bookstore and always kept at least one copy of the hefty blue-bound volume in stock. I didn't so much as open it for years, although several people had taken the time to explain what it was when they requested it. In those days, I was all about literature and seldom read anything else. After my heartbreaking boyfriend and I separated, and my interest in things Jungian and occult grew, I could not imagine taking on another oracle. Astrology, the *I Ching,* and tarot had been difficult enough for me to grasp and now, with the ever-hovering holiest holies scatting like gnats around my various bodies, I was not sure I wanted to submit myself to spiritual discipline. But I did look through the course, discovering that it had a lesson for each of the 365 days of a year. So in Seven Stars Bookstore, some ten years after my journey began, I said to myself, well, despite the tornado of energy following me, okay, I'll give it whirl . . . (no pun intended).

MY COURSE IN MIRACLES

A Course in Miracles is about changing fundamental beliefs about what the world is. With one little step at a time, and a good deal more than twelve steps, the goal is to undo your ego's illusions and create reality anew. The book of lessons was not so much "written" as it was "channeled"; The author was supposedly none other than Christ himself. Some of the principles of the course began to sound familiar as I listened to John. He told us over and over that we don't know what we are, who we are, how large we are, or how much access we have to higher levels of spiritual thought. He spoke of the species as "dumbed down" to the personal ego, which mistakenly thinks itself to be separate from God as well as others—thinks itself alone and afraid. If we can trust enough to put ourselves in the realm of something higher, he explained, our fearful thoughts and behaviors will not wreak such havoc. He taught of a dispensation for Earth and the human race, a specific window of time. That time, he said, is coming now.

I began to come often to hear John at Seven Stars. I met other "regulars" and learned that they were from all paths of life. Like me, their suffering had sent them on a search. Some had had psychic experiences. Others just believed in John's gospel, his "good news" that the world will change because they know astrology or follow some other occult guidance. Some nights, John spoke about *Yeshua*, as he called Jesus Christ. He used examples from the New Testament, but he often scorned what the church had created in Christ's name. Christ had been misunderstood. He did not want to be worshipped as a sacrificial lamb. He wanted to show us that we are as powerful as he. He did not want to be considered a martyr, as much as to show that there is no death, that we are spirits occupying bodies. He had not come to revise Judaism or begin Christianity, but to demonstrate the truth. His true church is the heart. John told us the truth will come out; the truth "will set us free." I thought of Jung's famous line, "Thank God I'm Jung and not a Jungian," and imagined Jesus, looking back at what has been done in his name, gasping "Thank God I'm Christ and not a Christian."

Eventually, I began attending a private group that John led once a month at Gerry's house. For several years in the latter half of the Nineties, I made the trip. John's message was about "waking up." But it isn't easy to recognize the world as an illusion; it isn't easy to see how we create our own realities with unconscious fears, especially for so many of us who want different realities. I had studied the concept of the shadow in Jungian psychology—

that bundle of characteristics that is totally alien to the ego. I had identified many shadow figures in my dreams as well as in my external day world and, although it's impossible because the shadow is so unconscious, I tried to be more aware of what I was projecting. But often, it was only after some unpleasant dream or incident that I was able to see my own lack of trust and my fear.

John taught us how fear creates the circumstances we dread in our lives. He gave us exercises to separate us from our egos so that we could observe their habitual reactions. He counseled us to think of ourselves in the third person so that we did not mix our larger selves up with our limited egos. I sometimes walked around the house saying, "Deborah is depressed today but I'm not." Or "Deborah thinks she's a failure but I don't choose that." I sometimes paused, feeling like an idiot for performing such an exercise. "Deborah thinks she's an idiot for doing this exercise, but I'm not. Deborah is a freaking idiot, but I'm not."

We reported back to John when our experiments failed, when we did not feel like the gods we were supposed to be. How silly we felt denying the sorrows of humanity when we turned on the news. But John insisted that humanity is creating crises to push itself into transformation. He suggested, along with the famous bumper sticker, that we kill our televisions. He decried the media moguls who milked every evil to satisfy their greed for higher ratings, and he insisted the power-shadow of those in charge wanted to keep people frightened. John told us that those who do not resonate with the light may leave their bodies here or cause others to leave theirs, but that death is not an ending—merely a changing of form. They would see their mistakes eventually, and would have to balance them out in other bodies in any of the other numerous universes. In the meantime, our world will give up suffering, even as it suffers. I stopped watching television news when I realized that it often advertises more fear, the dangers of the common neighborhood or household gadgets, or actually gives ideas to those who are borderline insane—the snipers, the bomb makers, the disturbed, enraged adolescents.

Much of what John said makes sense only if we begin to think differently. But we are habitually trained and we continue to give our energy to worries and upsets and spin out the same scenarios that sent us searching in the first place. He encouraged us instead to "fake it till you make it."

I found myself worrying about the accumulating mileage on my car and then my car broke down on a highway far from home. I was frantic, but I practiced John's mantra: *I accept this situation in peace.* The tow truck came, the bill came, the car was not too bad. I thanked the universe for showing me how my thoughts had power, both to stop my car and then to lessen the trouble. Incidents such as this one continued. The challenge was to take every negative situation and be grateful for it, to see the silver lining in it, even if it was only that we created it to see why we created it.

One winter, I planned to stay in a friend's house in Maine while she was away. When I arrived late at night, I found the door, which was to be left open, locked. I sat in my car and closed my eyes. *Be still and know you are God,* I repeated like a litany while trying to think of my next move. It was too late to go back to Boston or call my ex-mother-in-law. And I was too money-conscious for the last resort, a motel. When I felt somewhat calmed, I closed my eyes for a meditative moment and saw the image of my friend's cat coming out of the bulkhead—an image I had seen several times in previous summers. I jumped out of the car, walked to the back of the house, and felt around in the dark for the handle of the bulkhead. It was open! I stumbled my way up the stairs and unlocked the front door. Why not choose faith? But still, sometimes, I forget and curse everything, finding a self-pitying solace in depression, alcohol, and country music. John said that too is a choice.

John was so often loving that, at times, he brought tears to our eyes. One night, he spoke about how he and the other spirits learned from us as well—that we made them remember the sorrows, the illusions, of being in this dimension. He reassured us continually that there is no failure, and no going back. Because there is no time, the planet is already transformed. "You've already done it! Catch up with yourselves!" he hollered out loud, making us laugh along with him.

This group became a very important part of my life. I made some new friends I could really talk to about these issues—issues in which few people in the outside world have any interest at all. Again, when I tried to tell the uninitiated, they just waved their hands at the ugliness and insisted that the world was not better, but as a popular movie might say, "worse and worser." Then I myself became dismayed, for they appeared to be right. I figured going to hear John regularly was like being in AA. Faith isn't rational. You have to take one day at a time and stay in the program.

One evening, a particularly difficult individual came to a session at Seven Stars. He was crippled by anger, involved in a custody battle, convinced his adversaries were especially evil and should be wiped off the earth. John tried to get him to see that his own hostilities were being mirrored back to him, that he was caught in a self-defeating battle, that he was fueling the hatred, that he needed to separate himself from his ego's desires and fears in order to allow the dynamic of the relationship to shift. But, like many people, this person couldn't give up his control and his investment in the right outcome, couldn't trust the universe enough to let the action evolve on its own. He became hostile and somewhat abusive to John and the room crackled with tension. John remained placid and loving, repeating the same message in ten different ways before he ended the session. After about two hours, Gerry's energy waned and, like any clock-watching therapist, John said, "We have to stop."

Usually when a session ended, before people left, they milled around discussing the night's issues among themselves for a short while as the tapes were being made. Gerry's head often drooped and he sometimes fell asleep and even snored for five minutes or so, until he shook himself abruptly awake. Then he usually had a cigarette and gabbed with the rest of us.

This particular night when Gerry awoke, he put his hands to his eyes and felt tears. He looked around at those of us who were still there and, in an irritable voice, commented, "I feel awful. What the hell happened?" The hostile individual had already left, so we filled him in on the verbal beating he'd taken as John. He shook his head, clearly in a bad mood, and declared that he didn't want to hear the tape. Packing up the tape-duplicating machine and the recording device, he stormed out without saying another word. He was obviously no longer John; he was a flawed human like the rest of us. Someone suggested we send him some light on his long ride home to Worcester—a habit that John encouraged us to practice that involved encircling ourselves and others with white light for healing and protection.

THE MEDIUM AND THE MONAD

When I picture Gerry and John in my mind, I see how different they are. Gerry, an aging ex-hippy, father of three adolescent children, struggling to have enough money, fixing his own car, working on his modest ranch house, coaching his son's teams. He did private readings at $150 an hour, but the group readings at Seven Stars were relatively cheap at $10. He was quick to tell you, "John doesn't charge, but I do."

Gerry, the human being whose body John borrowed, was a heavy smoker. John sometimes complained that it was both difficult and painful to come into his body. We saw this as he came in. Gerry had his own problems and, as I got to know him, I saw how amazingly he changed when he became John. Gerry was not a conscious channel. He simply checked out as if he were napping. He listened to the tapes of the sessions, but could not remember his discussions as John.

I like Gerry a lot. But I love John. John is a huge presence, loud and garrulous and wise, clearly in control. Gerry is as world-weary as the rest of us. I eventually heard the story of how Gerry first channeled John. He was in the act of leaving a channeling session in California, when he was stopped by the channel himself. The channel paused in mid sentence and hollered out to Gerry as he and his wife were sneaking out the door: "Hey, you can do this too. You're a channel. You need to do this too!" Gerry and his wife ran out of the building and down the street laughing.

Several weeks later, however, Gerry decided to try it. It took them a long time to even understand John's voice, but they kept at it, as they knew something was happening. Eventually, John came through. In California in the Seventies, Gerry had quite a following as John. One night, he showed us a video of the early John on a talk show and we all laughed hysterically. John was quite awkward in body at first and his voice was quite a bit stranger than now.

When he first began to channel, Gerry remained conscious. John told him they had known each other in a past life and that, in between lives, Gerry and he had made this arrangement. The more confusing issue was the way John addressed Gerry as "Thomas," which was the name by which he had known him in the other life. This was *not* Doubting Thomas, the apostle, however. He said this Thomas had been a thief and made occasional jokes about it. Furthermore, they had met in a life when John was not John the Apostle! All this was enough to boggle the mind.

Whenever John spoke of Gerry during a session, he referred to him as Thomas. But when John spoke to us about himself, he always used "we" rather than "I." Over the years as I've heard other channels, they've always used "we," and I've learned that this standard "editorial we" refers to the monad, a network of extensions that make up the soul. Each one of us is actually plural, part of a soul family that consists of our own soul extensions living simultaneous and parallel lives along with our material life. Sometimes we have feelings that seep into us from these other extensions—intuitive moments when we are aware of other aspects of our soul family. These are called "bleed-throughs."

REALITY INSIDE OUT

In a private session with John, he explained to me that some of the spirits around me were indeed me (as the psychics had said)—that is, me from the future. I thought of my poem: "The Future that Brought Her Here." How had I found that title? Was it given to me? The poem was about my first adult experience of alternate reality. I thought of something else. I remembered standing in my apartment one day looking out the window, my body doing its usual morning buzzing. As I watched the wind in the trees, I remembered a dream I had in childhood.

> *I AM DANCING AND DANCING, joyously, ecstatically, like a tree in the wind. The music is the "Dance of the Sugar Plum Fairy" from the* Nutcracker Suite. *The background of the scene is a rich yellow and, for some reason, I catch myself saying jaune, the French word for "yellow." The trees are thin and black, swaying and dancing in complete joy with me.* ❧

Now I wondered when and where I had known that world. It felt very real.

Here I was—gathering precious pearls of wisdom from a teacher who was no longer human—a spirit who visited my friend's body. I was trying to learn how to stop thinking and *"just be."* How to stop creating my own suffering. How to refuse depression and use my power to choose. How to withdraw my responsibility for others' demands and behaviors and accept them as they are. How to be polite but honest when I don't like something. (John thought we are all hypocrites, liars, and fakes—which to some extent is true, I must admit.)

There was no doubt that my reality was inside out. I was going out of the mind I had spent forty-seven years cultivating to think rationally. Now I was regularly visiting a spook, surrounded by my own spooks. And yet my life made more sense than it ever had before. Life in general made more sense. I thought of Paul Gauguin's famous Tahitian painting "Who Are We? Where Are We Going? Where Have We Been?" For thousands of years, people had no answers to those questions. Most stopped looking for the answers. But John's theories made more sense than the philosophers I had studied in college. God, Goddess, the Source, the Force—whatever we wanted to call it didn't matter to John. And it is all the same thing, all one, all *Love.*

Everything else is a lousy choice humanity invented by viewing the illusion of separation "as if" it were real. This idea that we are all one, all parts of God who is nothing other than love is reinforced by many creation myths that contain a "fall" from an original Paradise. For example, in the Jewish Cabala, the Light is split into individual sparks and the spiritual journey is to follow the path back to the Light. God evolves as well. We are those evolving parts of God. The power that we refer to as God wants to know itself better. In our world of duality, we can only know something by experiencing and understanding its opposite. God is One. Yet God chose to imagine itself as individual personal egos split off from One. The illusion has become our reality. John reminded us that Christ said, "Be in the world, but not of it."

Didn't John Lennon also receive the true message in his songs "All You Need Is Love?" and "Imagine?" Do we need countries and borders? Do we need the divisions of organized religions and rules to believe ourselves loving and behave as such? It seems to me that the separate religions have only set us against one another other. Reprehensible, hateful acts have been committed in their names. John's information enlightened me with its absolutely simple assertion that *nothing is real but love.* Not fear, not suffering. How naive that sounds. But if we can stop the cycle of action-reaction, embrace non-violence as other great leaders like Gandhi and Martin Luther King, Jr. did—though both were murdered—if we know that the body and death are just illusions, doesn't that make it easier? Wouldn't forgiveness be easier altogether ?

If only humanity can learn to believe, to believe while still inhabiting the illusion. Jesus and Buddha transcended others' anger and abuse with great self-discipline and effort. If only everyone could, I thought as I listened to John. Well, first things first—if only *I* could.

Chapter 8

IN THE HOLOTROPICS

I have lived on the lip
of insanity, wanting to know reasons,
knocking on a door. It opens.
I've been knocking from the inside.
RUMI, *UNSEEN RAIN*

The flyer came in the mail, unsolicited. Gabriele's Bed and Breakfast in Provincetown held weekend workshops for women. I stood in the alcove of my Brookline apartment and read the description of "The Holotropic Breath Workshop" with interest, because I had sold some of Stanislav Grof's books in the bookstore I owned years ago, and had leafed through them myself. Grof was a California psychologist on the cutting edge at a time when a thousand and one different types of experiential approaches to psychotherapy surfaced in the the 1970s. The innovators of these techniques began to go beyond Freud's "talking cure" into more emotional experiences to find healing. New terms like EST, Rolfing, Transactional Analysis, Psychosynthesis, Gestalt, and archetypal and transpersonal psychology were coined, and their popularity provided evidence that people were hungry for introspective healing that included experiental dynamics. As I continued to read the specifics about the workshop, I felt the brochure had been sent to me for a reason. I had never been on Gabriele's mailing list before, and I've never had another mailing from there since. I had recently been experiencing so many "coincidences" that I felt as if I were leading a double life—English professor and poet in the work world, wild dreamer and visionary in my private world. But visionary of what? Aliens? Angels? Alter egos?

Grof's research into non-ordinary states of consciousness led him to a specific method through which the mind and senses are altered using certain accelerated breathing techniques along with loud, powerful music. This technique produces visionary and emotional states formerly thought to be accessible only through the use of psychedelic drugs. The word holotropic means literally "moving toward wholeness," from the Greek *holos* (whole) and *trepin* (moving toward something).

Grof was a scholar-in-residence for several years at Esalen Institute in Big Sur, California—one of the psychological research centers that, in the 1970s, launched experiental therapy on a large scale. Grof volunteered for an experiment with LSD as early as 1956, and began his work with altered states from this experience. He engaged in professional discussions with many notables: anthropologist Gregory Bateson; Joseph Campbell, the world's foremost mythologist; Fritjof Capra, who found relationships between quantum physics and Far Eastern philosophy; anthropologist Michael Harner, who was initiated into shamanism in the Amazon and South America; the renowned spiritual teacher, Ram Dass; Rupert Sheldrake, the English physicist who does fascinating work in morphic fields; well-known scientific author Ken Wilbur; and Rick Tarnas, eminent psychologist and astrologer.

Grof claimed that altered states were generated in three ways: by the ingestion of chemicals (LSD, mescaline, psilocybine, or other hallucinogens), by what he termed a "spiritual emergency" (the spontaneous experience of non-ordinary consciousness as a result of physical, psychological, or emotional trauma or an addiction crisis), and by the practice of holotropic breath work. As I read some of Grof's books after the workshop, I realized that the experience of the transformation of my bedroom ten years before had been one of these non-ordinary states brought on by my extremely emotional mindset—Grof's so-called "spiritual emergency."

Grof's work raised questions not only about multiple realities, but about the relationships between the cosmic force and matter, between brain and consciousness, between the universe's destructive and creative energies, and between the ineffable experience of the Absolute and the horrifying Void. He found that the scientific vocabulary could not contain these experiences and that the paradoxes found in poetry and esoteric philosophy were more conducive to capturing in words what people experienced in these situations. He discusses these states in his book *The Cosmic Game: Explorations of the Frontiers of Human Consciousness.*

> The emotions associated with holotropic states . . . range from feelings of ecstatic rapture, heavenly bliss, and "peace that passeth all understanding" to episodes of abysmal terror, overpowering anger,

utter despair, consuming guilt, and other forms of extreme emotional suffering.[1]

Although these practices were new to Western medicine, shamans in
American Indian cultures, and cultures in Africa and South America had
evoked these responses through ritual healings for centuries. I felt compelled to try something new to communicate with the strange new energies
around me. I was aware of changes in my sensual perception. During my
regular twenty-minute meditations, I had begun to see differently. Besides
a vivid, rich purple light that seemed deeper than our three dimensions,
now I discerned more clearly the outlines of the figures around me. And
I physically sensed their movement in the air. Sometimes, I saw a piece of
their clothing very distinctly, usually a patterned shirt. I never saw distinct
facial features, except for one man—the owner of the huge eye that looked
back at me.

My apartment was extremely dry in the winter and, one afternoon, I had
a nosebleed that wouldn't quit. I had been prone to nosebleeds as a kid and,
as I had a cold, I had taken Anacin, which probably inhibited clotting. I lay
down on my bed with a wad of Kleenex and closed my eyes. I could feel the
spirits moving intensely around my head. To my surprise, I had a flash of a
very precise image. I was lying on a table and four or five masked surgeons
were leaning above me. It only lasted for a fraction of a second, but it was
particularly detailed and focused. I had never had this type of flash image
before. I then felt pressure inside my nose, a twisting and turning motion.
Through the deep purple light, with my eyes closed, I could make out the
shadowy outlines of what seemed to be human bodies—figures with heads,
shoulders, arms, and torsos—that were floating rather than standing. They
resembled the robed figures in the drawings and paintings of William Blake.
The pressure in my nose increased, as if someone had taken a clamp to it.
Most astonishing was that I could smell the odor of burnt flesh. The nosebleed quite suddenly stopped and I realized the bleeding had been cauter-
ized! I lay there a while longer, knowing that, somehow, these "entities" had
a hand, if not an instrument, in my recovery!

I also noticed that, during meditations, when I first felt the spirits
zoom in around me, they dropped something on my eyelids—an object
very distinctly applied to each eye, something round and small, like a stone.

---

1. Stanislav Grof, *The Cosmic Game: Explorations of the Frontiers of Human Consciousness* (Albany: State University of
New York Press, 1998), p. 6.

The visions that appeared behind my closed eyes began to change. On some days, I could see *through* my eyelids to the shadows of the furniture in the room. When this happened, everything was shades of grey and green and I could see fuzzy lines of energy, as if the objects themselves were quivering. I could make out, not only the shapes of bureaus and chairs, but the woodwork around the ceiling, even the definitive panels of the closet door. At the same time, I could also see the white outlines of bodies, human-size or even slightly larger, around my body. I could see them hand each other blocks of what I can only call "white light." They were luminous and bright white against the regular green-and-purplish vista of my closed eyes. The figures passed the blocks of white light to one another and then pushed them into various parts of my body. When they got close to my body and/or within it, I felt a sensation that ranged from that of a mild electric current to a momentary but discernible shock—at which point, I always shivered and cringed the way anyone does at suddenly being shocked. Although it didn't really hurt, it wasn't at all pleasant.

Over time, I became more and more acclimated to the blocks of light and didn't quiver as much. But at first, sometimes following the meditation, different parts of my body ached in the way you ache when you have the flu. More than once, I was unable to continue my normal pace of activity and actually took to my bed thinking I did have a flu bug. But the aches were gone within a few hours. I called David Hall to ask his advice and he suggested I tell my "spirits" when the feelings became too intense. They were quite persistent, however, and I found myself standing up waving like a mad woman to get them to stop. These sensations and visions continued for about a year and I was just feeling ready to move on to more clarity when I found Gabriele's flyer in my mail.

I had been to several psychics and healers since the new sensations began in 1994, and there was a common denominator across all these sessions. My soul had chosen signs of a physical awakening at an important time in human history. I was told I would be reclaiming powers I had lost in other lifetimes. As I read about Grof's techniques for healing trauma, I thought perhaps I could discover something about my proclivity for depression. Perhaps I could recover the adolescent self that had been traumatized by my father's breakdown and somehow repeat the trauma more consciously.

HEALING BREATH

Holotropic breath work is meant to lead you into internal experiences where the natural healing process of the psyche can be activated. We all experience what is appropriate for us at our particular stage of healing. Certain categorical themes recur, although many experiences remain unique. As I read the workshop description, I couldn't help but remember the intensity of sensations I had in my breath work with Jason. The shaking and release of cellular-level fears from my body had been overwhelming. I read in the brochure that the two workshop facilitators had been trained by Grof himself. With the intensity of the energies already surrounding me, I wondered what I would experience in such a session.

The brochure told me that holotropic breath work was done in pairs, in two shifts, with one person as a "sitter," available to assist the "breather." As in a past-life workshop I had attended at the Boston Jung Institute, one partner undergoes the experience in the morning, the other in the afternoon. A few phone calls convinced my friend Ellen, a massage therapist interested in body work, to go with me. Ellen had been in a conscious growth process for many years and, together, we planned a trip to Cape Cod for the weekend.

I first met Ellen when our sons attended a Montessori school together. She lived next door to me when I moved from my townhouse to the beach, before I relocated in Boston. Our sons, in fourth grade then, played together in the beach neighborhood, which included an old fort and a park on a cliff overlooking the bay. Strangely (or not so strangely), Ellen's partner had left her abruptly and secretly for another woman, and she was going through exactly the same kind of horrific heartbreak I had gone through in the mid Eighties. I recognized the synchronicity of our meeting and saw that my role was to help her through her crisis. We both survived and the heartbreak is a bond we have always shared. We spent several years communing in one another's living room or on the wrap-around porch of her house half a block from the beach.

Those days were many years behind us now. Although I was still without a partner, Ellen had reunited with a high school boyfriend and was currently in a committed relationship. She had continued exploring her personal growth as I had. We had both experienced the archetypal "Mad Woman"or "The Dark Side of the Great Mother,"as Jung might refer to it. Ellen's path was through Native American traditions and she had already completed a four-day vision quest in the Mojave Desert, where she fasted and hallucinated—something I felt was way beyond the scope of my endurance.

We left for Provincetown in the dead of winter, so the trip was a lot smoother than it might have been in summer traffic from Boston to Cape Cod. We flew across the bridges and, in record time, found ourselves cozily ensconced in a suite at Gabriele's that included a hot tub. On Friday night, we attended a brief lecture on the work by the two women facilitators. They explained some of the scientific background to prepare us for the journey. Back in our room, Ellen and I conjured up a great dinner at a little inn somewhere with a fireplace. Instead, we found only one tacky little restaurant still open at 9:30 at night. We promptly returned to our room, undressed on our terrace in the frigid January air, and immersed ourselves in the bubbling water of the hot tub. I remember sleeping restlessly that night, awakening many times to the commotion of air around me. It seemed my friendly guardians were gearing up for something big.

I faced the morning rather exhausted. After our lovely hostess, Gabriele, served a light breakfast and the group moved into the workshop room, I encouraged Ellen to take her turn first. Not having slept well, I felt I didn't yet have the energy for accelerated breathing. I just wanted to zone out to the music, which, we were told, had been selected precisely for its intensity (there were several sets of very large stereo speakers in the room).

To begin, one person in each pair stretched out comfortably on pillows and blankets. The facilitators showed us how to breathe and encouraged the "sitter" to prompt the "breather" if she stopped for any reason. They told the breathers to continue their specific breath work with their eyes closed for about twenty minutes to a half hour, after which they would probably find themselves in an altered space. They enjoined them to feel the experience as intensely as possible, and to keep their eyes closed. Then they warned the sitters not to interfere, even if the breathers began crying or hollering, or moaning or laughing. If, during the three-hour session, a breather wanted to walk around or visit the bathroom, they said, the sitter should guide her.

After the workshop facilitators had explained Grof's method, many of us exchanged anxious looks with our partners. "Yikes!" was all I could whisper to Ellen. Yet the environment seemed safe; we had guides and the leaders were trained to handle "bad trips." The previous night, we had all shared the reasons we were there. We were all seekers who knew our conscious minds had great limitations. We were women educated in psychology and spiritual philosophy looking for the next step in our individual development. We were women who had suffered emotionally and acquired a certain courage from having done so. Everyone there had undergone some form of therapy. Some were returning to experience holotropic breath work for a second or third time. And we were all willing to encounter whatever it was that would confront us. The facilitators had required a medical history from each of us, and we had each signed a release form.

Our workshop leaders told us that the domains reached through the holotropic process could spark feelings of memories in previous (or current) lifetimes, or even relationships to animals and plants—the remains of our links to the evolutionary process itself. Or we might experience a transpersonal realm from which we could view all of human history, with its dualities of good and evil, from an objective state of mind. Some breathers returned to a "perinatal matrix" and found themselves stuck in the womb with feelings of suffocation and the violence of a forced delivery. Many even rebirth during holotropic states. Grof explains that " . . . anything that we would, in our everyday state of consciousness, perceive as an object, can be also encountered as a corresponding subjective experience when we are in a holotropic state."[2] For myself, I expected some kind of emotional regression to my fifteen-year-old self that would let me grieve on a deep level for my father's death. Through therapy, I had connected my troubles with men to this first sudden abandonment.

Our workshop leaders also told us that people often reached mystical states in which they felt themselves merging with parts of nature and the vast expanses of the universe. As Grof says, "This work brings strong evidence suggesting that in the last analysis, each of us is commensurate with the totality of existence."[3] I interpreted that to mean we can become aware of our oneness with each other and "God."

Ellen and I exchanged a hug. I whispered "Good Luck" and saw to it that she felt as comfortable as possible. As the music began, she started her breathing. The loud and evocative music began with a combination of different cuts researched and recommended by the Grof Institute. The result was something overtly tribal—African or South American—with multi-vocal chanting in the background and a good amount of drumming and rattling.

After about ten minutes, I could see that Ellen was experiencing some of the anticipated physical side-effects, such as a numbing of the extremities and a dry mouth. She shook out her fingers, grimaced, and twisted her features, moaning a bit. I encouraged her to keep going by whispering to her

---

2. Grof, *Cosmic Game*, p. 16.
3. Grof, *Cosmic Game*, p. 16.

and patting her shoulders. After about a half hour, she began shifting her position and got up on all fours. She seemed to be straining different parts of her body, pushing and pulling herself across the floor. I tried to disentangle her from the blankets and periodically asked if she needed anything. We had a few big bottles of water and I offered her a drink now and then. When she seemed to be in pain, I tried to get close, but she pushed my arm away. She asked for pillows and wedged them against her stomach, then she beat a little with her fists on the floor.

As I looked around, I suddenly realized the level of noise in the room. Several of the women were moving about, held back only by their partner's hands. Others were lying down but dancing with their hands, shaking their heads, singing or wailing, groaning, or actually calling out, cursing or crying. It looked and sounded like *The Snake Pit,* an old Hollywood movie about an insane asylum. I knew what we were in for; I liked the edge and I found the scene both wild and amusing. But, although I observed the participants one by one, I could not imagine what each person was experiencing. Over the next few hours, which went by very quickly, I spaced out a few times, lost in the music and my own thoughts, as Ellen continued to struggle with her body, refusing my offers of help. At one point, she quietly mumbled to me that she felt as if she were in the birth canal.

It was then that I remembered that Ellen's son was born by Caesarean section and that she herself had been a forceps delivery. She had a scar on her shoulder from her own birth and that shoulder periodically ached when she was under stress. She was especially disappointed when she couldn't push out her own baby and had to submit to anesthesia. I found it fitting that she found herself in that dark cavity tunneling toward birth.

I also recalled reading some channeled material that stated that the most difficult thing we ever accomplish is to be born—that death is, more often than not, a delightful passage and something that we should not fear, having gone through it many times already. In this context, Ellen's thumping and bumping, rolling and kicking, moaning and hollering seemed perfectly appropriate. She kept reaching for her neck and pounding her chest, and I continued to remind her to breathe. I plied her with water when I could and walked her to the bathroom once or twice while she kept her eyes closed. The noise and activity in the workshop room was overridden by the very loud music. In a way, even the sitters were experiencing a non-ordinary event. We occasionally looked around and smiled at each other across the bizarre scene, which was at times humorous as well as serious, a scene out of Hieronymus Bosch.

The time passed quickly and the music continued as long as there were breathers on the floor. Then slowly, one at a time, the breathers began to open their eyes and come back to the world of linear time and common consciousness. As the women finished their process, the two facilitators walked around telling the sitters to have their partners lie quietly and calm down. When each pair felt ready, they were sent downstairs to another room where paper and colored pencils awaited. During this final part of the workshop, participants were instructed to draw a mandala of their experience. When everyone was finished, the session was processed by the group sharing the mandalas.

Some people described their journeys in explicit detail. Others chose to say nothing, simply holding up the drawing, then passing it around the group. I can't, at this point, recall the other journeys, but Ellen spoke of hers as a powerful rebirthing. She felt she had made a semi-conscious journey down the birth canal and, in that experience, she was able to heal both the sense of her own coerced emergence through the birthing process, and her sense of helplessness at her son's delivery. Her mandala symbolically showed both darkness and light, imprisonment and brutal arrival.

We enjoyed a light vegetarian lunch and took a break, some of us walking briefly outside in the sobering winter air. Then we went back upstairs and prepared for the other half of the participants to take their "trip." I was anticipating mine nervously. I remembered a previous past-life-regression workshop where I found myself as a French nun. As then, the thing I feared most was that nothing would happen. Ellen seemed refreshed and, good friend that she is, she was ready to be my caretaker.

MY TURN

I began the breathing and immediately found it uncomfortable. As I felt my toes and fingertips disappear, I also felt the sides of my face numb and my body begin to tingle and shake. I could feel the "active" state of the energies hovering above and around me. I silently told them to back off, but then called them back and asked them to keep me safe. I soon lost track of time and couldn't tell if I had just begun or had been there for hours. Eventually, I stopped my accelerated breathing and just let the music fill me. Bright lights splashed behind my closed eyes and psychedelic designs began to appear. I saw the perfectly symetrical, kaleidoscopic foldings and unfoldings of intricate patterns and geometric shapes. Two-color combinations dominated, shifting in pairs. Bright-yellow and black pulsing stripes and spinning flower shapes, waves of dark blue and then reds. I found myself exclaiming "Ooo" and "Ahhh," and dancing with my arms and hands.

The music was deep and vast, with woodwinds and electric guitars that seemed to be playing from inside my brain. I don't know how long this went on, but I was having a grand time when, suddenly, out of one tangled design, a shape began to form. It morphed into a clear blue eye, like the one in Magritte's famous painting. I felt transported and found myself moving quickly toward the eye, which came closer and closer, until I went through it, flying at thousands of miles an hour. I flew through doorways, one after the other, portals, cave-like entrances made of crystal, amethyst and quartz, glitter and gloss. A bright white light appeared in the distance, over the thresholds, light like the brightest Sun. Yet I could look directly into it, feeling, not pain, but warmth—and I could see a figure in the glare of the light, an angelic being spinning. I had a sensation of swooshing, swishing, faster than I could control. I went through archway after archway and finally saw huge landscapes beneath me, a bird's eye view of what looked like Ireland or England—cliffs over oceans and spacious green pastures of velvety textures. It was as if I were a plane flying over the whole continent of Europe. At times, I swooped in for a close-up, winging over turrets and courtyards in France, Italy, and Spain—through medieval cities with cathedrals and coliseums, knights and horses, huge brick walls, and dungeons and chains—then I soared back up to see forests and fields, a hunt complete with beagles and foxes—and then lions. As I flew, everything zoomed into hyper-focus, then zoomed out again. The colors were deep and flat, without variation—solid green, solid red, solid brown, extremely solid, flat, surreal geometrical planes. But the light remained luminous, almost as if there were a spotlight behind me, on the periphery of my vision—a radiant glow, a ring of fiery white.

Periodically, I returned to the archways, passed through yet more doors, and then onto a new scene. I recall one specifically Asian vista, with pagoda roof tops and troops of soldiers in bright satin pajamas of different colors. Then temples and Buddhas, sculptures like Shiva, black Bali-like monsters with open mouths, dragons and fangs. I have no idea of the sequence of these visions, and can only recall the details that flooded my eyes like a panoramic film. It was as if I could see from behind, from below, from above, *holotropically.* I suddenly understood it! I could think, I knew where I was—in this room as well as outside of it! Ellen leaned over periodically to ask if I needed anything, but I whacked her hands away and covered my eyes so that nothing would stop this Cecil B. DeMille production, this amazing view into—*what?*

Sometimes the eye returned, beginning in the distance as an abstract pattern, then moving closer and taking the form of a huge oval. I felt seen by it, penetrated—dare I say *loved?* Then a long parade of faces passed by, each one beginning in the distance, then flying closer and closer until I could see it close-up and put a name to it. There was Jesus just as I had visualized him when I was a child! Mary in her blue mantle, Buddha, Zeus, some Greek goddesses and Hermes and Dionysus, the Egyptian deities Anubis and Isis, the Celtic Lady of the Lake—each one looking right at me with love. There were more whom I can't recall, what seemed like people from all ages, archetypes from all walks of life. "Which life?" I thought. And I saw the man who was "the eye" from the chest up, with dark curly hair and a beard, a Nehru collar, and long patterned white coat. Then back to the doorways. It was extraordinary!

I rolled over on my side and, keeping my eyes closed, reached for the bottled water, which Ellen quickly put into my hand. I took a long drink, not wanting even to flutter my lids open for fear the visions would end. The last sequence was space, sky, huge and infinitely deep, stars pinned to a dark backdrop that hung like a dome over my face. Now and then, one star-like dot spiraled in close, shaking and quivering, then burst open into white light like fireworks. Gradually the explosion broke up into a white cloud against a dark-blue background. Then the eye returned again, moving in close, quivering and spinning like a star. Over and over I watched this routine, the music transporting me. Even when the drums were intense, there was nothing but joy—a vision of sheer joy, music and images perfectly synchronous. I simply felt seen, united, and loved, part of the rhythm, part of the landscape's unbelievably vast design.

Close to the end, I remember thinking that I didn't want it to stop and that only an hour or so had elapsed, so maybe I should go back to the breathing. When I finally opened my eyes, I saw Ellen there smiling, but the room was empty. Apparently, I was the last to finish and, although I felt that only an hour had passed, it had actually been three full hours! Somewhat unsteady on my feet, and with Ellen's help, I got up and folded my pillows and blankets. "You were really grooving the whole time!" Ellen laughed. I just beamed at her. "It was wild!"

I didn't know where to begin with the mandala. I divided it into four quadrants and filled the first with the giant eye. As I colored it in, I lamented the fact that I had not inherited my father's artistic skills as my older brother had. I didn't want to forget anything about the journey, but I didn't think I could do it justice. In the second quadrant, I drew the arched doorways on a smaller scale, dozens of them surrounded by sparkles and stars. I outlined them in different colors, one vertical rectangle within another, as if to give them depth. In the third quadrant, I drew the domed sky with stars everywhere. In the last, I drew the kaleidoscopic Kodachromatic designs using every geometrical figure I could remember: trapezoids, rhomboids, pyramids, triangles, and squares. I splashed in colors and squiggled lines all around them.

I simply couldn't begin to reproduce the faces or the numinous quality of emotion connected with them. But in the "show and tell" that followed, I added at the end—"Oh, and after I saw this huge eye, I saw Jesus and Mary and Buddha and all these Biblical and mythic figures and Egyptians." I caught one woman rolling her eyes at her partner as if I were not to be believed, and I felt strange and clammed up. But then another woman, who had come alone and done her trip without a partner, described her experience, which was cosmic and quite close to mine. She said she was comfortable and exhilarated as she flew through each vortex, that she felt beautiful and fulfilled the entire time. I felt that she validated my own experience, which had been so astonishing that I didn't know if I trusted it myself.

Later, when I read Grof's books, I realized that my trip was a transpersonal experience. Beyond the subjective, personal life, the range of experiences can also include meetings with archetypes. We can have powerful encounters with mythic and religious figures, both loving gods and goddesses and potent or horrifying demons—in other words, the whole nine yards of the Jungian collective unconscious. The archetypes lie like seeds at the bottom of the unconscious, but they are the bridges to higher realms. They represent our less-personal aspects, the places where we connect with what can be called our "oversouls," our multi-dimensional aspects—aspects of our monadic family that dwell in other dimensions, but serve as our guides. We can encounter these aspects in moments of transcendence and prayer as well as emotional crises. Grof's research indicates, as the name *holotropic* testifies, that the part contains the whole, that the universe's micro-/macro-cosmic relationship embraces our selves as reflective of every other aspect of our universe, and vice versa, so that everything is interrelated and codependent—a concept also known as "the butterfly effect." As Gerry/John had said to us often: "We are all God! There's only *one* of us here!"

As I read about the holotropic breath "trips" that others have had, I noticed that some people also witnessed the destructive impulse in imagination, in history, and in humanity. I was struck by the fact that my experience was particularly pleasurable, *beatific* really. I couldn't recall anything frightening and I was a person with fears. I think perhaps the guides around me were giving me confidence that I could trust them, nourishing me and deepening my well of faith. The only thing I can say for sure is that they were highly energized by the process as well. I was extremely fortunate, and feel grateful for having undergone such an inspiring trip. It was notable in that there were no fearsome images—serious expressions, yes, but not one negative emotion. Yet at the time, I had no idea what effects I would bring back into my normally limited quotidian perceptions. For the moment, I was content to quote Rumi:

> *Lo, I am with you always,* means when you look for God
> God is in the look of your eyes,
> in the thought of looking, nearer to you than your self . . .[4]

---

4. Moyne, John and Coleman Barks. *Open Secret: Versions of Rumi.* (Boston: Shambhala Books, 1984), p 50.

Chapter 9

THIRD-EYE VIEWſ

*. . . it may happen that you go through a phase when a strong vibration is automatically
and permanently switched on in your third eye . . . and it often has to do with
the guides pouring energy into your structure.*

SAMUEL SAGAN, *AWAKENING THE THIRD EYE*

I didn't find Dr. Sagan's book until I saw it in Dijon on my Black Madonna journey during the summer of 2000. Sagan is the director of the Clair-vision School in Sydney, Australia. Drawing on both Eastern and Western traditions, he wrote a very intensive manual for spiritual development and especially for opening the inner vision of the sixth "anja" chakra, or pineal gland. The book is quite complex, enumerating very particular exercises that demand time and constant practice—the kind of manual I can never follow. But it didn't take long for me to notice that I had skipped several stages. Something permanent had happened to me as a result of the holotropic breath workshop. I assume that my third eye would have opened eventually, since David and other psychics had told me I would be awakened, but apparently the workshop accelerated the process.

Admittedly, strange things had begun during my meditations before I attended the workshop. Behind my closed eyes, I saw more intense colors, as well as the shapes of beings around me and the layout of the furniture and objects in the rooms where I meditated. The best analogy I can offer is wearing those 3-D glasses from the Fifties on top of military night-vision glasses that help you to see in the dark.

After that weekend in Provincetown, it seemed that my third eye had been blasted open. I now had more and more strange visions, often just as I awoke in the morning. Ever since my holotropic experience, the single eye greets me after about fifteen seconds of meditating with my eyes closed. The scene is no longer in Technicolor, but it is clearly evident within the dark hues and cloudy shapes that usually greet my closed eyes. The outlines of the eye quiver and vibrate. Sometimes it moves with a floating rotation, moves backward into depth, and eventually I see another eye. As this eye retreats, I see a whole face, with nose and mouth, chin and hairline. The face belongs to a man, the same man I remember from my vision in the workshop; he is wearing a mandarin collar, but I can never see below his throat. Often, he turns slowly in my vision, and then I see the overlay of his face coming into view from another angle. I recognize that he is indeed a hologram.

The man in my vision has never made (eye) contact with me or shown any kind of emotional or personal recognition. Indeed, I have the impression *I* am spying on *him*, because he seems to be completely unaware that he exists inside my vision. Yet he looks completely alive. His mouth moves, opens and closes as if he were in conversation with someone, though I hear nothing. Only this year I happened to see a drawing of Djwhal Kuhl online and I did a double-take at the exact resemblance of the picture to my inner image. Back when he first appeared, it was all so strange that I finally went for a private consultation with Gerry/John, during which John confirmed that this image is related to my soul. He told me to think of the man as one of my guides and also to understand that some scenes are symbolic rather than actual. Though I pressed for exact details—Who? What? Where? Why? How?—John just said I needed to trust, be patient, and allow the unfoldment. At the same time, the depth of my vision behind my closed eyes increased. I perceived a dome-like valley within the three-dimensional abyss. Colors continued to change. If I am outside, for instance, on a sunny day, as I close my eyes and look, I see the eye, but now the background is bright orange or red or yellow.

There are patterns behind the eye as well. They look to me almost like repeating wallpaper patterns of intricate flowers. The man's face is translucent and I can see the patterns through him. Sometimes I realize that what I am seeing is a bird's-eye view of the top of his head and it is just his wavy hair making the patterns. Then the overlay of the eye begins close-up with the iris and slowly backs away so that I can see the entire eye, both eyes, eventually the face, always in a slow rotating motion with the patterns within it. It is so fascinating that I lie on my bed for long periods of time just watching the images change.

After several months, I began to view scenes through the eye, again similar to my experience in the workshop, though much less intense. The scenes, as in moving pictures, only stay for a few brief seconds and I need to flutter my eyelids about nine tenths closed to focus on them clearly. As I strain my inner vision to keep the scenes in focus, my forehead pounds with painful pressure. I stay with the vision as long as I can bear the pressure, which is viselike at my temples and in the center of my brow. The most vivid of these visions usually come after about ten minutes into a meditation or just as I awake in the morning. I gather from reading I have done that some of these morning scenes are simply *hypnagogic*—like fast-moving cartoons. But I had not ever before in my life had this type of vision.

Slowly, several new experiences occurred. First, the movies appeared as cartoons, which, I read, were perfectly normal for some people as they hover at the edges of sleep. But then I began seeing particular thematic cartoons. One was a Greek myth. I saw centaurs and images of gods and goddesses—Zeus, Dionysus, and others—lying around pillared palaces feeding each other grapes, gallivanting through the woods. I saw swans and unicorns and rare birds. It was a regular Disney *Fantasia!* I found it amusing and entertaining, but also certainly odd—and not just because it appeared spontaneously without my having willed it or thought it up. At that time in my life, I was compiling a collection of poems for a book, an anthology of contemporary poems about Greek mythology. I began the work in 1993. The spirits arrived in late 1994. It was as if they had read my mind. Or they were my mind! A part of it anyway. The book was finally published in 1999.

The story of how the book came about is rather magical in itself. For several years, I had been teaching works of the Greek playwrights Aeschylus, Sophocles, and Euripides, as well as *The Iliad* and *The Odyssey,* in a literature class. In order to give the students another perspective on our great legacy from the Greeks (the endurance of these archetypal themes and images), I sometimes brought in copies of contemporary poems that put the themes and characters in a modern context. Because I always keep up with contemporary poetry, I had noticed the popularity of myth poems and thought that, at some point, there should be a collection of them. I looked for one in libraries and bookstores, but was unable to find what I wanted. I then thought maybe I could put one together.

I first entertained this idea back in the early months of 1993 when I received a brochure in the mail from the Bread Loaf Writer's Conference in Vermont. I had attended the conference way back in 1977, my first step into the public writing arena. Still in my twenties, I had gone timidly, with my sheaf of unschooled poems, and selected the poet Mark Strand as my mentor. Strand was in his mid forties, tall, slim, and simply gorgeous. He strolled up and down the green hills of the Vermont campus like the Pied Piper, with young women trailing behind him. I got to know him better in the Eighties when he came to the Stone Coast Writers' Conference in Maine. But when I saw the brochure in 1993 (which, as a former attendee, I received every year), I saw that Mark Strand was going to be at Bread Loaf again. The staff rotates and, although some people return to teach every year, Strand hadn't been there in a long while. I didn't think anything else about it at first, but I believe my subconscious cataloged that tidbit along with the memory of a very beautiful poem by Strand entitled *"Orpheus Alone"* that had appeared in *The Best American Poetry 1990.* I loved the poem and read it now and then, both to myself and to my classes.

The same night that I looked over the brochure, I had a dream that I was at Bread Loaf laughing and talking with Mark Strand. A real feel-good dream. In the morning, I awoke thinking maybe I would apply for a scholarship to Bread Loaf. Although tuition had been only $400 in 1977, the two-week conference weighed in at $1500 in 1993. I didn't have that money to spare, but I had a number of publications in good poetry journals and qualified for the scholarship application. I thought Bread Loaf might be helpful, since I was preparing to mail out my manuscript of poems and could use some professional feedback. Also, I thought it would be nice to see Mark again and ask him about my idea for an anthology of myth poems. I already had the title, *Orpheus & Company,* inspired by Strand's poem "Orpheus Alone."[1]

As it turned out, I was awarded the scholarship and I received encouragement from Mark to do the book. I also met three other poets who were there on fellowships. They had each published a book with Alice James Books in Cambridge in the early Nineties. I had submitted mine to the same publisher and been told I was the runner-up finalist. These three poets encouraged me to resubmit. The next fall, Alice James accepted my manuscript. So the dream turned out to be auspicious on a number of levels.

WITH EYES WIDE OPEN

As I worked on the compilation of the myth poem collection, I also watched "movies" of Greek myths when I awoke in the morning! These were not daydreams or nocturnal dreams. They came unbidden and I was perfectly conscious as I watched them behind my closed eyes. After several minutes, they

---

1. The character of Orpheus is the tragic quintessential poet of Greek myth, and therefore of Western literature.

faded away. I also had other visions that occurred with my eyes wide open, usually after waking, often very early, around five or six A.M. These were neither nocturnal nor day dreams—I often went to sleep for a while when they were over. They were like movies behind my eyes, movies over which I had no control; they were dreamlike, although I was perfectly awake.

Then the more astonishing visions began. In these, I saw with open eyes things that I had never seen before. One morning, as I awoke at dawn and opened my eyes, there was a huge, transparent, floating Native American Indian in my bedroom. This was no dream. I knew I was fully awake. The image had distinctive heavyset features and was built like the side of a barn. He sat cross-legged, wore a blanket around his shoulders, and seemed to be engaged in silent conversation with someone else. He was completely translucent—I could see the rest of the room through him, the bureau, the closet door, and window behind him. He was in color, but pale color, faded, hazy blues and browns. I admit I was frightened. Yet it was as if he were in his own world and had just accidentally become visible to me, like tapping into a crossed phone line. I stared for several minutes, then got out of bed for a drink of water. I got back in bed quickly without looking around and pulled the pillow over my head. When I got up at seven, he was gone.

The mythological visions, which went on for a few months, eventually gave way to visions of Native Americans. I began to see scenes of Indians, tribes, and teepees through my closed third eye during meditations, and again in the early morning as I awoke. I saw big panoramic views of natural landscapes and what I supposed were reservations. I felt distinctly that I was in the American West of the 19th century. I remember asking myself why I thought "West" when, in the 19th century, there were Native Americans all over New England where I now lived. But I did think "West," and my suspicion was confirmed a few years later. I was born in the desert of southeast Washington State, so I recognized winter scenes of mountains and rivers, rocks and streams, of people wearing layers of very bulky clothing gathering wood, and of squaws with babies on their backs walking single file on footpaths through thick forests. The scenes were not in color, but more in shades of gray or even sepia, like old photos.

Occasionally the Big Indian appeared for a few moments floating in my bedroom as I slowly awakened in the morning. He was still visible for a few seconds when my eyes were finally open. I recall that a former client of mine at my bookstore, a prominent psychiatrist who was definitely on a spiritual path, once told me of an experience he had with a vision in an emergency room. The way he described his vision reminded me of the images I was now seeing. An Indian of a completely different time and place, transparent but substantial, simply floating on air. He did some research on the Indians who had occupied the territory, trying to discern if it was an actual ghost or if the vision was more personally related. Like him, I had no answers.

Naturally, I knew something had shifted with the energies around me. They were still working on my body. And my claire-sentience, my ability to *feel* psychically as well as physically, had also developed. More than once, as I was on the verge of nodding off to sleep while meditating, I awoke startled and utterly freaked out. I felt an arm that felt exactly like a human arm close around my ribcage and prop me up out of my slumped posture. It was so real, so tender and gentle, so loving, I wondered about angels. Were these spirits or angels? I remembered that, in my session with Jason the Spirit Cleanser, he said he was aware of at least two angelic presences and some spirit guides around me.

Then I began to feel the hands inside my abdomen when my spastic colon acted up. And I know how whack-o this sounds, but they eased my pain, seemed to massage the colon back into position. I had spent a lot of money with a nutritionist—for a while, taking all kinds of expensive herbs to rid myself of a case of Candida and get my stomach working normally again. That was when the spirit hands began to work on me, or rather, inside me. Finally, I stopped buying the expensive herbs and just asked the spirits to help when it bothered me. They began to help, but it was difficult at first. Lots of pain. I realized later that they were opening my third chakra, the solar plexus, where we keep our fear and power all tied up in knots. I feel the hands in different parts of my body even now, but I have to say, my stomach problem is much improved. I have changed some eating habits, but I still drink coffee, which before had been a major trigger for my spastic colon. I have also returned to eating many foods that I had cut out completely.

There were many times when I was curled up in pain on my bed. If anyone had walked in, they would have thought I was on the medieval rack, moaning aloud, holding my stomach. I could feel what they were doing and it was as if they were braiding and unbraiding something inside me. Since these sessions always ended with my stomach completely comforted, I trusted what was occurring.

Another bizarre example of this claire-sentience occurred when I was at the dentist. A bridge in the back of my mouth that I've had since I was seventeen came loose on a flight to Florida to see my mother. When I arrived, I went immediately to her dentist to have it reinserted. He applied permanent dental glue and pressed down hard on the bridge with his fingers. After about thirty seconds of pressure, he told me to sit there for a few minutes longer and let the glue set. I saw him leave the room, closed my eyes, and was praying that the glue would hold, as a new bridge would cost thousands of dollars. And then I felt a hand on my chin and one in my mouth applying pressure. I shot open my eyes, expecting to see the dentist with his hands in my mouth again, but I was alone in the room. I was flabbergasted and could talk of nothing else on the way back to my mother's. My mother had been cautious about my stories of the angels and spirits over the years, but, as she drove, accustomed to my strange tales, she simply rolled her eyes at me and said "Now I've heard everything!"

Yet these tappings and touchings and "adjustments," as David had called them, continued. Sometimes I awoke in the night feeling those arms across my body, as if holding it in position, while other hands seemed to be inside my body pulling strings of what I can only call "energy" through different organs. I must emphasize that this experience felt as vivid and real as live human hands. When I called David in another mini-panic, he said it was part of the "cleansing process" to open chakras and align meridians, and that I should not be alarmed. He called it psychic surgery and reminded me that it was occurring to lots of people who were awakening to higher vibrations, but that I just happened to feel if *physically*. I seriously wondered whether I had realized the extent of what I was requesting before I incarnated! Did I know it would be this totally isolating, uncomfortable, and just plain weird?

One of the first sections of my body attended to was my heart. I remembered what Jason said about allowing the sorrow to be released. It felt as if strings were tied tightly around my heart, pulled through, and then let go like a toy top, so that I felt a very beautiful loosening, an "opening," along with a sense that some beautiful elixir was being poured into my heart—a thick, smooth, cool liquid. I felt enormously loved and often cried during this process. I thought I was crying for myself, mourning my aloneness, my troublesome daily plight of being an exploited adjunct professor, overworked and underpaid, unappreciated in middle age without a dependable income or a partner, lonely, depressed, and sad. But there was something else "coming in" that contradicted my conscious emotional framework, a tremendous sense of gratitude and a feeling of being loved by an invisible world—by God, by Jesus and Mary, by the angels, by the Goddess, and by whomever else I had prayed to off and on since I was a child. I found myself feeling grateful for my students, grateful for my books and my own mind, grateful for my poetry, for my friends and family. I felt lucky. Impossibly lucky. I was so used to moaning about my plight that this contradictory feeling greatly surprised me.

I remembered John had also told me that I had "asked for this." I assumed at the time that he was referring to the information David had given me about the "deal" my soul made before incarnating. In the meantime, I joined John's healing group, where other people appeared to know that a global awakening was occurring. I attended the weekly session where Gerry channeled the spirit of John. I didn't bother worrying about the veracity of the spirit's identity, as everything he said was wise and loving and generally helpful in many aspects.

John said all of humanity is invited onto this path, but some forget or ignore the signs sent to awaken them. They are lost in the material world, "addicted to form," as he put it. But this was and is why we are here. *Every one of us.* To wake up, in this body, at this time. It is a great privilege to be on Earth at this time, he insisted. David even said there are souls queued up trying to be born here. (I wondered if this could account for the over-population.) John said that my soul had decided there was no way I would miss the boat to greater awareness and that it had arranged for me to be aware of the psychological awakening of the species *physically.* One morning, it came to me that I had also asked for spiritual help consciously *in this body, in this life.*

MEMORARE

On Christmas Eve of 1987, I was still living in Maine. My mother was visiting and she, my brother, and I all went to a local midnight Mass. It was tremendously crowded and, though we left home with a half hour to spare, there were few seats. I ended up standing throughout the service. I was tired in the way a lot of people are tired at midnight Masses. I felt the culmination of the season, the rushed shopping and wrapping, the sense of something missing, the anti-climatic semi-depression that is said to affect many during the holidays. It was yet another anniversary of my father's Christmas death and my birthday. The day after Christmas was always tainted with let-down and, since my father's death, with a little gloom. My son spent Christmas Eve at his father's, returning in the morning. But I found the holidays especially trying after my divorce. Even after my father's death, my mother always kept a lovely festive house with many of our friends and relatives dropping in. But over the years, my Christmas celebrations had grown smaller and quieter. My marriage was a thing of the past and my lover was long gone. My sense of family was fractured and I sentimentally looked back to my childhood, when I had seemed so much happier.

I had just completed the sale of Anastasias's, the bookstore named for my mother, because it hadn't produced enough income to support me. I was tired of scrambling for money. (Little did I know the situation would worsen over the years). I had decided to take a few months off and study things Jungian. I leaned against the wall of the church, spacing out to the priest's predictable homily, and spoke directly to Mary. I told her I would do any-thing, *anything* required of me, but please, *please*, lead me somewhere, to some greater use in the world; please show me what to do. I felt I had something to offer, but did not know what or how to deliver it. I recited the prayer called the *Memorare*, which specifically requests the Virgin's intercesion: "Oh Mother of the Word incarnate, despise not my petition and in your mercy, hear and answer me ." It was one of the few prayers I truly loved. Whether I thought it went directly to Prayers-Granted Central or nowhere at all was irrelevant. I knew it couldn't hurt to try.

Five years later, I had moved to Boston and settled into teaching as an adjunct at several different colleges. I was paid by the course. I had been teaching an overload—five courses a semester and three in the summer—for many years. I thought that, if I ever got a full-time job, it would be a piece of cake! Within course parameters, I was able to teach some of the material I was interested in. I created courses and actively read criticism. My classic freshman composition class was based on readings related to the creative unconscious. In that class, I taught Jung's *Man and His Symbols* and later a few of Hesse's novels that illustrate Jung's concept of the shadow. I knew that, like myself, once they understood what happens in our natural psychological process of projection, these students would have more empathy. I knew they could avoid rancor for others if they owned up to their shadows rather than projecting them outward. I believed that projection could be bred out of us, generation by generation, so why not start now?

I loved the students at the art college, because each of them had already made the decision to focus on their creative talent, which is a difficult choice in a world that defines success by security. Each time I saw him, David insisted on telling me that my teaching was "very, very important." Once he even said that the students I was given were souls I had had as students in other lives! And in those years, I did, by and large, have wonderful, interested students—artists and musicians who often thanked me for the course and told me I had changed the way they thought about their dreams and the world in general.

One strange example of this, one of many, occurred when a distraught and anxious student came to me one morning after a class in which a paper was due. He asked to speak to me in private and told me that, over the weekend, while he was "playing a gig" in New York, his dog had run away. He said he was so upset he could not finish his paper. Now I had heard my share of excuses about dogs eating homework, but I knew this student was conscientious, and I could see how seriously concerned he was to find his dog. He said he had spent an entire day posting signs and pictures of the dog in his neighborhood. I told him he could have an extension on the paper, but that he must come to class.

As I started to walk away, down the hall to my office, I suddenly stopped and called to him. On the spur of the moment, I had a stray thought and made what I'm sure must have seemed a strange suggestion to him. I suggested that he visualize the dog in a meditation. I told him to imagine light around the dog, and to talk to it in his usual way, telling it he would find it and that the dog should head for home. He stared at me thoughtfully and said, "Okay, I'll try that." I walked away thinking, "He probably thinks I'm nuts."

Amazingly, two days later, this same student caught me again before class. He was ecstatic and said he had found his dog through my suggestion! He and his girlfriend had practiced the meditation for a full ten minutes. He said that, as soon as they finished—in fact, he stressed that the *very moment* they finished—the phone rang and a woman who had seen one of his flyers said that she had his dog. Over the years, there have been several occasions on which these kinds of suggestions have saved my students from personal distress. We sometimes discussed dreams and I had each of them keep a dream journal. I usually had them apply some Jungian principles to one selected dream in their mid-term conferences. Naturally, we worked on writing problems, but the thematically based course allowed the students to open up to the creative unconscious in other ways, as well as in their art and writing.

Though the financial situation I was in at the time was difficult, I continued to teach because I couldn't bear to do work that wasn't aligned somewhat with my own interests and, truthfully, I wasn't trained to do anything else. And I wanted to write in my spare time and teaching was supposed to give you more extensive time off. In reality, each year I had only August free for my writing. I managed to keep my writing on track by isolating myself at writers' colonies during August, by keeping my friends at a minimum, and by only joining groups and workshops that fed my own inspiration. It was a life I chose for myself, even if I was sometimes lonely. I decided that, if I was ever going to meet a partner, it would have to occur within the flow of my own chosen activities. I did have several groups of acquaintances with specific interests—the dream group, the peer workshop, my publisher's editorial collective, my women colleagues, my neighbors upstairs, my dear college crowd, my son and his friends. And I had my invisible guides who helped to keep my inner life incredibly rich. I took time to listen to my intuition, I played with divination techniques, and I learned to trust the irrational.

I soon forgot my request and promise to Mother Mary that Christmas eve, assuming it would never be answered. Despite my publications, my ship didn't come in. I bounced from school to school, drove an hour to teach an hour-long class, had cash-flow and budgeting problems, and was increasingly tired of working so hard for so little. Yet it occurred to me that this, what I could only call a *miracle* that had happened to me—this awareness of other disincarnate entities in my household and about my person—these new physical sensations, these strange visions were *a gift*. They had to be purposeful. I just didn't know what to do with them. And there were only a few people I could talk to about them. David became a very special confidant, because he acknowledged, respected, and verified what was happening. And John's interpretation (though he himself was a spirit borrowing Gerry's body) was invaluably validating as well.

Chapter 10

BURNING DOWN THE HOUSE

I saw grief drinking a cup of sorrow
and called out, "It tastes sweet,
does it not?" "You've caught me"
grief answered, "and you've ruined my business.
How can I sell sorrow, when you know it is a blessing?"
RUMI, *BIRDSONG*

From my analyst RB, I knew that therapy is about being re-parented. But even though he is my age and I had been drawn to his charismatic brilliance ever since he "cooked" my dream of the Black Truck, I knew that I was too realistic either to fall in love with him (he was *very* married) or to imagine him as my father. Yet the unconscious has its way of fooling us. And my work with him was marked by many dreams about my father. I hadn't dreamt of Daddy for twenty years or so, and the new contact that was revealing itself in my dreams surprised me. When I began seeing RB weekly, however, my father figured in my dreams on a regular basis, often in a wounded condition. I felt some responsibility to save him, as I did, more or less, with most of the men in my life. But there were some other unexpected healing signs as well and, over the years, his image seemed to be healing itself.

As the long poem I had drafted about his afterlife neared completion, I remembered a lovely dream I had had a few years back in which Daddy bought a huge building just so I could have a place to write. At the time, I attributed the dream to my positive transference to RB and the deep work we were doing together. But, like my dream of the one-eyed Asian man, this dream seemed prescient of things that would not become relevant for several years. Now I think the size of the building was indicative of the length of the poem I was to write. The unconscious, you see, is not circumscribed; it can predict the future, as well as reach deeply into the past. I didn't yet know I was to inhabit this poem intensely in the years that followed.

When David told me I had a "legacy" from my father, I was really baf-
fled. Was he picking this up from me—the day I stood in front of my Dad's
self-portrait and blamed him to his Fauvian-painted face for my taste in
men? Or was there something really coming down from some other dimension of the dead? It didn't seem to matter. I carried my own guilt for blaming
my father for my over-emotional relationships. Since my mother had moved
to Florida from New York back in the Seventies, none of us went to visit his
grave any longer. When I had my first visit from my spirit friends, I assumed
the energy came from my father. So I stopped in at the Unicorn Bookstore
in a Cambridge suburb and had a brief psychic reading.

The woman, who claimed to work with the angels, said she kept seeing a
grave site and flowers. I immediately thought about the cemetery. My father
died so young and so unexpectedly that my mother didn't have a burial site
arranged. He is buried in Flushing, New York with his parents and I don't
even know where. I was afraid that, if I drove there, I'd get irretrievably
lost. My mother had even discouraged me from going there. Nonetheless,
I discovered the address of the cemetery and the location of the plot and
sent flowers. Then, on an impulse, I sent some flowers anonymously to my
temporarily estranged brother for his birthday. If nothing else, these gestures
made me feel as if I were entering a realm of forgiveness and self-forgiveness.
Despite all of this thinking about what I could do to lead my father's soul to
peace, however, I think I realized I was going to write this poem mostly for
my own healing. Now, when I reflect back on this period of my life, I can see
how many signs pointed the way.

Every January, just after my Christmas birthday, I go an astrologer and
have my solar return chart read, which gives me the themes for the coming
year. And in January of 1995, I was told "you're beginning to heal your
father this year." This reminded me of a dream I had in college, from which
I awoke hollering to my roommate about purgatory. Although there was
no physical likeness, upon awakening, I irrationally but immediately associated my father with a black man in the dream who reached his arm out
to me in a plea for help. It was what Jung calls "a big dream," with archetypal figures and completely realistic feelings lingering for a long time. It
was so vivid, in fact, that I recall it perfectly today. I'm not sure the dream
came, as most dreams do, from my own inner issues. I don't recall anything
significant at that time. But I count this dream as one of a half-dozen "big
dreams" I will remember forever. It felt like a message from someone in
real trouble.

I kept thinking that maybe purgatory is that bardo state where souls in transition can get lost because the illusions, projected fears, and guilt of the egoic world are still with them at death. These fears are then recreated instantaneously, especially by souls who die unexpectedly and are not aware they are dead. One of the goals of the Tibetan Buddhists is to dream lucidly, so that, at death, they can negotiate the illusory images of the bardo passage precisely and without fear, and pass through the transitory state into spirit and light as easily as possible. I also surmised from what I'd read about near-death experiences—and from the many times John told us that there is no death, only change—that, in other worlds, thought manifests into form *immediately*. And in the bardo state, it seems that the forms created are still dreamlike, illusory, *samsara*, as the Buddhists say.

John spoke of the linear narrative imposed here on the Earth plane. One of the reasons we don't understand that we create our own reality here is that there is a time lag between cause and effect—that and, of course, because we aren't always aware of what our unconscious mind is up to. Because we've set up time as a construct, and because we play at life with rules that our bodies have to get or be somewhere, the "time" it takes to manifest a desire or fear on this plane is much slower. This keeps us from realizing the causal relationships between our conscious and unconscious wishes and thoughts. But in other dimensions, the same rules do not necessarily hold. This premise gave me the idea that my father, out of his own guilt, could have himself created a purgatorial reality at some point after his death. No doubt he was sorry for deserting us when he woke up dead, so to speak.

I had also read that some near-death experiences that involve attempted suicide are horrific. Because they seek to negate the creative life impulse, these souls come in contact with destructive impulses. And because of the energetic Law of Attraction, suicides often come into contact with other suicides, drunks with other drunks, etc. When they reach the other side, addicts still hunger from their addiction *as if* they have bodies, especially if they don't know they are dead. (Dante was right-on in his *Inferno*, assigning each sin to a specific level in purgatory and to a corresponding punishment.) John insisted that there are always other guides available and ready to counsel confused souls, but these souls can still create their own hells or purgatories, which frighten them as much as you might suspect, even though these creations are just as illusory as the hells we create here on Earth. Or rather, just as real as they *seem* to us. All the pain we feel when our bodies are injured is also due to our steadfast belief that we are our bodies. Essentially, we have created the "pain body." As we know, various people have been able to transcend physical pain. Walking on hot coals without burning has empowered many of our contemporaries.

Johh told us that, in sudden massive disasters like the 9/11 attack, when many people die at once, there are actually "spirit hospitals," because so many spirits believe they have bodies and that these bodies are injured. This collective belief actually manifests. When they realize they that are now spirits living in another dimension, they leave and go about their evolution into existences not so different from our own. There are schools and activities and even movies on the other side as well.

The order of events after death has always confused me. When does the Life Review happen? Before the tunnel? After? These memories are spoken of as common events in the books that relate near-death experiences. Of course, we can't expect to discover the truth of life after death with exactitude. Yet, however the experience really plays out, I think we can imagine infinite *possibilities* for life after death. And I realized I could play with these imaginings in my poem.

John also discouraged us from wanting to know all this information. Since we are multi-dimensional beings, he said, our soul extensions are active on many different planes, and there is no way to understand completely or explain the death experience. John constantly assured us that the only real thing in existence is love. The Beatles had it right: "Love is all there is." Sooner or later, a soul makes this discovery, only to give it up again in another physical incarnation. Because I am curious and never stop speculating completely, it occurred to me that the state of "enlightenment" may occur when each "aspect" or extension of the soul fully awakens to the reality of love and the illusory quality of everything else that appears real, and then makes contact with the other extensions of the monad up and down the halls of time.

John assured us again and again that dying is easy; the more difficult thing is to be born. Moving out of the body is a great release; moving in takes a lot of adjustment. And imagine, after living for nine months in unity with your mother's body, having to separate into your own body and negotiate that birth canal! I remember Ellen's experience in the holotropic breath workshop. Birth is a challenge as well as an imprint! Reading about the experiences of others in near-death experiences or prenatal holotropically altered states gives us a vast spectrum across which to imagine.

In one of Robert Monroe's books on his astral travel, he observed a soldier who had just been killed trying desperately to get back into his body. Obviously, the sudden realization that *the body is not what we are* is a difficult one when we are so completely identified with it. In the practice of Korean Dahn Hawk yoga, practitioners often say "I am *not* my body but my body is mine." And the experiences of meditation also help us realize that we are more than just our bodies and thoughts. John often spoke of the body as a room we might rent in a hotel. I have even used that image in my poem about my friend Judith's death.

THE FACE OF GOD

I began teaching the poetry of Rumi in one of my literature courses because it is extraordinarily beautiful and concise, and because his subject matter relates to many of these esoteric ideas. Rumi is considered a fully realized being who came to his enlightenment in mid life as the result of a heartbreak. He had a mysterious teacher, a "vagabond saint" named Shams (which means "Sun") whom he called "Friend, " or "the Beloved." Through his relationship with Shams, he learned of unconditional love for everything— every person, every plant, every insect, even every sorrowful negative aspect of life. By transcending the state of duality or the poles of opposites, by suspending judgment and accepting everything as it is, Rumi reached an ecstatic joy, but only after suffering the pain of separation from Shams. Harassed by Rumi's followers, Shams disappeared and Rumi, in his own bereft loneliness, composed his exquisite poems. When Shams returned, Rumi became enlightened. Evidently, Rumi's jealous followers eventually murdered Shams, though no body was ever found.

Rumi recited his poetry extemporaneously. Like Christ and the Buddha, he never wrote a word. Everything that comes down to us was transcribed by his disciples. He emulated the practice of the "whirling dervishes" by holding a pole and walking in a circle around it with his eyes closed as he spoke his poems. Like many mystics, Rumi saw the face of God in everyone. I find his poetry mystical and paradoxical. It contains one simple theme, his philosophy of Universal Love:

> If they ask what Love is
> say: the sacrifice of will.
> If you have not left your will behind,
> you have no will at all.[1]

---

1. Kabir Helminski, *The Rumi Collection: An Anthology of Translations of Mevlana Jalaluddin Rumi* (Boston: Shambhala Books 1998), p. 40.

This short poem tells us about both aspects of "will." On one hand, it is equivalent to "ego," or desire—that which needs to be left behind, to be "undone," as John put it. And it takes a lot of will power to sacrifice ego. It's personally difficult to deflate your desires, and it's downright scary to turn off the inner voice of your needy ego, which tells you what you need to be safe. But the ego lies. We don't need what it tells us we need. The hardest thing is to transcend the fear, for fear is at the bottom of every selfish, hurtful, or destructive act.

Rumi's ideas parallel many of the truths that John taught us. Rumi also speaks of two worlds, a world within this world, a world underlying the illusion of this world. The conflation of the true world with the illusory world of our fear-based manifestations keeps us from seeing that there is only love. Rumi resonates with Buddhist teachings about keeping the mind free from its usual muddle in a poem where he states: "Think of nothing but the source of thought." He parallels Christ's admonition to "Be in the world but not of it" with his lines: "Abandon life and the world, and find the life of the world"[2] And many of these poems echo John and *The Course in Miracles*, which emphasizes the veil over our eyes, that we see through a glass darkly. Rumi says "Know that your life throws a veil over your path." We are here to wake up in *this* body, to recognize how much larger we are than our own individual egos, which become completely identified with the body, safety and security, and the fear that we are not safe enough, rich enough, important enough, loved enough.

The bibliography of books on and by Rumi has exploded in recent years. In 1987, I first heard him mentioned in a workshop at the Boston Jung Institute on the subject of "Divine Love" given by John Ryan Haule, who wrote a book by the same title. The modern mystic Andrew Harvey claims that Rumi is the best-selling poet in this country right now because his "Springtime" has come. He is, as Harvey says,

> . . . an essential guide to the new mystical Renaissance that is struggling to be born against terrible odds in the rubble of our dying civilization. Rumi is a stern, gentle awakener and doctor of souls trying to help us recover the vision of the enlightened heart before it is too late and we destroy ourselves and our planet. [3]

All major religions have esoteric branches that say the same thing: we all have access to divinity because we are all aspects of God. The fact that this belief

---

2. Andrew Harvey, *The Way of Passion; A Celebration of Rumi*. (New York: Tarcher/Putnam, 1994), p. 291.
3. Harvey. *The Way of Passion*, p. xx.

appears in them all, to me, increases the odds that it contains truth. The fact that many esoteric religions were secret cults also shows what a threat that truth is, for how can hierarchies of power rule over us if we all have access to truth and divinity within ourselves?

Like Christianity's Gnosticism, Buddhist philosophy, the greatest Hindu texts, and the teachings of the Jewish Cabala, Rumi's Sufism, the mystical branch of Islam, transcends the intellect and all dogmatic prescriptions and hierarchical intercessors and brings us into direct knowledge of "The Tao," "God," or "Divine Love." He eschews the structures and strictures of traditional religions. This stance is, of course, revolutionary and puts him in good company with the alchemists and other secret societies, especially those of the Middle Ages and the Renaissance—the Cathars, the Knights Templar, and the Rosicrucians. And let us not forget that the men who signed the Declaration of Independence belonged to a secret society called the Freemasons, a later derivative of the Rosicrucians. Have you never wondered about that single eye above the pyramid on the dollar bill? The true teachings of Jesus as shown in the Gnostic gospels are much the same as Rumi's lessons, and we shouldn't forget that Christ was a political threat, not only to the Romans, but to the high priests of Juda.

Rumi says "Why use bitter soup for healing/when sweet water is everywhere?"[4] We have created bitter soup by thinking that the machinations of the world are beyond our control. We can make sweet water in our own lives by faith alone, by accepting our "bitter water" in peace and then imagining sweeter outcomes. By visualizing and asserting them as already manifested, these outcomes can come into being. *Poppycock!* the minions cry. Nonetheless, we must undo our neural pathways and create new ones by sticking with a risky faith and giving all our heart to it in order to see it is true; it will only become true as we recreate our beliefs. Much of the "New Age" is actually just a return to this older age, examining what has been hidden, going back to a pre-Christian era—as far back as the Orphic cults of the Greeks and the sacred knowledge of the Egyptians. This knowledge is dangerous to those in power, and we must realize that the world is not ready to give it credence. But living in fear only creates fearful outcomes. The time has come for this to change on a massive scale. People meditating and visualizing in great numbers do indeed have the power to move mountains.

---

4. Rumi, Moyne & Barks, trans. *Unseen Rain; Quatrains of Rumi.* (Boston: Shambhala Books, 1986), p. 57.

Whereas some of the mysterious writings of those who believe that we have direct access to our divinity are convoluted and difficult (to say the least), Rumi speaks quite simply and elegantly: "This is how I would die/ into the love I have for you://as pieces of cloud/dissolve in sunlight."[5] We must be willing to go out on a limb:

> From the wet source someone
> cuts a reed to make a flute.
> The reed sips breath like wine,
> sips more, practicing. Now drunk,
> it starts the high clear notes.[6]

The reed must fill itself with music. We cannot annihilate the ego instantaneously to believe in the Self. The reed must be cut from its usual environment or mindset, to inhabit new breath. Rumi often uses the metaphor of wine or drinking as a way of disorienting the ego from its normalcy and its tendency to "wrong-think." Once drunk, once freed from the regulations of fear and "shoulds," it has an opportunity to reach a new level.

According to Harvey, Rumi's assessment of the state of being human can be broken down into three stages. The first is early childhood, when we are our most pure and luminous selves, until we undergo an inevitable primary wounding experience. We all have one at some point, even if it just inheriting the teachings and fears of our parents. This wounding, what psychology often refers to as the "narcissistic wound," causes us to erect "the false self" of stage two. Psychologist Alice Miller's best-selling book *The Drama of the Gifted Child* supports this idea.

This false self is erected to survive in a world of "shoulds" and "should nots." Most people spend the rest of their lives in stage two, defending the values of the false self's beliefs and building up security for the ego. Harvey thinks we are living in a stage-two world, but that there are more and more people who have come face to face, through crisis, with that false self. They have to live through the horror of a loss of identity before finding themselves at stage three. The increasing incidents of crisis and fear mongering are pushing more of these stage-two lives into growth. Harvey says:

> If you are lucky, that breakdown will happen early because the pain
> of childhood or the painful contrast between your inner self and the

---

5. Rumi, Barks Coleman, trans. *Birdsong: Rumi, Fifty-three Short Poems.* (Athens, GA: Maypop Publishers 1993), p. 30.
6. Rumi, *Unseen Rain,*, p. 35.

outer world will become so great that you'll be haunted by fears of suicide or driven really to look at all the facts of your life.[7]

SATURN'S RETURN

Astrologically speaking, our Saturn return at age twenty-eight or twenty-nine often triggers a natural reassessment of what we are doing in our lives. Whether you "believe" in astrology or not, think about where you were at this age. For me, this was when I discovered the true cause of my father's death and when my marriage collapsed. At this age, I also ventured forth for the first time publicly as a "poet" by attending the Bread Loaf Writers' Conference in Vermont. Many people will say this was a time for them to take stock of their direction, a time when new decisions were made. But surrounded by a belief in "scarcity," as well as other false prescriptions and stage-two standards, the majority of people readjust only as much as is necessary to keep the approval of a stage-two world. Harvey goes on:

> It is best . . . to squeeze it (the breakdown) into the last days of
> your twenties and make it prolonged. So prolonged, in fact that you
> will have to begin the search for another reality, seriously and pas-
> sionately.[8]

If you are lucky enough to crash down into an entire questioning of the way you live, either as a young adult, or later during a mid-life crisis (what is called the Uranus opposition at age thirty-eight to forty-two), you may find yourself drifting into stage three.

The end of stage two and the beginning of stage three are often marked by visions, synchronicities, dreams or dream series, numinosity aglow in the midst of the humdrum daily life. This is certainly how I was moved into my own quest. Sometimes, an extraordinary meeting with a mentor will initiate the seeker. The combination of my breakup with C and my discovery of RB's alchemical dream workshop turned my life around. Yet, even when my "spirits" arrived, I was still trying to sustain a stage-two ego.

In Rumi's case, his initiation occurred on his first meeting with Shams and his conversion was immediate. Prior to this, he was a respected professor of traditional Islam, stepping easily into a comfortable life, a role his father

---

7. Harvey, *The Way of Passion*, p. 13.
8. Harvey, *The Way of Passion*, p. 13.

vacated for him. His love for Shams was not carnal, but the neediness most of us experience in coupling was there:

> After being with me one whole night
> you ask how I live when you're not here.
> Badly, frantically, like a fish trying to breath
> dry sand. You weep and say,
> *But you choose that.*[9]

How many of us choose sorrow and depression when it may be just as easy to visualize the most positive outcome. By choosing something other than the expected grief and longing and the demands for security that the ego presents, we chain ourselves to a false sense of wholeness with another. Relationship wholeness is not two halves coming together, but two wholes in synch. When you realize this profundity at the root level, a shift can occur.

Extrapolating from Rumi's writing, Harvey explains:

> This is a moment of terror, shock and ecstasy when you know, because another human being is incarnating it in front of you, that everything you have understood about the world, about identity, about the nature of reality is a stupid fiction of your false self. [10]

This happened to me personally at several different junctures. But each time, I didn't trust it enough and tried to readjust to what I thought of as "the real world." Finally, at thirty-seven, when my relationship with C terminated, I hit bottom. I readjusted slightly for ten or more years and then picked an unforthcoming, ambivalent man and bottomed out another time, despite my new "senses."

Indeed, that so-called "real world" is not real at all. In my numinous dreams, in my experience years ago with visions and visitations, I was finally given the opportunity to see through the ethers to the beings who surrounded me. Yet I was still dragged, kicking and screaming, through stage three. Apparently, my soul had made a total commitment to awaken in this lifetime, which had nothing at all to do with my personality and conscious mind, or what I thought I wanted. I assume that is why, unconsciously, I never "allowed myself" to be comfortable in my struggle for financial survival. And even after my holotropic awakening, I still did not

---

9. Rumi, *Unseen Rain*, p. 25.
10. Harvey, *The Way of Passion*, p. 14.

know how to shift my depression. It took years of searching, scrutinizing, and listening to John, years of meditating, years of risk-taking, and a few more bad decisions and mistakes with much doubt along the way to learn to trust the natural beneficence of the universe. You don't have to be willing to die, but you have to transcend the fear of death. And I wasn't so much afraid of dying, as I was of suffering. I thought then that perhaps if I put down on paper in the form of a poem this kind of a journey—only from a soul's position in the afterlife, specifically an imaginative journey taken by my father—I could clarify some of the ideas in my own mind, as well as redeem him in my heart.

At the point when we realize the charade of the stage-two world, Harvey tells us, we can arrive at stage three, but this difficult, uneven crossing requires us to pass through a conflagration of the ego. As he puts it, "Transformation is a huge task, hugely beautiful and hugely difficult."[11] But as Christ said, "Seek, and you shall find." I was seeking, had been seeking for many years. Some are able to struggle through stage three to its close—which, again according to Harvey's interpretation, is a radiant realization—but only after trial by fire.

> The agonies of the false self are paltry, suburban melodramas; the agonies of the spirit are played out in the immense theater of the Divine and they mirror the struggle ... for the victory of Light in this dimension and in matter. . . . What happens in stage three is that the false self is burnt alive.[12]

To burn up the ego cannot be a pleasant experience. Most of us can't even abide an insult, and our egos rule our reactions almost instinctively. But when we suffer from a traumatic event in our lives that appears to come from outside of us, that is a sure sign that the ego needs to let go. From here on, it's an in-again/out-again relationship with that surrender. The more resistance you give, the more the crisis persists. I am reminded again of Jung's notion that what is not made conscious on the inside happens on the outside as fate. This notion also supports Rumi's idea of the world as a mirror.

John told us amazing stories about the initiation of Christ's apostles. They awakened at once on the Pentecost, found themselves seeing the radiant light, speaking in tongues, ebullient, living fully for a few minutes in

11. Harvey, *The Way of Passion*, p. 16.
12. Harvey, *The Way of Passion*, p. 14.

recognition of their own radiant spirits. But the awakening moment is not sustainable. It was the *memory* of that truth that sustained them through their hard tasks and their eventual martyrdom. He insists it was not easy. One does not stay in that enlightened moment forever. Even Christ had his troublesome times. He too had an ego that he had to hone, refine, and transcend. After all, he was a human being as well as a god. As we all are.

Jesus was a highly evolved soul who had trained himself both before the incarnation and while he was here. There are eighteen years of Christ's life that are unaccounted for in the gospels. He is twelve in the Temple, amazing the Rabbis with his questions and knowledge. Then his mission begins at the age of thirty with his baptism by his cousin John. There are occult documents that track him in India, where he was called *Issa*. He may have studied meditation and learned from the Buddhist tradition to go beyond fear and above desire. It is likely that he knew Plato's work and was familiar with Hellenistic culture and history.

John told us that, for healing to take place, faith is needed from both the healer and the one who is wounded. Healing is a *co-creation*. Some of Master Jesus' healings failed. We protested to John that none of these are in the New Testament. He laughed and said "and why would we write about the *failure* of miracles?" Their calling to convince the faithful was difficult enough as it was.

For a "miracle" to take place, we must be in the present moment, forgetting all past beliefs and future anxieties. It takes tremendous faith to live in the moment, yet that is what is demanded. For only in the moment can you change the habitual way you think, create new neuropeptides through an emotional leap into faith, and then make room for something new to manifest. Your old belief systems and habitual worries will pull you into your projected future and keep you from living in the moment. This is a constant battle and we must be vigilant, because the old belief is so subtle. Miracles occur in synchrony with natural laws. But stage three is not a full-time picnic either. Here's Harvey on the further delights of stage three:

> Stage three ends—and the mystical traditions agree on this—with the direct vision of the divine nature of Reality and divine nature of the Self . . . a direct vision of the Divine Light, . . . as a state of grace and nature. . . . It is a white Light . . . manifesting everything. It is the Light of the Divine Mind.[13]

---

13. Harvey, *The Way of Passion*, p. 16.

Harvey insists that, once it has come up, that light cannot be permanently snuffed.

THE LIGHT OF FAITH

For years, I only saw the light that Harvey described in dark rooms with my eyes closed. But recently, it is there spontaneously in my peripheral vision. At first, I was alarmed enough to have my eyes tested for various eye diseases; I checked out fine. The light alone replenished my faith. I was finally moving out of doubt and into certainty, although my regular day world still dragged me back into depression. I was less lonely, but still alone, still struggling financially. The new man in my life was not fully present and did not boost my self-esteem. I allowed my emotional attachment to betray me once again. But all the while, I kept rereading Rumi's poems.

> My ego is stubborn, often drunk, impolite
> My Loving: Finely sensitive, impatient, confused.
> Please take messages from one to the other,
> reply and counter-reply.[14]

Harvey tells us that the only way to reach stage four is by blind faith, because you constantly fall back into the fears and expectations of the ego. You have no previous history of success and, basically, you don't believe in your miracle-making capacity. The pattern of the past, the attempt to be safe in the future, can, will, and *does* keep you in this dumbed-down mind and body that believe they are being attacked from the outside rather than attacking themselves. Every negative thought about yourself is a killer. Every negative thought about others is also a killer, because we are co-dependent, because we are one. *As you judge, so you will be judged.* And the hoarding and greed provoked by fear throw you back to stage two in a nano-second.

By practicing your own Last Judgment, you can reach Stage three—a state of acceptance for whatever comes your way, positive or negative. And only by being in that non-judgmental state can you manifest the reality you want. Rumi often uses the metaphor of drunkenness for the confusion of the self's changing circumstances, as well as for the ego's war to stay in con-

---

14. Rumi, *Unseen Rain*, p. 57.

trol of the heart, or Self. And there are times when, paradoxically, the ego knows it is challenged.

> Glass of wine in hand, I fall.
> get on my feet again, dizzy, deranged,
> then sink down demolished,
> not in this place any longer
> yet here, strong and sober, still standing.[15]

We must change how we feel. We must *imagine* that we feel better than we actually do. Our depressions damn us. Look at your dream life and all those annoying or threatening characters, and you will see how much you really judge.

For years, I have actively worked on my dream images to see what fears and projections are represented there. And still, the ego continues its hold. I've tried to react to each one of life's unfortunate glitches with conscious acceptance, while still feeling my ego in the midst of resistance. But I do believe that holding the thought "I accept this in peace" minimizes the trouble with the flat tire, the towed car, the missed plane, the problematic relationship. I thank the angels that I have not had to be tested by the house literally burning down. But I think, as devastating as each and every tragedy appears, there is a reason for it. By holding to the idea of each and every one of us living a divine plan, I hope I can pass that test. Only recently have I actually trained myself to feel better by simply faking it.

For this huge change into which we, as a global society, are now entered, there is nothing ahead but risk-taking and faith. Many of our systems (education, health care, finance, energy, government elections, manufacturing, food production) are caving in because it is time for new, simple, more compassionate systems, community living and off-grid patterns. Until we fully believe in our power to create reality and seek equity for everyone on the planet, we will not find solutions. By stage four, Harvey says

> You know that the false self is constantly tempting you to dance into new shapes . . . You can be trapped and caught and humiliated again and again by shadows and desires, but the game is so obvious, the illusions so transparent, that you start laughing even as you fall.[16]

---

15. Rumi, *Unseen Rain*, p. 15.
16. Harvey, *The Way of Passion*, p. 9.

And what becomes apparent is the sense of humor the universe has—its ironic synchronicities, the little messages you are handed that you still refuse! The ladybug on your steering wheel, the entrained birds taking off overhead, are the signs you may have asked for to affirm your will. Six hundred years before Freud, Rumi uses the house as a symbol for the personal ego.

> Desperation, let me always know
> How to welcome you
> And put in your hands the torch
> To burn down the house.[17]

The enlightenment Rumi speaks of here is more available to us because we are in the endtimes *now*. In the past, we had great teachers, but they were lamp posts on the way. Harvey says that Rumi is one of these lights in the dark. To transcend the dualities to which we have become accustomed, and to reach the new state of being human as well as spiritual, the ego must be willing to undergo an annihilation. That's why it's so hard. We cling to our limited identities and hold onto our junk-strewn world like children with their teddy bears. When we let it all go,

> the miracle happens—the power to cognize non-duality directly,
> humorously, normally, arises in the divinized mind. . . . The miracle
> is that we are, each of us, the source of the whole universe . . .[18]

I also found substantiation for Rumi's philosophy in Grof's book, *The Cosmic Game*, which speaks of the tacit contracts we seem to make when we agree to incarnate on Earth. We don't see that we are here playing roles together, participating in a collective consciousness that can and will evolve. The reason for our blindness, as Grof says, is that we make the game so perfect. Only by agreeing to play with such full-functioning rules can we challenge ourselves to find the way back to Eden. Grof believes the task is no less than to accept and love the whole catastrophe of what we've created universally, for that is the only way we can undo it and create something different where each of us in a body will be fully realized. This means "Let it be." Tolerance, forgiveness, blessings for the horror . . . then move on. As Shakespeare and many other brilliant minds have intuited, the world is indeed all a stage. When we cross over to Hamlet's

---

17. Harvey, *The Way of Passion*, p. 9.
18. Harvey, *The Way of Passion*, p. 138.

"undiscovered country," we realize that we have merely forgotten our true state as a piece of the godhead venturing out to experience itself under new circumstances.

Grof's book has the same underlying theme as Rumi's teachings, or Christ's teachings, or those of the Buddha. We are all one. We are all God. We are playing at having fallen, having separated, having circumscribed our powers. Someone said: "We are not humans having a spiritual experience. We are spiritual beings having a human experience." The ultimate test is to love our downtrodden, ugly, cranky neighbors, our rude customers, our angry drivers, not just our families and friends. But must we accept violent dictators, marauding crowds, rivals, tyrants, thieves and murderers, liars and thieves? Suicide bombers? The Taliban? What is underscored over and over is that, while we don't need to tolerate their behavior, while we can accept that we must deal with them in such a way as to protect others, we must also have compassion for their ignorance and fear, because it is the same as our own.

Reflect what you want reflected back. *Do unto others.* Only by changing your own fear into love can this occur. Only if you know beyond a doubt that death is not the end can you transcend this fear, this greed, this clinging to material things. The great mythographer, the late Joseph Campbell, said the most important teaching of Christianity is to love your neighbor. Most of us find this pill a little hard to swallow sometimes. But John's message is also quite clear. He emphasizes that we do not have to die willingly to become realized beings. The Second Coming is not the arrival that fundamentalist and traditional religions are awaiting. Christ Consciousness is available to everyone now. It is a resurrection in the heart, not on the cross. And the transition has been made easier in this era. For the first time in many millennia, we do not have to die first before we can move to a higher dimension, if we just ask the spiritual world for help.

Once upon a time, I was too educated, too "intellectual," too "rational" to ask or to believe. Not once, but several times, I was brought to my knees and my childhood faith helped me learn to believe differently. Now I am fortunate enough to see with my eyes that the help is indeed here. Feeling worthy of it is the final crossing. Perhaps Rumi has been resurrected after eight centuries to say it for us plainly, with absolute certainty:

Nail me down in a box of cold words, that box is your coffin.
I do not know who I am.
I am in astounding, lucid confusion.
I am not a Christian, I am not a Jew, I am not a Zoroastrian,
And I am not even a Muslim.
I do not belong to the land, or to any known or unknown sea . . .
My birthplace is placelessness,
My sign to have and give no sign . . .
I am the life of life.
I am that cat, this stone, no one . . .
I see and know all times and worlds,
As one, one, always one.
So what do I have to do to get you to admit who is speaking
Admit it and change everything!
This is your own voice echoing off the walls of God.[19]

I began to embody these themes in poetry, the firewalk that would burn up my previous beliefs in the limitations of the rational world and open my personal entryway into forgiveness, self-forgiveness, and release. Many a morning, I have awakened, buoyed somewhere between a dream state and another reality, to recall this poem:

You must ask for what you really want.
Don't go back to sleep.
People are going back and forth across the doorsill
where the two worlds touch.
The door is round and open.
Don't go back to sleep.[20]

19. Harvey, *The Way of Passion*, p. 139.
20. Moyne, John and Coleman Barks, *Open Secret; Versions of Rumi*, p. 7.

Chapter 11

INTER/ECTING WORLD/

If you see a wall and it is protecting you from unending darkness,
you will not want to go there. But if you see a wall that is blocking the light,
you will want to go there in order to remove the wall.
MICHAEL SINGER, *THE UNTETHERED SOUL*

In early January 1996, my plane landed in Seattle after several cancellations and delays due to unusual storms. We drove two hours to Port Townsend through raging wind that jostled the compact car from lane to lane, passing downed trees and areas sodden with flooding. Flashing a weary smile, a young woman handed me some papers, a check for the month's food. Rather than say good night, we both laughed and said, "Good morning!" She'd waited patiently half the night to deliver me from Seattle to the grounds of the Centrum Foundation for a month-long writing residency.

The sun came up the next day at five A.M., the sky, a fingerpainting of mauve and tangerine. From a lone cabin atop a hill, my expansive vista included wind-torn grasses and the churning Pacific below. A few other buildings slept in the distance. From my cabin window, I could see the edges of town beyond the fanned curl of beach. I flicked on the heater in the knotty-pine wall and hastily unpacked. Disregarding the hour, I set up my computer, determined to dive into writing after some decent sleep, despite the howling winds outside.

I hadn't been asleep long when I heard a crash. I crept out of bed and tiptoed into the living room to find that strong gusts had shaken the frail walls sufficiently so that the curtain rods had blown off the four small windows in the front of the cabin. Three thousand miles from home, half-asleep, I barely noted my half-dreamed, unbidden thought: "Well, I guess Daddy's here." I went back to bed and slept until mid afternoon.

I had come across country to the state where I was born with the intention of writing poetry about my father—a subject I had avoided since my teens. Determined to make peace with his ghost, I spent the first few days, almost unconsciously, submerging myself in my interior world, sustaining a waking dream in which my psyche was replenished. I was solitary, not lonely, experiencing one of my most nourishing phases.

My claire-sentience to subtle changes in my environment, my extra-sensory intuition through which I can *feel* shifts in energy, had continued to develop, and I noticed almost immediately how much it intensified on my arrival on the West Coast. Once inside the cabin, I believed there were multiple intelligences around me—spirits of living organisms, others who'd occupied this space, perhaps the ancestors of the land, insects in the walls, my father himself—or maybe it was only my belief in these correspondences that eased my writing while I was there. I wanted to prove the validity of these new-found senses, like Darwin playing piano notes for the earthworms to test their sensitivity to sound.

Yet I had only the phenomenon of my humming ears, my breathing skin. And there was also something more primordial occurring beyond my usual creative process. Perhaps the spaciousness of the West was more conducive to stirring these nascent senses. Somehow, silence, sudden communions with nature that took place on my daily walks in synch with the unraveling of poems, all provided a private covenant with *otherness* that transcended my own subjectivity. My heightened sensitivity to the biosphere will forever be intertwined with the green grounds of the Centrum Foundation.

Every morning, gazing out my window over oatmeal, I watched five or six deer as still as statues on the chartreuse lawns. I never saw them move, but when I looked back minutes later, they were gone. Evidently, they knew when the world around them slept and, like dreamy apparitions, they disappeared into the dawn. Beyond that bluff, distant waters slowly cinched in the January breakers, lapping the shore and leaving a wide path of tangled seaweed. If I left the cabin on time, I could walk all the way to town along the scrubby beach.

Every few days, I followed the tide into the quaint but upscale town and returned on the bus laden with bags of veggies and grains. Sitting on a bench with my parka open, my scarf loose, warmed by the waterfront sun that was often radiant despite what I'd heard about Washington winters, I sliced a kiwi over rice cakes, nibbled on goat cheese and almonds, red peppers and pita bread. So pleased just to *be*, I realized how often during my routine at home I ran to survive my schedule, meting out my weekends as if two days of rest could even begin to penetrate my shutdown senses or alleviate layers of city stress. But here, a sensory reciprocity enveloped my solitude.

I thought sorrowfully of the town in the high desert beyond the mountains where I'd spent the first six years of my life—Richland, Washington—that had since become dangerously polluted from the burial of radioactive waste. The physicists at Richland had played a role in building the atom bomb and there was something incongruent now about my reverberations with the natural landscape and my knowledge of the contaminated land where I was born. Like many, I have adapted to cement beneath my shoes and, in imperceptible increments, have lost actual contact with the land itself—the potent Earth thrumming beneath the soles of our feet. Like the natives of many primitive cultures, I believe the land holds the energy field of all the creatures who have ever inhabited it.

On the quiet paths around Fort Worden, the abandoned World War II fort where the Centrum Foundation is located, I stilled myself to become like the deer, focusing with all my senses opened, grounding this new energy. I tried to tune in to the faint buzzing in my body that was becoming so familiar—currents that passed along my own acupuncture meridians. For the first time, I could relate physically to the interdependence between humanity and the living organisms of soil and rock. Although I'm not sure I understand what I experienced, I know that, in that place and time, I accessed new senses.

I recalled my own trauma around my father's sudden death. And I thought a lot about my father's life, how he came out here to Washington as a young doctor before the climax of the war, uninformed about the secret project to which he was assigned. How he and my mother, in their mid twenties, made lifelong friendships with the physicists and physicians who lived in government housing in a makeshift village in the desert. How, when he revealed his suspicion about his work, he was told never to mention it. How my East Coast parents, still young and adventurous and in no hurry to leave their new friends, extended their stay in Washington for ten years, skiing at Sun Valley and summering in Priest Lake, Idaho. My brother and sister and I were all born there.

I remembered coyotes howling at night, and how Kayo, our collie, learned to mimic them. I recalled witchy tumbleweeds that frightened me, and cowboys who yodeled from my parents' monophonic console. How I held the album covers in my lap and delighted my father by memorizing the words. I remembered yellow snapdragons and the variety of my father's rose bushes. How the corals were my favorite; how careful I was not to touch the thorns, picking bouquets and prancing around the lawn in my lavender sunsuit while my mother hung the wash. I swore there were fairies among the evening fireflies and, when my family still teases me about the "imaginary" friends of my early childhood, I am forced to think twice about the ambiguity of my experiences. Home movies helped imprint these images, and I felt, during this retreat, as if I reawakened to that magical child. In 1954, my family came east to New York, where my father's Italian clan were rooted.

In the blustery turbulence on the plane from Boston to Washington, I had called on God to steady the wings and addressed my deceased father personally, pledging to set us both free. I visualized him through a number of casual, but unforgotten, images: Daddy laughing on the phone; Daddy on the den couch watching live television with me the morning Lee Harvey Oswald was shot; Daddy crooning Sinatra on our many family road trips; Daddy leading a family march to the soundtrack of *The Music Man*. I reveled in these happier times, then entertained darker images I felt I must penetrate as well. It no longer mattered to me how well I could describe the subject that intimidated me. I knew I must try, despite any fears that might arise.

During meditation, I imaginatively drew a figure-eight of light around my father's head and slowly enlarged it, cranking it brighter, spinning it around the image. I began using this technique years ago after studying healing with imagery and energy. The visualization often helped me discover trapped swells of incarcerated grief, as if the "pain-body" existed in the cells of my chest. Then I'd tear up, sigh, and breathe deeply.

In 1963, when Daddy died, we knew nothing of the need to mourn, so I followed my stoic mother's example. She just courageously went on. I now know that we heal by re-experiencing emotions through concrete images that shift the ingrained neuron paths or thought processes. Now I believed I could alter the images that had wounded me by re-imagining them in a forgiving context.

Outdoors, I immersed myself in Centrum's natural world, with long walks through the damp, gamey woods around the fort, drinking in the warm January light and sheltering in the splendid rows of poplars and pines. One misty afternoon as I wandered the thicket of paths, fog skirting my feet and grace hovering in the atmosphere, I stumbled on "Memory's Vault," the sanctum of poet/publisher Sam Hammill, whose press was in another building on the grounds. I was astonished by the site, a meditation in itself.

Two imperious stone thrones preside over a modern Stonehenge set within a Zen garden on a bedding of green and tawny rocks. Five monolithic slabs are engraved with beautiful human longing: Sam's five poems of sea and rain, animals and air. I felt his call to the sacred, suddenly grateful for the central tragedy of my life—my father's passing. I realized it had gifted me with a treasury of conscious wealth and made me a poet.

Light drifted across clusters of fresh holly, wild pachysandra, and patches of lime; mosses draped in the crannies of bald branches, clinging to bark in the storm-downed birch. The woods, beaten by winds, seemed to savor its own survival. Worn paths obscured the tangled foliage, but I was beckoned in by huge ferns, gloss on wet leaves, scurrying ants. Once I stopped dead on a path where a cylindrical crystal shone in the sunlight. I drew closer and saw a spider web beaded with dewdrops, a numinous glow rimming it inside and out, like a Grail cup I could drink from.

Later, I found steps up to the fort. I peered into ghostly dungeons, rooms where old admirals made plans. Descending stairwells that led to a bluff, I walked till lost in the scent of mud, the climate nesting its breath in my hair. I knew I couldn't wander forever, as the sea would eventually appear on one side or another, so I felt an exhilarating freedom in being lost. These woods were sanctified, emptying my day-world mind, offering kinship with nature's communal mind, that realm where the unconscious rejoins its organic source, before being alienated by civilization.

MORPHIC RESONANCE

When the Sun lowered itself and the clouds were tinted violet, I headed back to the cabin to meditate. Once stilled, I became immediately aware that the *chi* around my body had thickened. I underwent a fresh sensation, as if blanketed with stretchy, netted energy. I could extend my hand in front of me and push the field of air around my palm, almost like static from a balloon stuck to my hand.

Was this my projection of the moving energy field around me, one based on quantum physics, that hypothesized connection between science and faith? Was this what made me aware of invisible dimensions? Could my unconscious mind have given me "the butterfly theory," its understructure showing the interdependencies of intersecting worlds? Or was my experience influenced by British physicist Rupert Sheldrake's idea of "morphic resonance," in which the present overlays the past?

Einstein helped us understand that time is a construct; everything is happening all at once. String theory posits that we may live on a membrane surrounded by parallel universes vibrating at different frequencies in other dimensions. These strings pulsate in patterns like those of a violin, and there appear to be worm holes that provide access between dimensions. Some theorize that the Big Bang stretched the fabric of space and that layers of reality piled up in "super symmetry." *What the @,$?&# do we know?*. I can't help but think that there were relationships between my intentions and the fields of tactile power around me, simultaneously intimate and impersonal.

My uncanny sensations continued daily. I imagined that my father was among a team of energies helping me process my dormant grief into poetry. I was closer to my father's spirit here in the West, where he had grown into his own artistry—his surgery. And he wrote poetry as I do. I wondered if the charged density in my *chi* had anything to do with my long-overdue receptivity to my repressed memories. I also suspected that the recent rainstorms had charged the air with more negative ions, which heightened my sensations.

When I recall this pilgrimage, I see rows of aspen lining paths against the blues of Puget Sound. Ferry boats trudging toward the sprinkling of islands in the distance, triangular wakes like veils trailing behind. Even under overcast skies, a kind of cleansing. And when the clouds did clear, the days were warm, the Sun magnificent. Tucked in the northwest corner of the country, standing on land closer to my birthplace than I'd been in years, mutually rooted with my young father, I felt, through my perception of an associative empathy, a palpable connection to the most basic nurturing sources.

Before I left my cabin, I improvised a ceremony to release images that had haunted me and, possibly, my father as well. I lit candles, burnt sage, and invited him in while I read my poems aloud. The homemade ritual helped ground my intentions. Though distant now from traditional religion, I had always had an *a priori* knowledge of eternal existence.

When I left the Foundation, on the flight back to Boston, I thought about my father's transition. Since his death was induced by an overdose, I suspected the crossing into afterlife was rough. I wondered if my own pain had tied him down. I had read about near-death experiences—how unresolved grieving can tether a soul to its last earthly identity. I believe William Blake's "doors of perception" open the more we unconsciously inhabit the *belief* that they do. Our environment can speak to us. By developing intuition in stillness, we allow our bodies to relay information.

The search for the lost father is archetypal. Many of us, marked forever, spend our entire lives searching. Perhaps there is no difference between what we do and what we imagine we do with the presence of that absence.

The following year, I was awarded a poetry fellowship from the National Endowment for the Arts for ten of the poems in the sequence I wrote while in Washington. I trust that my father and my mysterious senses came through for me in the seamless boundary between dimensions, between past and present.

Chapter 12

THE WORLD'*S* VEIL

A POEM SEQUENCE ABOUT MY FATHER'S DEATH
AND IMAGINED AFTERLIFE

. . . and I will give a white stone, and on the stone is written a new name
that no one knows except the one who receives it.
REVELATIONS 2:17

i. The Sorrow of the Body

Always at the edge of morning, where the curves
of the moon had blended, he expected clarity,
an exact latitude where color smudged the sky.
From where had the thought of paradise

descended? Behind the water tower, the dirt cliffs
hung over the polluted bay. Their depressions
matched his own and he was drawn to drive
beneath them while the city's beaten horizon

suggested this human tie to time was wrong.
Why did his dreams persuade him of huge, bottomless
stairways inverting the proper proportions
of space and rain? And what did it mean

when he woke in a trough of sighing, unaware
of any image for his ache? What held him aloft
were ineffable reaches across the geographies,
to imagine them within grasp, as if they were facts,

as if he could lance the body's gravity,
withstand its tug when the colors
of the quarry rocks embraced each other,
when the sky at evening drained its pink

and green and gold into the small
receptacle of a planet whose belief
in its own isolation sets a world to yearning—
Sweet yearning

for the beauty of touching with the heart
what the mind did not
in creating the sorrow
of the body.

ii. *Being*

He thought he could cut the cord to his regrets
by curing the world of its wounded.

He didn't know what he railed against
was its unfit heart. The lie it had sworn by—
this wormy marriage of life to death. He wanted

to dissect the body's burden, explore its incarcerated
god, *Spirit* draped in the body's grace. To wrap sun
beneath skin like a beacon and pivot each muscle,

distilling a glow deep in the veins. He thanked the body
for its blood, delicate cartilage like squid, wedged
nodes of marrow, appendages . . .

Dispensing medicine to carry the body's cargo
would not delay aging, but like anyone,
he wanted to prolong the music of youth.

Playing the staff of his wife's neck
as she sat in the freshly cut grass
lifting an infant to her shoulder,

he'd have willingly taken the toddler's steps
over and over from beach to ocean, believing
the waves' illusion of movement on damp sand,

not knowing earth's borders from water's,
not knowing his own, knowing nothing at all—

being.

iii. What Held Him Aloft

for so long was how whole he somehow
knew he was. Not how his mind saw it,
the fractured past tethered in place.
He was amazed that he had made, after all,

children. Amazed at the body's responses
to love. How he honored the systems, the networks
of veins, the vapors and tremors of passion—

To lift the scalpel, to stitch the torn sinew of people
with families and names, to deliver them back, this
was a reason, *an answer*—enough to keep him in balance,

enough to replenish his well of faith. He'd look at his
own hands in wonder, envision the satiny heat
of healing, his own Hippocratic certificate,

an entitlement worth a life.

iv. To Rule the World

Under his dominion then,
an intravenous needle would deepen
the light in the crevice
between membrane and mucous.
One touch of his speculum and Spirit would open
inside, where he could probe a vibration
into song. He knew this was all anyone wanted—

to make music from misery, to hold the note
of compassion for invasions of pain.
What the world did to the body was shameful
but he understood through connective tissue,
the vascular system's muted blues
so close to the skin,
the intricate hints at the body's veil—

Yet he misunderstood the mind's power, its
paranoia, didn't know why—
when he lowered his intuition
down the crack of the mind,
he was confused by the distance back.
To live inside loss was to believe
you were nothing

more than human, to rule the world out
of your life, until you were nothing
but cavity, matter, lacking Spirit's
eternal ember, which is light, *life*,
the soul in the body's world.

v. *Lost in the Call*

The yacht club docks shimmered whiter
     against those glazed summer nights,
wives in spaghetti straps with champagne glasses
     fluted to match their shapely heels,
fumes of dusky *Taboo* and
          Chanel in the air.

While Como and Crosby crooned
     their hi-fi foxtrot and money chimed
through the lair of paper lanterns,
     the effervescent surgeon carried
a habit in his pocket.

Though for a time he could sing, samba,
     even fandango with the sucking monkey
on his back, the pills added up, multiplying
     the swarm of moons pulling him under
the malted bay.

And there in his head both sibyls and sirens
     warned and lured. *What path to travel?*
Who could he call?
     Where was the cure?

vi. Can the Soul Be Insulted?

He dreamt of a rosebud broken through the sidewalk
in front of his old Brooklyn home. Something doomed
he wanted to water, force-bloom to a hothouse aura,

one small miracle in Caesar's world. He dreamt of tumbling
a wad of cash from his wallet, a confusion of Wall Street
and the Aqueduct Race Track, Lord & Taylor, Sears or

Sacks—an endless list of modern comforts: tvs, convertibles,
cruises. If his soul was insulted, it must have turned
the other cheek, its resistance less than the rose-

beaked wren whose tail he chased nightly, tossing salt.
He dreamt he was starving at a banquet, trampled
by maestros in tuxes and wingtips, contessas'

furs and sequins, crawling past loud greedy
guards excessively fed—the flesh gone to famine
when the soul's left for dead.

vii. The Day of His Passing

He drove his two older children to the high school went home and
painted with dissatisfaction then followed his wife around the house as
she did her chores When she said she was going for groceries he pan-
icked begged to go with her without confessing his concerns Unaware
he was desperate she refused and he was abandoned *addicted* to the
secret of which she had had but myopic glimpses He went straight to
·the medicine cabinet wrote himself another prescription Maybe he
forgot how many pills were a limit forgot the toll morphine in Demerol
takes— but maybe he knew *yes somewhere he knew* And when his daughter called after school wanting a frock for the prom she'd been asked to
he only seemed slightly distracted offering charge cards

Then he left in his sports car for the pick-up where he ordered
apple pie at the drugstore coffee shop a drive from which he did not
come back since his body stopped when his lungs collapsed.

viii. Death's Dreams: In the Beginning

In the beginning
after the crash of the astral firmament,
after the end of his three-dimensional world,

above the fog of fragments and etheric arrivals,
the old geometries dissolved, recombined
into new alignment.

And ruin departed
dragging its bag of grief, his breath
quickening like intimacy redeeming the air.

And he sensed the ancient tinctures there
as if he were witness to the birth of extinct
plants. Apparitions appeared in the rivers

over which hung trees blossoming stars
whose light shone like evening windows
in his memory's home. Each awakening,

an invisible impulse, entered his body's
sleeve of chakras, those wells of magnetic
photons snaking the temple empty

of bones—where filaments glowed
in a pillar of light, their source,
inexplicably known.

ix. Death's Dream: The Clearing

He was so far up in the mountains,
layers of blue haze, the tops of trees,
pine, fir, birch and beech—as if seen

from a plane. A thousand arms held up,
palms open, bent at the wrist and quiet snow
poised still in the air like dusk, a grainy otherness,

when someone said they were serving heron,
and he saw Heron! *Blue*, with the head on,
the eye still as it lay on its side, restless

like a fish (though he thought to himself—*bird*)
as if he'd been swollen with heron
and all reminiscences, nostalgias

released from the breast—as if he had *lived*
in the fish-eyed bird, knew what the body felt
paralysed on the platter. And he knew

he would partake in libations,
drink from the decanter—
If he bowed his head in clear intention,

this tie-dyed belt of light
would cinch in the clouds—
all heron on earth would wing to a clearing,

fish would leap in the frequencies
of waters, while the snows resumed
their white contritions.

x. After

the first beautiful blitz of death, rain
and a tenderness he forgave
in every breathing thing.
Hyacinths. Marshes. Garlic.

He could see that the world
continued in its ignorant mirage,
its traffic and horns—limousines
disguising death

as something wrong
instead of different, the world
with its games and time,
holidays and baths.

He circled the similar towns, somnambulant
spirit unable to speak or to alter any outcome,
in sympathy with martyrs, the uselessness
of war, the dwindling forests . . .

Only his various isolation pursued him:
a carcass in a butcher shop,
pink streetlights after hours,
a spatter of water rounding a corner, then gone.

The weather of death was not a place,
not even a planet—yet the world kept on
turning its raincoat collar, rubbing its
damp hands as if ruin were certain.

There was no death after his death,
just a frequency, unfamiliar—still
his voice would not go back; he could not
reappear to tell them he felt the old

Sunday desires, that he was unprepared
to cross—Nor could he tarry forever entangled
with matter in earth's circumscription
where ruin was futile, finality, nowhere.

xi. *Life Review*

Buoyant in the cusp of a cone, funneled by magnetic force,
it was as if he rode a raft above—something other than air,
(ether, he supposed) and when he was poised at the reach of a gyre,
and lowered onto a platform, he saw a small assembly

in robes of sculpted white-on-white brocade. Above, the glow
of receptive faces, one figure in stunning silence, gestured
toward a director's chair. The others too took places
as the room defined its borders with a screen.

He was unsure, how much time had elapsed, when
he had eaten last, if he was dreaming—was the hour
day or night? Then candelabra dimmed, chandeliers
recessed into the ceiling and a film began with his name in lights.

xii. Forty-Seven Years

As he watched his brief life leaf by
like a scrapbook's turning pages—he felt something
settle within the empty space that he'd displaced: *warmth*
from his immigrant parents, *love* from his brothers,

cousins, wife; he physically *felt* how he'd been their rising star,
the only one to sail through college—their pride
in his publications, his poetry and paintings. Then he saw
himself drafted west in the years of the second world war—

an army doctor attentive to burns, experiments
with the bomb. Now the affluence in the fifties—
Chief of Surgery, and at the sudden death of the father
he'd always longed to impress, he felt the growing yen

to return to New York. Jump cut to the fifty-three caddy,
all five of them singing *Young at Heart*, the speedometer close-up,
needle tapping 100 miles per hour. Expanse of desert
fading from focus, prairies and plains. Ohio. Pennsylvania—

the Holland Tunnel, at last—New York, new homes
on Long Island's northern shore, and just as he wondered
about his fall—the scenes of his migraines began.

xiii. Migraine

What brought on the spumy aura in the air,
   the almost euphoric spell which preceded
     primitive armies above his eyes, spearing the skin?

   Nauseous, fumbling for keys in a dark garage,
     he dropped his ebullient persona
      and ran for a bathroom stall.

     The film rewound, then chugged fast-forward in an assault,
      camera zooming through hallways
       distorting his children's faces, silence

      ovaling their mouths, his wife drawing the shades,
       the weight of a ten-ton towel over his eyebrows—Shots
       of shelves, montage of bottles spilling pills,

    samples to tranquilize and wide-angled labels smeared
     with promises to sedate. Slow-mo pan of his addictions,
      the monstrous man he'd impersonate—doors

  slamming, locking, when his wife flushed the contents of a vial.
   Something blackened the space that was his body
    when each of his children froze in still-life,

     blinking, turning away—his wife's strength,
      a swaying building in an earthquake—
       At last the screen dimmed into darkness,

    the cries ricocheted in his head,
     the whole family's feelings reverberated as *his*—
     in this low-lit room

      with strangers
       who sustained him,
        in silver rays of empathy and solace.

ixv. *Instantly through Thought*

His sorrow was heavier than his guilt
but each hung like a small dark
garment in a closet,
so this was hell.

However passive, however
Accidental—his soul knew,
even at the threshold of amnesia,
he'd accomplished his death

by his own hand.
And when he felt himself
occluded, a rancid star, pulled root,
too lucid in the aftermath,

the sound and shape of his thinking
warped and wafted like blown sand
until he forced his mind to create
a cage of safety,

one sacred cell, free
from self-hatred. *Yes,*
there were guides to aid him
but because he felt unworthy,

they took on the grotesque form
of lepers, roaches, rats—
Perhaps the question was
whose judgment he awaited

in this prison he'd custom-
designed, building his own
bars one at a time
instantly through thought.

xv. Self-fulfilling Prophet

It was not that he questioned his own
dead carcass but some nights he
found himself choking from thirst

in a bushy circular pit he remembered
from Dante. Here other homeless junkies
tore at their clothes in delirium tremens

or paced back and forth on leprous stumps—
Times like this he felt alive, horrifically alive.
Other nights he buzzed with slaphappy crews

of good 'ole boys, until their skin would boil
with sores he'd seen as an intern only in photos.
Then he'd leap to the street,

begging strangers for tongs and gauze,
flagging down drivers and cabs which never stopped.
Only vacuous eyes met his shouts, skittish

with ticks or comatose; he'd search
for shelter in boarded buildings
where demons crawled

barbed wire like thorns,
garbage and vermin lining the walls.
Then he'd slide down the stains of a door,

pull his knees to his throat like he did as a kid
of five or six—stripped of his
tear ducts, unable to cry,

the guilt of his shame
feeding his crime, his
unforgiving

fix.

xvi. *Faith Must Be a Fortress*

But when the diamond of his eye
revealed conscience as counterfeit,
he saw that he was *not* his thoughts.

Without the body's encumbrance,
he saw that the mind was flawed,
a deformed crystal, thinking itself

severed from others, torn from whatever
was God. By some imagined sin,
it thought of itself as *separate,*

same mind he had always clung to,
always known. And if he believed
that he was lost, indeed he was—

and streets grew Kafkaesque
with hedges, shadows, sinister
thugs. But where was a roadside

phone booth, hospital, tow-truck?
His dread seduced him through a vortex
producing what he feared. Yet when he

dared reverse his thoughts, *Paradise*
was a bridge across the maw of his inferno,
and *Faith*—an acropolis of roses and blue

ions sent him warm, communing rays.
Confused, his disembodied mind doubted
again while vegetation withered

to streets wet with filth; hooded youths
skulking the gutters of a dicey
neighborhood. And he recognized

for the first time that he was *damned*—
Not by the mafia he thought was God
but by his own brutal judgment.

xvii. *Third-eye View*

Alone, he closed his non-corporeal eyes
in the night wind and saw the face of a sphinx.
Nothing more. Not a landing to stand on.
Not an entrance to choose, nor a door to imagine
behind. The eye of the sphinx
in the mind he saw through. Was it truly *other*,
or merely another sporadic reflexive
of his own sorry mystery?

Face of a sphinx. Pyramid eye of a dollar bill,
luminous through the darkness, wavery
as wind, giving history a lifetime survived
by the stare of Horus, what sands leave
in a twine for aeons to find . . .

He felt the eyes behind his mind
meld and dally on the runway of his brow.
At least there was somewhere to reach for,
something to soar with, leveling view,
both telescopic and holographic

above this unfocused abyss—this
capacious eye, a transparent mirror
somehow—unblinking, but wet—
maybe a hint, maybe
something to lift
the veil.

xviii. *The Wedding of Self to Selves*

An open arena played on the monitor of his brain—
glossy and beveled chinks of sun, aeolian
instruments in the backdrop. Despite his penchant

for dark, he conceptualized different wishes
within the montage. And through this new eye
he perused the operas in ripples like waves from a coin

tossed into a well. Left defenseless by beautiful music,
he admitted the voices of patrons who merged
as lost parts of himself. The more he accepted, the more

he ascended from his cot where he saw his ensoulment
pooling above the bedding of self-contempt. Voices
explained they comprised his dimensional unit,

the higher octave of each earthly history, his future, his past.
If in his recent life, he negated his worth, here beyond death
he'd return to the essence he'd always been.

Through the crack beneath his door, crepuscular streaks
leaked like a shoreline where breakers plumed
over sand. He rejoiced in the scene of his childhood beach,

Coney Island, and over the boardwalk,
he painted the weather his favorite palette
while his voices disclosed that he had full control:

No one but you creates your view. Though hidden
and buried, *Spirit* was carried, released
in a marriage of self to selves.

ixx. *To Forget You Forgot*

Grapes fermenting in heat. Grace
transfiguring each little scarab. Fixation of light
into matter. How sensibly he could imagine
Spirit's evolution now. From the oversoul's mountains,

clouds skimmed the capstone, unveiling mansions
of his Father's house. The Cabalist's challenge: descent
and compression. *Embodied* in this vehicle
he'd studied in med school—The gnosis of healing:

to *remember and return.* He understood at last
the mind's concretion of body, how utterly
man made his world from his Word. *Beliefs*—
fears, or curses, anything held

and pondered with passion, eventually hardened
into form. His intuitive spark had always examined
the body for its enigma, something perpetual,
yet abstract—but how did you locate *that?*

Cut through the heart or the grill of the brain?
To swim the film of the flesh was to journey away
from repose, caught in the warring opposites, contusions,
lymphomas, gall bladder stones—to *fall*

from transcendence, then land in that alien craft,
that closed, paradoxical shell, misplacing
your source like an Alzheimer address—
To forget you forgot— To create out of fear.

Husking the pod of the mind's illusions
this was the worthy surgeon's task. And he carved
his first window in a wall of his bunker, built
from a thought just beyond it—a vineyard of lapis

and tourmaline grapes, each silvered vine,
a nirvana of light—same light he'd sought
when he'd carved and cut

those essentially bestial bodies.

xx. What If Man Made the World as It Is?

Blessed with the impossible thought of green stars,
he stood by his bed and tested his power, laughing
as instantaneous stars burnt and fell like emeralds

through his roof. Was this the unfinished evolution,
the Creator's one intervention: *Remember the God
in each of you?* What if dark thoughts

walled the cities, corrupted children, enscripted armies,
shot neighbors and strangers, cried *victim,*
pointing a finger, pinning the world on God?

At once he saw through the lie of the third dimension,
saw its reality was *off.* Sculpting his stars into one,
he willed it *red,* reshaped it, cutting a square

at the top, boxing its ears to an orb,
throwing the whole thing out the window
as a radiant exclamation!

What if fear made the human world as it was?
Wouldn't it follow that only fearless
love could change it?

xxi. *White Stone*

In one instant with his will, he created
a hill to hike, because The Ones-With-No-Names
explained the light body needs exercise

and he wanted to stretch, to make a sky
of his blue-hued sparkle, climb a pile
of earth-toned rock which reminded him

of the west he had loved and been part of.
Those long drives into nothing but faded cactus
and craggy hills that hung and tumbled

over the low dust-span of road. Out of habit,
he searched for rattlers, pulling his boot up
and then he spied it—a glowing stone,

white as the light which shone through each being
made of matter, white and oval and speaking
a language he might have invented—

He closed his translucent fingers
and heard the rush of his name
like the whisper in which flowers grow.

Bowing his head in self-forgiveness
for his plight which had lifted and flown,
he toasted a canteen to *The Powers that Be*—

And in that fully lit moment, he knew his
true Second Coming, the grace
which would weave its gloss in time

around every soul.
Each unique
with its white stone.

Chapter 13

∫PIRIT RULE∫

The light of the body is the eye: If therefore thine eye be single,
thy whole body shall be full of light.
MATTHEW 6:22

As I was leaving David's Cambridge consultation room after one of my bi-annual visits, I went to give him my customary hug and he jumped back, saying, "No, not today. Your energies are so intense, they've given me a horrible headache." Then he flung his hand to his head and practically pushed me out the door. "It's as if they lay right on the skin," he added.

I knew what he meant. Hadn't these energies given me flu symptoms? I had to laugh. It was a most apt description of how I felt their presence. I was used to them, but David, who got information about them from his own guides, did not have the same physical experience. My spirit friends were making him ill! Somewhat bewildered but amused, I smiled and waved from down the hall, commenting to myself, "I guess my spirits are in a league of their own."

It was in that session that David told me that some of what I was seeing was *symbolic*. This was helpful, because it gave context to the mythological figures.

"But what about the Indians?" I asked. Whereas the mythic characters were cartoonish, the Indians appeared more like photographs. The information he was given about my visions characterized them as views into what we might think of as "past lives." But he explained to me again that, since time is not real, but a construct, and since everything is happening at once, there is no past and these aspects of my soul—my *soul extensions*—were living in parallel dimensions now. Therefore, they were really representative of "parallel lives."

"Whatever!" was all I could say at the time. But I did understand more and more that our sense of what is "real" is a limited bare-bones representation of a much bigger picture. We are much larger beings than we imagine.

Later that year, I had one more consultation with poet Kurt Leland, who is also a channel. Kurt has some respectable credits in poetry and I was thrilled to find someone in the spiritual business who was also in the poetry business. Kurt channels an entity named Charles, whose wisdom is more "intellectual" than John's—more, dare I say "scientific"? Charles bears some resemblance to Seth, the being whom Jane Roberts channeled in her two best-selling books *Seth Speaks* and *The Nature of Personal Reality*. Like Jane Roberts's Seth, Kurt's Charles, is concerned with dispensing information about the levels of learning that we make on the Earth plane, the configuration of the soul's inherited characteristics, the layers of the experience and orientation of the soul, and how our personal and collective reality comes about through our own thought projections.

Charles even gave a name to the process I was undergoing. He called my third-eye visions of past/parallel lives "ranging," and defined it as a communication between different aspects of the soul extensions of my monad. This ranging also included the vision I had of a male guide, the spirit whom I thought, from my automatic handwriting, was perhaps an aspect of the monad of Djwhal Kuhl. Charles indicated that I had advanced to a level where I requested this "Ranging" process before I came into this life. The process was intended to help me keep my faith and assist me in making the leap to *perfect trust* in my intuitive, psychic self. Charles said I had been allowed to grow at a level that was usually only possible *between* lifetimes—that, in one lifetime, I would change my consciousness completely. I must admit, however, that I have found the transition to perfect trust rather shaky, to say the least. And I am far from having created the ideal life I want.

When I went to see Charles, I was particularly depressed. The spirits had been with me for several years already, yet my daily life was still burdened with making ends meet. Charles explained to me that my defeated beliefs were polluting my energy field and blocking more fruitful results for my efforts. I complained that it was increasingly difficult to believe in myself when the world did not seem to want me or my miracles, much less give me an average teaching position with an average income.

Charles gave me an exercise that I still practice, and it did produce results eventually. He told me to lie down and feel all my negative beliefs, all my fears, and place them in my solar plexus. Then he told me to name them, one at a time— "I'll never get a decent job; I'll never find a partner; I'll never have enough income"—and after each declaration, to add " . . . but I don't choose this." The goal is to avoid denial of my very real feelings, but also to blow them out of the field. I follow this with positive affirmations, whether I believe them or not.

This exercise convinced me that the idea of "magic words" is legitimate. Certainly negative thoughts can create a morose energy field that can then attract only more darkness. Therefore, reciting different thoughts aloud may possibly overcome the habitual thought forms. "Abracadabra" and "Bibbidy-Bobbidy-Boo" have a historical basis, after all.

Years later, I came across a marvelous book by Gregg Braden, *The Isaiah Effect*, in a Logan Airport bookstore. The book is about ancient prophecy and how we can manifest what we need through prayer *scientifically*. He connects quantum physics with the art of affirmation in an entirely understandable manner. He also acknowledges the existence of other dimensions in which existence is not perceptible due to the high vibratory rates of light frequencies. Following up on what cosmologists commonly call "The Big Bang" of creation, Braden explains that the vibration of the universe's expansion exceeded the three-dimensional laws. As it began to expand more quickly, he points out,

> 90 percent of the universe literally vibrated itself into high states of expression! It is this 90 percent that may represent the place where the parallel universes of quantum theory live.[1]

This idea lends credence to more metaphysical speculations. For some reason, by "ranging," my soul was allowing me to view short scenes occurring now in these other dimensions. After several more months of scene changes in my third eye, including some very amusing visions I hesitate to talk about because they are so absolutely silly and unbelievable (suffice it to say Spirit has a sense of humor), I decided to have a one-on-one visit with John again.

PARALLEL LIVES

I slipped into Gerry's office and chatted with him briefly about what would transpire in the consultation. After he explained to me how to work the tape machine (because he said John doesn't get into "touching things"), he sat

---

1. Gregg Braden, *The Isaiah Effect: Decoding the Lost Science of Prayer and Prophecy* (New York: Three Rivers Press, 2000), p. 99.

quietly holding his quartz crystal in a meditation until, with much coughing and throat-clearing, John settled into his body. John goodheartedly scolded me for having to "know and understand" everything. When I complained about the intense physicality of my experiences, he admonished me for not appreciating the love I was being given. He then went on to clarify some of my concerns.

"The man you are seeing during meditations is your own inner teacher, a higher octave of your soul."

"So, does he have a name? What should I call him?" I asked.

John looked away, was quiet for a moment, consulting the ethers, then gave me his response. "He wants you to call him Brother."

"Really?" I asked.

In the early Nineties, in one of those family dramas in which you're not quite sure which one of you started the trouble—trouble you may try to fix, but somehow can only exacerbate—my older brother and I had had a misunderstanding, a falling out. This brother had been my literary mentor/tormentor as we grew up, and he was a very important person in my life. Perhaps as another remnant of my father complex, I felt I had struggled for his approval uselessly most of my life. No doubt, we were both hurt very much. I know I felt sick about it for quite a while. But, in any event, there had been an extended silence between us. I looked at John blankly.

"That's strange, because I have lost all communication with my older brother."

"Yes," said John. "You know there are no accidents, Deborah. Don't focus on that. You have other work to do on your own."

"Yeah . . ." I said uneasily. I did know this was true. A lot was left unanswered there, but I changed the subject. "So what are these fast-motion movies I'm seeing behind my eyes?"

"Many of the movies, as you call them, are symbolic and there will be some that show the lives of your soul extensions, those in other timeframes, who are living their experiences in the now as you are living yours. Past lives, you like to call them. Parallel lives is more appropriate. You will be called to other places where the energies will be more conducive to the movie, the show, the whole production so to speak, so that your energy can be stepped up. There is a purpose behind this process that you will understand eventually."

"Other places? Why? Do they work better in certain locations?" I asked.

"Just understand that they work like radio signals, sometimes better here than there. They need tuning. *You* need fine-tuning."

"But what about the bizarre and sometimes scary images I see with my eyes open in the early mornings?" I asked. There had also been occasional demonic faces that appeared. Every so often, whenever I felt uncomfortable, I pulled my head under the covers and called on my angels for protection, as David had advised.

"These images are produced by your ego. Your own fears. Say 'no' to them if they do not please you," John said in his dismissive formal accent. "They are nothing, ephemera, illusion like the rest of the world humanity has created. They do not exist. Remember, the world is inside you. They're your own thought reflections. Your vision is being adjusted; it will take time."

"Right, just say 'no'," I repeated, knowing the general success of *that* campaign. I didn't understand how to differentiate between the visions that were symbolic of parallel lives and those that my ego created in an unconsciously fearsome state, but I assumed these latter were something like the images of the bardo period, when a soul crosses over.

John's answers to my questions often left me unsatisfied, not exactly because he dodged them, but because he sometimes gave me the impression that I didn't need to know the answers. He frequently went on to give me good advice about the fact that we live in an illusion. He said I must straddle a couple of worlds right now, accept them all, and know that I was guided. He suggested that I keep focused on my writing, that I sit down with a blank paper and see what happened. I sensed he was getting at something specific here.

I wondered if the writing was to come as my poetry usually comes. I simply hear a line in my head and begin to write. I don't usually stare at a blank page and wait. I don't have that kind of time. I can feel when a poem is coming on and my creative process is to resist it until it bursts through. I gear up by being physically active—vacuuming or washing dishes—until I begin to feel the first line formulate in the back of my head. Only then do I go to my desk and eke out a first draft. Then I sometimes stay up for hours and make the time for it. I often cut that first "given" line entirely as I revise the poem, but I always need it to begin. At the time I wondered what John was insinuating. It later occurred to me that John may have been referring to this book you are reading now.

One day, I picked two tarot cards and asked for information on my nurturing relationship with the spirits. The cards that came up were two of the Trump cards—the Hermit and the Magician. As I read information on their significance and shuffled them back into the deck, I started writing a poem in my head. Two short pieces came out easily. I had already written poems for the Hanging Man and the Fool, so I added these two to the sequence.

Writing these poems helped to inform me about the archetypal energies represented by the cards. I have experienced all three stages except for the Magician. Will I ever be the Magician? I identify him with the alchemist of Jungian psychology. I'd certainly settle for that. Over time, I felt these forces in my life more particularly, and I was inspired to articulate these archetypal energies in order to experience them more fully and finish the set. Here's my poem.

Tarot

Though their purses shrank, their souls gained in stature.
—C. G. JUNG

Hanging Man
All my earth reversed in an instant. As if I stepped
on the nerve of the universe—can never return
to leveled view. Strung by one welted ankle,
here surrender is survival, *absolute*, almost virtue.
What did I know erect but the cage of myself?

Magician
I know the game. Breath, flint, spark and a fired seed,
I contain all possibilities in my hat. An egg, a rod,
a drop of water. I'm syzygy through space.
the drive of sap through branches—my release?
Call it *mana*. Call me the unborn who emerges
out of nothing. I purify the cauldron, coin the lead.
Go ahead—Ask me to resurrect your wasted world.

Hermit
I carry my own light out of the hypnagogic gloom.
No sun, or star—Still, my bare beam opens direction.
Flanked by forests, cloaked from contact, I stoop
on my staff. Birds drop berries and secrets
seal this path from evil. How the nights are patient,
gentle—tamping my thoughts.

Fool
The unnumbered, *zed, void, squat*—I'm out
of the loop—no name or home, one of the passive
poor. Treading the air from nowhere
to the first heaven. I'm all paradox. Buds blossom
when I pass, hobo's bundle on my back, ferrying
to another shore. Wanderer on pilgrimage
to the 10,000 things. I have nothing to do
but ascend.

I am especially fond of the Fool, who, as in many fairy tales, is the dumbling son who finds the magic goose or treasure by meandering off the beaten track, trusting his sense of the universe's guidance rather than the controlled desires of his ego.

John reassured me about something else that day he spoke so sincerely to me. He said I would eventually have a partner, the partner I longed for. He chided me for being such an idealist. I had met no one new in years and, while friends encouraged me to try the personals or online dating, I honestly didn't want to make a project out of my loneliness. There weren't enough hours in the day as it was, and I think I did have a sense that, if it's going to happen, it'll happen by itself. John said the relationship might take time to manifest on the Earth plane, but he said it was "already done." I found that terrifically uplifting.

Though John's love and encouragement always came through, I left this particular consultation with my hungry mind wanting more, dissatisfied and impatient to keep on keeping on.

WHAT YOU RESIST PERSISTS

Both John and David had told me that I would be healed and I would be a healer. But what did "healer" mean? They both indicated that one of my guides was what they thought of as a "VIP." Evidently, he had worked with me in other lives when I still had my now-lost psychic power. And, as John said, he had been my teacher between lives.

From what I understand, we've all been victims and victimizers, and we're all tired of having played so many parts in so many different lives over the last few millennia. (Yes, there was "time" before our recorded history. Many psychics refer to life in Lemuria and Atlantis, the two continents that sank and disappeared in a catastrophic war that Edgar Cayce made famous in his voluminous writings.) John insisted that it was time to awaken *now*. Yet so many of us are still asleep. How would this awakening happen? How could it happen? And what exactly was it that was happening to me? What was I supposed to do?

John always insisted that I should stop worrying and just *be*—allow everything I confront to work itself out. This "allowing" was an interesting concept he mentioned now and then, explaining that, through our egoic control, we don't always "allow" ourselves to heed the advice of our guides—advice that often comes through subtle synchronistic hints—and to accept what comes without denial and avoidance. One of John's cardinal rules was: What you resist, persists.

In our Healing Group sessions, John encouraged us to follow our daily duties and accept in peace whatever comes, whether we like it or not. He told us we could state preferences in prayers or affirmations, but to be open to accepting even the most dreaded situations. These are created, he said, either by our unconscious or our higher selves for our own growth, or by the collective unconscious, which is difficult to avoid. Always remember, he enjoined us, that they are illusions. Resisting them, complaining about them, or avoiding them will only create more of these situations. John also recommended that I continue with my dream work, for any effort to make the unconscious conscious is always an important step in learning to create reality.

Although I found that I looked forward to my meditations—indeed, actually felt the increased energies distracting me if I tried to put off a meditation—since the spirits arrived, my meditations had changed. My mantra didn't help me drift into the theta state as easily, and I sometimes felt I wasn't in meditation at all, just taking time out to see the inner show of my third eye. To counter this problem, I wrote out some affirmations and thanked the higher powers in advance for giving me a restful twenty-minute vacation. I called on my new Inner Brother, the Spiritual Hierarchy, the Theosophical Brotherhood of Light, Jesus, Mary, the Angelic Community in general, the specific archangels Gabriel, Michael, and Raphael, the ancient gods and goddesses, Hermes and Orpheus, and the gods of writing to aid me in my ascension process. As I recited this prelude to my meditations, I felt energies zooming in around me. I actually felt the weight on the bed increase. Intermittently, I began checking out of consciousness altogether, as I had in the past. Sometimes, when I came to at exactly at the twenty-minute mark, I was aware of having seen images that I couldn't recall.

One day, I decided to sit down with the blank page and see if I could do some automatic writing the way the poet Yeats had done with his wife. I asked the energies to come in and guide my hand. As I felt them zoom in around me, the air vibrated all around my hand, which I let move across the page. Beneath my closed lids was Brother's eye. I felt my rather shaky hand writing a capital D very slowly in script. I half assumed I was pushing it, the way I always felt when playing with a Ouija board—a game, by the way, I have disliked ever since a freakish incident back in college when a group of us screamed in mass hysteria when we thought we had contacted a dead P.O.W. who claimed there would be nuclear war. (This was during the Vietnam War, when one of our greatest fears was of the next world war against communism.) I was afraid to allow any spirit to inhabit my hand. Yet I had invoked protection; I had learned to trust the process of visualizing white light around me.

After I felt the letter D completing itself, I expected the word I was writing would be "Daddy." Much to my surprise, however, my hand seemed to move of itself and continued writing the letter J, again in script. And after that, very slowly, there appeared the letters "W ," "H," "A," and "L." I lifted my hand to write a new word. The second completed word was "KUHL." *Djwhal Kuhl.* I had seen this name before, but it took me a while to place it. Djwhal Kuhl was a member of the White Brotherhood, a Master Avatar and the spirit guide behind the channeling of Alice Bailey—an English theosophist, one of the majors authors of *The Secret Doctrine,* an esoteric guide to awakening. Bailey, with her guide, wrote more than twenty volumes of philosophy in the late 19th century. I had browsed through some of her books in bookstores in the past and even purchased a few, only to find them unreadable. As in much channeled writing, the language is convoluted, heavy-handed, and archaic. Combine that with the baroque 19th-century style and you'll be asleep in no time. Then I remembered that David had once told me that I had been a pupil of an Indian guru in between lives.

Though I was happy to listen to John when Gerry, as a full-bodied medium, channeled him to teach our group, I did not feel comfortable with the idea of channeling writing myself. I considered myself a writer, with my own ideas, even though John told us that most of our best ideas are given to us from our higher selves, other members of our monad who are in spirit rather than in body. Being struck with an idea still left room for personal creativity, but the idea of straight dictation did not appeal to me. John indicated that I should write, but he also told me that whatever resulted would be my own work. This conundrum became clearer to me when I understood that there are levels of higher selves. Still, I did not want my physical hand moved by another's impetus.

I thanked Djwhal Kuhl for identifying himself and asked him to help me with my own poetry in my own words. Then I closed the notebook and never attempted that process again. But the more I looked at the image of the man in my inner eye, the more I began to think of him as Djwhal. After all, he was wearing a Nehru collar, was dark-skinned, with dark, curly hair. It clicked one day that I was told to call him Brother because he was part of Theosophy's Brotherhood of Light, a group of higher beings about whom I had read who were said to oversee the planet's ascension. Perhaps, if he had been my teacher before, he was my teacher still. I knew from my astrology chart, which I had been told is weighted heavily by masculine planets, that I had had lives on Earth as a male. Hadn't David said that, in addition to having been martyred for my pagan powers, I had also lost my psychic ability by abusing it when I was in a male body? But David indicated that, in between lives, as Djwhal's student, I myself was a Brother.

SPIRIT VOICES

Life proceeded "normally" for a while after this experiment, and months went by with my visions continuing, the scenes varying and changing over time. I had some singular "movies" that I saw only once, but that remained memorable. I recorded everything in a journal, along with my dreams. As in my holotropic trip, I saw the Colosseum full of lions. I saw the insides of dungeons. Then there was a scene that came and went of French aristocrats at a ball. I say French because I recognized the Louis-esque furniture, gardens like those at Versailles, and 18th-century three-cornered hats. Sometimes, there would be a hunt scene, with men on horseback swinging their crops, attired in caps and jackets, knickers and boots. And sometimes there were soldiers in formation with three-cornered hats. There was also a theater scene of a ballet. From the way the camera of my inner eye zoomed around behind stage, I got a ballerina's view of the audience. Then occasionally, there was a detail of the orchestra pit, mostly in the string section. I suspected these "films" were from past/parallel lives.

In college, I majored in French because I loved the sound of the language, which always come easily to me. Even back in seventh grade, when I learned my first French words, I felt a familiarity with the sounds, the feel of the vowels in my mouth. And though I lost a lot of the language from lack of use, I always loved speaking French—from junior high through graduate school at Boston College. I reviewed French history and strained my brain to figure out if these images were all from the same century. I had taken dancing lessons as a child—ballet and later jazz— and any kind of dancing had always been a favorite pastime. At three years old, I declared to my parents that I would be a dancer. Somehow, by the time I was twelve, I had grown out of it. Ballet was so strenuous, and by that time I really enjoyed doing the Watusi and the Twist. But from my twenties into my fifties, I preferred to exercise in dance classes—from jazz, modern, aerobics, and disco to ballroom and Neuro-Integrative Aerobics, my current passion. The foot work and body work come easily to me, and dancing has been one of the joys of my life.

In the French ball and garden scenes, there was one particular couple that was always hugging and touching and kissing. I found this entertaining and wondered how I figured in the picture. Which one was my soul extension? The woman or the man? Then again, I never knew what to expect. In one meditation, I saw my long-gone dog, Tasha, running in a field, happily jumping over a fence. She had disappeared from my ex-husband's house many years ago when he agreed to take care of her while my son and I went on vacation. We had missed her sorely and mourned her deeply. I was touched by the image and relayed it to my son. He was now in college and I was open about what was happening to me. He even came to meet John once or twice and had an interesting reading with him in which John told him about a past life we had shared as medicine men in Madagascar in 650 B.C.E.

One June morning in 1996, I awoke trying desperately to remember a pedestrian dream in which I was teaching, when I suddenly saw an image of the Egyptian god Anubis floating at the foot my bed. I recognized his jackal head and typical Egyptian posture. He was holding what looked like a wand or staff, which he ceremoniously lifted and pointed at me. The image, just as distinctive, dignified, sober, and translucent as that of my previous friend, whom I simply call the Big Indian, faded after a few moments. I had seen him with my eyes open. I was so startled, I never did write down the teaching dream. Later that day, I looked up Anubis in several books. He was a priest of the dead and the initiator of Egyptian mysteries. He is related to embalming rituals and passage through the underworld.

I understood the god's significance in several ways. My dear college friend Judith crossed over to the other side a few weeks later in the TWA 800 crash over Long Island, New York. Was this a message from the underworld? For a long time, I thought the visit from Anubis was a prescient announcement. David Hall had also predicted "the loss of an old friend." It sent me into a tailspin for several reasons. First and foremost, of course, was that we had lost this gorgeous, fun, brilliant, creative woman and that she left behind young children, a husband, a huge extended family, and numerous friends. Her well-attended funeral was both heartbreaking and heartwarming. It was followed by a long big-chill weekend with my college friends. To this day, her memory is fresh to all of us and we miss her dearly.

Another symbolic meaning for Anubis' visit involved his role as an esoteric mentor. With my increased sensations of lovely liquid light pouring into my various chakras, I speculated that I was being "embalmed" to convince me of my immortal soul. I spent time in the underworld during my depressions and dwelled there most consciously and extensively in my dream image work. I thought that perhaps the image of Anubis anticipated my own healing powers to raise others to awareness. Maybe he had appeared to remind me of my own weird "initiation." This concept took several forms over the next few years, and now I know that it was the infusion of light that my soul selected to feel *physically*.

I learned, after a while, that the universe has a very odd sense of humor—wry, almost dry at times, and at others downright silly. As I observed synchronicities both from daily life and from puns in my dreams, I began to get a sense of the way spirit jokes with us. At other times, I saw how serious it could be. Spirit doesn't create our fate; it just reflects back to us how we create our own. And it's there for us, if we ask.

Chapter 14

MY HOLY LAND

It depends on what you mean by angels.
What I mean by it is a form of consciousness
that is higher than human: non-human intelligence.
It's more of an energy than anything physical.
RUPERT SHELDRAKE, *THE PHYSICS OF ANGELS*

In her life, my mother had a handful of psychic experiences, probably the most blatant being the vision of my father two years after his death. Occasionally, she told me of a dream that related to me. Once she mentioned that she'd dreamt my car was sinking in quicksand. There was no one in the car; the scene only contained a driverless silver Ford Escort. A week or so later, I totaled the car, skidding in the rain on a busy parkway in Cambridge. Thankfully, no one was hurt, but it also began a difficult period for me. So when my mother phoned in March of 1997 (three years prior to my trip to France) and said she had dreamt that she should take me with her on her upcoming trip to Israel, I teased her and said that, if she had the nerve to tell me such a dream, surely she *must* bring me along. She laughed and mentioned the expense involved and, of course, I knew my demand was unrealistic.

She knew, however, that I placed great value on dreams and my dream work, though she never seemed to understand its purpose. Once, when I was visiting her in Florida, I practiced the dream-work technique I'd been trained in on one of her dreams—a dream about her long-dead and distant father who, in the dream, simply hands her a flower. She agreed to sit with me for an hour and revisit the dream, which she thought odd, as she had never dreamt of her father before. I tried to move her into his image as we worked in soft voices with our eyes closed, but she was completely unable to leave her ego, even imaginatively. Perhaps this is why she, like many people, is so resistant when I speak of reincarnation. She insists she simply couldn't be anyone but herself. "Look, we live, we die, we go to heaven," she told me. End of story.

The value of meditation, ultimately, is to recognize that we can leave the ego. Perhaps that is why I find Jung's practice of active imagination effective. In any event, my mother's dream of her father and the flower was strangely prescient, because, unbeknownst to either of us, it marked the beginning of a long period of suffering for her. In our work that day, the closest she could move into her father's psyche was to say, "It's as if he is comforting me about something." I think she was a little afraid of her pre-cognitive experiences. In fact, she was wary of my psychotherapy. Period.

After the take-you-to-Israel dream conversation, we dropped the subject, chatted for a while about other things, and then hung up. A week or so passed. Then, on a perfectly ordinary Wednesday afternoon, I received a phone call informing me that I had been awarded an individual artist's grant for $20,000 from the National Endowment for the Arts for the poems I had submitted. I had completely forgotten I had applied. I had been submitting applications to the NEA ever since my journal publications qualified me as eligible seven or eight years back. The application was long and tediously detailed, but I nonetheless filled it out routinely once a year, understanding that, even though it was probably futile, I could never win the grant unless I applied for it. It was the sequence of poems about my father's afterlife that I began in Washington that won me the grant. I immediately phoned my mother. "What would you say," I asked her, "if I told you I can afford to go with you to Israel?"

Conveniently, and one might say synchronistically, someone had dropped out of the group, leaving an empty place. And, remarkably, the trip was scheduled for twelve days at the end of May—in my small window of free time between spring and summer sessions. At the time, my mother was eighty-one, the eldest member of the church group that had planned this visit to the Holy Land. She was in perfect health, yet admitted to me that this would probably be her final trip after a lifetime of travel that began when she became one of the first airline hostesses in the 1940s. After my father died, she took a trip abroad each year.

Most of the group going to Israel belonged to her Catholic parish in Pompano Beach, Florida. One of the parish priests, Father Joseph (who was originally from India), was going to accompany the group, and hoped to say Mass daily at various sites. The "tour" was not something in which I normally would have participated, but there were several compelling reasons to go: the uncanny dream, the right timing, the idea of making memories with my mother on her final trip abroad, and my own renewed interest in the personage and psyche of Jesus Christ and the mysterious Magdalen. I never hesitated in thinking I should go. I hadn't even thought about what I could do with the grant. I was heavily into my credit cards; I needed a new car; I very much wanted some time off to write. But, despite the fact that I didn't like tours (much less Catholic tours!), in my mind, as in my mother's dream, the trip to Israel was a foregone conclusion.

As my mother and I planned for our trip, I realized with some dismay that I had to travel as one of the traditional Catholic pilgrims from Holy Cross, my mother's church. I did not share this church's understanding of Christianity, having read the texts of Nag Hammadi and studied the mystical aspects of other religions. I was curious about how my current psychic sensations and my own private understanding would play out in the Holy Land, or literally *on* the Holy Land. Despite my ambivalence about traveling with this group, I couldn't help but believe that this ancient soil—literally this holy *land* was one of the places to which I was called. I didn't care if I was a "cafeteria Catholic," picking and choosing what I liked of the doctrinal buffet. I did not want to play the hypocrite, but I truly felt that, no matter what I had taken from the Catholic ritual I grew up with and still admired, I could attune it to my renovated beliefs.

I had heard, of course, about the new "Christ Consciousness" on the planet, and my quasi-mentor John had much to say about "Yeshua" and the revisionist history created by the early Church fathers. At that time, I was also rethinking the Magdalen, her gospel, and John's version of her relationship to Jesus. I had read several channeled books on the subject, including Edgar Cayce's, and was fascinated by the story I kept encountering, which turned out later to be substantiated in the French legends. John confirmed questions about the marriage of Yeshua and Mary, but he often waved away discussion, preferring to stay with his message that Christ Consciousness is becoming available to the human species, and that it has nothing to do with dying on a cross. It has everything to do, however, with the symbolic resurrection of the light body and the mind's return to the awareness of its oneness with All That Is.

John said, basically, that the so-called "Second Coming" would be signaled by the reemergence of ancient esoteric teachings that had been wiped out by the persecutions engineered by the Church hierarchy in Rome. The human race has forgotten its spiritual origins, its golden age—forgotten what it was and is. Thanks to these recently discovered gospels, we now have another view. The importance of Jesus Christ on Earth is that he demonstrated a direct model for the evolution of humanity. As John said in his own gospel, "The truth shall set you free." As Jesus says in the Gospel of Thomas,

> [The Kingdom] will not come by waiting for it. It will not be a matter of saying "here it is" or "there it is." Rather, the kingdom of the Father is spread out upon the earth, and men do not see it.[1]

The evolution comes from the suspension of judgment, from forgiveness of sin (which is nothing more than ignorance), from brotherly love, and from the understanding of Oneness—all of which sounds simple, but, until this time in history, has proven impossible.

LIVING TECHNICOLOR

Fortunately, the trip took place in 1997, during Bill Clinton's administration, and the Israelis and Palestinians were closer to a peace agreement than they had been in a long time. Since we were leaving from Miami, I flew to Florida from Boston the day before and then traveled with my mother to Miami. After extensive delay and intensive interviews by Israeli officials in a private room at the airport, we learned at the last minute we would fly to New York and leave from there. I suppose this may have been to throw any possible hijackers off track. But the net effect was that, by the time our huge plane took off, we had already been through a full day of travel.

Temperamentally, I am nothing like my mother, who is calm and composed, and can fall and stay asleep anywhere, anytime. I never sleep on transcontinental flights and always need a few days to adjust my problematic sleeping habits to a new clock. Melatonin gives me nightmares; Ambien did not yet exist. So, despite a few Excedrin P.M. tablets and two stiff belts of scotch on the rocks, I was wide-eyed throughout the nine-hour flight. When we finally did land in Tel Aviv, Emile, our annoyingly perky Israeli guide, told us that we could not get into our hotel rooms until late afternoon.

We left the airport at 11 A.M. Emile piled us onto a bus and immediately began speaking through a microphone, acquainting us with our new environment. The usually enthusiastic church group was made up of a handful of middle-aged couples, but also contained a teenager and his mom, a few sets

---

1. Robinson, James M. gen. ed. *The Nag Hammadi Library in English* (San Francisco: Harper and Row), 1978 p 138

of sisters, a few single men in their thirties and several single women, and mothers and daughters like ourselves. Just about everyone was exhausted and totally uninterested in the busy noise of an average business day in Tel Aviv. We, for the most part, ignored the overly enthused Emile and his unlikely friend, our Palestinian bus driver, the jovial Ahmal, who chuckled constantly and appeared to be the only one listening. Our heads bobbed sleepily along with the bus as we drove through the city.,

Personally, I was horrified that Emile actually intended to take us to see some sites—to get off and on the bus, walk the streets, climb stairs and hills—when I hadn't slept in over thirty hours! But here we were, en route from Jaffa, forced to stop and view a church where Saint Peter had had a vision in which he was asked to teach the word of God to the heathens. Father Joseph, in his sweet manner and sleep-deprived haze, began asking about the possibility of saying Mass. I elbowed my mother and groaned, already forgetting my pledge to honor the Catholic rituals.

We were promised lunch and marched onward into the church like somnambulant Christian soldiers. I immediately slipped into a pew, trying to adjust my eyes to the relative dark after the hostile sun outside, which had seemed to be stabbing its flashes of fire deliberately and ruthlessly at my throbbing head. On previous trips abroad, I had always taken the opportunity to crash for several hours immediately upon arriving at a hotel. To have to wait for most of the day was nothing less than torture. My mother sat down next to me and then knelt to pray. Still half-sitting on my backside, I could only slump a little to my knees and close my eyes—not out of any piety, but from complete exhaustion.

Strangely, however, I did feel spiritually moved. My claire-sentience of the spirits around me was especially acute and I was immediately aware that my sensations were heightened. I felt that tapping sensation in the air, an idea I associated without thinking with the flapping of wings. That was the first time a new vision occurred. In the little church in Jaffa, somewhere south of Tel Aviv, behind my closed eyes, I was pulled through a series of distinct doorways or vortices, one within the other—almost exactly the way I had experienced them in the holotropic breath workshop. Although I had sought no altered state, done no breath work, summoned or invoked no special assistance, I felt afloat and gripped the back of the pew in front of me tightly with my hands. This was not mere fatigue. It was the same floating sensation I have when I meditate, only about three times stronger. Keeping my eyes closed, I saw a wall of stone that kept shifting and opening to tunnel views, faster and faster.

Suddenly, it opened completely to a huge panorama in Technicolor. "A Bible movie," I said to myself. "I'm in a freaking Bible movie!"

I saw behind my closed eyes a group of women in long sweeping clothing balancing big baskets on their heads and walking single file along the seashore. At the water's edge, they stopped and began washing the clothes in the baskets against the rocks. *Whoosh!"* My ears buzzed and I felt a cool fluid within them. Then the scene lost focus and returned to the tunnels of stone. As soon as I focused in on the stone walls again, it was as if an inner camera shutter opened in a different direction, revealing dusty kiosks and shopkeepers, a kind of open air market. It was very crowded with people attired in Biblical apparel bargaining and beckoning, with donkeys, camels, goats, and geese straying among barrels of what appeared to be feed and food. Both of these scenes lasted only about ten seconds each. There were no sounds at all. My head was splitting from the effort of trying to maintain the view. Then I shot my eyes open and looked around the church.

Various pilgrims were admiring the windows and iconography, and some were saying the rosary before a statue of the Virgin. My mother was still, her head bowed. I wondered if she were sleeping. Craning my neck in different directions, I experimented, closing my eyes and opening them at regular intervals. It seemed that I could see through my eyes again, could see the light beings around me. Were these light beings my guides or angelic beings rooted to a numinous place? I was clueless.

Some of the figures were wreathed in pastel colors. They seemed to be made up of separate particles, pixel-like. And yes, some had wings. When I closed and opened my eyes fairly quickly, I caught these moving figures against the backdrop of the actual walls and aisles and ceiling lines. But when I kept my eyes closed for longer than six or eight seconds, I was pulled into the vortices, then the tunnels, and then delivered in living color to a Cecil B. Demille production that also lasted but a few seconds.

Because of the Bible views, I thought of the film *The Ten Commandments*, and of how when my parents had taken us to see it as young kids at Radio City Music Hall. I couldn't have been more than ten. I was awed by the scenery. But there was one particular scene that struck terror into my heart. And this same scene that had been directly threatening to me as a child now came to my mind as I sat, half-slumped in the pew in Jaffa. In it, if I recall correctly, an elderly slave woman is about to be caught in a closing stone wall. I believe a bit of her clothing became trapped and she was anxiously looking around for help. The stone wall itself seemed familiar to me and I felt as if that woman's terrified heart beat within my own chest. Now, I felt as if I had been there, in that scene, with slaves overseen by swarthy, muscled men pulling on the ropes that closed the wall. I don't think I was conscious of that thought as a child, but I always remembered that scene. In the ensuing years, as films (and I) became more sophisticated, I have watched the epic again on television and remarked to myself how silly I was to be frightened, how phony the scenery looked after all. Yet each time I happen on the film, I try to determine, somewhat neuroti-cally, whether that scene has been shown or is yet to come. If it is yet to come, I wait for it anxiously. As I experienced my astonishing inner panorama in Saint Peter's Church, the memory again overwhelmed me.

Again, I must assert that I know the difference between visualization and imaginative fantasy, as I have engaged in the latter all my life and honed it especially through dream working. But something totally unbidden—a vision of such precision and detail that I couldn't have summoned it forth—took place in that church. Had I not had the holographic breath workshop to orient myself, along with the strange sightings that occurred often enough in my bedroom after the workshop, I would have been very upset. As it was, I didn't doubt myself at all, and I grew all the more curious about my relation-ship to this troubled land, Israel.

British physicist Rupert Sheldrake's theory of "morphic resonance" pro-poses that there is an intelligence immanent in nature. In his book *The Presence of the Past*, he discusses the possibility that people entering these morphic fields can experience the memories of those that lived and died there. In Virginia Lee's interview with Sheldrake, he explains his theory:

> The whole idea of morphic resonance is that the past is potentially present everywhere, and that you gain access to it by resonating with it. And out of that grows the future, which is open and undeter-mined.[2]

In *The Edges of the Civilized World*, poet and essayist Alison Deming quotes David Abram speaking of the perception of spirit in nature where

> ... phenomena can be hidden not just within the past or the future, but also within the very thickness of the present itself, that there is an enigmatic, hidden dimension at the very heart of the sensible present.[3]

---

2. *Common Ground*, Summer issue, 1997.
3. Alison Deming, *The Edges of the Civilized World* (New York: Picador, 1998), p. 22.

Before I read this passage, and before I was at all familiar with these controversial theories, my encounters in Israel simply came as raw experience. For some reason, I was able to see into the memories of the very mud, clay, and rock that made up this land.

WITH BOTH FEET ON THE GROUND

By the time of my trip to Israel, my third eye had been active for three years during meditations. I had become accustomed to the odd, amusing, and sometimes scary imagery to which I bore witness. Once when I was speaking to a Cambridge psychic in casual conversation in the Seven Stars bookstore, I asked if he had ever heard of visions like mine. He scoffed and told me he had demonic faces before him half the time! I was content with that and didn't ask again. John and David reassured me that I was both sane and safe, and that was what I chose to believe. But here, with the chakras of both feet standing on the sacred *temenos*, I realized this was a whole new movie. The focus was much sharper; the colors were deeper. I found myself wondering how I was going to correlate my own amazing vision with the full-bodied Catholic nature of this journey.

After we left Saint Peter's Church, we passed through the town of Caesarea, a town Herod rebuilt and named for his emperor, Augustus Caesar. The town was the capital of the Roman government of Palestine for 500 years. It was eventually destroyed by the aggressive Beybars and wasn't rediscovered until 1956, when archeologists excavated the Roman amphitheater and ancient aqueduct. As we walked around the aqueduct and snapped photos of the sea behind it, I closed my eyes again, this time lifting my face directly into the sun. Once again, a scene opened to me, this one of a walled city with darkly clad women (I assumed Muslims) carrying what looked like baskets of food to and fro. It seemed to be a different, more contemporary scene than the Biblical vision I had had in the church, but I lost it too quickly to determine anything. Even with the bright sun reddening the background of my closed lids, the dark robes had appeared distinctly.

I didn't mention my vision to my mother until later that afternoon, when we finally got to our hotel and I could write it down. She shook her head, smiling, and said, "Just don't tell people; they'll think you're crazy." As a child, I had been pegged "the dramatic one"—the poet, after all, the family's drama queen. I was certain she didn't believe me. And yet it made me angry to think that. She said what she always said: "Why would this happen to you and not anyone else?" She shamed me for thinking I could be worthy of something this numinous. And, in truth, I asked this same question of the psychics I sought out to help me name the experience after I got home. They all told me the same thing: "You and your soul have chosen this particular awakening. You have had these powers in other lifetimes. You are worthy of this experience, as *everyone* is."

There was no doubt of the religious devotion of my fellow travelers, and yet I wanted to tell them my own heretical version of the meaning of Christ's life and death. I wanted to tell them that the race was indeed evolving and, from my intense experience, I was living proof. Of course, I was not going to try to convince anyone of anything, but I did believe that I might have come here to be initiated into another phase of the mysteries. I was so tired, however, that I didn't have to trouble myself with these thoughts for long.

Our first hotel was in Tiberias, a small city some 600 feet below sea level overlooking the west side of Lake Kinneret, or what is known to Christians as the Sea of Galilee. It is not, in fact, a sea but an exquisite jade-green lake. Because of its beauty, Josephus, the ancient historian, described Tiberias as "the ambition of nature." Herod Antipas founded the city, naming it for the Roman emperor and building palaces, baths, and temples. When the Jews were expelled from Jerusalem, Tiberias became the center of Jewish intellectual life. Maimonides, the great philosopher from the court of Saladin in Cairo died and was buried there in 1204. The Galilee Valley is especially fertile and beautiful, nourished by salubrious hot springs. The lake itself was a focal point for travel between nine different cities at the time of Christ. It abounded with catfish, mullet, carp, and other species. The stories of the Gospels occurred here. And here, fishermen still use nets to comb the seven-mile wide, thirteen-mile long stretch of glassy water.

From our hotel window, my mother and I tried to imagine the landscape in the first millennium without the busy tourist establishments that crowded this side of the lake. We took a walk around the grounds that night and sat in a café on the shore listening to rowdy rock music from a huge boat deck packed with young people. Our waiter explained that these were students who had just graduated from high school and would be drafted into the army in two days. This was the annual send-off blast for the young women and men. We were somewhat dismayed when we learned that they would be partying into the wee hours of morning. The noise was considerable and we faced a number of grumpy compatriots the next morning at our early breakfast. Yet we had to consider: There was an ongoing guerilla war in the

Middle East and these young people would soon be conscripted into one of the best-trained armies in the world. They deserved one night of fun.

The Israelis are not overly friendly, even to Americans. I asked one unsmiling waitress about the formality, the restrained almost disdainful attitude that was sometimes visible toward tourists. She only replied, "We live under a lot of tension." I have been through most of western Europe, and was accustomed to striking up conversations with the locals. When I was younger, of course, it was easy to spend time with other youths at some beer garden or local haunt. And I can still sometimes be amazed that my own naiveté and joie de vivre didn't get me into trouble. Yet here, I didn't mind the shelter of my little tour group, especially when we passed through the many checkpoints into the Palestinian territories where most of the Christian sites are located. One day, we were stuck in traffic for half an hour and had to change plans when word came back that a bomb had been found on the road.

In general, leaving the Jewish sector and entering a Palestinian town like Bethlehem was always a shocking change of environment—from affluence to rock-bottom poverty. In Palestine, the streets are shoddy and narrow and the houses are ramshackle, with tin roofs. In Tel Aviv, the streets are lined with flowers, the houses built of graceful sunlit limestone and gated by extravagantly designed wrought iron and sculpted hedges. I found I felt compassion for the Arabs as underdogs even as they hassled us, chased us, and plied us with their wares—"My mother made this rosary with her bare hands!"

From Tiberias we went to the smaller town of Cana, where my mother posed for a picture with her $2.00 bottles of Cana wine in front of "The First Miracle Shop," a tacky little place with tons of olive-wood rosaries and crosses adjacent to the bins of wine. I didn't bother relaying the possibility that Cana may have been the site of Christ's own wedding. And I didn't realize then how involved I would become with that story in the next few years.

Later, in the bigger city of Jerusalem, we encountered young men and women standing on street corners, waiting for buses or subways, dressed in fatigues, carrying knapsacks and rifles. And there was always a palpable tension in the air, even though this was four full years before 9/11.

THE PRESENCE OF THE PAST

My first day in Israel convinced me that the ground we stood on held many vibrations, many secrets with living ancestral energy, and that it carried, not only the spirit of those before us, but historic memories as well. The very atmosphere of Palenstine is weighted with its own heavy karma from the myriad conquests of the land, each victorious army devastating the monuments of its predecessors. City built on ruined city built on ruined city—for more than 3000 years. I saw many ongoing excavations. We visited one in Beit She'an, where I walked among the reassembled Roman mosaic streets of a walled city and climbed to the top of an amphitheater. Palestinian soil has been turned over thousands of times over three millennia to unearth the strata of entire civilizations that lie deep beneath it. I felt as if the land itself had senses.

I became dizzy trying to follow the overwhelming history of this small, but persistently significant, region—an area barely the size of the state of Rhode Island. From Joshua crossing the Jordan River to overrun what was then called Canaan in 1250 B.C., to the Philistines founding of Palestine; From Saul's reign and the ancient kingdom of David to Solomon's building of the Temple; from the division of Israel and Judah to the Assyrians' conquest of the north; from Nebuchadnezzar's destruction of Jerusalem to the Babylon captivity of the tribes. Then came Alexander and the Ptolemies of Egypt, the Syrians, and the loss of Palestine to Pompei in 64 B.C. Herod the Great ruled until 4 B.C., when Jesus lived, and Hadrian followed, ushering in the Byzantine period with its dark Madonnas and gold-leaf paintings.

After Constantine's conversion under his mother, Queen Helena, Christianity flourished in the region. Many of the churches we would visit were built in this era. Later came the Persian and Muslim conquests, and the eventual defeat of the Crusaders by Saladin. Then Mongol tribes and the Ottoman Turks held the small country for 400 years, until the Allies took it under the British Mandate in World War II and the United Nations partitioned it and turned over its administration to both Israel and Jordan. In 1948, the Jewish National Council established the State of Israel. Since then, the region has been riven by conflict.

Throughout the incredible sweep of this history, how many monuments and works of religion or art were destroyed, buried, and lost as new cities were built atop them? And how many of these cities were themselves then destroyed, buried, and lost in succession? There must be a residual consciousness held deep in the very soil of this region of all that has happened here.

I once read—in one of what I call my "voodoo-hooey" channeled books—that there is a portal over the Middle East, a doorway to other dimensions, that accounts for this tumultuous history. The premise is that there has been a continuous struggle in the other dimensions for control over this planet, and that many so-called visitors "clothed in flesh" have passed through this portal from other realms. In the legends, the ancient Egyptians and the Atlanteans before them knew of the portal, through which knowledge of sacred geometry and the secrets of the architecture of the pyramids were passed, and the laws of the lost Arc of the Covenant conveyed.

Through the portal, alien beings come and go, leaving behind both gifts of truth and falsehoods and superstitions—like the burning chariots seen by the prophet Elijah, who mistook them for gods. This is the setting for Armageddon, where the forces of light will line up with their flaming swords against the sons of destruction, and for other strange mythic stories like those found in the Dead Sea Scrolls in 1947. Over time, these legends have carried the human imagination right up through the dusky heavens, spiraling out into space and emerging in strange theories like those of Van Aicken, Barbara Marceniak, and Barbara Hand Clow. For myself, I couldn't help but feel the mystery of the land and the vibrating tensions in its atmosphere as distinctly personal and not entirely unfamiliar.

Chapter 15

THE GIFT OF TEARS

*Angels themselves could be thought of as a particular manifestation of the
activity of these fields, just as photons are a particular way of thinking
about the activity, the energy, carried in electromagnetic fields.*
RUPERT SHELDRAKE, *THE PHYSICS OF ANGELS*

This sense of mystery and tension stayed with me throughout the two weeks
of my trip to Israel. No matter where we were, Father Joseph said Mass
every day—inside the Church of the Holy Sepulcher, one of several markers
of the place of Christ's death; in the Church of the Dormition where Mother
Mary died, adjacent to the upper rooms of the house where Joseph of Arimathea made arrangements for the Last Supper; in the Church of the Pater
Noster on the Mount of Olives where Christ first delivered the Lord's Prayer;
or at the Church of all Nations at the Garden of Gethsemane, with its 3000-
year-old trees. And at each new site, when I closed my eyes, my extraordinary
experiences continued. I entered the inner theater of tunnels and saw swirls of
pearly-winged angels until vague biblical pictures came into view. I could only
sustain them for half a minute at the most (if that!), as my forehead felt the
pressure in the third-eye area, giving me intense momentary shots of pain.

I experienced two different types of visions: airy figures of light and the
"bible movies" I described above. The light visions occurred mostly when
we were inside the churches—beings of white light and a pastel pulsing of
light that sprouted wings. When I closed my eyes almost all the way, leaving
that slight flutter at the tips of my lids, I saw the space as it was through my
closed eyes. I could recognize the shadows of people in front of me, occasionally even identifying them, flipping my eyes open to see if I had guessed
correctly. The layout of the altar, the statues, the crosses all appeared with
blurred boundaries, but were clear enough to recognize.

Then the airy figures came and went, flitting about "on high" in glowing
light-blue or pink or golden light, some with silver mixed in, not unlike swirls
of mother-of-pearl. Two of them often flanked Father Joe. I had no doubts

about the goodness of this man, but I also wondered if these airy figures invoked a field around him that helped transform the ritual of the Eucharist. As I watched people go to communion through my mostly closed eyes, I saw angels among them.

The second type of vision I experienced in Israel—my "bible movies"—aroused my curiosity and frustrated me to no end. They continued, but I couldn't sustain them. They came and went quickly, in flashes. They usually began in the imagery of stone walls that became deep corners and emptied into vortices within vortices, eventually opening broadly, widening to a vista that made me gasp. In the next moment, they blurred and were gone. The movies appeared less frequently than the light beings, but when they did, I could find no way to control or explain them.

I too went to communion every day. Although I may be a pagan, a romantic heathen, and a blasphemous heretic, I had no fear that I would be struck by lightning. These are not, after all, the days of the Inquisition—at least not yet—and I refused to be held back by dogma. I thought about the rituals and sacraments that, at several points in my life, I had rejected. But now, as I witnessed these fields of light, I wondered if prayer and invocations to the gods actually *do* summon a change in atoms and molecules. Besides, my long-lost childhood love for Christ was suddenly activated in this intensely spiritual environment. I could not hold back tears of joy as I felt what I can only call a further opening of my heart.

What happened to me during this trip was profound. I felt this joy—this *love*—as a literal part of my body, the old cliché of my heart. And I wept. I wept constantly, finding dark corners, retreating behind my sunglasses, and sniffling and dabbing discreetly at my eyes. When there was music or singing, my heart ached as if I were separated from a lover, even though I was no longer pining for any particular man. I experienced the ache that my favorite poet, Rumi, describes as a yearning for the Beloved. I think my heart remembered *union*.

More than once, my mother caught me crying and didn't quite know what to say. I simply chased her away by whispering, "I'm seeing the angels." She just shook her head and smiled affectionately, as if to say, "Oh, my crazy daughter!" My mother is a traditional Catholic and has only recently stopped questioning my meditations. "Why don't you just pray?" she frequently asked. "This is how I pray," was my only answer. Although that is not the *entire* truth. When I meditate, I enter a void where the universal energy can flow through me. And that is not the same as asking for help or expressing gratitude, which I do as well at other times.

I am reminded of Saint Francis and the "gift of tears" that he and so many other saints experienced when they became one with the love of God. I cried through my meditations for the first two years after the energies first appeared around me. It was *physical.* Something was triggered—some meridian or acupressure point—and the tears were a cleansing release. I also cry immediately following a massage. While I didn't trouble myself with questions of sainthood, I did feel opened to a kind of self-forgiveness—a compassion for my own suffering that was different from self-pity—that I had not known since I was a child. I repeatedly, instinctively, forgave myself for my woundedness, for giving into depression too easily, for sometimes doubting that there is a larger plan at work, for all my grand sins and all my peccadilloes.

The tears I shed in Israel were not about finding religion, but about the "revelation" (and I don't use that word lightly) that we are all worthy and loved. Revelation occurs when blinders fall away, revealing the truth behind the veil. I felt loved completely and wholly in a way that sustains me even today, despite my heartbreaks. I was simply overcome with a spiritual emotion the intensity of which I hadn't previously known. Even the mystics have no vocabulary for it, because the feeling is beyond expression; only mystic poetry can contain its paradox. All I could give in return were tears.

In a study of Saint Francis, John Haule, the Jungian psychoanalyst, describes the saint's ecstasy as a process he could summon that took him from tears of pain to tears of joy. Francis was a wealthy young hedonist who considered himself a sinner. While I do not compare myself to Francis by any means, I do believe what I have been told by the psychics and channels—that these states of contact with the universal divine are indeed more accessible to us at this particular time in history. We need only ask in order for them to affect us and I had been desperately asking for help for a long time.

CAPERNAUM

Capernaum, with its beach roses and hilly lawns, was my favorite spot in the Galilee. I especially loved the Mount of the Beatitudes, which proved to be as green and hilly as any young Catholic child who heard the story would imagine. It is currently crowned with a beautiful domed church built by the Franciscans. The Franciscans have unearthed some of the ruins in Capernaum, among them what is said to be Saint Peter's home and a third-century synagogue supposedly built over the one in which Jesus spoke. On the rocks are engravings of both Roman and Jewish symbols—the Star of David, the palm, and the Menorah.

During Christ's time, merchants traveled through Capernaum on their way from Damascus with exotic clothing and spices. The Church of Saint Peter's Primacy, the traditional site of the loaves-and-fishes miracle, stands on the shores of another lake in the Galilee—Tabgha, a Greek word that means "seven springs." There, in the ruins of a Byzantine church excavated in 1932, a well-preserved mosaic exhibits two fish on either side of a basket. A new Greek Orthodox church was built over the site. I was struck once again by the association of wells and springs with miracles. The power seems to reside in the Earth! We walked the lovely lawns along the lake at Capernaum and took a boat trip across the water, during which my mother leaned over to me and suggested with a wink that I try walking on it.

Capernaum is rich with miracles. When Jesus left Nazareth because he was not recognized or accepted there, he went to Capernaum and made it his base. Here, he healed Peter's mother-in-law, the centurion's servant, the crippled man, two blind men, and Jarius' daughter, among others. He preached in the synagogue. Eventually, however, he cursed the city for its lack of hospitality. He was human, after all, and we can assume he didn't spend every second in higher consciousness.

One afternoon, Father Joe said Mass in the garden on the Mount where Jesus gave his famous sermon. He focused his homily on the blessings that Christ gave there, particularly the one for the "poor in spirit." I couldn't help but think of our modern world—so superficial, mundane and materialistic, governed by fear and greed, lost in its rational brain, with too many of its people cut off from the bounty of faith. Myself among them. Poor in spirit, if nothing else. And yet these too, according to scripture, would inherit the Kingdom. The Gospel, Christ's "good news," is that we are *all* saved. Indeed, we were never lost. Our own thinking has kept us lost in an illusion. It may take good karma and a few life cycles, or perhaps many lifetimes, but we are *saved* nonetheless!

In his best-selling book, *The Seat of the Soul*, Gary Zukav speaks of the law of karma as an "impersonal energy dynamic."[1] Unfortunately, he claims, we too often take this dynamic personally as a result of our interactions with life. This leads us either to anger or depression when we suffer what appear to be injustices. Christ seemed to say that there would be an end to this cycle.

---

1. Gary Zukov, *The Seat of the Soul* (New York: Fireside, 1990), p. 127.

It is empowering to think that we ourselves have some control over how we will experience the ascension process. But, although I wanted to hold on to the sense of the sacred I felt as I traveled through Israel, I have always found it difficult to maintain a consistent faith.

I seemed to be living in an ironic "Catch-22." If I hadn't believed, would I be seeing what I was seeing? Was it belief that made my visions visible? Was it belief that created them? It was not imagination. These visions were not something I could call up or erase at will. Without faith—the willingness to risk faith—the visions would be obscured. Of that, I was certain. But I had only recovered my faith in desperation. I remembered that I had threatened God, Goddess, the Powers that Be, by saying: "Dammit, if you want me here then you're going to have to make me want to be here. " I had begged for my depression to be lifted. But what of the position of skeptics who held to their skepticism? How will they ever *see*?

Perhaps it is only a matter of belief—of being willing to suspend the limitations of our customary senses and be open to seeing in an another way. I found my mind going round and round, for I couldn't prove anything. I could only believe. I even felt guilty that I had been given my own proof. But why me? Was humankind really recovering original powers that had been lost through a metaphorical fall? Here, on Earth, in one of the most war-ridden, karma-loaded parts of the world, the blessing did not escape me. Even the poor in spirit are loved.

In the still, mild late-afternoon air of Capernaum, one of our group, a lovely red-haired Italian woman, sang a gorgeous "Ave Maria" while we received communion. I returned to my stone bench and watched a bird light on the makeshift altar as everyone clapped for Father Joe—a regular Saint Francis himself! *This* I vowed to remember.

MOUNT TABOR

When we left Capernaum, we head for Mount Tabor. On the way, we passed through Magdala and I was extremely disappointed that we did not stop there. During Christ's time, Magdala was an important city known for its fleet. This was Mary Magdalen's birthplace. I thought to myself that the very meaning of her name, "the tower," indicates the power that Mary gained as a disciple. In the tarot, the Tower is struck by lightning, an image that intrigues me on several levels: the destruction of the Gnostic message by the Petrine church, and the opening of the crown chakra and the final revelation of rising kundalini energy. Both meanings, though opposed, seem accurate.

As the road up Mount Tabor was too narrow for our bus, we took cabs from the small village of Daburieh (my own namesake!) up to where the prophetesses Deborah and Barak commanded the armies of Israel against the Canaanites (Judges 4:6). The mountain is 1600 feet high and the ride up the curvy S-turns of the road caused my mother and me to laugh hysterically as we flew into each other in the back seat while dust poured in the open windows and the wind ravaged our hair. The Palestinian driver seemed determined to give us a ride we would never forget. At the top, we disembarked unsteadily, composed ourselves, and marveled at the view. Of course, we knew of the mountain's other—*New* Testament—significance as the site of the Transfiguration, when Jesus chose to show himself to James, John, and Peter in all his "glory" (light body), with Moses and Elijah suspended in the air. As we stood at the summit, I once again closed my eyes and was swept into vortices of light. The moment felt so numinous, I eventually wrote a poem about it, as if I myself had been transfigured. The poem served as a safe vehicle for my experience. When I wrote it, I felt that I could not speak aloud about the moment. Poems are often an effort to capture subjective magic, and here the transformative medium of poetry served me well.

Transfiguration at Mount Tabor

Matthew 17:1-8

Dizzy from the Palestinian taxi,
above the bowl of sanded vistas,
my mother and I recalled how Jesus
took Peter, John and James
and walked the twists of this very mountain
stepping into the sky,

dazzling the disciples
with his altered state—hair haloed,
robe kindled in gold, and how Moses
and Elijah stepped out to either side
of the fan of flames,

so that three men made of light
spoke as if on a street-corner
leaning on lampposts—

while the witnesses gaped . . .
Peter babbling on about pitching tents
for their unexpected guests . . .

*

My mother stood a long time
in her imagined sins, pages
of her prayer book leafing in the breeze,
while I moved deeper in through the weight
of my body, then out beyond
the mountain's crest. Fixed
on the point of a sword-like cloud,
I walked the plank of my own
unorthodox belief
and I did not scold myself

for the thought that I was part
of God. I went spinning out and out,
leaving my head and trunk
on the escarpment, went out and back
to the prelapsarian ungendered *All.*
For several seconds I was *gone* . . .

Afterwards, I kept silent, told no one,
because when Moses and Elijah left
the radiant vapor of their cloud,
Christ returned to his own dense flesh
and said to his stunned friends:
Tell No One What You've Seen This Day

as they followed him through scrub
and haze all afternoon, hiking
back down the lilied footpath of Tabor
and on to supper with the others
in the blue breadbasket of Jezreel.

Jezreel is the largest valley in Israel, spanning the Galilee mountains and the mountains of Samaria in the south. It abounds in regional trees—olive and oak, pine and willow—with exotic biblical flowers of saffron and pomegranate, rose and rue, and the herbs of mustard and myrrh, mint and mandrake. I think the view from this mountain and the state of awe that I felt standing at its summit were among my most treasured moments in the Holy Land.

JERUSALEM AND JERICHO

During our second week in Israel, we stayed, I'm sorry to say, in the Jerusalem Holiday Inn. The view from our room was not nearly as scenic as the one in Tiberias, although we could see the golden Dome of the Rock, that gorgeous and controversial mosque. From here, we took several long day trips south through the Judean Desert to sites along the Dead Sea. I was continually struck by the poverty of the Palestinians and the Bedouins, who still live in caves. We passed outposts of tarped and tented hovels, clotheslines strung with colorful rags, burnt-out car carcasses, and always a plethora of barefoot children running and waving.

Ahmal, our bus driver, stopped so we could take some pictures of the strange moonlike landscape. Out of nowhere, several Bedouin boys came running up to me, pulling at my skirt and asking for money. When I gave them a few shekels, they burst into tears, crying, "Dollah, dollah! " I had to smile at their selectivity. Who was it who said that "beggars can't be choosers"? Feeling like an exploitative American, I promised them "dollah" if they would pose for a picture. As I focused my camera, a shepherd and his dozen or so sheep moved in the dusty distance. Otherwise, there was nothing between us and the horizon on either side—just rock and craggy yellow mountains with ledges and deep holes amid cavernous drops. I assumed these young boys had come from somewhere in this vast emptiness. I've been to the deserts of the southwestern United States, but this is a different landscape entirely. Now, years later, I shudder at the fact that these very boys, provoked by the circumstances of their poverty and envy, may have grown up to become suicide bombers or militant radicals.

We stopped again at the Mount of Temptation, where Jesus is thought to have confronted Satan. Although no one knows the exact spot, a sixth-century church now sits over the cave where, it is said, Christ stayed during his forty-day fast. My many conversations with Gerry as St. John had given me a different, perhaps "Jungian," reading of that temptation. In my version, it is his own all-too-human egoic fear that Christ encounters in his retreat. He knew it was the ego that he had to overcome; transcending this byproduct of his humanity was his real challenge. Moved by the astonishing landscape, I composed another poem that imagines that confrontation.

The Shadow of the Valley

First night with no moon. Heat so deep
it sucks a Bedouin oasis. Dead Sea,
perfectly still where Jesus stands.

Snake-oil spokesman for illusion, Satan
paces behind him. *You can be richer, stronger—*
It's us against them, he says and Jesus
lets him talk awhile, even listens.
The breath scalds, a smoke of moths—

he's not above his shadow's fears,
weeps at the vision, Jerusalem villas
and courtyards burning, the garrison looting,
skewering children. And he knows *Satan*
wants him weak when he offers Caesar's kingdom.

So when Christ looks down, his sorrow dangles
over limestone, fashioning the city out of air—
Lately wavelengths with the other world
have been erratic, channels jammed,
currents crossed and that image of a crucifix,
nothing he cares to look at. The demon laughs,

sputum flies, brush fires brew where it lands
and rodents gallop—*You're not real*
unless I say so, Jesus answers.
And Satan flares his bat cape, spinning
off the parapet, to fall like dust
on Jesus's sandal. Like ash and bone
spaded by sun. Sulfurous scent

of storm and wires shorting out—
Christ stumbles on his shelf of shale,
whispers *Be Gone—my troubled twin,*
my withered angel, lost semblable,
forgiving
the dark part of himself.

✻

Jericho lies below Jerusalem, some 3000 feet into the sun-parched region of the Jordan valley. It lies between Jerusalem and the Dead Sea, the lowest place on Earth—1300 feet below sea level. Jericho is among the oldest known places on the planet. Objects excavated there have been dated as far back as 7000 B.C. Many of our group wanted to see the place in the Jordan River where Christ was baptized by John, reputed to be about five miles east of the town. (How can they know where that is? I asked myself. Didn't Heraclitus say you can't step in the same spot of the river twice?)

The River Jordan is, of course, famous in the Old Testament as the body of water the Israelites crossed with Joshua. In any case, our driver Emile informed us that the location lay in territory known as "No Man's Land," an area made off-limits for both Jews and Jordanians in a border settlement. We could look across the river to Jordan, which was a good deal greener. Still, Emile pointed out the strafed trees and blasted plants that were testimony to the war that had raged there.

So we stepped into the Jordan River at the only point to which we had access—a tourist trap replete with soda merchants and camera shops. I watched as many of the group waded in to scoop up the healing water. Mom and I had brought a couple of cosmetic containers and empty water bottles. I strolled into the cool green water, lifting my skirt to mid-thigh, to fill the containers with liquid I could throw on my face during hard times in the future. Someone began to sing a sort of gospel hymn and, for the moment, it seemed right. I was willing to give this a nod. Maybe the pure faith of the people around me set it up, but there was energy there. I felt a little like a barometer, tuning in with my eyes closed. We snacked at an outdoor café overlooking the river and, from there, went on to Qumran, a most significant parcel of ruins asleep in its small capsule of sacred time that spoke to me with an intensity I couldn't have anticipated.

QUMRAN

The scriptorium ruins at Qumran may be where the Dead Sea Scrolls originated. It was founded in the second century B.C.E. by the Essenes, a mystical Jewish cult. Mary, Joseph, and Jesus were all said to be members of this cult. After much research, I have come to believe that the occult teachings of man's divinity were transmitted to this cult from Egypt and carried forth to Gaul after Christ's death.

The Essenes left Jerusalem for the desert to live a quiet life of study, meditation, reflection, and prayer. They took vows of poverty and charity. Josephus called their lives Communities to Perfection. At some point before the great Roman destruction of Jerusalem in 70 A.D., the Essenes hid their most valuable possession, seven scrolls of scripture, in clay vases in the caves of the overhanging cliffs somewhere to the west of the Dead Sea. Most of the cult was massacred by the Romans under Titus.

The community center at Qumran was excavated in the 1950s. Objects like ceramic bowls, clay writing tablets, and desk-like tables and benches were uncovered. What's left of the structure is the outline of a few rooms, stone seats, and tables. It appears that part of the community may have lived underground inside the Earth Mother. The ruins are surrounded on three sides by a vast and empty desert with one view toward the Dead Sea. The scrolls that were found there speak of a battle between Darkness and Light that was anticipated to be close at hand. Some reflect Egyptian beliefs in the transmigration of souls and the sacred mysteries of death and rebirth. Is it not significant that these scrolls were found within two years of the Gnostic gospels, just fifty years before the start of a new millennium?

The Essenes appear to have strong links to the Western mystical traditions that were condemned as heresies in Medieval Europe. Three years after my trip to the Holy Land, when I traveled to see the Black Madonnas of France, I came across legends that link surviving Essenes to southern France as forerunners of later Celtic communities connected to the Grail stories, some of which are French in origin.

At Qumran, I was more emotionally moved than in any other place in Israel. I loved the remains of the room known to be the scriptorium, and effortlessly imagined the white-robed figures of the Brotherhood of Light writing on parchment and hide. When I closed my eyes, I was swept once again into visions of tunnels, then underground walls with figures in white robes appearing from hallways and turning corners only to disappear again.

I felt the numinosity of the place and half-consciously began picking up stones and putting them in my pockets. I brought the stones home with me because I wanted to hold on to a piece of that special place. I was so attracted to it that I enlarged a snapshot I took of the ruins—a few steps by a water cistern—and framed it for my mantelpiece. It's just a small and simple picture in an inexpensive frame, but I'm drawn to pray whenever I gaze at it. When John later confirmed that I had lived a past life as an Essene in the time of Christ, I understood why I was so moved.

From Qumran, we went farther south to the Dead Sea itself. The bizarre world we crossed was once the bottom of the ocean. We drove over a kind of moonscape—truly God's country, bumpy and rocky, dried and deserted—until we came upon a beach resort and disembarked to do the traditional mud-smearing and bathing in the saltiest water in the world. However, neither my mother or I could stand it. My legs burned as soon as I waded in, and I spent the next twelve hours lathering them with expensive Dead Sea cream to kill an insidious itch. Yet many of our group swam, including Father Joe, who bobbed about like a buoy on top of the salt. Nothing lives in this water and the idea that it has salubrious qualities is amazing to me. Despite its incredibly high concentration of calcium chloride, magnesium, sodium, and potassium, I wanted no part of it. I kept thinking instead of that curious community of Essenes and the mysterious peace I felt there among the stones.

MASADA

Our last day trip was to the Fortress of Masada, the site of a heroic stand by the 900 Jews who took refuge there against the Romans. Once a retreat for powerful Romans, the site was fortified in 40 B.C.E. by Herod the Great as a stronghold against Mark Anthony. The summit itself is huge—two and half miles long—and cut out of the mountains some 2000 feet above sea level. The Jewish leader Elazar Ben Yair and his patriots captured the fortress from the Roman army in a surprise attack in 70 A.D. The Roman General Silva then surrounded the fort with eight military encampments whose outlines are still visible in the sand today. Masada is now known as a noble shrine to the 900 Jews who committed mass suicide there rather than surrender to Silva and become Roman slaves.

Josephus tells of the last days of the Jewish survivors. When Silva's armies surrounded the stone structure, the 900 held out as long as possible then divided into groups of ten. Each group cast lots to choose an executioner. The executioners then regrouped and continued the ritual killing until only one remained. This last survivor checked to confirm that the entire community was dead, then set fire to the fortress and threw himself on his own sword. When the Romans finally stormed the walls, they found nothing but the charred remains of bodies.

The fortress itself is difficult to reach. We had to take a cable car to get up to it—not unlike a scary ride at an amusement park. We went in groups of four. My mother elected not to go, as there was still climbing even once we left the cable car. Here too, half-consciously, I picked up rocks thinking I would give them to my Jewish friends at home, feeling the intensity of pressure in the air and around my body. I expected to see ghosts but, when I closed my eyes, I was once again lost in the labyrinthian stone underground. It wasn't so much that I wondered whether I had had a life here, as that I suddenly understood that there really was no such thing as Catholic or Jew or Essene or Muslim or Roman or anything else. We are all connected. We had all probably had lives as members of these communities. I couldn't bear to think of the intolerance that rends this country and the ignorance of those who cannot believe beyond one lifetime. These are the unfortunates who give in to cycles of vengeance and hatred.

Emile, who had quizzed us in Biblical history throughout the long bus rides, awarding tiny crystals and gemstones for prizes, blasted the song "O Jerusalem!" as we left Masada and headed toward Jerusalem to see the Citadel—the Tower of David that was built by Herod the Great and said to have been spared by Titus in 70 A.D. when the city was razed.

SITE SEEING

We spent the rest of the trip in and around Jerusalem at the many controversial sites within the old walled city—at the temple ruins, the magnificent Wailing Wall, and the large esplanades of the Dome of the Rock. We saw so many sites—the Pool of Bethesda, and churches like Saint Anne's that were built by the Crusaders in the 12th century—that they began to run together in my mind.

I meandered through the Roman triple gate known as the Ecce Homo, named after Pontius Pilate's famous words, "Behold the Man" (though the arch has no real relation to Christ's passion). The arch is actually part of the church of the Sisters of Zion, which is said to house the judgment seat that John speaks of in his gospel as the place where Jesus was tried. In the floor, carved on the paving stones, are the remains of a Roman game, the same game that Matthew and Mark tell us the Roman soldiers played when they gambled for Christ's robe.

We followed the path Christ took with his cross, passing among Arab shopkeepers hawking their wares admidst the wonderfully seductive mid-Eastern music that blared from each kiosk, seeing what we could of the stations that were incorporated into buildings. We visited the Garden Tomb just north of Damascus Gate that is believed to be the place of Christ's burial. I had serious doubts about the authenticity of certain places that were claimed as the actual locations of various stories, and I used my sonar sentience to judge for myself. Here, I half hoped to see Mary Magdalen in the famous *Noli Mi Tangere* scene, but I had no breakthrough visions. So I wrote a poem that gives my own personal perspective on a truth she may have known.

Noli Mi Tangere

There was a presence before the stone.
A pressure so much larger than human
wounds. My mind let go into the crags
of sorrow and I grew
this cavernous heart. It was a tomb
but also a garden. One is the other
always. The spirit rises. The body stays
and blooms. I took him
for the gardener as the roses were wilted
on the lattice near where he stood.
He'd been broken and nailed
but nothing showed. Not one thorn,
not one bruise. The light stunned,
magnetized me while reaching
for his robe. He threw out his arm, a bolt
of lit wires; shocked, I fell back.
I wanted the warmth
of his skin, to rest my head there,
but how removed he was,
glowing from his brow, both palms.
No seams for the ravaged
flesh. The shade of white

on his garment, almost gold
like the air behind his head
when he taught us Truth.
No one dies. No one
ever dies. No one
is alone.

The painters only saw my body
as pulp, pigment and bone, the thick
color of my hair. But I was traveling
without movement, statue-still,
and my head knocked
the sky. His gaze
limbered my knees
and the suns in his eyes burned
through mine. I came to myself
alone, stupefied, not knowing when
he'd gone. And I ran to tell the brothers
we must *choose* belief,
despite the fears which fool
our senses, the fear
which covered Eden up.

*

My mother and I shared many laughs as well as many moments of awe and deep faith on this trip. We were united in our reverence and in the sense that we each had somehow known this world before. Despite my mother's insistence that she "could be no one else," she confirmed in herself a similar familiarity to the one I felt for the country. My visions were not as vivid in Jerusalem as they had been in the Galilee and at Qumran, although the image of the stone walls still persisted.

Although we used Jerusalem as the base for our explorations, I felt I did not get enough of it and wanted to return some day. We did view models of what the city was like at the time of the second temple; its lovely white buildings and intricate layout brought back to me the thought that "the city" was the center of spirituality in the old world. When I think of Jerusalem now, I see the nervous expression on the young Israeli waitress who could not smile and I think about the hungry faces of the Bedouin boys in my picture who must be teenagers now. When I think of the cycle of calamitous events that have occurred since then, I wonder if all these young people are still alive. I wonder if the boys are terrorists.

The last time I was able to close my eyes and see angels was at the airport. I imagine that angels are legion in that weary country, with its long war-ridden history, its caves of secrets and legends. They send what light they can to the troubled people on both sides of the checkpoints. They weep, perhaps, as Christ wept when he foresaw the Roman sacking of Jerusalem. They weep when they see the Holy City as a war zone, the scene of carnage from suicide bombs. They weep because they know—as we all know—that it is not for the last time.

Chapter 16

ROCKY MOUNTAIN HIGH

Once trust began percolating back into the soul again, humans would behold the liberating of those colossal earthly powers that now lie silent under the spell of our bad faith.
CALVIN LUTHER MARTIN, *THE WAY OF THE HUMAN BEING*

As soon as I returned to Boston from Israel, I called Gerry for an appointment to ask John about my Biblical third-eye visions. I drove to Gerry's house west of Boston and entered the usual chaos of his kids and pets. We scooted into his little office off the living room. Whenever Gerry held his crystal and breathed heavily as he went into trance, I loved to look at the photograph of him in his John persona in his long, white, gauzy shirt and pants on top of Mount Shasta the night of the Harmonic Convergence in August 1987. He is standing with his followers on this very sacred mountain in California, on this very special day—a day whose significance I only understood afterward as the opening for, and arrival of, legions of angels bringing the new light photon wave to Earth, the official beginning of the Age of Aquarius. Even his facial expression is different from that of his Gerry persona. On this day, I sat there marveling at the two of them, and the whole idea of the body as a garment for spirit.

When Gerry completed his transformation, John asked to hear my story. He looked blankly up into the air as he always did when reading the Akashic records, trying to answer particular questions about past/parallel lives. Edgar Cayce described the Akashic Records as the recording of every act and event that has ever taken place in time and space on Earth. I always picture these records as being held in the mother of all computers. John turned back to me with raised eyebrows and told me point blank that I had lived three past lives in the Holy Land. One of these, he said, was during the reign of the second Herod, during Christ's ministry. He told me I was a thirty-eight-year-old Essene man named Morab who developed an interest in Jesus' message and followed the crowds to witness his Sermon on the

Mount. I couldn't quite get my mind around the idea that an aspect of me had attended the famous sermon, and I joked with John for a minute, saying I hoped I got plenty of the loaves and fishes.

But when I look back at my experience in Israel, this information seems particularly resonant. I can see it as an explanation for my long love affair with Jesus. I always saw him as nurturing and felt a kinship with his message, especially the beatitudes ("Blessed are the meek, for they shall inherit the earth"), which were spoken in Capernaum. Other women who came of age with me during the Seventies' feminist revolution had problems with Jesus as a masculine figure and many turned to the ancient goddesses instead. But I never had a problem with Jesus being a *man*. To me, he embodied the quintessential feminine characteristics—openness, tolerance and acceptance, the passion of a burning sacred heart. Later, when I had my own encounter with the goddess material, it fit comfortably with my relationship to Christ. I didn't see any necessity to give a gender to the godhead. It is a force, after all, a conscious energy that can take whatever form it chooses.

It was at the Sermon on the Mount that Christ taught the Lord's prayer. Even before I was old enough to understand the concept of microcosm as a reflection of macrocosm, I always felt the protective spell of those words, ". . . *on Earth as it is in heaven.*" Now I realize that heaven on Earth is not impossible to imagine. As Joseph Campbell says in one of his videos on the study of myth, Heaven is *no place.* Heaven is in our consciousness. It is up to us to wake up from ego consciousness, and visualize and create it here. The Dalai Lama, as one of the enlightened, sees through the illusion and says there is only peace in his world. The rest is our illusion. Bloody painful illusion it may be, yes, but don't give it full credence. Help the hungry, clothe the naked, but don't retaliate against the perpetrators of evil. Rather, we must stop the cycle of fear.

I felt most moved in Capernaum and in the desert village of Qumran. I didn't tell John that, yet he confirmed that I was seeing images of a past/parallel life as a male member of the Essene community in Qumran. When I asked about my mother's history in Israel, he said that she had been a Roman centurion in the garrison at Capernaum, but one who was interested in Christ. He said many Romans did become followers. I had to laugh to myself and couldn't wait to tease my good Catholic mother, telling her that she was one of the pagan Romans.

I received further information in a reading I had a few years later with Kurt Leland, whose other personality, Charles, corroborated much of David's information, telling me I was an old soul who had had many down-trodden lives, the result of misusing psychic power. This lifetime, he said, was very much about understanding that human beings do have control over their reality and can work with the creator to realize it. I was content with these explanations, and the information helped me considerably to feel comfortable with my experiences. Even though I still did not really understand *why* I was seeing the visions, I felt the courage of my convictions.

OLD SOULS

I have always felt rootless, as if I could move anywhere and make a life there. I still did not feel I had found my "geographical place" in the world. Actually, it wasn't until my first trip to the Mediterranean at the age of twenty-two that I literally felt that the ground beneath my feet in France and Italy was home. David Hall often told me that I would feel more comfortable in the Southwest where many "old souls" lived. Charles said they also lived in northern New England, parts of California, and near the mountain ranges. I had always loved Maine and was more attached to New England than to New York where I grew up.

In 1998, I finally completed the poetry anthology I was editing and sent it along to the University Press of New England, a consortium of several university presses including Dartmouth and Wesleyan. The book brought together my two major interests—poetry and mythology. I was fascinated by the poetic interplay of human reality and the archetypal forces that Jung identified as vehicles for imaginative transformation. Over the years I worked on *Orpheus & Company*, I spoke to many poets whose work I had solicited. I struck up a correspondence with Mark Irwin, a poet from Denver when I inquired about the area of Durango where he had spent some time. I had fantasies about moving back out West.

At one point in our exchange of notes and letters, Mark invited me to come out to Colorado. He said he had a favorite place to write in a small town called Antonito, about forty miles north of Taos, New Mexico. His good friend, Reyes, owned a ranch there that had belonged to his mother and Mark always had an open invitation. I decided to take Mark up on his offer. I had a spring break in March and would go to the ranch to rest and write. I didn't think about where I would get the money to travel and worried a little about it all ending up on a credit card, but this particular trip beckoned to me uncannily. After all, I had a place to stay for free. And then I remembered that my dear and generous college friend, Camilla, had offered her frequent-flyer miles "anytime before the end of the year." I have been so blessed with my group of college friends. We see each other regularly, despite the forty-plus years since our graduation in 1970. We even joke about being buried together! One phone call and I had free plane fare as well.

I had never met Mark, but had read his three books and surmised that the individual who wrote such beautiful, heartfelt, and tender poems had to be trustworthy. There's something about poetry that cuts through the fabric of the personality to the real essence of a person, and I had faith in that. I was curious about him and pleased at his open-handed gesture.

When I arrived in Denver that mid-March afternoon, snow flurries were whiting out the landscape. Mark had suggested I take one of the shuttles to a nearby hotel lobby, where he would meet me. I piled into the very crowded shuttle and closed my eyes for a brief meditation. Right away, I knew something was happening again with my third eye. Not that I had expected anything new. Yet the West was a complete surprise.

In the shuttle bus, leaving the boonies where the Denver airport sits, the volume of whooshing and buzzing around my head was so intense that I had to close my eyes. I was catapulted immediately through the eye looking back at me, through the arches and vortices where I slowly identified a new scene—one of scrubby mountainsides, hills and rocky passageways, a distinct old "cowboy movie" landscape with arroyos and mesas. Very slowly, I discerned some figures walking single file along a pass. As they came into view, I recognized them as indigenous characters. It was a winter scene, with snow on the ground and heavy garments packed around the bodies of both male and female figures, three or four of whom carried a canoe. The view spun around and faded in and out.

The experience itself was very similar to the one I had had a year earlier in Israel. I thought to myself, "Okay, I 've been summoned here to experience something again." I pondered how the trip had come together so easily and wondered if there were some connection between going to specific geographical places where I may have had other lives and the alignment of the energies David was always talking about. My claire-sentience had picked up changes in the atmosphere when I was in Port Townsend two years earlier on my writing fellowship, but that had only been a *feeling*—a sense of the energy fields becoming denser. I had experienced no visions there. But, in Colorado, I suspected there was a hidden reason for my visit.

I recognized Mark from his picture on the back cover of his most recent book. A slim, handsome, serious-looking man who appeared to be in his early forties. He appeared to be looking for someone, so I approached him to introduce myself. We exchanged a slightly awkward hello, dragged my bags outside to his Ranger, and drove to his house outside of Denver. There, I met his lovely partner, a beautiful artist and elementary school teacher named Lisa. She did not have the week off, but Mark and I were free to take the six-hour drive the next morning down to the ranch in Antonito. I had a photo he had sent me of the ranch on my refrigerator, the stucco structure awash in a sea of Southwestern colors—burnt sienna and teal shining beneath an afternoon sun. I was anxious to see those colors, realizing they might tint my third-eye view.

From our conversation at dinner the previous night, I gathered that Mark knew a number of very successful poets, and that he was an intellectual critic as well as a poet. I was delighted that he praised my anthology, saying more than once that there were many thematic anthologies, but that mine was "classical" and a substantial contribution to the tradition. *The Harvard Review* had called it "an important book," and I was quite pleased that it had already earned some respect. We swapped stories about other poets we'd met, about art and music, and about our personal histories. Both of us were without secure tenured jobs and commiserated about the politics of academic institutions. Mark had a Ph.D. and four books to his credit—or nearly so, as his latest was due out in a few months. He had, at one point, actually quit a tenure-track teaching job to move to the mountains. He had lived in Eastern Europe and been the recipient of awards and fellowships. He often had semester-long appointments as a visiting poet at various universities.

Before we left for Antonito, Mark amused me with his domestic obsession. He was enthused about growing wheat grass and making juice from it, describing all the salubrious properties of his homemade drink and making sure he brought enough for the duration of our travels. He chopped the mass in a food processor and swore by it as a miracle drink. Just the color of it made me turn green and I declined a sip as he transferred it to the thermos. But somehow the obsession immediately endeared him to me.

Throughout the ride to southern Colorado, I periodically turned my head away from Mark and closed my eyes to see if the Native Americans were there. I must admit that I was amazed, as we drove through the Colorado landscape, at the specificity and accuracy of detail of my own inner landscape. I recognized the Western mountainscape from the terrain of my own visions. Although, in Israel, my visions had been vividly colored, more on the scale of a grand spectacle, my visions in Colorado were greyish-green, as if displayed on an early Fifties black-and-white TV.

What was remarkable was the movement—streams flowing and winds waving across foliage that parted as if a comb swept through it. The scenes kept blurring in and out of focus and kaleidoscoping into different close-ups. Seasons seemed to change from one scene to the next. I saw a stream and some young Indian men fishing, then the scene blurred, wafted off into spinning lines, and opened into another panorama of an Indian village or men on horseback. The views were "shot" from a bird's-eye view, as if I were holding a movie camera and flying over geometrically shaped sections of land like the pieces in a child's puzzle. I had all I could do to act natural.

Mark had an itinerary planned out. He wanted to do some cross-country skiing and hiking, and we stopped at several points to climb and walk. The temperature during the day sometimes rose as high as 75 degrees in the mountains, although during the night, it went down into the thirties. Our first stop was in between two mountain ranges—the Sangre de Cristo to the east and the San Juan range to the west. Mark wanted to show me Ohaver Lake just south of Monarch pass. He was very thorough in his preparations and reminded me several times to bring sunscreen and layered clothing. He also appeared annoyed that I didn't bring a camera. Actually, I didn't have a camera, but I felt as if I were behind one when I closed my eyes. As breathtaking as the mountain paths were, I was more intrigued by my inner scene.

At one point, Mark went on ahead of me. When I was alone, I sat down on a rock and shut my eyes to follow my own internal scenes of indigenous people. Again, they varied. Sometimes Native Americans rowed in canoes, sometimes they walked. At times, it was as if I were a director, panning across an encampment complete with teepees and smoking fires. Just as in Israel, there were pearly-white spinning circles that eventually formed transparent figures that I can only call "spirits." My body felt the density of the field delivering its pressure, along with minor electric shocks.

I remembered the figure of the big Chief who had appeared in my bedroom several years before. I had even seen him with my eyes open on a few mornings as I awoke. He had come more than once, but had finally stopped appearing. David claimed that one of my guides was a Native American. But truthfully, I didn't especially relate to Native American spirituality. My friend Ellen has done many Native American retreats. She has experienced sweat lodges and the like. And to her credit, she actually went off into the Mojave Desert by herself on two separate vision quests, fasting for four days and consuming nothing but water. Her spirit animal came to her and her connections to nature deepened. I had always been interested in her studies. She taught me about the medicine wheel and the symbolism of the directions, but the American Indian tradition did not feel like home to me. Perhaps I had had only one life as a Native American, since I always felt more European.

Yet here in Colorado, the visions made me aware of the historic land in the same way I had been made aware of it in Israel. I kept thinking of the ground itself—the *soil* beneath my feet and the historic imprints it held. Perhaps I had once been a white man with an attitude of entitlement, of "manifest destiny."

DOORS OF PERCEPTION

Rupert Sheldrake speaks of "morphic resonance" as a material phenomenon that holds the spirits of memory. The great shame and tragedy of the Western expansion in the United States—the almost total eradication of the Native American tribes, their nature-oriented religions and communal values—kept crossing my mind. Somehow, despite the destruction of a whole way of life, some of the wisdom of the spiritual relationship between humankind and the land, the Shamanistic practices, the medicine and magic, had been preserved and passed down. I wanted to learn more.

Several years later, in 2001, I happened upon a remarkable book, *The Way of the Human Being*, by Calvin Luther Martin. Martin, a former professor of History at Rutgers University, engaged in studies of Native Americans that so affected his life that he left his teaching post and moved into indigenous communities in Alaska and the Adirondacks. Living among these native tribes, he wrote their stories. Many of these tales inhabit other realities—realities that defy Newtonian physics and the world of otherness that "civilized" man has created. His work has brought him into quantum physics and the theory that matter and energy "shapeshift" from one state to the other, that we co-create our world with universal forces.

Martin calls this process "superposition," the potentiality of many states co-existing at one time and place. These superimposed potentials, he claims, account for the mythic presence in the stories of indigenous peoples. Martin weaves the ideas of physicists like MIT's Alan Lightman and Princeton physics professor John Archibald Wheeler into his discussion, quoting Wheeler as someone who sees that "the mind asking the questions" affects its own experiments: "In some strange sense," Wheeler concludes, "this is a participatory universe."[1]

Martin, like many mystics, goes on to speculate that the universe is not outside of us. Drawing on Wheeler's article, "Bohr, Einstein, and the Strange Lesson of the Quantum," he underscores the mutual interaction between humankind and the world.

> Mankind, it seems, has an unavoidable role in creating the reality of the universe. There was a time, continues Wheeler, when scientists imagined the universe as something outside them . . . "without personal involvement."[2]

In an earlier era, in a time when humans lived with a greater respect for and understanding of the plant and animal worlds, Martin maintains that "Grace" abounded and that some indigenous people knew how to mine the universe, "always in the strange reality of the Gift." He quotes Wheeler, whom Alan Lightman has called "the greatest living expositor of quantum physics," wondering if, at this distance from the determinism of Newton's laws, we are destined in the future to recognize the theory of superposition: "And on the way, (will we) all say to one another, 'Oh how simple' and 'How stupid we all were!' and 'How could it have been otherwise?'"[3]

Quantum physicists' "String Theory," or the "Unified Theory of Everything," as a *Nova* program called it, posits that we may live in a membrane surrounded by parallel universes inside higher dimensions. In this theory, "strings" of experience vibrate in patterns like the strings of a cello or a violin. These physicists theorize that the Big Bang stretched the fabric of space and that layers of reality may be piled up in "super symmetry." They speak of electromagnetic forces that could be *1,000,000,000,000, 000,00 0,000,000,000,000,000,000,000* (Thirty-nine zeros!) times stronger than gravity. Teams of physicists in the United States and in Italy are currently working competitively to prove this "Mystery, Magic, Matrix, Mother of all Theories."[4] Using atom smashers, they accelerate electronic particles and

---

1. Calvin Luther Martin, *The Way of the Human Being* (New Haven & London: Yale University Press, 1999), p. 91.
2. Martin, *The Way of the Human Being*, p. 91.
3. Martin, *The Way of the Human Being*, pp. 86, 96.
4. Brian Greene, *The Elegant Universe*, Hour 2, Nova PBS.

collide them at high speeds, causing them to release what they call a "vanishing graviton." Martin concludes that some Native American philosophy is contained in a "paleolithic mythology" that recognizes the shape-shifting potential of matter or mass as an energy field. Brian Greene's book, *The Elegant Universe*, explores this possibility, which may help explain some of my own experiences. Was I seeing through "worm holes" as I "ranged" from one dimension to another?

This idea recalls Sheldrake's "morphic resonance." Mystics would agree that *all that is* is interconnected. In his explorations and conversations among the depressed and highly alcoholic people who are the descendants of a culture previously in harmony with nature, Martin discovers a connection between contemporary physics and the remnants of aboriginal American religions whose adherents have, to a lamentable degree, lost their powers because they have lost their *belief* in these powers. Yet some remain intact:

> Witness the perception of Uncle Bul, a contemporary Australian aboriginal elder who declares that he can tell "where the animals are by dreaming them. He joins his dreams to theirs." In his trance visions he sees the animals in their spiritual rather than physical forms "hanging on a web of *intersecting threads*". Other elders say "they perceive the animal ancestors as *fields of resonance or vibration*"—as a kind of music.[5]

I italicize the phrases above because they are made up of words I might have chosen to describe what I feel sentiently in my own conscious visions. In discussing superposition, Martin stresses the "non-locality" of matter. *Many dimensions, many mansions, superposition, super symmetry.* Like the mystic poet Rumi, Martin sees that on some level we are all one . . . all *love*.

> The message is riveting and is fundamental to our own cherished religious tradition: offering a civilization strangled by fear, measuring everything in fear, the "chance to love everything."[6]

By the time I happened upon Martin's beautiful book, I was already convinced that the phenomena I continued to experience—my perceptions, these fields from a past that is not actually "the past"—were either adjacent

---

5. Martin, *The Way of the Human Being*, p. 99.
6. Martin, *The Way of the Human Being*, p. 107.

or overlaying energy fields. If, as quantum physics tells us, the energy of scientists or observers of experiments affects the results, can it not also be true that any belief held firmly and clearly will have the same power?

Sheldrake talks about collective memory stored, not in genes of organisms, but in fields. Therefore, these so-called "past/parallel lives" I was seeing through my forehead were not necessarily mine; they could be more of an attunement to the memory of a place. Just as Jung believed that evolution is an ongoing process, it appears that the universe itself is conscious. Many of us are intentionally changing—can change and will change—our reality on this planet by affirmation and visualization. I believe that what the psychic poet William Blake called the "doors of perception" open as we inhabit the belief that they will. I believe that the sacredness of our environment, this Earth, can speak to us, just as developing intuition allows our bodies to speak to us. We are returning to the laws of magic, which is really just the changing of consciousness at will, a holistic harmonious way of being human. Our excursion into the faithless, rational, left-brained incarceration we have imposed on our species and on civilization, our belief in separation from our true source, and our lack of unity with one another has run its course. It is already over for many awakening souls alive in the present. As John told the Healing Group: "There's only one of us here!"

ANTONITO

Mark and I couldn't get to the lake that day, as the path was closed. He was especially disappointed, but I was so overcome by my newest visions that I didn't mind at all—although, once again, as in Israel, I felt compelled to keep my secret. The road trip with Mark took us to another wonderful spot owned by his friends, an area known as "Love Ranch." This is a gorgeous glade of mountaintop cabins, falls, and streams below Mount Antero near Chalk Creek Canyon. Mark told me Chief Antero, for whom the mountain was named, had been a peacemaker between the white settlers and his own people. Here at Love Ranch, we wandered through a cluster of a dozen little log cabins with amazing views.

We peered in the windows at the cozy fireplaces and blanketed beds. Mark showed me some photos of his parents, who had rented a cabin only last year. He was still grieving from the death of his father just a month or so earlier. While Mark loaded up some jugs with the fresh mountain water, I walked around in the woods, again checking in with the morphic fields.

The resonance was as strong as I'd ever felt it. The whooshing sounds in my head were a kind of low hum—the music of the spheres. Poets have always known that language and sound are sacred, the *word* itself an opening to infinite possibilities. I was determined to write something that could describe the sense of altered reality I was feeling. I searched continually for the right words.

Back in the car, I drew Mark into a conversation about his father that led me to share some thoughts on life after death. I talked about my own father and the long poem I'd written about his death and afterlife. Soon, I was telling him about my Jungian studies, the occult traditions I had studied, and my interest in dream work. Mark then told me about an old man who had cured Mark's back ailment by the laying on of stones. I could see from his interest in herbs and his healthy "wheat-grass juice" that he was open to what we call alternative thinking. I found the combination of his interests delightfully paradoxical. On one hand, he was extremely intellectual and very opinionated about literature—especially about what constituted good poetry—and I respected the authority in his voice. Yet he had this other quirky side that came out in his relationship with nature. He was much more open-minded than I thought he might be toward my own interests in the occult and white magic. I thought to myself that perhaps there was hope for the academics and intellectuals after all!

When we arrived at the Reyes' ranch in Antonito, it was close to nightfall and very cold. The population of the little town was largely Latino, and appeared to be living in obvious poverty. But at the spacious ranch just outside the town, the house was lovely and well kept. There was a wood stove for heat, and Mark told me to set up my mattress about a foot away from it on the floor while he took a back bedroom. I have had a lot of experience with wood stoves and fire building, but he was amusingly particular about how the fire should be made and I let him handle it. The house itself was big and old and comfortable, a regular Ponderosa with a homey kitchen. Wonderful Mexican candelabras and colorful pottery bedecked the many shelves and counters. Interesting books and journals lay piled on every surface of the family rooms.

Reyes, a philosophy professor who taught in Durango, was attending a weekend retreat at a place called "Jesus in the Desert." How fitting, I thought and I vowed to go find it myself someday! Just looking through his books made me feel a kinship with the spirit of the house. It was obvious that he was concerned with soul work and the house was one of the most soulful places I've ever entered. I felt so grateful to Mark, and yet I also felt that some other agent beyond Mark had engineered my visit. I felt the same peace of mind that I had had during my month in Port Townsend two years before. Most of all, I loved how the light purled through the many king-size windows in the daytime. It was as if the sun were white instead of yellow, its radiant light in keeping with the house's provenance.

Chapter 17

THE ORACLE OF THE BODY

*. . . the whole idea of morphic resonance is that
the past is potentially present everywhere and that you
can gain access to it by resonating with it.*
RUPERT SHELDRAKE, *COMMON GROUND JOURNAL* SUMMER 1997

Obviously a morning guy, Mark awakened me each day with a kind
of "up and at 'em" attitude. I, on the other hand, am not a morning
person. I needed coffee to get going, but Mark did not drink coffee and
infrequently drank alcohol. I insisted he take me to town to get my own
poisons, however. I like my decaf coffee and, on vacation, I like my evening
wine. At first, I felt as if I were corrupting him, but it was not too difficult
to get him to join me for some wine. Each evening after dinner, we had ice
cream, talked about writing, and listened to Mark's favorite Mahler CD.
As the stringed instruments filled the room, I felt a kinship with Mark,
the comfortable couch, the pictures on the wall, the spiritual magazines,
and the photos of Reyes and his children, as if, in the depths of the music,
there were some kind of correspondence with the house's past.

We separated during the day to do our work. Mark was wrestling with
a long poem and obsessing somewhat over his newest book. I was still struggling with the "father poem" and where and how to fit it into my current
poetry manuscript. I wrote some straight descriptive poems about the landscape I could see out the living room window, but didn't feel overly moved
by any of them until I began a poem that included my visions. I needed to
speak about the mystery taking place within me.

We both took frequent walks around the fields, and my poem came
from these walks, from the contact of my boots with the dirt. Reyes leased
the land to some ranchers and it was calving season, so there were a lot of
new calves struggling awkwardly to stand. I watched groups of them from

afar and listened to the lowing. I never thought that mooing could be so sonorous, so soothing. I'd take a few steps, stop, and, with my Buddha eyelids, scan the fields. It felt important to listen as well. To close my eyes and see within how the listening seemed to coax the visions into view.

Mark was very concerned for the wild cats that were undernourished and living in the barn. Coyotes prowled at night and would find them excellent prey. We bought cat food when we were in town and he fixed them delicious meals with some of our left-over salmon. The cats were both skinny and skittish, and Mark spent a good deal of time peeking out of windows and around doors to see if they responded to his offerings. He was extremely sensitive to natural creatures and I found this very tender and compassionate side of him touching. Although I am not a cat person, I liked watching him watch the cats.

And he was quite the fastidious guide for sightseeing. When we were out, he instructed me to "climb up that hill and look at that gulch." Even when it was my night to play chef, he definitely expressed his preferences, telling me how to cut the eggplant! I chose to be amused by his "orders" and kept thinking how strange it was that I was here with this very serious man about whom I really didn't know very much. I wanted to coax out his silly side and lighten him up, but, occasionally, it bubbled up on its own. It was evident from his very winning smile that he was easier to get to know than I had first surmised, and that what sometimes sounded like gruff instruction was really only an expression of his concern for details.

In the evenings, the stars were incredible. I thought of them as little decimals of time sprinkled into the transparent mesh of the infinite sky. I had seen many New England starry nights, but never star power quite like this. I wrote several drafts of a poem describing the skies. The dark canopy behind the stars seemed to me so black that, if you stared long enough, it would bleed into maroon. I could trace the networks pasted on its surface, as if the stars were strung together like lights on a Christmas tree. The more we looked, the more hallucinatory the whole cyclorama became, as if it had a certain mass. Mark had a star guidebook and we turned it upsidedown and sideways under the flashlight, trying to read the constellations. I cared less about them than I did about the energy that was pulsing there, so many light-years away. And yet I could feel it, almost rhythmically, the whole breathing spectrum, as if it were in my body.

I saw the night as a linkage of wine-red fingers and indigo arms lifted ever so slightly off black velvety walls, so that there were multiple darknesses of different densities, dimensions, and depths. It was as if we could catch the star-song as a tuning fork catches a timbre. I thought that, if we could only be quiet enough, we might hear the same vibratory canticle tissuing deep in our ears, the same cello hum of those strings that make up the eternal OHM—the intake and outlet of God's breath, as it is said. There was magic here, both inside and outside this house—a natural consciousness in the landscape both above and below our physical bodies. Macrocosm and microcosm.

DOWNLOADING FROM THE ANCESTORS

We took a day trip to Taos, which was somewhat crowded with tourists, but lovely nonetheless with its dusty roads and upscale shops. And in the old hotel where he used to stay during his time in the Southwest, we just happened upon a wonderful exhibit of paintings by that scandalous literary lion D. H. Lawrence! There were framed newspaper clippings from the early part of the century written by journalists who felt the paintings were pornographic and shocking. The pieces themselves were mostly realistic, wildly colorful nudes. Big bare-breasted women sketched in postures not dissimilar to Gauguin's Polynesian ladies. As I recall, there were several paintings of couples, indicating some tension beneath the attractions—that ever insoluble conflict or power struggle between the sexes—that is so much Lawrence's subject and trademark.

Often, in my own judgment, the phallic symbols were a little too obvious in the background and Mark agreed with a chuckle. But we were both impressed and surprised that Lawrence was a good visual artist—an amazingly multitalented man, one who was not afraid in his writings to ponder the mysteries between a man and a woman's sexuality at a time when American censorship standards were rigid. Yes, traditional religions had certainly defined and distorted American views on sex.

Taos is, and has been, a flourishing community of artists and writers for most of the last century. Mark had spent a session as a writer in residence there some years back. Of course, there have been many famous inhabitants of Taos, not the least of whom is Georgia O'Keefe, famous for her cattle skulls and fetching flowers. Martin says that, for the Native

Americans, animal bones, especially skulls, contain the animal's imprint, its power—which may account for O'Keefe's obsession with her white skulls, as if they held a little morphic resonance themselves. Before we headed back to the ranch in Antonito, we ate lunch in a funky little café and wandered through some galleries and craft shops.

On the last afternoon we spent at the ranch, I took a glass of wine to a sunny corner outside the house and watched the sky as the sun slipped behind the mountains—a spectacular light show unfolding from salmon and tangerine to mauve and pewter, the mountains in the background showing shades of violet and taupe. In a nearby cottonwood tree, Mark pointed out a whole cocktail-party conversation between the twenty or thirty red-winged blackbirds who'd alighted there. I moved my chair every few minutes to catch the last rays of light before the breezes came up and the cool night slithered in. When I closed my eyes with my face to the falling Sun, behind the colors, the eye looked back at me.

On the way back to Denver, we stopped in Salida, a newish artisan community where Mark had bought land and was building a small vacation house for himself—a place to get away and write. The town was charming and we visited some more galleries, talked with the locals, and ate in a trendy restaurant. Mark was proud of the work he had done so far on his studio and we surveyed the view from the hill where his land sits.

By the time I was ready to leave for home, I had already spent several days writing umpteen drafts of my favorite poem of the week, which I eventually whittled down and called "The Oracle of the Body." The poem speaks of the body itself, its mass and matter, contacting the mass and matter of the soil where other spirits still linger in the wheels of time. It seemed to me the body acts as a vehicle, and *oracle*, through which the secrets of time, whether so-called future or so-called past, can pass into the *now*, the everlasting present. I was still having a hard time conveying my own experiences, which were felt through my body but engineered from some other interplay with the consciousness of nature.

Poetry, of course, constantly presents transformations, mild miracles and images that act as visions. Now, in light of Martin's book and my encounters with the quantum physicists, I feel even more so that the words of poets are often received as gifts from the muses or gods of our magnetic energy fields, as they are invoked by us in the act of writing. I believe this is akin to the process through which my visions are received. Jean Houston calls it "downloading" from the ancestors and the archetypes.

Martin's *The Way of the Human Being* reflects back to a time when people could change themselves into animals, a shape-shifting that the most skilled shamans still recall. He speaks of that earlier timeless time:

> ... when magic words were made. A word spoken by chance would suddenly become powerful, and what people wanted to happen could happen and nobody could explain how it was.[1]

I wanted my poem as a container for the experiences I had walking around Reyes' ranch with my eyelids quivering open on one scene one moment, and then another, inwardly viewing a superimposition. But somehow, this was too much for the parameters of the poem or, at any rate, beyond my talents to deliver. I eventually realized the major experience in the poem—that is, my perception of the Indian women spirits—did not have to be named as a vision. It finally occurred to me that I didn't have to spell out the occasion of the poem; it could just happen. Then the poem became more flexible. I went through many drafts before another poet, a year later, helped me to complete it. But this is another strange and synchronistic story in itself.

On the way back to Denver, Mark and I stopped again in a scenic area where a plaque commemorated a 19th-century woman for her spirit and independence. Mark went off skiing for a while and I wandered the woods, watching the light burnish the trees and lift the spring temperatures, the melting snow becoming run-off that trickled down into the many creeks and streams. I found a log, sat down, and closed my eyes, perfectly content to be outside in this mountain air wearing a simple cotton turtleneck and down vest, lifting my face into the warm sun. I felt a little sleepy and tried to meditate, but as I began reciting my mantra, I was distracted by another scene taking place behind my eyes. This one was different.

An old railroad track came into view and, far in the distance, a figure was pumping a bar up and down on one of those railroad handcars you see in old Buster Keaton movies, or in cartoons from the early days of television. A bluish-white spirit in the form of a man was working the handcar with muscular arms, moving it along the track. He came closer and closer, until he went right by my field of vision and I was left observing his retreating back, shrinking smaller and smaller, until all I saw was the empty track. I placed

---

1. Calvin Luther Martin, *The Way of the Human Being* (New Haven & London: Yale University Press, 1999), p. 130.

this image in the era of the Gold Rush, late in the 19th or early 20th century. There was no rhyme or reason I could fathom why my imagination would have been concocted such a scene.

When Mark returned, I told him about the image. I had freely shared my experiences with him after he gained my trust with his story of the stone-healing treatment. He had been very accepting and made no judgments. As I mentioned the latest vision, he told me that there used to be a railroad in the spot where we were standing. This statement convinced me that I was actually seeing the morphic field that belonged to the land. I wondered if I were the man himself, as I had wondered if I had had a life as one of the Indian squaws or braves tramping through the woods with a heavy burden on my back. The idea that we are all one—all species, all flora and fauna, all the sacred elemental incarnations, wind, fire, water, earth, wood, all *now*—became less and less of an abstract concept for me and more an experiental phenomenon.

My affection for Mark grew as the week unfolded, and I am still so grateful for my visions in that magnificent landscape. I was not ready to relocate out West at that time, but I did feel I'd been drawn there for some purpose. Perhaps only to deepen my faith. Perhaps only to write my poems. Perhaps to further align my *chi* meridians. Perhaps only to encounter this special man whose poems I love.

Back in Denver we had a lovely dinner with Lisa, and I left the next morning for home. Coincidentally (or not), on the flight home, I ran into a woman I knew from the art college who had been visiting her mother in Oregon. Her plane stopped in Denver to pick up those of us headed to Boston. Nancy offered me a ride to my doorstep from the airport and saved me the thirty-dollar cab fare. The trip had only cost me pocket money!

THE ONTOLOGY OF FEAR

Once I returned to Boston, my visions of the indigenous people were gone and, again, when I meditated, my third eye replayed the French scenes. This was puzzling, but I had no choice or control over what went on there. A month later, the tragedy at Columbine High School occurred and I called Mark, who I knew would be emotionally devastated by it. That this same land could produce such chaotic destructive energies was upsetting and unbelievable to us both. As I have spoken with more and more people who understand the way the planet's energy is shifting, I have come to realize that humanity's transition is going to be very rough at times. People who do not resonate with the higher frequencies can lose their balance, as fearful and confused spirits from the lower planes are more present among us. Entertaining the dark side at this time will invite more darkness in. It makes me think that some of us get "contaminated." Yes, we truly do get "possessed" at times. And certainly the fanaticism of terrorism can create a field for dark and confused energies.

We live now in a fallen world. The gifts from the Earth no longer support us, because we have used them with an attitude of entitlement, without proper understanding or gratitude. We have hoarded and exploited them out of fear and a belief in the scarcity of resources, rather than a belief in an abundant Earth. Martin calls this "human-scaled superposition" and speaks of "an ontology of fear." It has a snowball effect. It is the world created by left-brained rationality, overlaying the primordial world of the ancients . . . or

> . . . the bizarre reality that Melville, in a brilliant insight, called "No Trust." No faith in the Spirit of the Earth, in its common-wealth of grace, capitulating to the doubt, the dark itch, that our kind stands apart from the rest of it, and it—the earth—moves its slow thighs by a consciousness (if it has one at all) that is not kind to man.[2]

There seemed to be no human explanation for what went so terribly wrong with the two boys from Columbine and the many other grisly school shootings, but perhaps there is a spiritual explanation.

The Law of Attraction is activating more quickly on the planet. Judging others will only bring judgment back on ourselves and negative thoughts will attract negative spirits, as the membranes between several dimensions are much more open now. This means that confused spirits trapped in the astral plane have more access to intervention, just as there are more spirits also assisting the human ascension process. This is why, as the species heals, there will be an equal amount of chaos stirred up within those participating in negativity and fear. September 11th alone has set off eight years of our media and leaders preaching fear. Retaliation in Afghanistan and Iraq have only created more rebounding karma. The anger between the Israelis and Palestinians shows us the error of an eye-for-an-eye philosophy. As these

---

2. Martin, *The Way of the Human Being*, pp. 191, 184, 188.

tragedies continue and the media broadcasts them, the entire global community has access to the negative emotions involved. The global village is quickly becoming polarized.

And perhaps there are spiritual side effects to these tragedies. Oklahoma City, Columbine, Virginia Tech, and other tragedies; the sudden, premature, "accidental" deaths of superstars like Princess Diana and JFK Jr.; the overwhelming disaster of 9/11 and the continued terrorist activity in Iraq; the bombing of the Bali nightclub and the train bombing in Madrid; the millennial weather that has caused hurricanes, tsunamis and floods—these losses create collective mourning that can be healing, as whole communities ritually grieve together.

I remember David telling me that "many souls will be leaving," and John's words "you can pass into spirit at any time." Perhaps those left behind feel the tragedy more. However, in order to heal, people need to mourn and feel release, to clear out repressed sorrows and denials. Collective grieving is powerful. The opening of the heart and the raising of kundilini energy can be emotionally as well as physically overbearing. But if we are all clearing karma right now, it's understandable that we will find ourselves in a very emotionally intense period. Eckhart Tolle says, in *The Power of Now:*

> This suffering is inflicted not by God but by humans on themselves and on each other as well as by certain defensive measures that the Earth, which is a living, intelligent organism, is going to take to protect herself from the onslaught of human madness.[3]

I also remember John telling our healing group there would be many Earth changes, but that, in the end, "She will be fine!"

My experience in Colorado will remain one of the most memorable and beautiful of those I've had to date. I feel that the Native American spirits I saw through my third eye are a part of the Earth's protective penumbra. Mark's spontaneous invitation was fated and his hospitality renewed my faith, leading me to see into the fields that overlay our own reality. Mark's poems celebrate the Earth goddess, *Gaia,* with gorgeous language, grace, and one man's passion for the feminine principle. In my opinion, he has been given the words to speak truly as an oracle for the Earth. Here, the demarcation between Earth and the feminine is blended as well as blurred:

---

3. Eckhard Tolle, *The Power of Now* (Novato, CA: New World Library, 1999), p. 187.

Flesh

Of this world I live for—a woman you named
earth, a man you called flame. —Where are you
now? And who are we without these wolves we call
bodies? I remember in sunlight the webbed, half-
finished chrysalis shining on a log as a cloud
passed and a shadow, briefly, grew. And I remember
leaving, how I rubbed her body with a page of sunlight
whose every line I knew till she became a story
I could not enter. I remember the airports and train
stations, the rising and falling and encircling of arms
reminiscent of a field at sunset and the air's fresh
slaughter of wings. I remember and in remembering
begin to loft through the air, seeing the pollen, yellow,
everywhere in dusk and the colossal mouth of green,
growing, calling. I see our voiceprints on leaves losing
color and the precise lanes of our bodies moving
toward autumn where the animals stop, look and say
once without speaking through the air's gauze of snow
where everything appears to be either angel or skull.[4]

BIRTHING THE ORACLE

A year after my trip to Colorado, I spent the month of August on a writing
fellowship at the Vermont Studio Center in Johnson, Vermont. VSC invites
a prominent visiting writer to serve as Writer in Residence for a week or
two so that other colonists can meet with her or him and receive feedback
on their work. Forest Gander, who held a position at Harvard, served as
Writer in Residence during the first half of my stay. Forest is interested
in weaving scientific information and speculation into his own work, and
he appeared to respect my venturing into uncharted territory in the long
poem about my father's afterlife. Much of his own experimental work does
the same thing. During the second two weeks of the program, Olga Brou-
mas arrived. Olga is a well-known and spiritually conscious poet, and also

---

4. Mark Irwin, *White City* (Rochester, VT: BOA Editions Ltd., 1999), p. 57.

a translator of Greek poetry. She directs Brandeis University's Creative Writing Program, and harbors another identity as a massage therapist/ body worker on Cape Cod.

I had been reading Olga's wonderful work for years and introduced myself to her at one of the communal meals. We spoke of her body work and I talked to her a bit about my energy fields. It was obvious to me that she knew frequencies were being lifted on the planet and that humanity was undergoing a spiritual expansion. She put my hand on her heart and asked me to send her some energy. When I did, she closed her eyes and attuned herself, throwing her head back a little, uttering "Ahhh . . ." as she said she felt energy. While other people in the lunchroom eyed us warily, we set up a time to meet and discuss my writing. She had been meeting with all the poets and the word was out that, at the end of each session, she offered a foot massage. Such a generous and surprising gesture!

In reflexology, the bottoms of the feet correspond to the major organs and meridians of the body, and it is a good practice to massage your feet regularly. When I massage a certain spot on my foot, one that corresponds to the descending colon, I can relieve my bouts with a spastic colon, a condition that has plagued me since adolescence. So naturally, I looked forward to a session with Olga. When I showed up at her door, however, she had other plans. First, she talked about my packet of poems in general and encouraged me to explore these spiritual and occult subjects more freely. Then she helped me tweak a few syllables and finalize my *Oracle* poem, suggesting that I invert the lines and read the poem from the bottom up. This did not work well with the entire poem, but with certain parts, especially the ending, her idea really gave the poem more mystery and depth.

When our discussion was over, she told me she was not going to give me a foot massage but wanted to do some cranial-sacral work around my head. She said she had "received a message" while we were talking to give me this work. I was beside myself with curiosity, but also extremely pleased to meet someone in the academic poetry world who also embraced the psychic world. I had never heard of cranial-sacral work, but have since discovered that it is a popular healing modality used by many body-work practitioners.

I lay on the floor as Olga worked her hands about an inch away from my skull. I could feel my spirit and angelic guides move in immediately to assist with her motions. Soon the magnetic field was very strong and I saw deep, rich, purple (physically healing) energy through my closed eyes. It felt as though a layer of very thick, cool, dark purple air were sponging my brow and the back of my head. The density of the air around my head increased significantly, as if it were a cloud. I relaxed and almost fell asleep. She worked for about twenty minutes and then, gently and gradually, stopped. As I slowly sat up and sighed, she told me that, in the process of her work on my energy, she had received another message, this one directly for me.

"You've been seeking information," she said, "but it is time for you *to act* on the information you have." Olga also suggested that I might benefit further from sacral-cranial healing. She gave me the name of a professional woman in Somerville, a practitioner with whom she had worked.

Olga's poems are beautiful and her translations from Greek poets are excellent. She has a very physical approach to poetry and emphasizes breath work as she recites—each syllable, each word, becoming a living entity birthed from her throat. I was delighted to have met her in such meaningful and intimate circumstances. Still, I was puzzled by the meaning of her message. I thought I *had* been "acting on the information." I was writing the poem about the spiritual world and my father, which felt more or less finished. I had written a few miscellaneous pieces about other spiritual experiences, like the ones from Colorado and Israel. I had also written some poems about meditation and the occult arts, as well as some revisionist New Testament poems that I was pulling together in my new manuscript. Not only was I using the material in poetry, but I had gone to Vermont primarily to work on a novel treating these themes.

Olga's message to act, however, helped to increase my trust that the work done on my body was a powerful means to break through the emotional fields of my depressive blockages. When I returned home, I revisited my poem "The Oracle of the Body," the one I had begun in Colorado. I wanted the last words of the poem to be geographical. The idea I wanted to convey was how very sacred the land is. And I appreciated Olga's suggestion for reversing the order of some of the lines in my revision. When the poem was complete, I sent it to both Mark and Reyes, certain they would understand and appreciate this idea of standing on sacred ground, perceiving the spirit of those who have gone before us. A few lines from Eric Gamalinda's beautiful book of poems, *Zero Gravity*, served well as an epigram for the emotion I felt in my own piece.

The Oracle of the Body

. . . and in our poverty
there will be much to give
and more light than we can imagine.
—ERIC GAMALINDA

Coagulated dust, Colorado rock
flood the instep of my boots. Cattle low
to roots of trees and quartz
which lie like a neuron network
in the lap of mountains. Something stirs
the sagebrush. The cows themselves,
without reflection, step aside,
sensing the presence passing through.

I follow, drawn but aimless in the limited
light of all I know, when the oracle
calls forth from visible earth
invisible bodies, light as the birds
we share the air with. We willingly
empty the mind of objects, thoughts,
emotion, and turn like a naked Francis
to feed stray apparitions, shedding the cloth
of manmade world. We share the poverty

that gives as if from that bottomless
basket where bread and fish made manifest
the intention of a man who read in the sunset
a synchronous heaven and earth—
Yet we have learned nothing worshiping him
instead of becoming the love that he is
amongst those who "will do these things also."

The numen of those who vanish
births a door in my forehead,
a gnosis of new senses
sending up my blood and bone,
this land of manure and mud as my body
conducts the core and I open

my palms to the earth I am
under the lavender bowl of sky, under all
that is given freely, far from the careless slaughter,
far from the urban confusions—here at the border
of northern New Mexico, here at the ranch
on the edge.

Chapter 18

THE GNOSTIC MARY

. . . the Black Goddess has experienced good and evil, love and hate, truth and falsehood
in the person of her sisters . . . she will lead man back to that sure instinct
of love which he long ago forfeited by intellectual pride.
ROBERT GRAVES, *MAMMON AND THE BLACK GODDESS*

My third eye opened of its own accord after I took the holotropic breath workshop. But when I traveled to other territory, I seemed to step into Sheldrake's field of "morphic resonance," where the past still hangs in the air. I was able to pick up these morphic waves and tune into them visually. In Israel, I saw Biblical vistas; in Colorado, I tuned into Native American old souls.

Both before and after my trip to Israel, I had pursued my interest in Gnosticism. During the monthly meetings of his healing group, John occasionally spoke of his life with "Yeshua" and the apostles. He indicated that the Roman fathers of Christianity inaccurately interpreted Christ's mission and told us stories of the disciples' bafflement at some of the teachings about healing. We nagged him to discuss this, and, finally, he said outright that Mary Magdalen had played an important role in the early ministry and that history had been rewritten to excise many of the esoteric ideas in Yeshua's message. John's teachings to us closely paralleled *The Course in Miracles*, the book whose practice I was following. On my own, I began to read about the Essene community, the branch of Judaism to which Christ and his parents supposedly belonged. These books led me back to that group of texts previously encountered through my Jungian studies known as the Gnostic gospels or the *Nag Hammadi Library*.

This collection of strange texts was found in a buried urn in an Egyptian man's backyard in 1947, two years after the Dead Sea Scrolls were uncovered in Qumran. We assume the Gnostic gospels were buried by the Essenes, because they were deemed heretical. Along with some apocryphal texts that embrace a whole cosmogognic myth, they include gospels by apostles other than Mark, Matthew, Luke, and John. Most Christians are not familiar with these other gospels—those of James, Philip, Thomas, and, most notably, Mary Magdalen, who is referred to as the "companion" of Christ. I became fervently interested in Gnosticism and the Magdalen cult, which is still celebrated today in Southern France. John's gospel refers to "the disciple that Jesus loved." Although most historic scholars have speculated that John is referring to himself, one begins to wonder if Mary Magdalen is the hidden reference here.

To be a Gnostic is to have direct experience or knowledge of God. But if we can have such commerce with the eternal, why do we need the intervention of clergy? We can see how threatening these beliefs were to those in power in the early centuries of the newly established Roman Catholic Church. Christ himself never created any dogma and we know that, throughout the first four centuries, there were diverse forms of early Christianity that vied with one another for ascendancy. The Gnostics stressed "spiritual vision"—seeing through a higher mind, or perceiving intuitively through the heart. Their emphasis is on direct experience rather than the witness of another. The Gnostics encouraged creative explorations of the divine that were expressed individually and could thus differ somewhat from one seeker to another. Naturally, this threatened any kind of man-made Christian "laws."

I felt a kinship with this material, especially with the gospel of Thomas—a group of sayings, some of which are contained in the synoptic texts, with different wording and sometimes different connotations. Many of the concepts in this gospel parallel the lessons of the contemporary *Course in Miracles*, like the idea that enlightenment entails a conscious dying to the material world, which is created by unconscious guilt.

In Gnostic texts, Christ transcends his suffering on the cross because he understands the illusion of what humankind has created. His body reacted to it, but there are hints that Christ was able to dwell in the light body. A document called "The Acts of John" speaks of Jesus as " . . . a spiritual being who adapted himself to human perception."[1] There are also suggestions that he survived.

Those who say they will die first and then rise are in error. They must receive the resurrection while they live.[2]

---

1. Elaine Pagels, *The Gnostic Gospels* (New York: Vintage Books, 1981), p. 87.

2. James Robinson, gen. ed., *The Nag Hammadi Library* (San Francisco: HarperCollins, 1981), p. 477.

I wondered if this "resurrection" had to do with developing senses and interior vision. Could this renewal of the "body" relate to the "subtle body" or invisible energy body and learning to place our consciousness there? I was immediately struck by how much these ideas resembled teachings of the mystical poets I had studied, specifically Rumi's Sufi philosophy.

Harvard Divinity scholar Karen King analyzes and researches Mary's gospel in her book *The Gospel of Mary Magdala; Jesus and the First Woman Apostle.* She admits that we do not know the actual author, but estimates the influences and date as sometime between 32 and 325 C.E., going on to say:

> It does appear however, that our author was familiar with traditions found in the Gospel of John and perhaps the letters of Paul. If so, that would put the gospel sometime after 90 or 100 C.E.[3]

This is long before the Council at Nicaea, when early Christian factions were supplanted by Roman Catholicism, and where all but four gospels were rejected in an effort to institutionalize the Church. This official dogma overwhelmed the Gnostics and other early groups that interpreted Christ in nontraditional ways. We know that the conquerors write history, but fortunately these and other texts that were deemed heretical found their way into urns buried in Egypt.

King also sees evidence that the beliefs of late Gnosticism were influenced by Platonism and Stoicism, and a respect for direct revelation from visions and experience. For instance, Acts 2:17:

> I will pour out my spirit upon all flesh, and your sons and your daughters shall prophesy, and your young men shall see visions and your old men shall dream dreams.

In Mary's gospel, Mary herself is the one with the inner vision of the Christ.

Although she weeps from his criticism, she stays centered before Peter, who is suspicious of her claims. When they express anxiety about their safety in light of Christ's recent crucifixion, it is Mary who encourages the frightened disciples to go out and preach. The authority she takes shows her power. It is evident through these texts that women played a key role in early Christianity. According to many historians, Mary Magdalen was venerated as a wise teacher with esoteric access to the resurrected Christ—a truth that

---

3. Karen King, *The Gospel of Mary Magdala: Jesus and the First Woman Apostle* (Santa Rosa, CA: Polebridge Press, 2003), p. 183.

has been kept from the masses and one that undermines the dogma of the traditional Church.

Elaine Pagels' book *Beyond Belief* addresses the power struggles in early Christianity and tracks, through the writings of the fourth century, how the official followers of Christ were required to pledge submission to the "One Holy and Apostolic Church" by reciting the Nicene (or Apostles') Creed. Mary's gospel, which values her visionary experience, was too threatening for the Church fathers. Whether or not it was actually written by Mary Magdalen is not as relevant as the fact that it was written at all and has survived as a fragment. "In this case," Pagels points out, "Mary Magdalen received *direct revelation* from 'the Lord,' and claims that Jesus authorized her to teach."[4]

Mary is related through conceptual and iconic imagery to the great goddesses of the past—the mythic mother of Gnostic wisdom, Sophia, and Isis, the great feminine energy of ancient Egypt. The gospels show that Mary was a distinct part of the disciple community and that some of the men resented her. There are specific references to Mary in Philip's gospel:

> And the companion of the [Savior is] Mary Magdalen. [But Christ loved] her more than [all] the disciples and [used to] kiss her [often] on her [mouth]. The rest of the disciples were offended by it [and expressed disapproval].[5]

HOLY BLOOD, HOLY GRAIL

The three authors of the historic study *Holy Blood, Holy Grail*, a best-seller in the United States and France in the 1980s, adhere to the thesis that Mary Magdalen is the "lost Grail" of the European mythology of the Rose. This book, like others that have been published since, (especially Dan Brown's best-selling novel *The Da Vinci Code*, which credits *Holy Blood, Holy Grail*), suggests evidence of a heresy that follows European bloodlines and secret societies. This tradition persists throughout the south of France, where the Grail legends were plentiful in medieval times.

Although one of the early societies, the Prieuré Notre Dame de Sion, has been exposed as a hoax, I don't believe the baby should be thrown out

---

4. Elaine Pagels, *Beyond Belief: The Secret Gospel of Thomas* (New York: Random House, 2003), p. 63.
5. Robinson, *The Nag Hammadi Library*, p. 138.

with the bath water. Let us not forget the power of the Roman Catholic Church, which may have had influence both in setting up and exposing the Prieuré. No one can do more than speculate about the truth of this confusing mix of history, mythology, and legend. But we know for certain that there was a heretical tradition, and that there was a corrupt and punishing Inquisition. (Even Dante throws three Popes into his *Inferno!*) Could the rumored "treasures," "magic elixirs," and "grails" hold the secret of our own human access to divinity?

> The research of the *Holy Blood, Holy Grail* authors indicates that the 11th and 12th century heretical movements kept alive the views enumerated in the first/second century Gnostic Gospels, which . . . had a strong female inspiration, that of Mary Magdalen. In exactly the same period the icon of the Black Madonna arose in great numbers.[6]

I had already followed the research of Margaret Starbird, originally a traditional Catholic woman whose first intention was to disprove these heretical assertions. In the first of Starbird's studies, she traces the heresy back to the Marseille tarot deck, where she decodes a story in the images. Her references also extend to the beautiful tapestries of Cluny, where the story of the "unicorn" (which is often taken to be Christ) and the "lady" is literally woven into the gorgeous wall hangings.

Elaine Pagels and Karen King have also written of the influence of women in early Gnostic circles. In France, the common legend is that Magdalen was Lazarus' sister and possibly Christ's wife. Other writers in search of the Grail bloodline have said that Lazarus, Mary, and Martha were originally from a wealthy family in Bethany, and that it was their family money that financed Christ's ministry.

Moreover, there are still numerous questions about the circumstances of the Resurrection. But whether as a vision or in the flesh, no one disputes that it was Mary who first saw the "risen" Christ. The questions have led to suppositions in the French legends that claim the Magdalen is Christ's wife, and that she may have had children—the bloodline ultimately leading to the Arthurian stories of the Fisher King. "Holy Grail" is itself an interesting translation from the original French, *sang real*, which means "real blood." French legend says Magdalen came to Marseille with Joseph of Arimathea

---

6. Deborah Rose, Travel Notes unpublished, pages unnumbered.

after Christ's death. Two different towns there, Saint Maximin and Vézelay, still claim her relics. She is celebrated over an entire region.

The secret tradition is preserved in the story *The Golden Legend*, which was, in its time, a record of the "lives of the saints." According to this legend, written in 1265 by the Dominican Archbishop of Genoa, Jocabus da Voragine, Marseille was the place of many Magdalen miracles. Here, Mary, the widow of Christ, who came from Marseille, "preached against idolatry," taught the Gnostic truths, and eventually retired to the cave of Sainte Baume, where she lived for some thirty years more.[7] In the legends, the angels take her up to heaven seven times a day to feed her nectar and to commune with the divine. I have wondered if the foundations for this legend could pertain to meditation and out-of-body experiences.

When Mary was dying, the legend says she came down from the mountain into her small village. There, she was given her last holy communion by the Archbishop of Aix-en-Provence, Maximin. The town itself is named after the Archbishop—Saint Maximin-La Sainte Baume—and, amid the lavender fields outside the town, there is a cross and a statue to mark the place where Mary allegedly died in his arms. The latter part of Maximin's own name—*La Sainte Baume*—recalls the balm, spikenard, that Mary used when she anointed Jesus on Holy Thursday. The legend suggests that Mary's brother, Lazarus, whom Christ had raised from the dead, accompanied her to France and became the first bishop of Marseille. Her sister, Martha, is said to have "settled in Tarascon where she quelled the Tarasque, the dragon of the Rhone," which is also highly symbolic.[8] Mary retired to a cave set into the mountain at La Sainte Baume, where there is now a chapel in her name.

According to British Jungian Ean Begg's classic work on the mysteries surrounding the dark Madonnas, Cassianite monks guarded the Magdalen's tomb from the early fifth century. Not until later, however—in the 13th and 15th centuries—were other relics found that supported the legend. Some of these were moved to Vézelay, which is the other village dedicated to the Magdalen. What is curious is Begg's notation that "Some fifty centers of the cult of the Magdalen also contain shrines to the Black Virgin."[9]

Like most mythic material, these legends have variant stories, one of which is that Mary of Magdala had royal blood and was a daughter of Eucha-

---

7. Ean Begg, *The Cult of the Black Virgin* (Herndon, VT: Lindisfarne Books, 2006), pp. 97–98.
8. Begg, *Black Virgin*, p. 99.
9. Begg, *Black Virgin*, p. 99.

ria, a term applied to Aphrodite. Another claims she, her brother, Lazarus, and her sister, Martha, owned seven castles, in addition to the village of Bethany and much of Jerusalem. Her own dwelling of choice was Magdala (which means Tower), a mile from Gennesaret on the Sea of Galilee.[10]

Begg interprets some of this material symbolically, as part of the secret tradition. Starbird draws attention to the Tower card in the tarot, which is struck by lightning. The divination behind this card, Arrien tells us, is about restoration and healing. "The Tower is a symbol of the change and awakening that is required to dismantle that which is artificial, false-to-fact, or conditioned within our natures."[11] This representation of the lightning-struck Tower, or the power of Magdala, carries the message that Mary was one of the few apostles who understood that the original sin that evicted us from Eden, with all our baggage of guilt and shame and fear, was only the sin of ignorance—the ignorance of equating ourselves completely with matter, or our basic belief that we are our bodies. The destruction of the Tower "symbolizes a casting out of those remaining aspects of the self which are capable of fragmenting our essential unity of being."[12] In Greek, the word *harmatia* means "error," "missing the mark," "a turning away from truth," rather than the intentional wrongdoing implied by the word "sin."

In the traditional gospel, Jesus casts seven devils out of a woman often associated with the Magdalen. The mystical number seven, which we find associated with castes and demons, also alludes to the

> . . . planetary stages on the journey of the soul into and out of incarnation, according to the religion of Ishtar/Astarte/Ashtoreth, a teaching which was assimilated by some Gnostic groups. Astarte, among her many roles, is the goddess of love, in whose temples sexual rites were performed.[13]

Perhaps this accounts for Mary's alleged prostitution. In the Gnostic tradition, the feminine wisdom called Sophia is both virgin and whore, recalling one of the Gnostic texts entitled *The Thunder Perfect Mind*, a poem I find aston-

---

10. Begg, *Black Virgin*, p. 97- 98.

11. Angeles Arrien, *Tarot Handbook: Practical Applications of Ancient Visual Symbols* (New York: Jeremy P. Tarcher, 1997), p. 82.

12. David Fontana, *The Secret Language of Symbols: A Visual Key to Symbols and Their Meanings* (San Francisco: Chronicle Books, 1993), p. 177.

13. Arrien, *Tarot Handbook*, p. 99.

ishingly beautiful (quoted in the following chapter) because of its capacious and paradoxical all-embracing feminine voice.

MUNDUS IMAGINALIS

Like many young girls raised Catholic, I was equally drawn to and horrified by the adulteress whom Jesus saves from stoning. The possibility that Mary was a pagan woman, specifically one in the line of Isis' priestesses, makes much more sense to me. When Mary anoints Christ with the rare and expensive spikenard oil on the night of the Last Supper, she performs the sacred Egyptian ritual conducted prior to a royal death. The church has never explained this detail, even though it appears in the approved gospels. Judas complains about the extravagance and Christ rebukes him. In her own gospel, Mary is speaking directly to Peter and the apostles about secret teachings she received from Christ's apparition after his death. This posits the idea of an interior communication, a Christ within, a *daimon*, a word that gained its current sense of "demon" only in the Middle Ages. To Socrates and the Greeks, *daimon* meant "guide," or access to immediate inner truth. This divine concept would have been revolutionary to the patriarchal fathers of the Church, which may account for the fragmented remains of some of these texts. To men who misunderstood Christ's cryptic messages, men who were trying to institute laws and regulations within Christianity, Mary's "daimon" loomed as a threat.

In the Gospel of Mary, we see Mary as a disciple and teacher who claims to have had direct communication with Christ's spirit after the crucifixion.

> Mary said to them: "I will now speak to you of that which has not been given to you to hear. I had a vision of the Teacher, and I said to him: Lord I see you now in this vision." And he answered: "You are blessed, for the sight of me does not disturb you. There where is the *nous*, lies the treasure."[14]

Mary has an individual encounter with a vision of Yeshua, the Christ. She meets him in what the Jungians call the *mundus imaginalis*, or on a level where imagination yearns for the infinite beyond the known world. It is her faith, her quest made up of desire and imagination, where the *nous* exists. As Jean

---

14. Jean-Yves LeLoup, *The Gospel of Mary Magdalene* (Rochester, VT: Inner Traditions, 2002), p. 31.

Leloup puts it in the introduction to his commentary on Mary's gospel, "The imagination is the sympathetic resonance of the invisible and the visible, of the spiritual and the physical."[15] This validates the imaginative function as a means to manifestation in the material world. It also implies faith in the imagined. As quantum physicists have found, a witness to an experiment actually alters the outcome of the experiment. There appears to be a link between will and faith, which, under the right conditions, can manifest in matter and create our projection of reality.

In her gospel, Mary is respectful to the other disciples, but it is she who teaches them a woman's way of knowing. "In Jungian terms she is an archetype. In orthodox terms she is an icon. Both of these words mean that she is a doorway to another dimension . . ."[16] We can't forget that she is the first witness of the resurrected Christ in the famous Easter morning scene. He tells her not to touch him.

We further deduce from her gospel, in a discussion with the apostles about the secret teachings, that they do not understand the esoteric truths about the soul's journey. In a parable, she tells them that the soul must pass through many gateways, knowing itself loved and whole and worthy despite the concepts of sin and punishment so common in the laws of Judaism. Peter has an especially hard time accepting Mary and her insistence that Christ warned against making more rules and laws. In Karen King's analysis,

> The true model for leadership is the Savior, the teacher mediator of divine wisdom and salvation who cautions his disciples against laying down fixed laws and rules that will come to enslave them.[17]

Mary displays herself as courageous, while the apostles fear how the populace may condemn them as it condemned their Master. According to King:

> Peter sees only that Mary is a woman, not that she is a spiritually mature disciple . . . Levi's correction of Peter helps the reader to see one of the primary ways in which people are deceived by the body.[18]

---

15. LeLoup, *Gospel of Mary Magdalene*, p. 18.
16. Rose Notes, p. 9.
17. King, *Gospel of Mary Magdala*, p. 189.
18. King, *Gospel of Mary Magdala*, p. 187.

I wanted to write a poem about this powerful scene to honor Mary's open presence and confidence among the apostles. We may regret that Mary weeps in the face of Peter's attack, yet the gospel ends with her encouraging the others to get on with their work of spreading Christ's ministry. "The Gospel of Mary instead suggests that the story of the gospel is unfinished," King tells us, and that "the body is not one's real self."[19] Here we see the Gnostic belief that the earthly world is an illusion or, as we might say today in psychological terms, a projection created out of guilt and fear.

In my poem, I used the setting of the upper room where the apostles received the Holy Spirit at the Pentecost. According to the Gnostic gospels, Christ visited the apostles many times after his death and Mary was among them. She tells the apostles that "The Savior said, 'All natures, all formations, all creatures, exist in and with one another, and they will be resolved again into their own roots . . . ' "[20] This concept alludes to the spiritual nature of the soul incarnated into matter, which will dissolve or decay in death while the spirit returns to its root realm in another reality. In Mary's gospel, Christ describes the soul's ascent after death. When Peter questions the veracity of Mary's report, she is defended by Levi, who reminds him that the Master loved her best.

I wanted my poem to reflect Mary's special relationship with Jesus, her understanding that sin is nothing more than ignorance and that it is our manner of thinking that projects our illusions about reality into what appears to be real. At death, we eventually become aware of our inherent oneness and goodness as aspects of the divine. This journey after death—what Eastern religions call the Bardo state—is easier if the soul has learned its lessons consciously, while incarnated in a body. This is an essential message for the new paradigm. In my poem, Mary understands the illusion of sin and the power of belief creating reality.

---

19. King, *Gospel of Mary Magdala*, pp. 189, 124.
20. LeLoup, *Gospel of Mary Magdalene*, p. 25.

The Gospel of Mary

My brother Peter, Do you think that I thought this up myself or that I am lying about the Savior?
—The Gospel of Mary

I was not alarmed when the doves continued to coo
though their wings were burning.

I was on fire too.
It was morning. I was there

with the eleven. We gathered
in the vestibule of the upper room.

Our breath thickened, colors deepened.
For just one instant I saw the root of love

staked through everything. But so few
of them received the vision at its core.

They tried to *think* it through. It was not
for thought. It was more

for holding and becoming. Light
brandished from our fingertips

like swords of warrior angels.
When it extinguished,

I flashed my ordinary hands
and we all laughed.

Because they asked, I told them
what he said to me in private,

I didn't say he'd kissed me
on the mouth. I told them how

I met the savior *inside* my head.
How our thoughts entwined,

rising like bean stalks
through swatches of clouds.

How he said *thought*
created matter, and that fear

is ingenious for damaging the world.
He said *Here is the soul, here the Spirit,*

the mind—
a naive child between them.

I drew a diagram in air of the soul's
escalation, my fingers sparking

the seven heavens. I tried to show
what rushes naked, leaving the body

like a town one no longer cares to visit.
How the soul, small and homeless,

remembers then, and rejoins Spirit.
How, in the aftermath, oblivion

is transient, and darkness is illusion,
both habits to be broken.

Peter and Andrew debunked
my "strange ideas" and woman that I was,

I wept. Levi stepped in and calmed the others
the way the savior woke in the rocking

boat and calmed the sea. They all looked
at me in wonder. I spent the rest of my life

on earth infused with his apparition
because I *thought* that I was worthy.

*

One of the major problems in traditional Catholicism is that we have been imbued with the concept of our *unworthiness*. And in order to manifest abundance as true co-creators of our reality, we need to feel worthy. Instead we are taught that suffering, martyrdom and unworthiness before our God is the appropriate orientation.

THE SHADOW AND THE LOST FEMININE

Carl Jung was one of the original owners of the Gnostic gospels, the most famous of which is the Gospel of Thomas. Jung bought the texts on the black market and had them translated from the Coptic, and their teachings influenced his psychology tremendously. The idea of individuation, the evolution into wholeness, is supported by a number of sayings in these gospels, which begin where the other stories end—that is, after the death of Christ, when his disincarnate visitations begin.

Jung's exploration of the *anima*, or feminine soul, led him to understand the two poles of the archetype: the light goddess, fair maiden, ethereal woman who inspires men; and the negative *anima*, the dark devouring earthbound goddess, the hag and the raging, scorned woman. Jung felt Christianity was an incomplete mythology due to its partially excised feminine power. Only Mary the Mother is revered in the traditional Church. The dark feminine associated with the body, sexuality, and sin is rejected. Ean Begg paraphrases Jung's position:

> The idea that the meaning of life has to do with the projection and reintegration of the soul, sketched in early Gnosticism, 12th century poetry and in later alchemy, was not made conscious until Jung. [21]

---

21. Begg, *Black Virgin*, p. 133.

Begg and Joseph Campbell both suggest that the 12th century gave birth to a new way of looking at the male/female relationship. With the emergence of the Black Virgins, Begg sees "something like a quantum leap in consciousness, and understanding of the symbolic significance of the relationship between the sexes."[22] Campbell, in his *Power of Myth* series of interviews with Bill Moyers, speaks of the troubadours and love that was based on the heart, transcending social law and church dogma. Begg sees the troubadours in the 12th century as creating a new myth for "soul-making" through love. The knights performed feats for their idealized women, who were unobtainable, usually because they were already married, as was Guenevere to Arthur. Lancelot's pursuit and Guenevere's infidelity brought down Camelot and the Grail was lost. In the 12th century, idealized romantic love becomes the goal of the male/female relationship. Yet this goal is unobtainable.

Jung was aware of a split in humanity's psyche and sought to redress it by honoring the dark matter of women that the Church sees as a source of sin. This idea, however, was also misread and is only reemerging in our own times.

> But courtly love was to prove an idea whose time had not yet come and, after Dante and Petrarch, the allegorical inspiration ran out of steam, to become little more than a literary convention.[23]

This split in the two aspects of the feminine becomes evident in the witch trials in Europe, headed by the Inquisition. These occurred when the Church's shadow, its "*witch*" so to speak, was projected outward onto the bodies and souls of actual women. The Black Virgins are associated with Mary Magdalen as symbols for the truths that must remain occult or hidden. The underground stream kept them alive despite terrible repression. The blackness, according to Begg, shows these truths as "unmanifest and unrevealed."[24] They are from matter, the Earth, the womb of the Earth. When I read Beggs's book, I recalled my dream of excavating the dark woman in the cave. Unconsciously, my inner Black Madonna was already present.

"Khem" is the name for Egypt. The word "alchemy," the work *against* nature (read as matter) that must come through nature, thus has Egypt as its root. Indeed, the earliest references to alchemy are found in Egypt, although

---

22. Begg, *Black Virgin*, p. 131.
23. Begg, *Black Virgin*, p. 133.
24. Begg, *Black Virgin*, p. 143.

most of the translated writings date to the Middle Ages. (Egypt was also where the Gnostic gospels were discovered.) Alchemical experiments, then, coincide with the rediscovery of the feminine principle. "The great age of the Black Virgin," Begg tells us, "is the twelfth century, but legends about her hark back to the dawn of Christianity, the dynasty of the Merovingians and the age of Charlemagne."[25]

These ideas made a deep impression on me. I had vivid third-eye visions at the ruins of Qumran in Israel, where the Essene cult retired from secular living. And when I traveled through France, I became aware of a French connection. I wondered if I had been on this journey before in other lives. Or was I merging with the other multidimensional aspects of my "monad," who were currently living these parallel lives? Or was I wandering into morphic fields that held the unresolved past in place? My curiosity drove me to more books exploring the occult origins of Christianity. And, shortly thereafter, another synchronistic opportunity fell into my lap.

25. Begg, Black Virgin, pp. 144, 133.

Chapter 19

WOMEN CLOTHED BY THE JUN

The underground stream of the West—witchcraft, alchemy and most forms of gnosticism and heresy—is essentially a feminine stream. Its goal is to undo the process of alienation; to get back to kinesthetic origins . . . the True Self.
MORRIS BERMAN, COMING TO OUR SENSES

A s I stepped into the small café in Cambridge, I immediately spotted the auburn-haired woman who was organizing the Black Madonna journey to France. Deborah Rose flashed her huge and generous smile at me from across the room. As I approached her, we introduced ourselves, ordered some fruit and cheese, and then spent the next few hours head to head in the world of fallen Catholic women.

A graduate of Colby College and a French major like me, Deborah, who was exactly my age, had been giving workshops and writing articles about her experiences with the Black Madonnas. She had already taken several trips to Europe, some alone and some with other women, to view the statues and meditate in the Madonnas' presence. Deborah said her own direct involvement with the Black Madonna had been extremely personal and that she was looking for a "transformational" experience within the group. I didn't have to clue Deborah in on the idea of an evolutionary leap or an ascension process. Clearly, she was already on that path.

As a body worker, Deborah was well aware of the meridians and the need for releasing negativity at a cellular level. She also understood intuitively that the feminine way of knowing is an idea whose time has come. Ever since the late Sixties, when the radical women's movement erupted along with the sexual revolution and the fight for civil rights, the first wave of Aquarian chaos had been breaking existing value systems of race and gender. All three of these revolutions will take another few hundred years to be refined, but there is really no going back, no matter how hard the conservative sectors of the population push. In the next 2000 years of the Aquarian cycle, new systems will evolve. Men like Jung and Begg were substantially ahead of their times. Deborah and I both shared Begg's belief that "the one-sided patriarchal system is dying, and to cling to it is now a psychic sin."[1]

We sensed a sisterhood based in our names right from the start of our friendship. Deborah is the prophet in the Old Testament who leads an army against the Canaanites. Deborah means "the bee." Mythologically, bees represent "ways of seeing," or "varied forms of perception." In the Greek tradition, the second of the temples built in Delphi was erected by bees to assist the oracular vision of the Delphic Oracles.[2] Because it collects its young from blossoms, the bee is associated in medieval lore with the Immaculate Conception, and with the *fleur de lis*, since bees live in that flower.[3]

The eminent Magdalen scholar, Margaret Starbird, remarks that bees produce "the delicious and valuable gift of honey," which symbolizes "the erotic secretions of male and female partners during coitus." She associates this "honey" with the spikenard with which Mary Magdalen anoints the feet of Jesus on Holy Thursday, recalling the Egyptian rite for a dying king.

Deborah and I shared, through our names, connections to the world of the goddess. And as for "Rose" (her actual birth name!)—the rose has long been acknowledged as the most flagrant (as well as fragrant) symbol for the hidden feminine. The occult tradition used it to signify the Magdalen herself—she who was the other half of the sacred marriage. The rose, a symbol appropriated by the aristocracy along with the French fleur de lis, is also related to the Chinese lotus, whose roots lie hidden in the depths of the most emotional element, water.

The Madonna sites were very popular in medieval Europe. They were connected with miracles, with commerce, and with healing and social progress. At the peak of their worship, the great Gothic cathedrals were constructed, each of which is associated with a sacred space related to a spring or a ley line beneath the foundation. These sacred spots date back to the Roman-Gaelic period, the earliest period of Christianity in France, when pagan practice and traditions were fused into the young religion. The energy grids of the Earth, or ley lines, are known for the springs beneath them, many of which are said to have healing properties. The pagans were well aware of these areas and constructed their altars to various goddesses on these locations.

---

1. Ean Begg, *The Cult of the Black Virgin* (Herndon, VT: Lindisfarne Books, 2006), p. 133.

2. J. E. Cirlot, *A Dictionary of Symbols*, Second Edition (New York: Philosophical Library, 1971), p. 24.

3. *Herder Symbol Dictionary* (Wilmette, IL: Chiron Publications, 1986), p. 21.

OUR LADY OF THE HOLY SPIRIT

The Madonnas, often portrayed as queens with children on their laps, are also commonly related to the heretical community of the Cathars, who were opposed to the Church of Rome. It appears that the Cathars followed the ideas of Mary Magdalen. Pope Innocent III launched the Albigensian Crusade (1208-29) to wipe out all Cathar opposition to the Church in the areas of the Languedoc, including the cultured cities of Toulouse, Beziers, and Carcasonne. Some 500,000 men, women, and children were slaughtered in this genocide. Some of the sacred mysteries of the Cathars survived and were passed on to the Templar Knights, the mysterious crusading warrior monks who financed the building of the great Gothic churches. The cult of the Templars lasted 200 years, until the last of them was tried and burned in 1308 as the result of a conspiracy between Pope Clement V and King Philip the Fair.

In France, the Cathar community practiced a religion of love dedicated to Our Lady and the Holy Spirit. They did not accept the Bible except for John's writings, including Revelation and some of the other books of the prophets. Catharism, which was also called "Christian Dualism," was repressed and its practitioners persecuted. The last of the community fell in a ruthless battle in 1244 on Montsegur. Montsegur is related etymologically to Mount Tabor, where I had my own strange out-of-body experience three years earlier, which is also linked to *Deburieh*, of which Deborah is a derivative.

The Cathars considered their refuge "the Gnostic mountain of the Holy Spirit." After Montsegur fell, some Cathars remained in Montaillou and the village of Rennes-le-Chateau, "where the most curious cult of Mary Magdalen has its centre."[4] A certain Merovée Levi is said to have "perpetuated the Merovingian bloodline"—a bloodline the Order of the Prieuré Notre Dame de Sion, which still exists in France today, takes to be the original bloodline begun by the union of Jesus and Mary Magdalen. Begg describes the Order as a secret society, "a political grouping with specific aims that is also interested in ancient esoteric wisdom and hidden mysteries . . . [and] passionately concerned with the cult of the Black Virgin."[5] The legend claims that Mary was with child when she arrived in Gaul as Christ's widow, and that the gypsies worship that child, who is called Sara.

Like Starbird, Begg feels the story of the Cathars and their tradition may have been told in the tarot, "which appeared in northern Italy, Marseille and

---

4. Begg, *Black Virgin*, p. 101.
5. Begg, *Black Virgin*, p. 14.

Lyons in the fourteenth century after the repression of the Cathars and the Templars."[6] Also interesting is Fontana's idea, "The Fool is zero, the one who abandons concepts about reality in favor of direct experience."[7]

The infamous psychic Nostradamus (literally "Our Lady") was known as a Merovingian "propagandist as well as prophet, descendent of converted Jews who adopted a masculine form of our Lady . . . ."[8] He predicted a "Grand Monarque" would rise again. According to Begg, this Monarque would be of the original Merovingian bloodline, the converted Jews, possibly of the community known as Essenes who set down roots in southern Gaul centuries ago.

Nostradamus also saw that, in the future, in the time that has come to us now, "the Barque of Saint Peter will be destroyed."[9] This "barque," or boat, is possibly the Petrine Roman Catholic establishment, and he may have been foretelling the recent sexual scandals among the priesthood. By denigrating sexuality for 2000 years, the Church repressed the significant dark sexual aspect of the Goddess. The resulting stipulation of celibacy for priests no doubt helped precipitate the ignominy of the sexual scandals which surfaced among Catholic clerics in the beginning of the twenty-first century.

Moreover, I find it curious that so many of these repressed secret societies connect back to our earliest history in Egypt—to the cults of Isis and later of Artemis.

Three pagan goddesses are associated with the iconic Mary: Egyptian Isis, whose image shows her with her son Horus on her lap exactly like the medieval Virgin and child; Cybele, who came to Rome in the form of a black stone, known as Magma Mater; and Artemis of Ephesus, who was brought to Marseille in 600 B.C.E. by Greek Phoenician traders. The early image of Mary as dark skinned, most likely as a Semite in the desert climate, was later "whitened" and made immaculate as the Virgin mother of Christ, "split from her earthly female body."[10] After the 13th century, Mary lightens and is lifted into the status of a sky goddess. But the differences are evident . . .

> When Mary appears as the black madonna, at the sites that I have explored, she has independence and power totally unlike her white counterpart. It seems that the blackness is the thread to the older

---

6. Begg, *Black Virgin*, p. 100.
7. David Fontana, *The Secret Language of Symbols: A Visual Key to Symbols and Their Meanings* (San Francisco: Chronicle Books, 1993), p. 179.
8. Begg, *Black Virgin*, p. 149.
9. Begg, *Black Virgin*, p. 149.
10. Rose Notes.

and deeper teachings . . . that a woman's body, like the earth itself, is sacred. . . . The mother of all human beings was African.[11]

The Gnostics united the dark and the light sides of the feminine and called her "Lady." She was associated with Saint John's image in Revelations 12:1 of a woman "clothed with the sun and the moon under feet, and upon her head a crown of twelve stars." Begg also refers to an image from the *Sforza Book of Hours*, which dates from 1490, that shows a huge penitent Magdalen, her long hair covering her, and four angels in each corner. The image resembles the World card in the tarot, with . . . a boat whose occupants gaze up in wonder at the heavenly portent, as does a bearded man in prayer on the land. Finally there is a rocky, brown mountain with a cave outside which are representative of a woman and child."[12]

The World card in some decks is known as the Universe—an essentially hermaphroditic image and a symbol of balance. Arrien describes the World card as a return "to the original vision or life force symbolized by the Egyptian Eye of Horus."[13] Horus is Isis' child and is known for his one eye, the same eye the founding fathers, (most of whom belonged to the Freemasons) put on our dollar bill, symbolic of the visionary third eye, an inner seeing. Yet the female figure is veiled "across the body . . . The veil reminds us that there are more mysteries to come."[14]

Begg's description of the bearded man on the World card made me wonder whether he is Joseph of Arimathea, the man who secured for Christ the upper room for the Last Supper and arranged for Mary's voyage to Marseille. Joseph comes to Europe himself in the legends and is sometimes associated with the Druids.

The statues that have come to be known as the Black Madonnas connect to the original teachings of Mary Magdalen. They were revered by both the Cathars and the Templar Knights. Mary's true role as a teacher of the hidden tradition became part of the heresy, hence her "blackness," as in "occult" or "hidden" on a symbolic level.

When I began to look for answers as to why the Black Madonna was black or brown I discovered a few books and articles that were

---

11. Rose Notes.
12. Begg, *Black Virgin*, p. 100.
13. Angeles Arrien, *Tarot Handbook: Practical Applications of Ancient Visual Symbols* (New York: Jeremy P. Tarcher, 1997), p. 98.
14. Fontana, *Secret Language of Symbols*, p. 179.

informative and quite provocative. I followed my interest and I was led deeper and deeper into a study of Medieval Europe, the Cathar heresy, Mary Magdalen and the Gnostic Gospels, the evolution of Christian art, and the history of Ephesus and the mother goddesses of Anatolia.[15]

This archetype appears to be alive today in the psyche of contemporary feminist spirituality and it is moving into the population at large. Black Madonnas abound in Catholic churches throughout the world, often suitably placed beneath the churches in the dark crypts closest to the earth. According to Rose, there are 450 images of a mother and child with dark skin.

THE FRENCH CONNECTION

When I met her in early 2000, Deborah was deep into her study of the Black Madonnas. She had already visited Cathar territory on her own. That afternoon in the spring of the millennial year in the little tea room on Massachusetts Avenue in Cambridge, I felt as if I had been initiated once again into a spiritual mystery. My own fascination with the Gnostic gospels, my several poems, and my efforts to live in accordance with the *Course in Miracles* came together with a commitment to join Deborah on her journey.

Of course, I wondered if my third eye would be able to detect the energy fields and "morphic resonance" of the Black Madonna locations. My French studies from college and grad school convinced me that there were more connections to be made. My intuition settled the situation; I had to go. I knew the opportunity had been presented at a timely moment, for once again I would be free from my teaching at the scheduled travel time.

The trip was planned for mid July, just as my summer courses ended. There were six of us, all looking for soul-making experiences to bring us further into the feminine heritage that was missing from our own religious roots. Deborah's itinerary took us first to Saintes-Maries-de-la-Mer on the southern-most tip of France, where gypsies still roam and sing of Mary and Martha's arrival with their servant girl Sara, who is always imaged as black. The three Maries, according to legend, are Mary Magdalen, Mary

---

15. Rose Notes

Salome, and Mary Jacobi—the last two thought to be half sisters to the Virgin Mary.

Throughout my pilgrimage in France, I found my own personal connections to French history through the new visions in my third eye. The possible line of my own incarnations—or an attunement to the past from the Essenes, to the Gnostics, to the secret movements in Medieval France—showed consistency. Still, there was nothing that I could prove conclusively. I could only follow my own intuitive messages and the inner images I was given.

I knew my initiation was an ongoing process, and that the spirit guides around me were changing my body. I regularly felt their hands on me and within me. I often felt magnetic tugs and found these spirits or angels or higher beings responded to my prompts. As I learned to ask for help, I trusted more and more what David and John had told me about my healing. When I ask, I literally feel the cool elixir and perceive, through my third eye, shadowy figures surrounding me, approaching me, moving their hands through me. Sometimes, the healing is only partially effective. I understand that its success or failure depends on how much the blockage of *chi*, or life force, has affected my material body. I was never all that far from depression but I can say that I now have senses I was not born with. And I am aware that many other people on this planet are receiving and *perceiving* healing in new and different ways. I am fortunate to feel the physical presence of spirits, while others must trust their faith alone. More and more, I understand "the resurrection of the body" in these symbolic terms. Through grief, strife, struggle, forgiveness, meditation, and body work, people can open their hearts and evolve. Perhaps it follows that, with aligned meridians and grounded energy, the human body can regain its rightful psychic heritage. It is only our idea of unworthiness that keeps us ignorant and in pain.

I wrote another poem about Mary, this time expressing more blatantly the forces of sexual desire and pagan power with which she can be linked. Was she Christ's wife? There are scholars who point out how unlikely it is that a thirty-year-old Jewish man of Christ's time would remain a bachelor. Starbird even mentions that it was law that a family find a wife for an unmarried man by the age of twenty, quoting Ecclesiastes 36:25 as her source. There is also speculation that the wedding in Cana, the site of Christ's first miracle, was indeed that of Jesus and Mary.

Mystical scholar Andrew Harvey doesn't mention a marriage to Mary Magdalen in his book *Son of Man; The Mystical Path to Christ*. Rather, he inter-

THE FUTURE THAT BROUGHT HER HERE

prets Mother Mary's role in the Cana incident as a blessing on the sexuality of marriage and he acknowledges the damage of traditional Christian "body hatred" and "contempt for sexuality."

> At Cana, Mary reveals herself as the Queen of Tantric ecstasy, the force of embodied divine love . . . This is the true 'Sacrament of Cana,' and when its full implications are embraced a worldwide healing of the body and of the many profound sexual wounds a patriarchal interpretation of Christ has inflicted on humankind can take place.[16]

Harvey goes on to speak of the "tantric aspect of the Christ-force" and it's relation to opening the heart. Growing up Catholic, many of us, especially female churchgoers, could not help but internalize the negative message of the Church's sexual shadow. I had always wondered why Mother Mary felt so concerned that Jesus make more wine available for the wedding guests at Cana. It is she who gently nudges her son to his first miracle. Of course, we will probably never know, but the truth might undo two centuries of misogyny and erase some of the damage the Church has done to women and the idea of healthy sexuality.

As a young woman, I also wondered about Mary Magdalen—this very important soul who chose to experience a life that would consign her to history as a whore. What secrets of the power of women and their sexuality did the Church of Rome find so threatening to its wealth and power? It is Mary Magdalen who applies the spikenard and then wipes Jesus' feet with her long hair. This rite for a dying king was reserved only for a priestess or a spouse. Whether Mary was a pagan priestess, a wife, or a powerful saint, she is associated with the power of the Black Madonnas. In the poem I wrote about her, I wanted to give her back the transcendent power of her voice.

---

16. Andrew Harvey, *Son of Man: The Mystical Path to Christ* (New York: Tarcher/Putnam, 1998), p. 189.

Magdalen

Matter gave birth to a passion that has no equal which proceeded from something contrary to nature.
—*The Gospel of Mary*

History named me a whore.
But history fears women with power

and finds an excuse. I was worse.
The Sorceress of Magdala, I knew the patterns

of imbalance which horn beam cured.
Tranquility induced by larch and beech.

Stirring palliatives of aspen and clematis
in a slow boil of weeds, I mixed elixirs for dropsy

and warts. When I taught, I taught throats to open,
intoning the centers along the spine

and I knew chants to extract the animal
rage from a lover. Thomas called me the thirteenth

apostle, unlucky, and Peter wanted me
gone. But Christ knew me as kin, knew history

would be unkind, that first night we talked
on my pallet after the crowd broke up.

My elbow brushed his as I shared the figs
hidden under my cloak. Our burden came clear

in the first taste of fruit. Even the air circling our limbs
slid into contours like caresses, each glow weaving

the other's shadow. Dark blew out the sky
and only the fire of our doubled ethers lit up the hut.

The method of love is not as important
as its transmission. And how bad is it—

for the gospel's infamous slut,
if the soul lives her purpose?

If the heart that has learned to transcend
transcends?

*

In my own readings and spiritual disciplines, I knew the power of transcendence through meditation. At the same time, of course, I have difficulty with the collective reality to which I contribute, and in which I participate. This reality ties us in the knot of our suffering, nails us to our sense of a limited corporeal body, and denies us direct acknowledgment of our own participation in divinity, so that we have no idea that our own collective fears and beliefs have created the world we so often call out to God to heal. Karen King expresses our worthy innocence.

> The Savior's teachings are aimed at freeing people from suffering and death, not punishing them for their sins. The Gospel of Mary has no notion of hell. There is no intrinsic value in the atoning death of Christ or the martyrdom of believers or the punishment of souls because there is no such thing as sin.[17]

This is the exact same truth that John taught us in our healing group. There is only ignorance and fear, which indeed can lead to evil actions in this reality. But it seems we have lost that truth by inflating the importance of the material world. How dismayed I felt watching *The Passion of the Christ*, Mel Gibson's film about the last twelve hours of Christ's life on Earth. Thousands of people attended this film, enduring the gory images, nailed to their own crosses of guilt. The misplaced emphasis on Christ's suffering rather than his resurrection has created our negative self-image as sinners. Had the Son of Man been lauded as an example of our own literal resurrection, had he been lauded as

---

17. Karen King, *The Gospel of Mary of Magdala: Jesus and the First Woman Apostle* (Santa Rosa, CA: Polebridge Press, 2003), p. 127.

an example of evolution that includes reincarnating and transcendence of the material body, then this would truly have been the movie of the century.

Thinking of ourselves as sinners may have some positive outcomes—like repentance, for instance. But we are more in need of *self-forgiveness* for our ignorance that we are all part of the godhead. We all have been wandering, spiritually handicapped by our own projections, ever since the so-called Fall. And it is up to us as a species, as parts of the godhead in our own right, to awaken from Adam's sleep.

Chapter 20

THE GIVER OF FORMS

For I am the first and the last.
I am the honored one and the scorned one.
I am the whore and the holy one.
"THE THUNDER PERFECT MIND," *NAG HAMMADI LIBRARY*

On the morning of July 18th, 2000, we arrived in Marseille jet-lagged but wide-eyed, picked up our rented van, and took off for Saintes-Maries-de-la-Mer, a coastal resort that was a key stop on the route of the medieval pilgrimage to Compostela in Spain. It seemed only natural that we begin our quest for Mary where the land meets the sea—"mer"/"mère." For me personally, the ocean has always been and will always be a source of inspiration. I have always lived close to the ocean, the original mother.

Cruising into the small coastal ticky-tacky, tourist-ridden town, we passed huge fields of lavender and sunflowers, wild pink flamingos, and the white horses that roam as freely as the gypsies that live in camps on the outskirts of the village. Near the brightly painted aqua-and-scarlet trailers, olive-skinned barefoot children lingered in wrinkled, boldly colored clothing. Hot-pink doorways and flowered tablecloths of yellow and red glowed iridescently under the bright Sun throughout the town. Even the twangy French spoken in this honky-tonk village charmed us immediately. Van Gogh's visions aside, midsummer in southern France is simply gorgeous; the light is extraordinary, and the sun doesn't set until well after nine P.M.

After settling into our rooms and crashing into sleep for a few hours, we met in the lobby to go out to dinner. Two Joans, two Deborahs, Katie, and Elaine. Our little group strolled through the outdoor cafés in search of some native seafood and found a quaint patio restaurant near the seawall. Rhone wine, cheap and plentiful, further heightened the mood, as we became acquainted with the roving gypsies who serenade diners in the evenings with the beautiful grief of their wailing, sorrowful songs. They appear each night in floppy felt hats and puffy-sleeved clothing accessorized with stones sewn into belts, jute anklets, and flaring scarves. They roam through the outdoor cafés and, at the least sidelong glance, approach the diners singing, accompanied by guitars and tambourines, or spoons and bells, until you pay enough to make them leave. Though persistent and pesky, I loved the distinctly foreign presence they contributed to the atmosphere. This was France, but not the France I had visited years ago as a student.

The gypsies, and their belief in the ancient story of the Magdalen's arrival in Gaul with her black daughter (or servant, depending on which legend you hear), gave another exotic edge to the windy little streets and tropical flora that mark this region known as the Camargue. In the spring, the town celebrates a festival in Sara's honor. They carry her statue from the church crypt to the ocean accompanied by hundreds of townspeople and reveling travelers. We were sorry to miss that procession, yet, as festive as we felt on our first night, we turned in reasonably early in order to be fresh in the morning to perform an initiation ritual on French soil. Young Joanie, my dream-group lady, always stayed out a little later than the rest of us, and entertained us over breakfast with her stories of dancing till dawn with campers on the beach. We dubbed her the "Partying Magdalen."

After breakfast on our second day, we headed down to the surf, a few blocks from the small hotel. Deborah pointed out a spot down by the jetty where there were fewer people. We climbed over the long rocks to a little circle of sand at the edge of the sea. There, Deborah led us in the first of our many self-designed rituals. Ringing her small Tibetan chime and burning sage for purification, she invoked the Great Mothers, or the feminine aspect of God. The Gnostics' beautiful poem, "The Thunder Perfect Mind," depicts a Supreme Being, an androgynous force, one capacious enough to hold both genders. In Gnostic mythology, there is a component of the feminine soul, Sophia, which means "wisdom." We passed the bowl of burning sage and each read a few passages from this mythic poem. As you read this excerpt, note the many paradoxes, which seem to express an ineffable truth in the way only myth and dream can.

> I am the wife and the virgin.
> I am the mother and the daughter.
> I am the members of my mother.
> I am the barren one and many are her sons.
>
> I am the she whose wedding is great
> and I have not taken a husband.
> I am the midwife and she who does not bear.

I am the solace of my labor pains.
I am the bride and the bridegroom,
and it is my husband who begot me.
I am the mother of my father
and the sister of my husband
and he is my offspring.

I am the slave of him who prepared me.
I am the ruler of my offspring.
But he is the one who begot me before the time on a birthday.
And he is my offspring in due time
and my power is from him.
I am the staff of his power in this youth
and he is the rod of my old age.
And whatever he wills happens to me.
I am the silence that is incomprehensible
and the idea whose remembrance is frequent.
I am the voice whose sound is manifold
and the word whose appearance is multiple.
I am the utterance of my name . . .

. . . For what is inside of you is what is outside of you,
and the one who fashions you on the outside
is the one who shaped the inside of you.
And what you see outside of you, you see inside of you;
it is visible and it is your garment.[1]

As we began our pilgrimage through France, we wanted to honor the truth of this poem and begin our journey with a significant ritual, grounding ourselves in the mythic world of our intuition. We passed the chime around the circle and each stated something personal about her intentions for the day, or about her developing relationship with the sacred location of the day. Sometimes, we posed a request to the feminine spirits that guided us.

I read one of my Magdalen poems and the other women picked out readings or merely spoke spontaneously. My personal intention for the trip was to discover something more about my own mystery, my third-eye activity. I wanted to know if it was connected to the mystery of the Black Madonnas and

---

1. James Robinson, gen. ed., *The Nag Hammadi Library* (San Francisco: HarperCollins, 1981), pp. 271–276.

the heresy of the Middle Ages to which I was instinctively drawn. I was turning a developmental corner in my own psychology, and I wanted to anchor it in the more general evolution of the species. I'd spent many years in the world of the intellect, the world of the fathers. The legacy of my own father and his sudden early death had made a strong impression on me at the age of fifteen.

I spoke of my own struggle with my masculine side, and my distrust of men and fear of abandonment. Afterward, we sipped from a small, cobalt bottle filled with a local liquor, then tasted a finger full of the "sacred" honey, which, in keeping with an ancient tradition, we poured on a rock for the goddess/mothers. We felt both solemn and light-hearted about the rituals, which we continually invented as we traveled.

What moved me emotionally and deepened me psychically throughout this trip was the power of the group experience and the not-infrequent synchronistic events that occurred in the immediate atmosphere and landscape—or, more precisely, the energy fields—that seemed to affirm our intentions. I had been stating affirmations before my meditations for some time and it seemed appropriate to state them aloud here with my fellow pilgrims.

GIVER OF FORMS

Feminine power has been part of the *zeitgeist* since the women's movement in the 1960s. The 21st century has been said to mark the return of the Goddess by astrologers and psychics alike. We knew it was feminine sensibility, embraced by both men or women, that would help to transform the planet. The Earth is feminine, and she has been degraded by wars, corporate exploitation, and profiteering. Her honor has scarcely been upheld in America, at least not since the Native American traditions lost touch with her powers as they were crushed in the 19th century.

The changes and upheavals of the Nineties and the storms, hurricanes, and tsunami of the early 21st century are evidence of the Earth's ascension process as well. Joseph Campbell, in *The Power of Myth*, tells the story of the Goddess as "The Giver of Forms." The feminine, after all, *is* the body, just as churches are feminine forms that represent the sacred marriage of spirit and body. It is woman who gives birth to humankind. It is the Earth that transmutes the form of the body back into herself at its death.

The Gnostic systems are largely mythic, yet they hold ultimate truth because the sense of knowing and understanding they are designed to convey is beyond the rational mind used to functioning in a world where opposite poles are never reconciled. In our dualistic universe, we find it difficult to hold opposites in tension. But in the worlds of myth, poetry, and dreams, the tension between extremities reveals a spacious reality. I remember reading that Einstein called the rational mind a faithful servant of the intuitive mind, yet today it seems more the betrayer.

In Jungian thought, the autonomous psyche may produce a unifying image from this tension, an image that transcends its polarities. In "The Thunder Perfect Mind," it seems the opposites are held in balance by the proclamation of the speaker's *I am.* The poem seems to give voice to *the Oneness that is All.* If we are all interrelated through the aspect of our own divinity, then this is the voice of the God/Goddess, the *All that Is* and ever will be.

The last 2000 years, the age of dualism and patriarchy, ended officially on December 31st, 1999, though the Age of Aquarius was already beginning in the 1960's. The feminine consciousness, like the New Age itself, was celebrated by many as a wave of light moving into the hearts and minds of those who were awake enough to feel it. Though many people think of the changing paradigm as something symbolic, there is an energetic reality at work, and we find, in these chaotic first years of the century, a polarization within the population. The dualistic splits of the Age of Pisces, an age of polar oppositions, has come to an end temporally, but there is no clear line to separate the ending of one age and the beginning of another. The most powerful institutions will probably be the last to go. How churches and political life and the idea of marriage and family will be transformed is still vague, although we already have hints in a new spirit of giving and the rise of Green businesses, community greenhouses and holistic healing alternatives. And even in the summer of 2000, I had no doubt that the process was already in motion whereby the new Aquarian spirit of freedom, tolerance, and equality would come into its full power, even as the last battles of duality are being fought. The Middle East, and Iraq specifically, is ancient Babylon. And, as we can see, Armageddon has begun.

On the beach that morning in France, we stood somewhat unceremoniously with our sage, honey, and liquors to liberate the spirit of the dark feminine locked in her Gnostic poetic mystery. Joanie, our Native American specialist, then taught us several songs. We sat on the rocks, warbling our new tunes both harmoniously and hideously off key, while the resort's early bathers looked over at us and smiled.

Having grown up both cynical and shy, I was surprised that I didn't find this scene corny. Perhaps it was my own opening heart, but, even as we broke into laughter, I was moved to tears, just as I was during the traditional Catholic masses Father Joseph celebrated throughout my trip to Israel. Yet here, I was even more at home with the evolving spiritual culture our little group created, and a new eclectic tradition in which I instinctively had faith.

My longtime psychic, David, told me once that I had been burned at the stake in a previous life as a punishment for speaking the truth. John had also indicated several times that I had been executed for my beliefs. I'm certainly glad that I have no conscious memory of these possible lives, but it does perhaps account for my panic disorder. I did have an immediate response to the legacy of the Essenes when I was in Israel. At the ruins of Qumran, I almost fell to my knees in grief. I didn't understand my reaction at the time, but when I returned home, I read about the Essenes and discovered a connection between the legends of the Magdalen in France and the legacies of the Essene community. I felt I must have had past lives here in France, or that I had aspects of my multi-dimensional identity currently living in medieval France. I had no reason to be drawn to the French and their language in high school, or when I selected my college major, but the language always came easily to me. I think I felt the faith of other incarnations still resonating at my core. In any event, I was grateful to be standing on French soil—or rather, ankle-deep in French sand—spiritually open to a deep appreciation for the Earth.

The sea was blue, the sun generously splashing down, the sky twizzling its reflections, the gulls friendly, and my fellow pilgrims already like family. We took the rest of the morning to swim, walk the cement wall, or sit on the beach in silence and immerse ourselves in the new land. Later, we gathered in town and went together to visit the dark-skinned Sara in the crypt beneath the church.

SARA'S MESSAGE

Sara is sacred to this little town, especially to the gypsies, who, in the ambiguity of the legend, consider her to be the daughter of Magdalen and Jesus. In the ceremonial procession every May, the gypsies and townspeople are accompanied by the wild white horses indigenous to the region and any other exotic animals that roam within their camps. Although we arrived two months late for this event, we still needed to see Sara, the gypsy goddess, in her natural home in the Camargue.

The little church in the center of town is a stone building with a medieval tower (Magdala means "tower"). In 1448, René d'Anjou, King of Provence, opened the crypt, which contains a huge stone known as the *L'Oreiller des*

Saintes, or pillow of saints. The stone is said to offer fertility and healing for the eyes (perhaps opening them to higher dimensions?).[2]

The artwork in the main church depicts three women arriving in a boat. Throughout this region, the Mary Magdalen in the legend is always associated with the boat that brought her. In this story, the three Maries—Mary Magdalen and the two sisters of Mother Mary—arrive in a crude, rudderless dinghy that somehow magically finds its way to the shores of Gaul, where Marseille (a short distance from Sainte Marie de la Mer) was a working harbor and a center of trade at the time of Christ. The details of the legend, of course, can no more be verified than those of Christ's miracles in Israel. But the art is lovely, and I bought a small statue of Sarah, the first of several mementos I collected to place in a shadow box later.

Down in the crypt, it is extremely warm. Tall white candles lit by tourists and pilgrims intensify the summer heat. Sara herself is surrounded by votive candles and written requests for prayer. After walking the small perimeter, I sat in a pew and tried to imagine this seaside village 2000 years ago. I prayed for changes in the world at large and in my own life in particular. Then I took a moment to close my eyes and focus on what was there.

The usual darkness was highlighted by the lights flickering in front of me. In the weeks leading up to this trip, I had been viewing my aristocratic French scene through my third eye on a regular basis. But I had a quick flash of intuition that there was something new coming into view as I moved through the eye looking back at me and entered the usual rotating vortices—deeper, deeper—until finally, a very fuzzy, but separate, scene arose out of the zigzagging lines. I saw a huge stone wall with stone stairs on one side. I was viewing it from the bottom up. I then watched a pale ghostly figure descend the steps and fade away. The scene ended in a few seconds.

In my mind, I heard the word "dungeon." I don't know why I chose to download "dungeon" rather than "crypt" as I sat in the basement of the cathedral. But, as I attuned myself to the *feeling* of the vision, it felt like a place of imprisonment. There were no windows and it was very deep. I jotted the memory down in my notebook, excited that I might have some glimpses into yet another life—one that took place in France and was somehow connected to the Black Madonnas.

Later that first night, after a wonderful dinner at a Greek café in the village, I had a strange dream. One scene occurred at what was supposed to

---

2. Ean Begg, *The Cult of the Black Virgin* (Herndon, VA: Lindisfarne Books, 2006), pp. 220-221.

be my father's wake. In it, I found myself with some of my college friends—obviously a "dream fact," as my father died when I was still in high school. But it was the next scene that intrigued me most.

I AM WALKING WITH THREE of the Rosemont women in a wooded area. We see the outline of a body in the leaves. I pick up a leaf and it is like a snake skin. The body, it is understood, has been "scooped out." Someone calls it a "phantasmagorique." Then I am at my father's wake, waiting alone to enter a hermetically sealed room where there is a discussion underway about the Black Madonna. I understand that it is dangerous if I get caught entering, as if this is an underground resistance meeting or a secret society that is outlawed. The other women, I understand, do not know that I am to attend this meeting. Then my father appears, but he is himself as a young man of perhaps twenty-five. He approaches me and tells me that "Nothing can be proven." ❧

During our ritual the following day, just before we set out for a day trip to Arles, I told my fellow travelers about my dream. Everyone pitched in ideas about the meaning. It was, of course, especially curious to me because of its forbidden and secretive elements. I explained to my companions that I had been having third-eye visions for the last six years. I explained that I had waited anxiously to arrive in France to see if my third eye would open and reveal visions as it had in Israel and Colorado. The group took in the information about my visions without any incredulity.

The French dream word "phantasmagorique" caused us all to laugh. I spoke the best French of the six of us, but I was myself quite rusty, while several of the women had taken up that silly "Franglais" habit of saying things in English with a French accent. We were all taken with the idea of the magic word "phantasmagorique" and struck by the secretive nature of the hermetically sealed room that appeared in my dream.

The dream began with three of my college friends who are very successful business women—women who are "making it" in the patriarchal world. But as the dream progressed, it seemed to move away from that world. The body I find is "scooped out" or absent. My sense is that it is feminine—someone who has been murdered, as in the stories we hear on the nightly news in which women are abducted by men, raped, slain, and left in the woods. This, apparently, was my unconscious rendition of what had happened to the archetypal feminine spirit under the misogynistic patriarchies. Woods, in mythic and Jungian terms, are always the locale of the deep unconscious. We see this in many fairy tales where sudden transformations take place in the forest. This sense of the dream surprised me, because I didn't think in these terms consciously. I did feel on this journey, however, as if I were entering a realm I had known before, one that was dangerous, dark, and forbidden to the common person.

Someone speculated that references to my father's funeral could indicate the death of the patriarchy. Yes, I thought, a collective symbol. However, I felt I needed to explain that I had my own father complex, and that I'd been exploring my relationship with my dead father for thirty years—not only in analysis, but through a long poem. I felt, rather, that my father being dead in the first part of the dream was the patriarchal father, the Saturnine presence I had struggled under in my unconscious. Yes, and I had hoped to release myself further from it by writing a long poem about him, which I had done several years ago. Now the appearance of the new, younger, more vital father was a great encouragement. This was my father before his illness and death. He seemed to be speaking to me from a place of deep knowledge—perhaps from the afterworld, where I had placed him in my poem. This young animus figure understood what was behind the door of the sealed room and appeared to know that, although the information in the room was powerful, "nothing could be proven."

It was as if faith alone were the only entrance requirement. And what was to be proven? The veracity of my third-eye visions? The theory that Mary Magdalen was the spouse of Christ? Was the Black Madonna mystery destined to remain a mystery forever? Even feminist historians and archeologists like Marija Gimbutas, who wrote about the earliest goddess icons, have a hard time proving that the matriarchal society that preceded the Biblical world is a fact.

We thought about this during our discussion of the dream and agreed that, by quietly honoring the Madonnas and goddesses, we, along with thousands of others on the planet, were bringing them back into the collective consciousness. This seems to have happened later—*literally*—with the publication of Dan Brown's *DaVinci Code*, the single biggest bestseller of all time. We did not need to prove anything historically. Belief would manifest outwardly only if we held it confidently within. True, the consensus reality created by the collective is a huge drawback for each of us. Yet the mere size of the consciousness movement, as evidenced by the huge number of Web sites, spiritual bookstores, and various new alliances and charities that are working for vast changes in world health and world justice, shows that we were not the only ones moving to create a new reality within the world's veil. The Mary sightings in Yugoslavia prior to the terrible wars there in the 1990s brought thousands to honor the mother. Since then, there have been all sorts of absurd Mary sightings—the Steak-and-Cheese Madonna, the Hospital-Window-in-the-Sun Madonna, Our Lady of the Tar Stain in the Parking Lot, and on and on.

The image of a snake skin in my dream was also a positive sign. This is an image of transformation that occurs naturally as the snake sheds its old skin and grows a new one. The serpent in Eden is a symbol of evil in general and Satan in particular. But in the goddess traditions, the snake is a sacred symbol. Even in Eden, the snake encourages the eating of the apple from the Tree of Knowledge, an act that leads to the end of Eden, to a world of duality, to good and evil and the necessity to discriminate between them. One of the *Nag Hammadi* documents called "The Dialogue of the Savior" gives a very solid reason for the need to pass through our dimension, where the duality of polar opposites is obvious.

> If one does not stand in the darkness, he will not be able to see the light. If one does not understand how the fire came to be, he will burn in it, because he does not know his root . . . If one does not understand how the body he wears came to be, he will perish with it . . . And he who will not know the root of all things, they (all things) are hidden from him. He who will not know the root of wickedness is not a stranger to it.[3]

And from the Gospel of Philip,

> Light and darkness, life and death, right and left, are brothers of one another. They are inseparable. Because of this neither are the good good, nor the evil evil, nor is life life, nor death, death. For this reason each one will dissolve into its original nature. But those who are exalted above the world are indissoluble, eternal.[4]

Rather than remain unconscious in Eden, humankind chose to enter a world where any level of evolution to higher consciousness must be consciously chosen, for we do exist in a world of evil (ignorance) and good (ethical integrity), and we do have to learn to align ourselves with one or transcend the temptations of the other. Such was the effect of the endowment of free

---

3. Robinson, *Nag Hammadi Library*, p. 234.
4. Robinson, *Nag Hammadi Library*, p. 132.

will. Therefore, an offering from a so-called Satan was necessary for us to become fully conscious of the illusory projections we have made of evil and good in our world—the world of the third dimension.

In our healing group, John told us that, after we left Eden, we forgot who we were—that is, sparks of the Godhead. We created the opposite of what we were so that we could know our own value, for how can we recognize light without darkness? Yet when we moved into the darkness, the fears created by separation from Oneness and imprisonment in an individual ego caused us collectively to forget. And, as in John's gospel, when we are told we come from the light, we can still find the light within. This calls for each individual's direct experience of the journey inward, as we're told in "The Dialogue with the Savior": "But I say to you, as for what you seek after and inquire about, behold it is within you."[5]

This message is repeated throughout the New Testament, in the approved gospels as well as those that were excised. Can this possibly refer to the inner light I see in my visions? For, even in a completely dark room, I can close my eyes and see a rim of light at the edges of my vision. I told my traveling companions about my own frustration with my meditation visions. I couldn't *prove* them to anyone. I couldn't *show* them to anyone. And I worried that, if I spoke of them, people would not believe me, or would believe I was crazy or making them up. After six years with no debilitating symptoms, I dispelled the notion that anything physical in my three-dimensional body was involved. No, all I could do was hold these visions with my own authority and describe them in words. They belonged to another dimension, the mythic world, even if they were only my own myths. I understood them as symbolic and revelatory, and I felt I was meant to share them despite the scorn or ridicule I might encounter. I am heartened by the words in the Gospel of Philip about the pearl cast down in the mud (or among swine, as we read it in the accepted gospels)—"it always has value in the eyes of its owner."[6]

This latest dream made me understand more fully that the "secret" aspect of this experience was implied and that I must accept others as they are. As Christ says throughout all the gospels, "Those who have ears, let them hear." I needed the right ears, and I wouldn't have listened had I not seen as well. My dream that night, with all its different levels, seemed to have

5. Robinson, *Nag Hammadi Library*, p. 232.
6. Robinson, *Nag Hammadi Library*, p. 137.

personal aspects for me and my journey with my father's spirit, as well as collective aspects for our group, for all women, and for humanity as a whole. The rituals and initiations had more influence than I thought and the magical ocean of dreams spoke to us in an affirming voice. As a group, the six of us were leaving the patriarchal world for a while, traveling in the belly of our rented blue van, already in the womb of the Goddess.

Chapter 21

THE MANDORLA

. . . in the ancient cults celebrating the sacred marriage it is always the bride who anoints her bridegroom in the actual nuptial rite—foreshadowing events consummated in the privacy of the bridal chamber.

MARGARET STARBIRD, *MAGDALENE'S LOST LEGACY*

We left the coast and drove the short distance north to Arles, drinking in the amazing colors of the countryside—the rich browns against the bold fields of sunflowers, the lavender and cypress trees that Van Gogh so often captured on canvas. The day was perfect, the sky glassy blue and cloudless. The town nested comfortably among red hills beneath the generous light. After wrestling for a time with the mysterious French parking meters, we headed on foot to the Eglise Saint Trophime, an early Christian church built in 1190, whose architecture is the epitome of Provençal Romanesque. Deborah's interest in the church focused particularly on the doorway that shows Christ seated in "the mandorla," known as an ancient feminine symbol of the vulva, " . . . the seed that is a doorway to a new world, one in which true feminine imagination is highly valued."[1]

In her appendix to *The Goddess in the Gospels*, Margaret Starbird speaks about the holy name of Mary and the significance of its gematria in the ancient Greek system of numbers. The name Maria is equivalent to the number 153, which relates in shape to "the measure of the fish," or, in Latin, the *Vesica Piscis*. The shape looks like this ◊ and, to Greek mathematicians and ancient geometrists, it designates the "womb or matrix of all geometric derivations."[2]

The mandorla is considered an opening, the almond-shaped vulva, a gateway specifically identified as feminine. It is also known in art as an "almond,"

---

1. Veronica Goodchild, *Eros and Chaos: The Sacred Mysteries and Dark Shadows of Love* (Lake Worth, FL: Nicolas-Hays, 2001), p. 105.
2. Margaret Starbird, *The Goddess in the Gospels: Reclaiming the Sacred Feminine* (Rochester, VT: Inner Traditions, 1998), Appendix III.

or in Italian as *mandorla*. In the Bible, the almond is considered an "awakener," as it flowers in January in Palestine. Starbird says the mandorla was the "matrix" (mother) from which all other geometric figures were derived. It was also known in the ancient world as "the Holy of Holies—the "inner sanctum." . . . The shape represented, quite literally, the eternal creation of the "Earth-Grail."[3]

For 2000 years, this idea was encoded in the gematria of her name. As I mentioned earlier, the anointing of the dying king, the act Mary Magdalen performs on Jesus the night of the Last Supper, was always performed by Egyptian brides. And here, in the image of the church doorway, is Christ seated *within* the mandorla!

As we enter the church, we enter the body of the sacred. The Black Madonnas, whose postures are straight and empowered, hold the child Jesus on their laps with a strong and stiff authority, like that of Isis' throne holding Pharaoh. Compared to the late medieval and Renaissance Marys, whose bodies curve, whose skin is lightened, and whose figures show soft vulnerability, the Black Madonnas are formidable in their appearance of strength. Starbird concludes that the messages of the excised Gnostic gospels were preserved symbolically in the sacred geometry of Gothic architecture and in the symbolism of the Black Madonnas. The early Christians took these older goddess forms and images of Isis and Horus and their pagan past to keep the fertility of Christ and the Magdalen's marriage alive, despite its having been erased by the Patriarchs.

It has been alleged that Mary Magdalen, a former pagan, is the link between the Essenes and the early Gnostics, as well as the lost Grail or the vessel containing the blood, the feminine counterpart, of Christ. In the legends, this bloodline flows into that of the Merovingian Kings and the tales of the Holy Grail. The followers of the Gnostic Magdalen flourished here. Starbird speculates that the bloodline was also kept secret for the protection of the family. Though historians have been unable to prove them definitively, we have to consider how these speculations would have significantly altered the institutions that grew up around Christendom.

We spent a long time in our private meditations viewing this image of Christ enthroned within the mandorla. When we left the church, we found the cloisters of Saint Trophime, which are steeped in medieval Christianity. There, Martha, the sister of Mary Magdalen, is portrayed repeatedly with

---

3. Starbird, *Goddess in the Gospels*, Appendix III.

the dragon she killed according to the legend. There is not much research available on the exact significance of this dragon. In Jungian thought, the dragon implies the ego, which must be overcome by the self. As Joseph Campbell interprets it, the ego must be subjugated to the whole person. Symbolically, the killing of a dragon is often about overcoming an inner obstacle, transcending the goals of the ego and dispelling its fears, usually related to some opinion the ego holds of its own importance or the fear behind that opinion. Perhaps in Martha's case, the dragon symbolizes the patriarchal tradition that these legends tended to undermine.

The paintings in the cloister date to the early medieval centuries and are a good deal faded, but Martha certainly has her own independent authority in these works. Deborah told us that the stories of Mary and Martha in France date from early Christian times, but did not gain real popularity and dominance until the early Middle Ages when the troubadours spread the songs of the Grail. We wandered from one painting to another, taken with the fantastical images—the "phantasmagorique" of my dream, I suggested, as we all laughed aloud. Later, we wandered in the outdoor shops and cafés, and sat for a snack in front of the Roman Arena, a smaller but still imposing Colosseum whose height dominates the town. I strolled along its periphery, amazed that I had not previously known there were so many Roman ruins in France.

THE KNIGHT OF LES BAUX

Our evening plan was to pick up some picnic food and have our supper at one of Deborah's favorite spots in the colorful hills outside Arles, an area called Les Baux de Provence. We battled our way through a crowded supermarket, splitting up to find designated cheeses, wine, and sausages. Finally, with our backpacks overflowing, we piled into the van and headed up the rocky hillside where Deborah, on a previous trip, had found the ruins of a fortified castle.

Les Baux is the setting for one of the famous courts of love that attracted troubadours from all over France. Here, they performed their songs and poems, and sought the approval of the court ladies who served as their muses. We were in the rural countryside within a half hour and, by intuition, Deborah led us toward her inspiring picnic ground. We carried our food from the van, following Deborah on foot up and down a narrow path, amid the weeds and grass of a steep hillside. We climbed for quite a while, teasing like nagging children: "Are we there yet? Are we having fun yet?" Occasionally, I found myself deep in fantasy, gazing at the countryside, imagining the era of knights in armor and the maidens to whom they dedicated their jousts and feats. Remembering the vision of my inner prisoner in the dungeon, I was now itching to study the Middle Ages.

I had taken an early-morning college course in medieval French literature, and I remembered now how I could hardly ever make it to class. For some reason other than the not-unreasonable time of 8:30 A.M., I just couldn't drag myself out of bed to get there. My dear friend and fellow French major, Betsy, knocked on my door three mornings a week to remind me that I had intended the evening before to make it to class. Knowing what I now know from my Jungian dream work about the resistance of the unconscious, and how truly unconscious that resistance is, I wonder if there was some latent memory of execution in another life that kept me away from those texts with their Provençal excess of vowels. Mother Consolata, Chair of the French Department (just think of the meaning of her name!), called me into her office and told me that, if I passed the course, it would be a "gift." Indeed, her gift to me was the worst grade in my college career.

We had been on our feet most of the day and looked forward wearily to a paper cup full of good Rhone wine. Finally, we passed the little chapel dedicated to Mary that Deborah had stumbled on during a previous trip, and, just beyond it, we set out Joanie's shawl as a tablecloth. Before eating, we sat in a circle, sharing our thoughts about the day and reading more poetry. Only Joanie and Deborah had read the rare out-of-print book by Robert Graves *Mammon and the Black Goddess*. (Graves is much better known for his classical study of *The White Goddess*.) But Joanie chose to read Graves' mysterious poem about the prediction that a Black Goddess would establish a new relationship between men and women, one not based upon patriarchal law:

> How shall he watch at the stroke of midnight
> Dove become phoenix, plumed with green and gold?
> Or be caught up by jeweled talons
> And haled away to a fastness of the hills
> Where an unveiled woman, black as Mother Night
> Teaches him a new degree of love
> And the tongues and songs of birds?[4]

---

4. Robert Graves, *Mammon and The Black Goddess* (Garden City, NY: Doubleday and Co., 1965), p163.

We discussed the enigmatic poem and the tradition of wisdom that was associated with the Provençal and Sicilian "Black Virgins." The symbol of the phoenix who dies and is born again every 500 years connects to the blackness of Mother Night, the woman who teaches the man in this powerful statement to redress the powers of the universe. "To lift the veil" in Greek translates to the word "Apocalypse."[5] Who then is this unveiled woman of the Apocalypse, imprisoned by a secret, who reads the language of the birds? Bird lore has often been associated with the oracle, and those who could follow the enchanted chatter were often deemed prophets during the Hellenic era. Later, in medieval fairy tales, princesses are often enchanted into sleep and silenced for indefinite periods.

Ean Begg quotes Jung in *The Undiscovered Self:* "We are living in what the Greeks called the *Kairos*—the right time—for a 'metamorphosis of the gods.'"[6] This reminds me again of Jung's argument that Christianity is incomplete, the dark matter of the female body having been rejected. In Mary's gospel, Peter does not believe that the Savior taught her esoteric truths in private. Elaine Pagels explains that "Mary startles Peter by saying that she knows not only what Peter did not happen to hear but also what Jesus chose not to tell him: 'what is hidden from you I will tell you.'" Then she relates her vision.[7] We concluded that it is Mother Night, the Black Madonna, Vierge Noir, the non-linear, right-brained, left-handed, intuitive, split-off feminine darkness that will reorient humankind into a heart-based evolution.

Obviously there was much confusion among Christ's followers after his death. Even before his death, Peter was critical of his confidences with Mary Magdalen. Peter complains to Christ about her participation in their conversations.[8] Jesus scolds Peter for his criticisms and Mary confides in Jesus: "Peter makes me hesitate; I am afraid of him, because he hates the female race."[9] This statement indicates that there were differing views of women's role in early Christendom. According to Begg:

> Triumphant Rome tried to exterminate the Church of Mary, but only succeeded in driving it underground. The rights of women

5. Margaret Starbird, *Magdalene's Lost Legacy: Symbolic Numbers and the Sacred Union in Christianity* (Rochester, VT: Bear & Company, 2003), p. 85.

6. Begg, *The Cult of the Black Virgin* p 127.

7. Elaine Pagels, *Beyond Belief: The Secret Gospel of Thomas* (New York: Random House, 2003), p. 104.

8. Robinson, *Nag Hammadi Library*, "The Pstis Sophia," translates as Faith Wisdom. This refers to Mary's presence as an apostle.

9. Elaine Pagels, *The Gnostic Gospels* (New York: Vintage Books, 1981) p. 78.

were likewise repressed, though in the Celtic world they retained many of their considerable ancient freedoms.[10]

Christianity succeeded in trampling out the Cathars, the Templars, and much of the ancient Celtic world, with its Druids and fairies and the Lady of the Lake. But the idea of a goddess was still evident in the continued reverence for the Black Virgins.

At 9:30 that evening, we sat on the hillside watching the daylight draining slowly from the sky. The flicker of lights dotted the windows in the houses below. This particular night was extremely special to me—the clear evening sky, the long day full of imagery and energy. I felt as if I could lie there on the blanket of grass with my paper goblet of wine for several more hours contemplating the history of my faith from an entirely new angle. I had missed my private time to meditate, but I closed my eyes off and on to see if images would come.

Since our arrival in France, through my third eye, I had been intermittently watching an aristocratic French couple, these scenes taking place at times on the grounds of a grand castle, something like Versailles. Sometimes I watched a fox hunt, complete with hounds and men in formal riding gear. Occasionally, I saw a military scene, with soldiers lined up on horses or marching on foot. I placed the time in the 18th century, close to the Revolution, because of the three-cornered hats and the aristocrats in wigs at the fancy dress balls. And now, lying in the hills outside Arles, behind my closed eyes, I was once again whirling though the doorways. Only now, I wanted to call them mandorlas, since their tops were rounded rather than rectangular. And my view drifted once again deeper and deeper down into that dungeon scene.

The image then backed up—that is, the stone wall appeared to move back, like a scenery change in the modern theater. It backed up and split, and, although I still saw an underground stone chamber, there was now a long corridor as well. Slowly, from out of the dark right-hand corner, around a turn in the narrow hall, came a man on horseback, his even gallop steady and strong. I squinted as much as possible, closing my eyelids in the manner of the Buddha, in order to see more clearly through my third eye. A painful, knifelike headache jammed through the middle of my forehead. I felt the density or pressure, the electromagnetic presence of my spirit guides work-

---

10. Begg, *Black Virgin*, p. 129.

ing around my head. Then I saw that my inner figure was wearing a cassock with a cross on the front. He slowed down, approached the foreground of the scene, and cantered on by, immediately fading out of view. I opened my eyes and rubbed my head, surprised to see the cassock and the cross. I felt I had expected something different—a suit of armor perhaps.

The other women were gathering up the paper plates, wrapping the leftover bread and cheese. It was now close to ten and still the sky had not completely darkened. It lay above me in a violet-blue dome as the lights from the valley sparkled more distinctly against it. I roused myself and shook out my hair. I knew the images were different from those of a dream. I didn't want to say anything to the other women yet.

I knew the Crusades had occurred over approximately the same 200-year period during which the Madonnas were worshipped. I also knew that many of the Crusaders, especially the mysterious group called the Knights Templar (those oxymoronic warrior/monks), had supposedly taken statues of the dark goddesses back to Europe from the Middle East when they returned from the ill-fated wars. The Templars were so called because they had actually inhabited the ruins of Solomon's Temple and were reputed to have a stolen a "treasure," which the Pope wanted to get his hands on. This treasure was rumored to be the lost Ark of the Covenant.

Louis Charpentier's book, The *Mysteries of Chartres Cathedral,* enumerates the many unanswered questions that remain about the legend of the Templar Knights. To begin with, there were apparently only nine knights who arrived in Jerusalem. Did they come as Crusaders? Crusaders, it would seem, would have come in larger numbers. And they were not themselves pilgrims. "What is more, they took part in no warlike activity," Charpentier observes. Charpentier suggests that the nine original Templars were on a secret mission to retrieve the Ark, which held, not the Ten Commandments, but "the Tables of the Law, the Logos, the Word; of reason, measure, relationship, number." He claims the Commandments were taught, written, proclaimed by Moses, not held in secret. But Moses assigned a Levite guard to protect the Ark, which contained "something extremely sacred . . . constituting a contract of power; extremely dangerous, and no-one had access to them, not even the Levite guard, but the High Priest alone . . . We are concerned then," Charpentier concludes, "with a divine law." [11]

---

11. Louis Charpentier, *The Mysteries of Chartres Cathedral* (Haverhill, UK: Research into Lost Knowledge Organization, 1966), pp. 49, 57.

Did Moses, the child adopted by Pharaoh's daughter, have access to the sacred geometry of the pyramids? This law was linked with specific numbers and measures, a "cosmic equation," as Charpentier puts it—"The Law of unity that rules the worlds, of relating effects with their causes and consequently of *acting* on the phenomena that the causes produce as they diversify into plurality."[12] (This is what we might call today the Law of Attraction.) Initiates had to decipher these laws from a cryptic numerical system that Charpentier says was later called the Cabala, or the heritage of the mystical way in Judaism.

Moses, who came from Egypt after all, quite possibly inherited some knowledge of the sacred dimensions contained in the pyramids, some of which were used in the construction of Gothic cathedrals like Chartres. We must remember that it was a Roman Catholic Pope who conspired with a French King to bring the Templars to ruin. I wondered about these paradoxical Crusaders, how they connected several traditions. And I made a mental note to look for more books on them while I was here in France.

After returning late that night to our beach-side hotel, we left our final day in Saintes-Maries-de-la-Mer open to explore our own rhythms. I spent most of the day by the sea and grazing in the shops—although I did visit the church again to meditate one last time in the presence of the statue of Sara. I re-examined the large painting in the upper part of the church showing Sainte Marie Jacobe and Sainte Marie Salomé in an open boat. One of them held an urn in one hand with the other hand raised in blessing. There was also an urn on the floor of the boat. The third Mary held her hands together in prayer. We would see throughout the villages we visited that Mary Magdalen is often depicted with an urn.

I mentally drew my connections. Was this urn another reference to the Grail? Was it there to represent the blood of the crucified Christ or the spikenard with which Mary anointed him on the night of the Last Supper? Were the secrets of the medieval heresy for which so many men and women were burnt alive also the deep secrets of alchemy—those suggested by the Gnostic gospels? That each of us has an intuitive gift to commune with higher aspects of the spirit world? That each of us has the power of manifestation through thought? That each of us, in fact, is a spin-off of the original Creative force? Wasn't this the salient secret of all occult traditions, that humankind could evolve to a state of divine enlightenment and exist

---

12. Charpentier, *Chartres Cathedral*, p. 57.

outside of the collective "illusion." That we can obtain the alleged powers of Jesus Christ to heal, to develop psychic knowing, and to abide in inner peace, understanding the oneness of all creatures?

In the Canonical gospels, Magdalen, like an Egyptian Priestess, applies the spikenard while Judas protests that she is wasting the pricey ointment. Christ rebukes him in this mystifying scene, insisting that it is proper to anoint him in this way. The urn represents Mary herself, as the vessel that has been lost in the Petrine Church, which wasn't established until the end of the second century.

And Mary's gospel exhibits her as a teacher of the *hidden* tradition. The restoration of feminine power to our overly masculine civilization—a civilization that appears to be headed for destruction, taking with it our feminine Earth and our original legacy—could fulfill the prophecies of Revelations. The "new heaven" may be reflected in the "new Earth." As above, so below.

While these thoughts steered our conversations at breakfast that morning, I wondered privately about my visions. The painting in front of me presented the French legend—the urn, the Grail, the boat, the body, the black (hidden) story of this Madonna, Mary Magdalen—and more significantly, feminine thought and intuition, which has been silenced for more than an aeon. I had no answers, but suddenly, the speculations appeared limitless.

Once again, I shut my eyes and looked through my forehead. I recognized the open arches through which my vision rocketed as the mandorla. The lens of my vision tightened, bringing the dungeon once again into focus. I watched the fuzzy pastel outlines spin, then form into the figure of the chevalier astride his horse. I wondered if he were a part of me, or I of him. Was his image symbolic of my experience in a past life, or a *parallel* life in a different reality? Does it matter that I know? The words of my recent dream came back to me. *Nothing can be proven.*

Even so, I liked it that he was there within me as I lay on the French terrain the previous day. He seemed confident riding that horse against the mountain-high stone walls. Was he later persecuted, incarcerated, his life snuffed out at the stake with his Templar brothers? I fantasized him in a castle with stables on the lower level, fantasized that he was heading out across some moat to fight for some "mysterious" lady or a principle that reached beyond the vicious politics of his time. Some principle deep within the symbolic mandorla fated to surface in the dawn of the 21st century. Some secret society I didn't know, but one to which, somehow, I felt I belonged.

Chapter 22

ROOTS OF THE GODDESS

. . . the Midi was, in the eleventh and twelfth centuries, Euope's cultural avant-garde;
it was the first region to break out of the "monochromatic unity" of the Dark Ages,
to awaken to interiority . . . experimental, open to new possibilities,
very much oriented to the mystical and mythological.
MORRIS BERMAN, COMING TO OUR SENSES

I see in retrospect that my trip to Israel was a necessary precursor to my trip to France. But when I toured the south of France with my women friends, I never expected to make the connection between an Essene life and the life of a Crusader. Yet these two visions had remained strongest for me.

We left Saintes Maries de la Mer on the fourth day of our trip to spend the afternoon in Marseille and then take off in the evening for the hour-long drive to Saint Maximin La Sainte Baume, one of the two towns that claim to possess Mary Magdalen's relics. As we stood with our "light luggage" in front of the van, it became apparent we couldn't fit it all in. Joan had flown in from Crete, where she lives in the summer with Nikos, her Greek husband. She was flying, with a whole summer's worth of possessions, directly back to Chicago, where Nikos would join her later. In any event, we had to tie some of our bags to the racks on top of the van. We scrounged around town in search of bungees and rope, looking like true American tourists from the Wild West as we strapped our bags to a coach with an intricate rope dance across the roof.

People stopped to make suggestions and some photographed us as we laughed and clumsily improvised. Katie became the official Priestess of the Roof Rack as the rest of us slowly let her take over. Katie was an outdoorsy, sporty woman, as was Deborah Rose. Little Joanie, distinguished from the taller Joan, coached from the sidelines. Elaine would most often rather be shopping, and I, a conceptual person, was pretty inept at this kind of endeavor. But I could see the larger picture and direct the show. With our bags finally secure, we snapped a few pictures of our Beverly Hillbillies van and took off in a cloud of pink dust down the road. On either side were low flats of sand where flamingo stood quietly against the sky. We wound our way back to Marseille, a two-hour ride, listening to a lovely contemporary song Joanie had found about Mary Magdalen.

Marseille, one of the oldest cities in France, was an active port even during the Roman Empire. The coastal city was originally founded by the Phocaeans, who had a special relationship with the goddess Artemis of Ephesus—the Anatolian Artemis. Like the more familiar Greek Artemis, she was a virgin, but is often shown with many breasts and associated with fertility. Her name is also related to Arcadia, which in turn brings up "ark," both Noah's and the Ark of the Covenant. The Phocaeans sailed adventurously around the region, where trading routes were numerous. Those who worshipped the dark-skinned goddess could very well have spread her statues throughout the region's markets, where they were deemed "Black Madonnas."

Begg claims the name Arthur derives from the Celtic *arto*, meaning "bear," or *art*, a stone, which could also indicate the Ark of the Covenant. David Hall had told me, in one of my readings, that I would pursue the Ark. Before I even walked through his door, he drew a picture of a long, horizontal stone box, saying it had come to him in his meditation for my reading. I thought, therefore, that Ark (from which the name Arthur may have derived) could also be related to the Magdalen through the Essene-Gaul-Grail connection.

The Greek Artemis is known as a huntress who kills Orion and sends him into the stars as a constellation. The Greek hero Actaeon was dismembered by his own dogs at her bidding. The older Anatolian Artemis and the Greek Artemis are both identified as protectresses of wild life, and as life-giving Black Virgins. And Artemis of Ephesus is also related to a mythic stone from a black meteor found in a swamp by Amazons.[1] Begg further associates the stone to the Grail, which we know also as a vessel, and I can't help but think of the medieval alchemists' quest for truth in the Philosopher's Stone.

Roman Catholic tradition has it that Mary, the mother of Jesus, passed the end of her life with Saint John in Ephesus. In 431 A.D., the Church of Rome raised her status with the Assumption. Artemis, her black predecessor

---

1. Ean Begg, *The Cult of the Black Virgin* (Herndon, VA: Lindisfarne Books, 2006), p. 53.

as a feminine deity, had her own cult in Ephesus 1000 years earlier. Moreover, there is a strange associative nuance to Artemis as the protectress of pubescent girls, and a negative attitude toward sexuality that falls to both Artemis and the Blessed Virgin.

Deborah Rose told us that Artemis was associated with forests, and that tree cults had grown up around her, like those of the willow, the hawthorn, and the yew—all trees of the underworld. Hecate and Persephone are underworld queens who are also part of the triple-goddess mythology: *She who rules all worlds.* We know that the Black Virgins are often found buried under or near wells on the ancient ley or energy lines that run throughout wooded areas. (These are called song lines by the aborigines in Australia.) The Madonnas now rest beneath the crypts of the Gothic churches built atop these pagan holy places.

Like Artemis, these Madonnas are severe and independent. "When moved against her will the Black Virgin resists by becoming insupportably heavy," Begg tells us. Furthermore, Artemis becomes Diana in the Roman world. She degenerates but persists in the Christian era as the goddess of witches, and Queen of the Night. Something of her tradition lives on in Black Virgins making them much prized by modern necromancers.[2]
Begg also remarks that the great Feast of the Assumption (August 15th in the Catholic calendar) originated most likely as the ancient festival of Diana. When Mary was given new status through the Assumption, she was referred to as *Theotokos*, or the Mother of God, in order to resolve any disputes about the divine humanity of Jesus.[3] Obviously, the significance of all these feminine icons overlap.

TRUE CONFESSIONS

When we arrived in Marseille, we parked the van near the waterfront and walked down the huge hill to find a place for lunch and found ourselves beneath Notre Dame de la Garde, the giant golden Madonna that stands over the church's basilica above the city. This golden (or white) virgin is called *La Bonne Mere* and she is the patroness of the city of Marseille. Deborah also pointed out a five-pointed Wiccan star carved on the pathway down the hill,. "That's a strange detail," I remarked. "Or *not!*" everyone chorused.

---

2. Begg, *The Cult of the Black Virgin,* pp. 55-56.
3. Rose Notes.

It was a gorgeous day and we couldn't help observing the number of men walking about wearing the classic blue-and-white sailor-striped boat-necked shirts associated with Marseille. The harbor is not picturesque in the traditional way of Mediterranean vacation spots. It is a rather rough-hewn, scruffy port, populated by laborers and some rather seedy-looking characters. We found our way to one of the many cafés on the working-class docks that overlook the masts of moored sailboats and numerous tankers. And though the restaurants were not glamorous, the food was plentiful. The French love to eat omelets for lunch, and the menu here had quite a list of them. Most of the dishes were served with some kind of fried fish. We ate heartily, having a carafe of oh-so-inexpensive wine as well.

We had come to see the old city and to visit the Abbey Saint Victor to commune with an important Black Madonna known as Notre Dame de la Confession. After working off our lunch by pumping our legs back up the enormous and extremely steep hill, we reached the cathedral. We found our Black Madonna deep in the cellar crypt. Deborah suggested that we sit with her, keeping an open consciousness, and offer up any negative thoughts that arose to the Madonna for transmutation.

This Madonna does not resemble the one that presides over the city from the hilltop at all. Far from glamorous or soft, she is plain and authoritative. Deborah told us that, in earlier times, a Demeter/Persephone ritual took place on this spot. Begg tells of the Candlemas procession that has replaced the Demeter/Persephone ritual in Marseille since the year 600 A.D. On February 2nd—better known to us as Groundhog Day, or the point between the winter solstice and spring equinox, "when deep within the dark earth, the life force quickens"—this Black Madonna, Notre Dame de Confession, is dressed in a green cape and lifted from her crypt to parade through town followed by a crowd carrying green candles.[4] The celebration is one of cyclic renewal. The color green, also the color sacred to the Egyptian goddess Isis, is a representation of the coming spring. The word *Theotokos* is inscribed on the Madonna's green cape. She sits up straight upon a throne just as Isis does, which gives her power and authority.

Before Deborah knew that fact, she said, her first experience with this Madonna was to spiral into negative belief patterns about marriage and men instilled in her unconsciously by her own mother. As Deborah put it:

---

4. Rose Notes,

In retrospect it is stunning to realize that my uncomfortable and unwanted feelings at this place were archetypal in nature: about a mother and a daughter, the mother's rage at men and her grief about her daughter's relationship to a man.[5]

Oh My God, I thought. How similar I felt descending into my own history. Here my soul-sister and name-sharing friend, Deborah, and I shared more connections. Though I can only speculate about my own mother's unconscious, unexpressed grief and anger at my father's death (or desertion), my unconscious appears to have picked up on something she repressed.

In the private mythology of my own dreams, throughout my therapy and afterward, the figure of my mother has been the part of me identified with a distrust of men. Certainly her own experience with my father must have wounded her deeply although she is not one ever to discuss that possibility, and I expect she would consciously deny it. Still, my mother never remarried and I was imprinted with her unconscious feelings. Whenever I confront her with this idea, she is quick to dismiss the pain, always more willing to see herself as strong and independent (and certainly she was!) rather than stricken by grief. She raised her four children with courage and it is only inside myself, through therapy, that I discovered this aspect of my mother's unconscious. To this day, whenever I meet a new man, my disapproving mother shows up in my dreams. Her consistent message is "Don't get involved; you'll just get hurt." How literally I have lived this.

Deborah's point in telling us her story was to encourage us to allow whatever came into our conscious minds to surface in our contemplation, assuring us that, later, we would find the meaning behind our thoughts. We were pilgrims, after all, and this was a holy journey for each of us. Despite our partying and playfulness, we must take everything concerned with our inner lives seriously.

I was overwhelmed by Deborah's statement that the Anatolian Mother Goddess lineage was probably the oldest known—reaching back to 6800 B.C.E., the date one archeologist attributes to a big-bodied mother giving birth while perched over a throne of leopards.[6] In Deborah's words, "Mary is the most recent in the long succession of mother goddesses from Anatolia." There is a connection between Ephesus and Marseille, since Marseille was discovered by Greeks who held the Anatolian Artemis sacred. What seemed

---

5. Rose Notes,
6. Rose Notes,

important was to understand the long lineage of goddess power related to this city.

The carved wooden Black Madonna wears a blue and green painted mantle decorated with stars. She and her son have dark-brown painted hands. I pondered her quietly, lit my candle, and thought of the line of female power that was represented here. What came up immediately and unbidden were my memories of guilt from my adolescence and onward—guilt for my own sexuality and sexual desire, which had been very intense in my early years.

Since about the age of thirteen, I had always had a steady boyfriend, a relationship that usually lasted for a year or two. I had always been drawn to express my passion, if not physically, then in poetry—corny poetry, I'll admit, but ambitious attempts nonetheless! Walks home from school often detoured into private spots and long wet kisses. I spent many Saturday afternoons writing love poems and many weekends partying with friends. I grew up fast in Manhasset, on the north shore of Long Island—a town referred to in a recent best-seller, *The Tender Bar,* as the heaviest-drinking New York suburb.

Manhasset was an affluent, sophisticated, country-club town. Growing up in the early Sixties, we had a certain amount of independence, even in junior high school, when girls walked up and down what was known in my town as the "Miracle Mile," a string of New York department stores. We collected in groups and hung out like kids do today at the malls. We usually met up with the boys somewhere during the day. At parties in finished basements each weekend, the lights dimmed and couples slow-danced and kissed languorously in the dark to the music of Johnny Mathis while parents drank martinis and whiskey sours upstairs. These halcyon scenes played out against a darker backdrop of political tension. Only a few years back, I wrote this poem in memory of the Cuban Missile Crisis and my first boyfriend:

The Day the World Froze

My first bona fide head-over-heels, whole-hog
detonation of the hormones: thirteen, walked home
by Jimmy Green—breathless autumn day,
sky festooned with the cinders of burnt leaves,
back when burning leaves was legal—that decadent
smell among kindred scarlets and yellows, vivid trees
crumbled against that utter blue, that early-sixties-suburban-
mother-station-wagon blue, that smoke-gets-in-your-eyes-
bliss that only adolescents know, singed October air,
and yes, a perfect day to fall in love, never mind

my dead-white lipstick or that my full slip billowed
in the breeze beneath my pleated kilt, never mind
the burgeoning blackheads on Jim's forehead,
we held each other at the street corner before parting,
how tenderly Jimmy handed me my social studies book,
slipped over my wrist his silver ID bracelet that read
JIM GREEN in Antique Roman letters, then we kissed
goodbye forever because this was the day the world froze—

Khrushchev's missiles poised off Cuba, their nose-cones
only ninety miles from the sunshine state; my parents,
Jimmy's parents, our teachers and principal fearing us all
annihilated that very evening before finishing our meat loaf.
Gone, poof—vaporized like ghosts, and Kennedy, our war hero
and first handsome president, so grave on the black and white tube,
his rugged hair, sincere eye contact with the camera, the whole
heightened world, a flying football—

while Jimmy and I kissed
with just a little tongue in broad daylight at the tip of my dentist's
driveway, then walked slowly backwards to our different neighbor-
hoods across the raked yards, finally turning back for one last look
to memorize each other's fresh, expectant faces, suspended
and shining against the ashen roses, the collapsing golden rod,
wispy wicks of dust and soot—Knowing, though we were much
too young to die, that we had known *love*.

I was a good Catholic girl on the one hand; on the other, I felt the draw and the strong sense of sacred mystery that seemed to fall under the heading of sex. I did not literally become sexually active until I was twenty-one, in the midst of the Sixties revolutions, yet those days and nights making out with my boyfriends felt very sexual. And the more sexual my feelings became, the more guilt I felt. Once, I even convinced one of my boyfriends to go to confession on a Saturday afternoon with me and we waited timidly in line for our turn to enter the dark and dreaded confessional, wracked with a sense of our stained souls. I also recall saying Novenas for forgiveness.

But here in the great Marseille cathedral, I looked up at this Madonna and realized I did not need to confess to her, or to any god, my sins of desire. It was as if Notre Dame de la Confession said to me: "Goodness girl, you've suffered enough over sexuality. Go on now, it's getting late in life; enjoy the pleasures of the body." Of course, I had been involuntarily celibate for a number of years and I was filled with a kind of deep longing without an object of desire. I hadn't been drawn to any particular man in a long while, yet I knew somewhere within that, despite my middle age, my relationship life would be renewed and my sexuality recharged. I laughed a little to myself about my own "middle ages" and decided I was in my own "12th century." After a time, I got up and walked around the church, my eyes half closed, trying to see what would appear.

The dungeon was ever there in my third eye. I let my mind drift. What had this knight done to deserve the dungeon? Immediately, I had the idea that he was punished unjustly—perhaps for sexuality, perhaps for keeping alive a forbidden tradition, perhaps for political moves. I was able to let myself go and just sense what I could. I wanted to trust that whatever came up was relevant. I then had a thought that startled me. Of course, it was about Mary Magdalen, the prostitute, the one who was almost stoned. She was deeply ingrained in the wound of female sexuality. In the legend, she came through Marseille, and Marseille is known in *The Golden Legend* as the site of several miracles.

Magdalen herself is also related to healing, to plants, to animals, and to growth or fertility in general. According to Margaret Starbird, she was held in high esteem for her regenerative powers. We already know that the idea that she may have been familiar with the Isis tradition is upheld by the story of the spikenard and the washing of Christ's feet the night before he was crucified. One of the Gnostic texts is called "The Gospel of the Egyptians." Was Mary harassed because of her priestess powers? Her pagan prostitution?

Was I, in a past life, that Templar Knight, killed in a plot by King and Pope for my heretical activities, accused of perversity for worshipping a woman? The Templars were accused of sexual deviance, among other charges. It didn't matter to me literally whether I was correct or not in fantasizing about my own past or parallel lives; what mattered was the *release* I felt from feelings of guilt. I let them go consciously and gave them to the Madonna.

Later, we gathered at the main entrance of the church as planned to take Deborah up on her suggestion that we walk to Place Saint Victor to visit the oldest bakery in all of Marseille, which is named *Four de Navettes*, or "Oven of Boats." This little bakery is famous for its pastry shaped like an elongated boat. Was it meant to imitate the boat that carried the Magdalen to Marseille? If you hold the pastry vertically, it resembles a mandorla, the oval shape of the arches in some Gothic churches that is metaphorically related to female anatomy. As we ate our snacks, we joked about the erotic paintings Georgia O'Keefe might have done of the mandorlas or our baked cookie-boats. Deborah told us that these cakes are traditionally eaten during the Candlemas processions. And, in Deborah's guidebook *Goddess Sites: Europe,* the editor stresses the vulva-like shape of the pastry!

About a month before we left Boston, we met at Joanie's place to watch a British video she had on the Magdalen. One of the major interviewees was a woman named Susan Haskins, whose book on Mary is well respected. While we were in the bakery, we recognized this very woman, with some companions who were filming the bakery sign and the images of the boat-like cookies. Deborah approached Susan and introduced herself. They knew of each other's work, and we were pleased to be introduced to the brilliant woman with long silver hair who was interested in setting the Magdalen record straight. To our delight, we found we were following the same itinerary and would all be attending the procession on July 22nd for the Magdalen's feast day. Weary but sated, we wandered back to the van to head for our next destination, the small village of Maximin La Sainte-Baume, deep in land of the Magdalen.

The next day, over breakfast in the apple-green dining room of a small but sweet hotel, we shared our stories about Mary Magdalen—who she was to us in our childhood, how the story of the prostitute about to be stoned horrified us and piqued our own fascination with her relationship to Christ. I knew I was not the only "recovering" Roman Catholic woman who had internalized Mary as a representation of woman's sexuality and the sins of the body in general. And I knew that I was probably not alone in my secret attraction to her, in the same way that I had interests in the prodigal son and other bad children of the Bible. When, in the Sixties, the musical *Jesus Christ Superstar* produced that beautiful song "I Don't Know How To Love Him," I played it over and over and sang it with my sister as she played the guitar. It *is* a love song, complete with its restrained passion and second-guessing questions—universal symptoms of Eros in action. It tells of every girl's first enchantment with the mystery of love. I find personal irony now in the song's words: *I never thought I'd come to this, what's it all about?*

Chapter 23

MARY'S MOUNTAIN

There were three who always walked with the Lord:
Mary his mother and her sister and Magdalen,
the one who was called his companion.
THE GOSPEL OF PHILIP

Saint Maximin La Sainte Baume is a tiny little village at the base of the
Sainte Baume mountains that houses the grotto that is considered, in
local French lore, to be the last habitation of Mary Magdalen. This town is
one of two in the region to claim her relics: her skull, assorted bones, and a
piece of a dress. We drove down the narrow cobblestone streets to our hotel
on the Avenue Albert, the main road through the town that ends in front of
the Basilica Sainte Marie Madeleine. After a calorie-rich formal lunch on the
fertile green terrace of our hotel, we retired to our rooms to rest, planning to
meet in the lobby to walk down to the church later in the afternoon.

In my room, I hung up a few of my skirts and hand-washed a few items
in the sink, then sat down to meditate. I immediately felt the presence of my
spirit guides as they zoomed in around me and poured the familiar thick,
elixir-like liquid over my head. Through my third eye, I continued to see the
dungeon, as well as another eye looking back at me in a kind of frame for the
scene. I asked for remembrance and understanding, although the mysteries
remained. Yet I did feel quite close to Mary and Christ, whom I had been
invoking regularly. I fell asleep immediately after meditating.

I'm not certain what I dreamt, but I awoke with an extremely sexual
arousal, to the point of an orgasmic physical reaction. This surprised me
completely! I had not been fantasizing about men; indeed, I could not recall
the last time I had felt sexual longing for anyone in particular. I hadn't been
in a relationship for several years, and the last man I fantasized over was my
analyst, RB, who had not been regularly in my life for some time. As a woman
approaching the change of life, my libido had lately gone underground. I

remember telling a girl friend, only half in jest, that I guessed I'd rather find God than get laid. I couldn't even connect any dream images to my feelings. I tried to shrug off the experience, but I kept thinking about it as I got up, brushed my hair, and got ready to meet the other women downstairs. There was something exhilarating, something of a gift, in my completely forgotten dream. Of course, I remembered the words of the Madonna that came into my head in Marseille: *Enjoy the body.*

I remembered a night several years back when I awoke with a sense that some invisible being had drawn me up with a kiss on the mouth. As bizarre as all this sounds, I felt again that I had been "touched" by an angel, but this time in a more intimate sexual manner. I concluded that the dream must have been resonating with the theme of the body that we had been discussing relative to the Magdalen and the split archetype of the Madonna/whore— Christianity's great mistake. I decided to share the experience of my strange awakening with the women of our group, but I saved it for our daily ritual circle before we hiked up the mountain the next day.

Although I have always enjoyed the playful part of my sexuality, I always considered sex a sacred experience. I felt it as an avenue through the body, leading to something eternal, God or the universe. I only became conscious of these feelings and found words for them when I underwent analysis. But when I think back to my girlhood, the feeling seems to have been there from the start. Brainwashed by Catholicism, my mother's generation, and the good-girl values of the Fifties and early Sixties, I was a romantic. Yet I came into my own sexuality in the late Sixties, when these ideas were considered old-fashioned. I scuttled the good-girl restrictions as quickly as possible, yet I always had a hard time with the thought of sex for sex's sake. Sex without love—some kind of deep love—seemed to me a kind of aberration. The feeling from this dream had been more tantric, exhilarating, more like sex with the Divine Beloved that Rumi described—"to empty the self/and have only clear being there." The dream had something otherworldly about it. Rumi again:

> Being is not what it seems
> nor non-being. The world's
> existence is not
> in the world.[1]

---

1. Rumi in John Moyne and Coleman Barks, *Unseen Rain: Quatrains of Rumi* (Boston: Shambhala Books, 1986), pp. 46, 32.

Just last year, I confirmed my intuitions about this orgasmic dream when I read the work of a woman who underwent a personal crisis during her psychology training. In her book *Eros & Chaos; The Sacred Mysteries and Dark Shadows of Love*, archetypal psychologist Veronica Goodchild speaks of the neglected dark feminine as "Clitoral Consciousness."

> The center of women's ways is not the head but the genitals, not the womb but the clitoris . . . as body . . . Woman become virgin again, woman-unto-herself, woman birthing herself.

Goodchild speaks of the necessity of a "fierce, instinctual, primordial love of being female," and of knowledge rooted in the lower sexual chakra that has been forgotten and needs recognition, lost as it is in the modern world of the patriarchy.[2] Rites and rituals related to what the Hindus honor as Shakti energy go back to the earliest mystery schools. Part of Goodchild's thesis is that the erotic is linked to chaos, not order. Like Begg and Graves, she stresses irrational knowing and non-linear thinking through the intuitive body.

I am comfortable with that explanation of my dream. The dream came to me at a significant time, in a significant place, and I can relate it to my own unconscious longing for union with something higher, just as easily as I can relate it to my interest in Mary Magdalen as Egyptian priestess of the mysteries and whatever legacy she has left to those of us on a spiritual quest.

Enlightened by a similar dream, Veronica Goodchild shared my experience. Her remarks on her own dream helped elucidate mine. She describes the process as ongoing in contemporary women who are willing to disconnect from patriarchal control to find looser, less structured ways of living—ways that allow creativity to arise, and help society break away from its ingrained stressful patterning to more immediate ways of living in the present and accessing the divine. This ability to disconnect from our habitual modes of learning is available to all of us, male and female, if we will only let old habits die and make room for a simpler, more meditative life.

This new, or rather rediscovered ancient, way of thinking is crucial in this transition to the Age of Aquarius. Freud's theory of penis envy, although appropriate for the marginalized feminine in his times, is outdated, Good-

---

2. Veronica Goodchild, *Eros and Chaos: The Sacred Mysteries and Dark Shadows of Love* (Lake Worth, FL: Nicolas-Hays, 2001), pp. 92–93.

child claims, and the "material, physical, natural, erotic, wet, wounded . . . dark" power of the revealed feminine will be restored to its proper place—

> . . . what needs to be done in awakening ourselves and the world to the secret center in the pelvic chakra that is seeking new expressions of life.[3]

Although Goodchild never mentions the Black Madonnas in her book, this prescription for healing resonates with everything the Madonnas represent. If we, in the United States, as a society, do not soon see the need to change our relationship with the rest of the world, our phallic-driven, materialistic civilization will crush us with its waste and its weapons, while killing the natural environment of the planet.

The very real danger and tragedy is that developing nations want to follow in our footsteps, seeking the very lifestyle that is threatening the world. When America did not attend the Global Environmental Conference in 2003, the word from our administration was that the American lifestyle was "non-negotiable." Yet the truth is that the American lifestyle as is—that is, with one or two huge, gas-guzzling SUVs in every driveway—is non-viable, non-sustainable, and, as many of us realize, doomed. We utilize 25 percent of the world's resources, which is completely disproportionate to the size of our country and our population as compared to the rest of the world. The feminine body is symbolized not only as the church; it is the Earth, for all are born into the world by way of it. And when we leave the world, the "matter/mother" of the body is returned to her. Best we tend our gardens well.

LIONESSE

We arrived in Saint Maximin La Sainte Baume on July 22nd, the Magdalen's feast day, in time to participate in the traditional procession of the relic from the Cathedral to the Dominican Abbey a few blocks away. Early in the day, our small group gathered in the lobby of the hotel and walked down the street toward the basilica of Saint Maximin. We wanted to visit the cathedral and spend some time with the images before parishioners packed the house that evening.

---

3. Goodchild, *Eros and Chaos*, pp. 105–106.

We entered the church and Deborah pointed out the stunning altar. Beneath a big beautiful dove, at the Father's right hand, is Jesus. To Jesus's right is Mary Magdalen. Her prominent place in this huge relief is astonishing. I had never seen her given such a place in any American church. Here, she is considered a disciple, with all the credentials of the four better-known evangelists. We could see the relic of the Magdalen's skull, which had been brought out from the crypt beneath the cathedral and placed in a large glass case with a helmet of golden hair around it. It was veiled, but we had heard there would an unveiling at five o'clock. Was the relic real? The actual blackened skull? I seriously doubted it, but I didn't really care. I've learned to live quite happily with mythic truth, but it was interesting to see and be a part of the veneration of this female disciple.

In the legend, the Magdalen is buried at Saint Maximin. According to Begg, the Cassianite monks from Marseille guarded her tomb from the fifth century onward. The relics that support the legend, however, weren't found until the 13th and 15th centuries.[4] Then, during the Saracen invasions, the relics are said to have been transferred to Vézelay, which we were to visit the following week. I thought of the importance of skulls in Georgia O'Keefe's desert paintings, how they hold the numinous energy of the spirit of the animal. Whatever this skull's power, someone had perpetuated its story so that the remains of the Magdalen's fragile bones would not be forgotten.

Outside the church, the entire town was getting ready for the celebration and we were amused by the irreverent commercialism rampant on this sacred feast day. There were rigged stages and platforms, musicians and balloons, and various carnival-like booths. We heard there would be dancing and even a rock band later that night in the many cafés that surrounded the rather smallish plaza.

Around five, we gathered with a huge crowd of villagers in the church for a Mass. The Dominican nuns gave out candles inside paper shades that were imprinted with the words to songs in the old Provençal dialect. A bevy of priests, altar boys, and girls led the procession, carrying the golden cage for the *le crane de la Madelaine.* Behind them, the throngs sang as the river of people flowed down the cobblestone hill to a side street where the Abbot would receive the relic. Our candles kept going out and we helped one another relight them—both strangers and friends. Deborah's whole shade caught on

---

4. Begg, *The Cult of the Black Virgin*, p. 99.

fire! We laughed through our singing, not sure exactly what we were singing, while trying to keep pace with the processional.

At the abbey, we entered through wrought iron gates into a yard in front of a building, where adolescent postulants giggled as the young Dominican monks sang in a small performance. Then there were several speeches by various town officials and clergy. Children were lifted, sparklers swayed, and everywhere raised candles contributed to the festive atmosphere. After an hour or so, we left the scene and walked the few cobblestone blocks back into the center of town in search of a café for dinner. It seemed as if the entire town were eating out, and all the cafés were bubbling over with waiting lines. Finally, we were seated. We dined well, but remained on the sidelines as the bands began to play and the youth of the village, all dressed very punky and so very French, began to fill the plaza-size dance floor.

About midnight, I wandered back to the hotel. The noise in the streets was enough to keep me awake for another hour. Fortunately (or perhaps *un*fortunately), my room was in the back of the hotel and I didn't have as much distraction as Joanie had. As she stood looking out her louvered window, some guys hollered up to her and she went out dancing till the wee hours. But we intended to hike Mary's mountain the next day, and I was feeling neurotic about getting enough sleep.

I lay in my bed that night, half dozing, and awoke to another strange experience. This time, it was a very brief dream that consisted solely of a lion approaching me and opening its jaws wide enough to put my whole head in its mouth. I was terrified by its maw as it moved toward me, but once I was enclosed in it, oddly enough, I didn't feel scared or threatened. There was something almost comforting about it. And it was one of those dreams that seemed absolutely real. That was all there was to it! One moment. The lion approaches, opens her jaws, and engulfs my head.

In the reading I requested when the spirits first arrived in my life six years previously, I remember David Hall's drawing of a lion turning its head and smiling. He gave me the drawing as the first image in his scrying meditation on me. I knew, of course, of the Lion as Leo, the astrological sign related to the artist. And my lion had seemed feminine. I assumed she had something to do with power—my own creative power perhaps. The Egyptian goddess Sekhmet is depicted as a lioness. Lions are often found on the feminine court cards in Crowley's tarot deck, specifically the Lust/Strength card, which is about overcoming primal instincts. Archetypically, lions represent royalty, power, and creativity, while, as members of the feline family, they are associated with feminine wisdom. David said the lion smiled and appeared auspicious. Without needing to analyze further, I drifted off to a dreamless sleep.

A few years later, I wrote a sequence of poems called "The Month of Slumber," about a time I had hidden quietly away to write for a month after having a bad flu. The poems reflected my new sense of the spirits' presence. Because I felt their origins were related, I included a poem about this dream in the series.

Léonesse

Not a cat, not a leopard, a lioness
walked out of my eye, halted
on furred paws. They covered

her claws, turning.
Her orange mane
swung like drapery

and when she opened her jaws,
I fell into darkness and close quarters.
Ripening fullness

inside her mouth. Her musk
was weighted, a cloud,
like the misty refusal of rain.

She licked my chin, my den
a warm furnace, heaved
in the height of her throat.

Heat ticked somewhere below
in the baseboards.
And the hands

of the dream held me
entranced in its print,
like a pinned insect

under amber. Sheltered
beneficence, brutal—
attractive, something

like love.

ASCENT TO THE GROTTO

In the morning, we bought some cheese, baguettes, fruit, and wine to take up the mountain for a picnic. We saw Susan Haskins, the film maker and Magdalen scholar, with her small crew at breakfast in the hotel and she asked to briefly interview us for her video. Outside in the plaza, we spoke one at a time about why we had come on this pilgrimage and what we were seeking. I mentioned the Gnostic connections, others spoke more personally, and Deborah gave some background for her Magdalen Tours. Susan said she hoped to include us in her film, although, to date, we still don't know if we made the final edit.

Our plan for the day was to drive up to a plateau on the mountain and then hike up to the grotto and come back down for a picnic lunch. Picnicking here and there helped to save money and the weather was glorious. The drive up the Massif de la Sainte Baume was winding and dizzying, with narrow S-turns that reminded me of Mount Tabor in Israel. It is one of the highest mountain ranges in Provence, its highest point close to 4000 feet. Deborah told us the forest is considered sacred and is under the protection of the government. There are atypical plants and animals there because of the amount of shade provided by the high cliffs. Local people believe that the forest is under the care of fertility goddesses, and Deborah recalled a sign she had seen in the museum on a previous visit that displayed a dark-skinned Anatolian Artemis sitting atop the plateau. In dream imagery, mountains are often symbolic of questing and spiritual aspirations.

Katie was our designated driver and we encouraged her with our squealing and warnings as she cautiously steered the van around some of the sharp hairpin turns. The road was so narrow at some points that, looking down, we could only see the steep drop beyond the road. There were no guardrails and, occasionally, poor Katie had to back the van up first to inch it around the turn. The more harrowing the ride became, the more we laughed and screamed, and we couldn't help reflecting that the spiritual journey often presents challenges like killing the Dragon of Fear. I had my head in my hands most of the way, looking down only at the floor.

Finally, we arrived at the splendid massif. We left the van with relief and went through the museum, where we watched a video in French before wandering into the small church, which houses several of the most exquisite murals. I stood in the doorway stunned. They were obviously modern, colorful, gracious. *And outrageous,* I thought to myself. You would never find such intimate art work in an American Catholic Church. One mural shows a red-haired Magdalen standing on a rock holding a cross, with her arm out straight, as if she is blessing and preaching to the sailors who are turned toward her in their sail boats. In another, she is obviously teaching; in a third, my favorite, she seems to linger in a stone doorway as she watches a Christ-like figure clothed in white walking away down the path.

Dare I say she looks exactly like a loving housewife watching her husband leave for work? The pastel colors and the house, with its raspberry colored roses against the mountains and sky, make it an extraordinary image. Her stance is casual and the scene overflows with tenderness. The mural covers an entire wall!

Behind the basilica is a fourth mural that shows Mary lifted to the heavens by angels, as is told in *The Golden Legend.* We sat in the lovely light-blessed room for a long time, lit our own candles, and admired the paintings and sculptures, and the vases filled with lavender placed here and there. Several nuns knelt and prayed the rosary aloud—a sweet, coiled lull of French vowels.

Once outside, we crossed the road and went into the forest to have one of our sharing circles. The chirping of cicadas and other insects was amazingly loud and birds called to each other across the trees. We marveled at the amount of sheer noise, yet, as soon as Deborah rang her chime, the woods fell instantly silent. We looked at each other in awe and burst out laughing, spooked by the sudden quiet. It was if the place were indeed enchanted and the insects and animals stood frozen and poised to listen. Deborah passed the chime to each of us and we spoke our intentions for the day. I told the group of my lion reverie and my dreamy sexual initiation the previous afternoon. Naturally, they loved it. When everyone had contributed a personal reflection, we adjusted our back packs and took to the trail. The rumor in the town was that the chapel path was closed due to rock slides. Nevertheless, fortified by our water bottles and chocolate bars, we decided to brave it. We poured out our honey for Diana, Mary, and the other mothers of nature, burned some sage, and passed the liquor, each of us taking a swig and toasting the goddesses in turn. As usual, the spirit in which we held our ceremony was both playful and reverent.

At various twists on the trail, we found wells and small shrines. Streams trickled and the sounds of the woods seemed to follow us. The sunlight's dapple smoked through the pines and maples and cooled the temperature of an otherwise oppressive sun. We came across a few other hikers and, although we were obviously Americans, we attempted to exchange greetings in whatever language we heard. Joanie sang for a while and the birds picked up again. The path was lined with a single-level stone wall; eventually, as the path became steeper, close to the top, the pattern of stones fell into place as a stairway.

It only took about an hour to reach the summit. Eventually, we could see the chapel above us, built into the massive side of the mountain. We crawled under fences and ignored the signs warning of rock slides. Sometimes, the quiet was palpable and I found a rhythm just listening to the sound of our footsteps and breathing. I remember feeling myself as part of nature's magic. The forest *was* indeed special.

When we reached the chapel, however, we were disappointed to find it boarded up. We had seen, in the store on the plateau below us, photos of midnight Masses that had been held in the chapel in previous years. I couldn't think of a more awesome place to celebrate the birth of Christ. This was Mary's cave, converted into a place of worship. It was frustrating not to be able to get inside, and we took turns peeking through the cracks in the boards. Three large crucifixes topped the stone building, signifying Christ between the two thieves.

After a rest and some playful picture taking, we all agreed that we felt more power in the forest than in this man-made building, and some of us started back down. Deborah, Joan, and Katy decided to hike further up, to the very top of the mountain. I wanted to be in the forest again with the woodsy aromas and the view of the plateau. Elaine, Joanie, and I sat down on the rocks and unwrapped our bars of rich dark chocolate. I thought of the Great Mother's dark body melting on our tongues. We savored each piece, ingesting it as if it were a sacrament.

Chapter 24

REJIDENT MADONNAJ

I live in a hive of darkness, and you are my mother . . .
You are the mother of thousands.
SUE MONK KIDD, *THE SECRET LIFE OF BEES*

When we returned to the mountain's plateau for our picnic under the trees, we befriended a young American college girl—a gorgeous curly-haired redhead named Erin. She was from Florida and had hitchhiked from Aix en Provence, the "Paris of the South," where she was staying with a French family. She wore a tank top and jeans, and around her neck she had several crosses and medals of Magdalen and Mother Mary. She approached each cluster of people, looking for a ride back down the mountain, afraid she would miss her bus back to Aix. We welcomed her to our picnic lunch and she seemed overjoyed to discover we were Americans. We were happy to help her and have one more Magdalen in the van. Katie once again maneuvered around the serpentine turns that were as twisty as the legends we followed. As it turned out, Erin did miss the bus, and we suggested she get a room overnight in the Dominican Abbey just down the street from our hotel. Tired from the long day of hiking, we decided that anyone who wanted dinner could meet in the lobby at eight. We invited Erin to join us.

By eight, only Joan and I had come to the lobby. As we strolled down the street to an outdoor café on the plaza where the crowds had danced the previous night, Erin caught up with us. We found a table, ordered some wine, and relaxed in the rays of the still-bright Sun. During dinner, I asked Erin how she became interested in Mary Magdalen. She indicated that she was on some kind of mysterious quest that she herself didn't understand. As the conversation continued, she said something like "I suppose I can tell you two, as I will probably never see you again. It's just that, well, I have visions. When I close my eyes . . . I see things." I put down my fork and stared at her.

"What kind of things?" I asked. "I see rooms, and people in rooms, and landscapes. They're not always clear; they fade in and out." I looked askance at Joan.

I had already told the group about my third eye and the dungeons, the history of my experiences in Israel, and the holotropic breath workshop. It seemed unbelievably synchronistic that this lovely, adventurous college sophomore would come all the way from Florida to this small village in France and meet another American woman who had similar visions! I was astonished, and burst out with my own story. She was totally interested, of course, and asked where she could learn about what was happening to her. She said she hadn't been born with this particular characteristic, but it had come to her spontaneously only a few months ago. "Nor was I," I assured her.

Physically, Erin appeared "normal," and she seemed perfectly sane and stable. She had taken several day trips away from the French family with whom she was staying and whom she loved dearly. Drawn to the stories of saints and miracles, she was led to Mary's mountain. She knew the legends and felt a kinship. We had a wonderful conversation and I encouraged her to seek some spiritual guidance when she got home. She said no one she knew would be open to her experience, and was amazed to hear my theories about the evolution of the species and the ascension process. She was not raised a Catholic, so she was even more surprised than I by whatever initiation she was undergoing.

I thought about the reactions of many of my friends to my experience; they warned me of brain tumors and other physical explanations. I suppose Erin could have had some abnormality, but I trusted that she had found us, found *me*, to share her experience. She was bright and practical and grounded as far as I could observe. We exchanged e-mail addresses, but when I returned home, I couldn't find hers and I never heard from her again. I sometimes think of her and wonder how she is faring. If there were some concrete explanation for her visions, I expect it became evident in time. But I couldn't help thinking that our meeting was arranged by some invisible power. How likely is it that she would run into someone like me who could give her a context for her visions? How likely is it that someone like her would validate mine? If the others had not met her, I might wonder if she were even real. As my dream told me: *Nothing can be proven.*

MADONNA ENTHRONED

After leaving Provence and making a play-day stop in the active city of Aix, the capital of Southern France, we drove north for a longer trip into the Auvergne, an area of volcanic stone and cones that make for an irregular topography. Le Puy en Velay, with its pagan green men carved into doorways, and its history as a home of the Druids, is a town Deborah Rose calls "magical." Here, yet another legend drew our attention.

After Mary the Mother appeared here in a townswoman's vision in 46 A.D., a series of miracles occurred that were associated with a black volcanic stone that is now located in the town's cathedral. Deborah remarks in her notes:

> There are stories of angels consecrating the building of the Cathedral. Joan of Arc's mother walked across France to pray here for her daughter's success. Five Popes and fifteen kings, hordes of crusaders . . . all came here to honor the miraculous *Vierge Noir.*.

En route to Le Puy, famished, we stopped at a roadside restaurant that seemed to appear out of the rolling fields of lavender. After a typical French lunch of omelets and salad, we inadvertently tipped the owner 20 percent when the gratuity was already included in the bill. We were piling back into the van when he came running after us with a huge bouquet of freshly cut lavender tied with a lovely yellow ribbon. We accepted it graciously, still unaware of his reason for thanking us so enthusiastically. Thereafter, the van reeked of lavender, until, overwhelmed with the fragrance, we ritualistically deposited the bouquet at a significant site in Dijon a week or so later.

As we approached Le Puy, we saw a huge statue on a hill overlooking the medieval village—a red Madonna called Notre Dame de France. The Madonna, which stands sixteen meters high, oversees the city, much as the Golden Madonna oversees Marseille, or our Statue of Liberty oversees New York harbor. Though she is colored red, she is very much a white Madonna, with feminine curves and a gentle face. You can actually climb up inside her, like Lady Liberty, and take in a panoramic view of the volcanic range.

We could see here that early Christendom had its roots in fertility goddess worship. The city shows a mixture of influences. Carved pagan men appear everywhere, covered with vegetation—in their grinning mouths and around their erect genitals. We strolled through the cobblestone streets of the old city past the Bacchanalian faces carved into doors, and eventually into the church. Legend has it that a stag once ran though the snow leaving a trail that marked the site for what became the church. The trail surrounded an old Celtic well and a rock. A sick woman in the village dreamt of a lady lying down on this black volcanic slab. When she awoke, she went to the rock, lay upon it, and was healed of her illness. Many "Fever Stone" miracles followed, as the wounded and ill drew up the salubrious waters from below.

Here, we examined the most famous Black Madonna in Le Puy, whose history is a story in itself. The Enthroned Black Madonna is actually a replica of an original that was burned during the French Revolution when the rebellious masses associated the church with the opulence of the aristocracy. The statue was recreated exactly from sketches—with a black face, long narrow nose, and circumflexed eyebrows below a crown that is like a warrior's helmet studded with gems and topped by a golden bird. The child's gown is deep maroon and patterned with Greek crosses. The Madonna's dress has lotus mandalas rimmed with fleur de lis. On the cuff of her left sleeve are lettered designs like the words in the Hebrew Cabala. The original statue has been traced to Jeremiah. It was passed to Moses' priests some 600 years *before* Christ. So she was a part of the Babylonian treasure smuggled from Jerusalem during the first or second Crusades. Her history is associated with Charlemagne, Clovis, and Constantine, and even with Solomon himself! I couldn't help but recall the "Song of Songs": "The eyes of many morning suns/ have pierced my skin, and I shine/ black as the light before the dawn."

Isis, the goddess of the Nile, held her son Horus on her knee exactly as the Black Madonna does. But the hands that hold this child are painted white at the wrists. Was this meant to represent gloves? And what's the significance of the child's black face and its own white fingers? One thought comes to mind: we are all issue of Africa; our mother continent is the Madonna body with its prolific womb. This child is not holding up his hand to bless the masses. There is no heavenly sky in his mother's slanted eyes. She is not humble or romantic, not wreathed with stars, but somber, carved from cedar, dark wood grown in dirt. The child simply sits on her lap as the Pharaoh of Egypt sat on the throne of Isis.

Now we can trace the long line of the sacred feminine from the icon of Mother Mary back to Isis. I think this was when it dawned on me that it was *all the same feminine, all the same mother, the Great Mother, the Devourer, Kali, Shakti, Isis, Diana, Hecate,,* each with her dark side inextricably linked to Marian imagery, whether it be Mary the Mother or Mary Magdalen. Cunneen tells us:

Statues of Demeter and Isis were black because they were associated with the fertility of the dark earth, . . . Such findings suggest that the black madonnas were Christian borrowings from earlier pagan forms that retained the power of their models.[1]

We could cite many different traditions here—African, Celtic, Byzantine. And the volcanic plateaus of this strange city give lie to the victories of civilization. As we are told in Revelation, this Earth will pass away. In the late 20th century and the first few years of the 21st, we have witnessed increasing numbers of fires, floods, hurricanes, earthquakes, tidal waves, volcanoes, and changing weather patterns. The Earth at Ground Zero beneath the Twin Towers in Manhattan shook to a seismic 2.3 on September 11th as the goddess Gaia or, Mother Earth, reacted to the massive weight and the rubble graveyard of so many innocent souls given back to the original mother. The archetypal feminine is calling out to be recognized. Like all mothers, she abhors both senseless killing and war. As in Israel, in Le Puy en Velay, I felt the energy of the eternal land—rock and soil turned over and over for centuries, swallowing animal kingdoms, whole tribes, and societies. Like the British poet Shelly's prophetic "Ozymandias," these primitive goddess/Madonnas speak from prehistory to remind us that nature is superior to culture.

> . . . My name is Ozymandias, king of kings;
> Look on my works, ye mighty, and despair!
> . . . Nothing beside remains. Round the decay
> of that colossal wreck, boundless and bare . . . [2]

LE MOULIN DES TEMPLIERS

We took the following day to drive to Clermont-Ferrand, the city of Michelin tires as well as Black Madonnas—an irony if I ever heard one! Here, the very first statue of Mary was carved in 946, an enthroned Madonna who served as prototype for all the others. Commissioned by the Bishop of the city, she was called *Mere de Dieu*. We visited two churches there and, in the crypt of Notre Dame de la Port, we beheld the Oriental Vierge de Tendresse, who dates from the 13th century, but is a copy of an original Byzantine icon,

---

1. Sally Cunneen, *In Search of Mary: The Woman and the Symbol* (New York: Ballantine, 1996), p. 177.
2. Percy Bysshe Shelley, *The Complete Poems* (New York: Modern Library, 1994), p. 589.

quite likely one brought from the Middle East during the Crusades. The statue was stolen in 1864, but the legend says that it "cried so much it was restored by the remorseful thief in 1873."[3]

It is perhaps fitting that the Madonna sits on a ledge in an uneven stone wall under a flight of dusty stairs—straight and stark, primitive and powerful, very dark, very black. At this site, there is also an ancient well from the Gallo-Roman era dedicated to the Earth goddess Cybele. Begg speculates that the earliest Blessed Virgin may have been found here.

In the nearby cathedral, we found a stained-glass window that follows the life of Mary Magdalen. What struck us repeatedly was how very unusual it would be to find such a window in the United States. The repressed heresies became part of the faith in France, yet Deborah, Joanie, and I—the three of our little party who were raised Catholic in America—had never been taught alternative legends of the Magdalen. And we were fairly certain there were no churches with stained-glass windows venerating her as a disciple and teacher. She reigns, in America, as the repentant whore.

Our trip continued through Vichy and Marsat, each stop chosen for its resident Madonnas. The Madonna of Marsat was a gorgeous golden sculpture. Though just as severe as the others, she was definitely the most opulently attired.

In addition to the more reverent rituals of our pilgrimage, we managed a lot of shopping, museum hopping and, of course, dining. Some of the images run together in my memory, but we did take time to wander about alone, to sit in cafés, to journal and think and read. Unlike my rushed trip through Israel, this journey's pace was leisurely. The days folded and unfolded into one another like the rumpled clothing from our suitcases.

My favorite city was the gorgeous, if slightly touristy (it was summer, after all) walled medieval village of Vézelay. There, we stayed in an old converted mill just outside the walls. The inn was owned by a woman we immediately began calling "Jackie O." because of an uncanny resemblance. The head of a lovely French family, she had renovated the mill into a charming country inn. A beautiful and active stream bubbled just outside our bedroom windows, beneath the small café tables where she served breakfast. Each room had a sink, shower, and toilet contained in an armoire! I simply found it to be the most peaceful and pastoral spot, with its overflowing gardens and charming stone walls. Sweet, unextravagant, simple, but elegant. It

3. Ean Begg, *The Cult of the Black Virgin* (Herndon, VA: Lindisfarne Books, 2006), p. 181.

was called *Le Moulin des Templiers*—the Mill of the Templars! So it was fitting that, here, my own inner vision clarified and sharpened.

I unpacked in my lovely room, lay down on the bed, and closed my eyes to perceive whatever I could. Immediately, I found myself in the dungeon. Yet this time, the dungeon did not seem a prison. Or perhaps this was a different underground chamber—again built of stone, but open-ended. When the knight flew by on his horse, he was closer, larger, and his colors were deeper. The stairway was gone. It was as if I had a more finely tuned screen in my eye. I saw that the red cross and white cassock were tightly focused and clear. Each time he passed out of my vision, my ears heard the same loud whooshing sound—not painful, but an uncomfortable shock, like a sneeze when you have a very bad head cold—*Kuh-Whoosh!*

I assumed, again, that this was another of my past/parallel soul extensions or a symptom of my developing sensitivity to morphic resonance. I was clueless as to why I had been called to bear witness to him. Still, I liked seeing him and, in my heart, I placed him in the story of the initiated Templars. I didn't realize until then that we had left Provence and Auvergne and come to the Languedoc, which is known as Templar territory—the world of the troubadours, those poetic word-weavers of romance and song.

As we explored Vézelay, I noticed the tremendous amount of Crusader statues, books on the Templars, pins and jewelry keyed to the Templar crest, histories of the Merovingian dynasty, fleur de lis, lilies and the related rose, rose-windows, and every other imaginable exploitation of the local symbols. I became curious about my vision and purchased a few pamphlets in French. I learned that it was on the steps of the great basilica of the church dedicated to Mary Magdalen that Saint Bernard de Clairvaux called for the First Crusade on Easter Sunday of 1146. The Templar cult began with nine warrior-monks and grew, over two hundred years, into a power that rivaled the Papacy. The Templar knights were highly influential on both political and financial issues, yet so much mystery surrounds their story. Exactly what were their closed-door rituals? Moreover, how were they able to inspire whole generations to construct the Gothic cathedrals that often took more than one lifetime to finish?

When, at last, Pope and King worked together to wipe them out, they had been accused of everything from worshipping a cat (a Satanic figure, but also the sacred guardian to Egyptian Goddesses) to participating in sodomy and urinating on the crucifix. These accusations paralleled some of those made against the Cathar community. Templars and Cathars alike were tortured and forced to swear that these falsehoods were true. If the alleged rituals included pagan sexual acts, they were most likely misunderstood. But where the Cathars were a community of men and women, ordinary citizens who had withdrawn from the laws of Catholicism, the Templars were monks, men who, one would expect, were instilled with the traditional laws of the Roman church. It is said that Philip the Fair, the King who conspired against them, had asked to become a Templar and was turned down. Not long after he condemned them to death, he fell fatally ill, though he was relatively young.

Questions as to how the knights came to occupy Solomon's Temple, why they suddenly abandoned it, and what their so-called hidden "treasure" actually was, remain unanswered. However, historians agree that the Templar cult was expressly devoted to Mary Magdalen. It's possible that the secret "treasure" consists of the lessons Mary taught about humanity and its separation from its divine nature. This is the lesson whose time has come.

> "Be in harmony . . . " If you are out of balance, take inspiration from manifestation of your true nature. Those who have ears, let them hear.[4]

---

4. Jean-Yves LeLoup, *The Gospel of Mary Magdelene* (Rochester, VT: Inner Traditions Books, 2002), p. 27.

Chapter 25

VÉZELAY

Nothing is owed to us, everything is given to us.
We were not created to possess, but to "be with"...
JEAN-YVES LELOUP, *THE GOSPEL OF MARY MAGDALEN*

While we were in Vézelay, I had a dream that I might not otherwise have noticed, because it was misleadingly filled with the residue of my daily experience.

> *I'M IN A BUS TRAVELING with several other women my age. We stop at a place where other beautifully youthful women (about twenty years old) come up to our car window. I know them; they are my (dream) cousins. They are all very giggly and seem to be having a good time. I point out the aura of one of the young women, which is light blue and radiant, to one of the other middle-aged women I'm with. There is also a redheaded young woman who chides me for not paying enough attention to her. It is as if I have forgotten her name for a moment and I am trying to recall it. I introduce the younger women to my friends. Then we are looking for money to pay a toll. We find that we have plenty of money. The young women are asking when we will come back to stay. The next scene moves to a restaurant where we are laughing and having a grand time. The waitress is an old black woman and she comes over with a tray of breakfast for us. Eggs. We protest that we haven't even ordered yet. She says benevolently something like: "Well, if you don't like this, you should know you can have anything, everything . . . whatever you want!"* 🌿

I awoke feeling buoyant and recorded the dream. I related the young women to Erin, especially the redhead. Erin had made an impression on me for a number of reasons. She was spiritually mature in a way that I've rarely encountered in a college sophomore. I love looking into my young college students' fresh faces, their smooth skin, their youthful innocence and curiosity. Sometimes, when I'm talking to a student one-on-one, I feel a pang of nostalgia for my own youth, as well as a wistfulness about my single status and a sense that I've somehow lost the best years of my life, sitting alone, my nose inside a book. But more often, I'm just interested in how these lovely young people are experiencing life, how they are often more aware than I was at their age. I feel badly for their troubles and want to say: "If you could just appreciate your youth" and "Your whole life is ahead of you." I don't say this, of course, knowing how banal those words sounded to me at various times when I was struggling in my own youth. With the narcissism typical of the young, I never found them particularly appropriate or consoling. As I thought about the dream, Erin's fresh face appeared vividly in my memory. But then there was another significance: Mary Magdalen herself is often described and painted with long red hair, as she is in the murals in the mountain chapel near La Sainte Baume. Considering the genius of the dreaming mind, I thought both of these references seemed appropriate.

There is a sense of doubling in the dream, with the middle-aged women and their reflection in youth-gone-by. This old/young duality seem to convey a cycling, or constant growth and rebirth. There is a joyous exchange of energy between the two groups of women. The confident black woman comes out of nowhere. I identify her as a positive shadow figure. Imagistically, she is more an Aunt Jemima type than a Black Madonna, but I love that aspect of the dream. She is American—*Southern*, to be specific. On the Native American medicine wheel, the South is the place of emotions and the heart. Visually, she may tap into an old stereotype of black women imprinted on me sometime in my early youth—the women in old films who are in service to white women, like Scarlet O'Hara's Mammy. But it is *she* who has the information. She is the wise African mother of the world. She is at peace with herself and happy, and encourages us to be happy! She seems to understand that the world is a playground, and she is perfectly delighted to impart to us this special knowledge: *We can have whatever we want!*

A few years later, I read Sue Monk Kid's novel, *The Secret Life of Bees,* whose theme centers around a trio of Black Madonnas living in South Carolina. The American Black Madonna was already seeded in the imagination of this fine young writer and, apparently, in the collective consciousness, for the book quickly became a best-seller and a popular film. I find that reassuring.

In my dream, I assume that paying the toll refers to the inner work necessary to change our thinking from fear to love, from unworthiness to abundance—a tricky accomplishment, but a practice we know is necessary. This is perhaps the most difficult task for a seeker of spiritual enlightenment. And, if the waitress is a shadow of my own ego, then I rejoice to think, at least on the unconscious level, that I have internalized the belief that I can create a life with an abundance of what is important to me. That I can bring into my reality anything, everything. This is the philosophy of *The Course in Miracles* and the salient teaching of many channeled writings of the New Age—Neale Donald Walsch's *Conversations with God*, Eckhart Tolle's *The Power of Now* and Wayne Dyer's *The Power of Intention*, all best-sellers.

I told the group about my dream and, of course, everyone was amused by the references to "traveling with other women in a bus." Nothing other worldly about that! We also recalled how, on the second day of our trip, Joanie had asked for *six menues* (apply Franglais) as we sat down to lunch. In French, the word for menu is *carte*. When the waiter approached with six omelets, we laughed at our error, realizing that *menu* meant the "special of the day." I remember being startled by the six omelet yolks, all that yellow against the provincial table cloth with its huge red and yellow flowers—a veritable cornucopia. Somehow, my unconscious had stored the image of the eggs and thrown it out as a symbol of embryonic changes and fertile offer-ings—the Resurrection symbols of Easter.

All of us (albeit sometimes skeptical about our own power) believed in "white magic" and had experienced the result of affirming our desires in at least some way. We understood that we could state what we wanted and put it out there for the universe to deliver. However, we all knew, as well, that tim-ing is key, because the cause/effect relationship on the Earth plane is much slower than it is in other dimensions. Yet a persistent practice and the right attitude can help enormously. John had taught me to state my preferences for what I want, but accept in peace whatever comes as a part of my growth. I kept this lesson close to my heart. If we can undo our negative thoughts by being positive 51 percent of the time, we can effectively co-create. The dream appeared simple and light, but it was also a collective dream, meant for our little group to share. Its message sustained me for a long time.

SIN OF THE WORLD

On our way to the lovely walled city of Vézelay, Deborah told us of Mar-jorie Malvern's book, *Venus in Sackcloth*, which maintains that a certain monk brought the Magdalen's body to Vézelay. An 11th-century rumor drew thou-sands of pilgrims there to see her relics. Malvern called the Magdalen of Vézelay a fertility goddess and mystical bride, as well as a miracle worker.

The town's church is at the end of Rue Saint Pierre, the main street of a village that is lined with lovely, if trendy, shops. The village walls give a sense of containment to the center of the town, which became a gathering place for the cult of the Magdalen. Saint Bernard preached here just before the Second Crusade. There is a statue of Mary Magdalen on the front façade of the church, and her so-called relics are kept in the base of one of the columns in the transept. It didn't matter to us whether the relics were authentic or not. We had all read Chaucer's "Pardoner's Tale" and knew that the market for relics in the Middle Ages was an exploitative scam. "Wherever you went in Christendom, you were sure to find the toenail of some holy person and the earlobe of another," Begg tells us quoting Pickett and Prince.[1]

In Vézelay's lovely church, the 12th-century sculpture in the basilica shows the Magdalen holding the jar of spikenard she uses at the anointing on Holy Thursday. The statue is a soft image, her posture curved and beginning to show signs of early Renaissance Marian imagery. Yet again I realized that, despite all the Catholic churches I've entered in my fifty years in the United States, I have never seen one with a large Magdalen holding this jar. The priestess has been reduced to a whore, just as the goddess Artemis has been reduced to her hounds. The Christians denigrated devotees of Artemis as "devil worshippers" and, because of her association with hunting hounds, called the pagans "sons of bitches," denoting Satanic leanings. Even the New Testament called for Diana's temples to be torn down (Acts 19:27). I wonder how many herbal healings and remedies were lost as these pagan healers were condemned and burned by the Inquisition.

I couldn't help recalling Mary's complaint in her gospel that Peter did not support her ideas. The Petrine Patriarchy may have been the first organized effort to counteract the teachings of white magic and manifestation techniques in order to disempower the masses. There was a definite misinterpretation of Mary's gospel, which defines sin primarily as the soul's move away from its natural divinity.

As LeLoup speaks of sinlessness in Mary's gospel, he quotes from it: "What is the sin of the world? The Teacher answered: There is no sin. It is you who make sin exist."[2] This leads me to wonder: How threatening was it to a clerical hierarchy for people to discover they were innocent of sin and had access to the divine without clerical intermediaries? Did the so-called pagan "witches" rely on these same manifestation beliefs and techniques?

---

1. Ean Begg, *The Cult of the Black Virgin* (Herndon, VA: Lindisfarne Books, 2006), p. 73.
2. Jean-Yves LeLoup, *The Gospel of Mary Magdalene* (Rochester, VT: Inner Traditions, 2002), p. 25

Did their healings support the idea that our bodies are meant to be balanced and that the tools we need to heal them are available by an understanding of the subtle bodies and application of preventive treatments? Treatments that could clear the "invisible" bodies before disease could penetrate the density of the material organs and the body of flesh? It it any wonder that women have never been given their rightful power within the Roman church?

I thought about the documentary film *The Burning Times* as I walked around the basilica. Joan of Arc was one among thousands who dared to follow the direction of her guides. I feel such pity for that brave teenage girl, whose voices left her when she was imprisoned and who went to the stake wondering if her own loss of faith, her own fear, had silenced them. I spent a good amount of time just looking at the intricate façade of the church, which was a beautiful Romanesque-Gothic frieze of Christ at the Last Supper. The cathedral at Vézelay completely captivated me with its ineffable scent of the Middle Ages and I perceived in the preserved town remnants of that era.

That night, we found a delightful café, where we sat under umbrellas as a light rain fell for the first time since our arrival in France. The young couple who owned the restaurant recommended some wonderful inexpensive wine. All the tables on the patio were filled and we communed jovially with the other parties, as if we were all feasting together within some Bruegel mural.

BRIDGE TO UNDERSTANDING

On our second day in Vézelay, it rained seriously for the first time in two weeks. The cobblestone streets and the outdoor cafés were deluged. I was sitting beneath an umbrella working on a poem when the unexpected afternoon downpour began. I found a lovely little tavern, where I noticed that the entire clientele was heartily devouring a thick porridge. I quickly found a small table and was lucky enough to order the last available bowl of the house specialty, French onion soup. Some of my companions walked in later and joined me at my table, but, to their dismay the soup was gone and they had to order another favorite dish—the popular *croque monsieur*—while I relished the aromatic broth and rich cheese topping.

Later that afternoon, the rain let up in its intensity and the Sun poked through the gray skies, but a light shower continued beneath the sunlight. We had gone our separate ways exploring the shops, and I had just sat down at another outdoor café to do some more writing when I noticed a numinous double rainbow peeking above the stone walls. It was extremely vivid and arched across the village from one end to the other.

I had once read that rainbows were seen as bridges between heaven and Earth, signs of the heavens' divine covenant with those of us here in the world. Furthermore, in many medieval representations of the Last Judgment, Christ is shown enthroned on a rainbow, representing wholeness and indicating "that a process is coming to its end."[3] Finally, there is a connection between rainbows and the Virgin Mary as the one who mediates and reconciles.[4]

This made me feel more intensely than ever that each event of this perfect day was laced with something memorable. Still later, the rainbow found its way into the poem I began at that little café. I wanted the poem to reflect the Magdalen's presence throughout the town, as well as in the church with its feminine mandorlas and bays. It seemed fitting that we had come to sit with her here within a walled city at the beginning of the Aquarian age.

Vézelay

Basilique de Sainte Marie-Madeleine

The stone cannot hold her.
It whispers and quivers
in the waxy-scented motes
of air. Like the tall blonde
candle-flame beneath her,
the wave of our postulant prayers.

She stands with her alabaster
vessel of nard to favor her master
in the ancient anointing
blessing his mission, the wedded
excretions between them,
fusion and fission of all that is—

sacred, profane—all displayed
here in the capital sculptures,
gargoyles and demons crouching

---

3. Gurd Ziegler, *Tarot: Mirror of the Soul* (York Beach, ME: Samuel Weiser, 1988), p. 111.
4. *Herder Symbol Dictionary* (Wilmette, IL: Chiron Publications, 1986), p. 155.

beneath Romanesque steeples,
Gregorian plainsong, tintinabulum
celebrated á *côté les anges,*
their halos and wings . . .

. . . we are one with all of these
things—as we follow Marie Madeleine
throughout France, her mélange
of reverence and sin, we are
toutes Vierges Noirs, daughters
of the interred feminine, cathedral
mandorlas cooking our souls, façades

of the bays like the folds of a woman's
hair. If I mention the lies
of the fathers, I must mention the fears
of ordinary men—must mention
forgiveness, rushing blood

shed in the heart. Both poles are wounded
and human—suspending the tension
like water on fire, the frozen
volcanic rock of the *Haute Loire-*

in this belle *paysage*
where six pilgrim women
this millennium year
stand before her in blue jeans
and sneakers, extolling
the Green Men next to Magi

in the windows, even the sirens
with serpentine tails—
as she looks out at us
one hand on her book,
and one on the skull, witness
for thousands, *les sorcières, les malentendues—*

Despite the shine of the Languedoc sky
in this outdoor café, tiny drops
rain down my page— broken chips
off an unclouded sun,

her rainbow is here—
strong feminine bridge
at the dawn of an aeon.

*

We spent another day shopping in the toney boutiques and then left the
quaint Templar Inn outside of town and the lovely innkeeper, who gave us
some fabulous white wine and other assorted goodies for the next leg of our
trip. The morning we left, we gathered after breakfast at the end of the long
gravel driveway beneath the trees, beside the pink and white petals of impa-
tience and the singing brook, and once again celebrated a small ritual. Deborah passed the chime to each of us to speak of our experience in Vézelay.
The clouds darkened again and we began to feel a light rain on our heads.
We finished our process quickly and dribbled some honey on the rocks near
the brook. Then we swigged from our cobalt bottle and piled into the van
with suitcases still strapped to the roof.

Every day, in my little room in the Moulin des Templiers, during meditation, I had watched my chevalier, in vivid focus and clear deep colors,
riding his horse through his stone underworld. Now I fancied him riding
through the bowels of Solomon's Temple rather than a French castle. One
guess seemed as good as another. I figured my best bet was to live in the
vision without forcing an understanding of it.

Chapter 26

DIJON

We are not yet in peace, for this peace is a process of becoming, a work that we accomplish—or rather that we allow to be accomplished—within us.
JEAN-YVES LELOUP, *THE GOSPEL OF MARY MAGDALENE*

When I remember Dijon, I actually think in mustard colors. In my memory, though I know it is not so, it seems that all the city's buildings are made of yellow stone. It is a far bigger city than some we had seen, but there is a homeyness about it. Or perhaps only I felt it was so special, because it was in Dijon that I really began feeling connections with the Templar knights. I was drawn to the history there quite intensely, my Crusader prancing across my inner eye regularly as I meditated in my luxurious mustard-toned room.

In Dijon, the Magdalens stayed in a fancy hotel and dined there for lunch the first day, paying outrageously for what was, I grant you, excellent *cuisine minceur*. The presentation of the food was, in itself, elegant artwork. The number of Limoges dishes we went through, each sparsely adorned with its decorative display, must have put the staff to work double-time. It's no wonder that the French are not overweight, despite all their cheese and pastry; their portions are miniscule, though there are often many courses. As voracious Americans, we virtually licked the plates.

My mustard-colored room faced the front of the hotel, looking out onto a fairly busy street. I laughed to myself as I hung a few hand-washed items as invisibly as I could on the balcony—a gesture I am sure the management did not approve.

It was in Dijon that I felt *compelled* to meditate more often. My spirits were absolutely hyperactive now, their vibrations fluttering around the edges of my body, and I took that as my order to sit still with my eyes shut. If I skipped a meditation, I paid with an intense headache. My visions were richer in color, but not the ultra-bright colors I had seen in Israel—more like milky, translucent pastels.

And here in Dijon there were two scenes that played repeatedly on my inner screen. First, the 18th-century lovers, those two overdressed aristocrats whom I had seen off and on in the embrace of a kiss for several years now—certainly prior to my having set foot on French soil. But now their scene was more intimate. "Oh no," I said to myself one afternoon, as I realized that they were in their bedroom and heading toward the bed! The furniture was ornate and reminded me of the white French provincial bedroom set I had as a child. I still use it, in fact—although since moving to New England, I refinished the pieces in a fruitwood stain. Still, the likeness was interesting. The wallpaper in the scene was ornate—a velvet-textured fleur-de-lis pattern that was similar to the paper in my parents' bedroom as I was growing up. My third eye panned the room very slowly, as if I were filming it. I watched the two figures in the bed and under the covers, but, to my relief, the view became increasingly fuzzy. "This would be the ultimate," I said to myself, "having my own x-rated French movie!"

I have my own biographical relationship with the fleur-de-lis design. My father's sister, Aunt Mary, was my "Miss Manners" as I was growing up. (She actually taught me to "cultivate" my sneeze.) Once or twice a year, she took me to the ballet with my other female cousins on what was known in the family as "Girl's Day." We always had dinner afterward at Fleur de Lis, a little restaurant a short walk from Lincoln Center. It was there that I first sampled escargot and frogs' legs. One Christmas when I was still in high school, Aunt Mary gave me a lovely 14-karat gold pin of a fleur de lis that has always been special to me. And so I recognized the wallpaper in this vision with a certain nostalgia. It also reminded me of the wallpaper my ex-husband and I inherited in the townhouse we owned years ago. When my baby cried in the middle of the night, I took him into the hall where, along the stairway, the wall was covered in large velvet black-on-white fleur de lis. My tiny son always stopped crying immediately and opened his eyes wide and stared. It was not until I came to Dijon that I learned that the fleur de lis is also an insignia related to the secret society of the Knights Templar. When I checked the history of the flower's significance, I found that, in the Middle Ages, it was associated with "the trinity of mind, body and soul, which come together only in mankind."[1] It also represents majesty and royalty.

---

1. David Fontana, *The Secret Language of Symbols: A Visual Key to Symbols and their Meanings* (San Francisco: Chronicle Books, 1993), p. 71.

The aristocratic couple in my vision, however, was from a completely different period in French history—the time just prior to the Revolution known as the Terror. I speculated that, if this was a past life and I had been an aristocrat, there was a good chance I viewed France for the last time on my walk to the guillotine. Maybe that accounted for my obsession about my neck.

Ever since high school, I have hidden my neck in the winter under scarves and high collars, so much so that I am teased about it by friends. I also suffered from strep throats throughout my adolescence and twenties. Each year, on the feast of Saint Blaise, my mother took us to have our throats blessed, and I continued to go on my own as a young adult. Finally, at twenty-two, I had my tonsils out. Yet my weak throat persisted as my Achilles heel, if that's not too much of a mixed metaphor. It occurred to me in my thirties, after I had had several years of therapy and regular meditation, that my sore-throat syndrome was waning. I rarely have them now, although I still wear scarves and high collars. Recently, I thought that having been beheaded in a past life might also account for my inability to speak up for myself! Sometimes I think I became a writer because I couldn't speak my ideas before a roomful of people without fear. To be counter-phobic, I became a teacher.

Watching this aristocratic couple waltz in their ballroom and kiss in their bedroom, I couldn't help thinking of Marie Antoinette—not that I had actually been there, but rather that I had lived in her time in support of the Ancien Régime. My middle name is also Antoinette, after my paternal grandmother. As a child, I had always been interested in the historic figure, and the infamous quip history attributes to the vain little queen: "Let them eat cake!" I think our lives leave us little hints about our incarnations and I'm not the first to find these synchronicities.

And so it seemed fitting that, in my luxurious bedroom in the hotel in Dijon, I watched this overdressed couple embrace and then disappear beneath the bed sheets and fade from view. Today, I think perhaps the image was there to foreshadow a new lover—one I encountered several years later with the same movie playing on my inner screen—perhaps the same soul of that other partnered life.

THE CHEVALIER AND THE OWL

The other scene I encountered regularly in Dijon was the one of my chevalier. Always the same high stone wall, a recessed part of a castle, or a dungeon, a very long narrow hallway of stone. And then, far back in the distance, a pearly light would spin closer, eventually taking the chevalier's form as he galloped full throttle on his steed. When he passed by, I'd try to follow him, but the pressure always made my head feel as if it would explode if I tried to keep focus. And the picture always would eclipse anyway as he rode out of view. There was no way I could catch his eye. I even willed him to see me or speak through my mind somehow. But I got no response.

Meanwhile, my private company of spirits was zapping me steadily with short puffs of wind-whooshing sounds in my ears and around my head. I felt as if the top of my head was covered in a viscous fluid, which then would harden, making me feel as if I was wearing a buzzing electric helmet. "Fine," I said to myself, "maybe I am or was some kind of a knight, probably a Crusader." But I don't understand, as few have, what these Templars were after before they were all executed. If these are past lives, I thought, I've certainly had some doozies. More like violent past-deaths.

Mary Alice Heyden, my astrologer when I lived in Maine, told me many years ago that I'd undergone many suffering lives. This derived in part, she said, from my Mars, Pluto, Saturn placements in the 8th house, the house of death and transformation. For no reason, when she said this, I thought about burning at the stake. When a Hawaiian healer I met at Jean Houston's Mystery School did a powerful session with me in which I associated to an execution, I had to work through my feelings, which were very angry—much to my surprise, more angry than fearful. With all apologies to my feminist self, I wondered if an angry reaction might be more natural for a man.

I always assumed that, if I'd been executed at the stake, most likely it had been as a female, a 16th-century "witch" (or healer). But now I speculated that, as a warrior monk, I may have been a defiant man. It was apparent to me that I'd had several lives in different epochs of history. Still another psychic body worker who helped in a session for grounding energy also spontaneously came up with an image of burning. He corroborated what David had said about my throat chakra being closed, as if I had been condemned for speaking. Now here I was discovering this inner Templar figure and learning that the last of the Templars, though male, though clergy, were condemned to die at the stake, losing their lives to smoke and fire. As for the aristocrats, their heads were rolling.

I found a very interesting bookstore just behind the famous church in Dijon. The entire shop seemed to be geared to the history of the strange Templar cult. Touristy, yes. Pink and green mustard jars of all sizes and shapes, Crusader figurines, Templar crosses, fleur-de-lis pendants, insignias on tapestry, Templar bling-bling galore. And this was years before Dan Brown's novel appeared. There were many different-sized Crusader knights, covered with their medieval mail armor or the typical white poncho emblazoned with the red Templar cross. And the books—histories of the Merovingian kings, histories of the Crusades, as well as studies of the occult roots of the Templars. It was there that I found Louis Charpentier's powerful book on the secrets of Chartres' cathedral, and where I first saw the book of instructions to open the third eye that I later ordered in English.

Browsing for a few hours, I read the theories about an ossuary containing Jesus' remains being buried in France on a mountain close to Rennes le Chateau. The French are familiar with the different heretical legends—that some of Jesus' followers came to France and that the crucifixion was a hoax. One such story told that Jesus came to Gaul with Mary Magdalen and t! the Templars, during the Crusades, stole his bones from the Holy Land and brought them to the Languedoc. These theories are practically clichés. Tales abound of codes found in sacred numbers and certain geometric plans worked into ancient parchments and esoteric maps. Naturally, these legends only raise the disdain of traditional Christians. By and large, however, it is the cult of Mary, not Jesus, that dominates the region. Yet one has to wonder about the origins of these stories. No proof, of course, but Alice's comment, "curiouser and curiouser . . ." comes to mind.

In this same crowded shop, I found a good number of owls for sale. The owl is significant because, on the left-hand outside wall of the Cathedrale de Bon Espoir, home of the Black Madonna of Bon Espoir (Our Lady of Good Hope), there is an owl figurine protruding from one of the stones. If you extend your arm overhead, the owl fits neatly into your palm. It is part of the tradition of Bon Espoir to make a wish on it. We watched one evening as local passersby reached up and cupped it for a moment, and then hurried on their way. I was particularly attracted to the owl. And how strange to find this completely pagan image built into one of the church walls.

In ancient Greece, the owl was auspicious, though in other cultures it is a harbinger of death. The stone owl at Bon Espoir was worn smooth and discolored from so many hands reaching up to it. Owls, as agents of evil—most likely those associated with the eventual denigration of women healers or "witches"—are also linked with many Roman and Greek goddesses. There is an old Christian legend that a rebellious child, one of three sisters, was punished by being transformed into a nocturnal bird deprived of the Sun—another patriarchal symbol. According to Barbara Walker, a slain owl's heart laid upon the breast of a sleeping woman would result in the woman's secrets being revealed through a "heart-to-heart" talk.[2] The genesis of the phrase "heart-to-heart" so delighted me that I found a lovely little brass replica of the cathedral owl in the store and purchased it as a souvenir.

When I think of the wisdom of Athena, and the connection between owls and oracles, I feel great affection for my owl. It was my idea that our ritual on leaving Dijon should take place at the foot of the owl, where we left the huge lavender bouquet from the restaurant owner in the Auvergne. The lavender had begun to come apart all over our van and we were saturated with the pungent aroma. Before we left Dijon, I also caught on film a particularly amusing image—a seriously tattooed and pierced young man with spiky pink-and-blue hair, dressed all in leather, his eyes closed in reverence, his hand over the owl.

ASCENSION AND ILLUSION

One of the most interesting museums we visited on our trip was the Archeological Museum in Dijon, which exhibited a beautiful statue of the Gallo-Roman goddess Sequana. She was unearthed in 1963, along with 300 *ex-votos* offerings for her healing miracles. Deborah Rose remarked that, in Montserrat the previous summer, she had seen many life-sized plastic arms and feet and hands, ex-votos offerings behind the altar to the Black Virgin. Though Sequanna is not a Black Virgin per se, she is related to them, in that she is a pagan image found near healing waters. Moreover, she is standing in a boat, like the images of Mary Magdalen. Sequanna ruled the Seine, whose source is not far from Dijon. The placard in front of her states that Sequana was the name of the original waters of the Seine and became the name of a feminine deity. By the sixth century, however, the name became masculine and Sequana was recognized only for her fidelity to a sacred husband—obviously an effect of the growing patriarchal power of the church. I was especially struck by the words that appear beneath the statue, as if spoken by the goddess herself: My rough translation from the French follows:

> When you see the first swallow [of spring], immediately keep still [as in quiet], run to a fountain or a well and wash your eyes, asking God that the swallows this year bring our eyes, no tears, no sadness.

Next to the bronze statue was an ex-votos left as a mask of the eyes. The swallow—a symbol of hope, spring, and resurrection in the Christian tradition—

---

2. Barbara Walker, *The Woman's Encyclopedia of Myths and Secrets* (New York: Harper and Row, 1983), p. 755.

was also an ancient companion of the Great Mother and sacred to Isis. Here, we can plainly see the ambiguity of Sequana's powers in a time when pagan goddess worship, though still powerful, was waning under the heavy-handed influence of the Christian fathers. Constantine converted in 306 A.D., quickly crushing all other forms of worship in the Roman Empire as heretical.

I was so taken with Sequana and her voice that I later wrote a poem, a kind of mourning tribute to the lost feminine, whose absence we feel profoundly in the modern world.

Bronze Goddess Speaks

Sequana, Gallo-Romain

There is too much woundedness out the window and inside the TV
where guards secure this blank room. Too much
pain trickling from the faucet in the toilette where water
will be the next thing these poor humans horde. I can
see from my boat they are a sad lot, and sinking. In 5000
years, life after life, no one has learned a thing about love.
    It is a fine ideal

for me to sit in the archeological museum in Dijon,
the stillness sanctioned by the embalmed air.
And I am here to overhear prayers and inspire new histories.
But even as legions pass, their thoughts flare in my hooded eyes
like 20th century weapons. Their tears deliver so much salt
each morning, birds convulse in the summer heat while insects

evolve new powers. Men scarcely stop to look me over,
though their hunger resonates like song lines through rocks
and soil. One young woman craves love, another success.
A dreadful girl begs for peace so quietly she doesn't hear
the scream in her voice, while all the Mother's estranged
daughters request the courage to bear the world.

Because I am ancient, most show respect, yet some
would sell me on the black market. Still others believe
prayer can help and those help themselves by believing.

Whether I listen, or not—is beside the point. Belief
is the point, though I am no longer what they believe in
and so tired of soaking up wishes like oils from Roman baths.

Dug up from earth, once I was charged terra but lost all strength
when wrenched from my pagan well, one of hundreds
beneath the Gothic Cathedrals. What I know continues
unchanged but changes nothing. If only they knew
the power of earth, how free they are
to love it—they might stop punishing themselves.

The Mother Goddess asks that we learn to produce only that which we need
in the moment. We need not anticipate or fear scarcity, which can lead to the
senseless oppression of others. We must trust that the Earth is here to sustain us. Tribes like the aboriginal Bushmen or the Montenards of Vietnam
model this lifestyle beautifully. Civilization and urban life have separated us
from this core belief that we can have what we need. When we work in balance with the universal Tao, what we need flows to us.

We spent a few free days in Dijon and I found myself walking around
lost in thought, sitting for hours at cafés, scribbling notes, going back to
the museum several times, amazed at the amount of ex-votos that had been
found. Obviously, these offerings had been created in tremendous gratitude
for the healing waters of the wells that lay along the ley lines.

Just down the street from the Cathedral with the owl there was a bras-
serie where I sat one day, my face in the Sun, my eyes closed, watching my
Templar knight on the inner screen of my eyelids. I felt lighter, believing that
perhaps my soul had traipsed through history, making mistakes no doubt,
but occasionally at least, living some of my lives imbued with the curiosity
to know what was behind the material world. It seems I have come into my
present life with that same question. I couldn't help but be struck by the
strange coincidence of my Chevalier appearing in my third eye just as we
entered Templar territory, and that his significance connected to the Black
Madonnas as well as to the early legends of the Holy Grail.

I read about the final Inquisition and the last Templar execution at the
stake on the Ile de la Cité in Paris. Jacques de Molay, the last Templar Grand
Master, was one of the casualties of this day. I was especially touched when
I learned that a handful of monks, in the dark of night, swam to the island
and carried back the bones of the dead in their mouths.

In his book on the mysteries of Chartres, Charpentier links the Templars to the Gnostics of Alexandria. There are correspondences between the Gnostics and the Essene cults as well. I contemplated connections between the Essenes of Israel and the Templars of France with amazement. Both places had triggered different visions for me. Different journeys, different countries, different times—separated by ten centuries or more—and yet each cult bore allegiance to a similar mystic philosophy. If the Templars had worshipped the Black Virgin and seeded her image throughout Europe under the wells and in the crypts of the cathedrals, perhaps my interest in the Black Madonnas and Mary Magdalen was all of a piece.

Knowing whether I have had actual past lives as an Essene or as a warrior monk seems secondary to the poignant experiences I had in Qumran and in the Languedoc region of France. If our new era indeed marks the beginning of an evolutionary leap for the species, perhaps I am being led, by whatever forces, to be bodily "zapped" by the vibrations or visions of a former existence. I am seeking this thing called "ascension," although I am still struggling with illusion. In any event, I was very definitely drawn to these periods in history, and something like a pure faith continues to well up in me and fill me with a sense of overflowing when I meditate. While my experiences intensify and I am raised mysteriously to some new level of trust, I sometimes feel like the bucket in a Rumi poem, at the bottom of a deep well, precariously hand-cranked turn by turn, brimming with new waters.

Chapter 27

PARIS AND CHARTRES

In Europe, places of Christian pilgrimage are nearly always sites that had been sacred to the Great Goddess before the advent of Christianity.

JEAN BOLEN, *CROSSING TO AVALON*

Joanie and Elaine left from Dijon for home, while the remaining four of us went on to Paris for the last week of the trip. We waved them off on the train and continued on our way to find more threads of the Magdalen mystery. We laughed as we sat on the Métro and passed the stations for La Madelaine and Saint Lazar. How many years ago had they been christened with those names—and *why?*

Of course, we visited the Grande Madelaine, the Cluny Museum, the Louvre, and the galleries at the Musée D'Orsay, where I rounded a corner into the Symbolism room and was taken aback to see in front of me the huge mural *Lamentation of Orpheus* by Alexandre Seon. A reproduction of this massive mural graces the cover of my anthology of poems on Greek myth. I have compassion for this Orpheus, the grieving father of poetry, and I wished I could begin to feel worthy of my own gifts and not, like Orpheus, be forever conditioned to sorrow.

I made several visits to Notre Dame on the Ile de la Cité and found much of the massive building eclipsed by scaffolding, as it was under renovation. The scaffolding itself struck me as ironic, as I wondered where the piles of straw and stakes had been erected to burn the last of the Templars. Could I be walking on the actual soil of my own execution?

I had time in Paris to synthesize my experiences with the Madonnas and put my own story together in light of the third-eye revelations. The lovely old church, Saint Germain des Près, was not a long walk from our hotel on the Left Bank, and I couldn't seem to kick the habit of lighting candles and talking with the Madonnas—black or white. I was drawn to this church over

away the layers of illusion, the many wrong roads we've taken as lightspirits into the illusion of dense flesh, the way out of the matrix we've been caught in. As Osho says,

> Man has been distorted. Man cannot be reduced to slavery if he is not distorted first. The politician and the priest have been in a deep conspiracy down the ages. They have been reducing humanity to a crowd of slaves.[1]

In all these meanings, the labyrinth was relevant to our own pilgrimage. We were breaking out of the mold that shaped our beliefs as young girls. And it is increasingly relevant to our present time for all of humanity.

Jean Houston, a world leader in the consciousness movement, has taken the labyrinth as her logo. I attended her mystery school the year before. On the first night of the first of nine weekend sessions, Jean laid out the rug she had made to order in the exact dimensions of the Chartres' labyrinth. Under low light, with candles, each of the approximately 200 participants took part in the ritual, selecting a guide for the year and sealing this association by walking the labyrinth. Jean announced our names and the name of our guides as we entered. I selected Hermes, Zeus' messenger, the god of writing. It was the year that my anthology of poetry on Greek mythology was published and I felt close to the Greek tradition. It was a beautiful, solemn, but heartfelt ceremony over which Jean, a lovely woman who has been at the forefront of the Human Potential Movement since the Sixties, presided as high priestess.

Now I was here in the famous cathedral walking the actual labyrinth. I tried to enter it in a quiet meditation as children squealed and hop-scotched around the periphery. When I reached the center, I paused for a few minutes to absorb the feeling of this celebrated cathedral. As I ritually grounded my preferences for my own unorthodox spirituality on the mosaic stones, I felt the essence of the entire journey was complete.

Jungian analyst Jean Bolen, in her book *Crossing to Avalon*, notes that the path of Chartres' labyrinth is 666 feet long and that this number is the sacred number of the Greek Goddess of love, Aphrodite.

> Typically the Great Goddess had a myriad of names . . . only instead of being called Isis, Tara, Demeter, or Artemis, her name is Mary.[2]

---

1. Osho. Courage, The Joy of Living Dangerously; Insights for a New Way of Living. (New York: St. Martin's Griffin, 1999). p, 89
2. Jean Bolen, *Crossing to Avalon* (San Francisco: HarperCollins, 1994), p. 25.

Aphrodite's symbol is the rose. In numerology, six is always the number of human relationships. The rose, of course, is often associated with love and sexuality. It is also significant that the labyrinth (labia?), when seen from above, appears as a feminine spiraling of petals. Now consider that 666 becomes a demonic symbol in later Christian theology. There are three rose windows of stained glass in Chartres. Thus the original pagan symbol, the labyrinth, is assimilated, but diminished in meaning—split into dark and light, the rejected feminine body pulled into the Satanic.

The location of the cathedral is also important. Like most Gothic churches, it is built above a goddess site. Bolen acknowledges the roots of the goddesses in Chartres, built above the pagan wells. According to Bolen, who was also influenced by Charpentier's book, the cathedral is erected over a Druid holy place and a well.

> Here, carved in the hollowed-out trunk of a pear tree, once existed
> a statue of a dark woman or a goddess with an infant on her knees,
> believed to have been made by Druids before the birth of Christ.[3]

Oddly enough, a few years later, when I was meeting with my regular Monday-morning free writing group—a salon-like activity in the Brookline home of the poet Barbara Helfgott-Hyett—the labyrinth found its way into my consciousness. This was after September 11th, and, as I wrote, something pulled into my poem memories of Igmar Bergman's greatest film, *The Seven Seals*. In the movie, a knight plays chess with the Grim Reaper as the plague sweeps through a medieval village. I did not know I was writing about 9/11 until I reached the last line of the poem, which speaks of the dance of life that includes the choreography of death. I wonder what other remnants of collective memory moved my words into the poem, whose title came later, when I discovered what I had written. The poem encourages that we continue to face life with a sense of molding it along with all the unfathomable larger issues that are in play, though hidden from us. There is no getting away from it. Once here, we must do our dance, however tragic it may appear.

---

3. Bolen, *Crossing to Avalon*, p. 29.

Down to Zero

We have no choice but to dance.

They dance in Pompeii, dance as the lava melts
the hill towns, rides roughshod over the homes.
Workers in markets, in gardens,

knot hands and dance into valleys
labor up knolls, as in the last scene
of *Seven Seals*. And lava
seals. And burnt steel seals

like candle wax; it erupts
and molds into edges, petrifying
the people. Still, they dance

through the labyrinth, serpentine
runny-rainbow, they dance
down to zero, their steps out of synch.

Some throw back their heads,
shut their eyes, leap and sing
in their dancing, hope to catch ledges
in clouds or in trees.

Those far from the doors
dance through tall ceilings,
down stairwells' black holes,

spiraled from towers,
they hold hands
and jump.

This grand cathedral, populated with thousands of figures—from those in
the stained glass to the sculptures on all surfaces—houses one of the most
renown Black Madonnas. And down in the crypt, another more primitive
Black Virgin quietly reigns. Louis Charpentier speaks of the mysteries of

Chartres as being in keeping with all its Templar connections. He claims that the sacred geometry within helps raise the consciousness of those who quiet their minds and rest on the ground built over the spiritually energetic ley lines. Charpentier says that the plan behind Chartres, and indeed behind many of the Gothic churches built during the influential times of the Templars, connects pilgrims and worshippers to occult truths about the true nature of humanity.

The light coming in from the stained glass windows moves in different arcs according to the geometry of the architecture. As the sun moves, the colored glass creates a rainbow of auras that affect the energy bodies of the parishioners. Charpentier even speculates that the original Arc of the Covenant may have been stolen and buried at one time somewhere under the foundation of Chartres! Was it for this reason that the Templars had inhabited Solomon's Temple? Phillip the Fair was convinced that the Templars had plundered riches and hidden treasures from the Holy Land. The wealth of these warrior monks led them to become the first bankers. They set up a financial infrastructure throughout Gaul by engaging whole generations of families in the work of cathedral-building. Perhaps that alone was their mission. Who knows what vibrations these caverns of sacred geometry have emitted for 700 years over the worshipping crowds? Charpentier speaks of the master craftsman behind this cathedral and speculates about his intentions:

> He was trying (and he succeeded) to construct an instrument of religious action, direct action, having in itself power over men; a power to transform and to transmute.[4]

I sat in various corners of the great cathedral where the light streamed in from the glass. I meditated on universal unconditional love, and prayed that my own tendency toward depression might be relieved. I prayed that my sense of exile and hopelessness might be lifted as I watched the way the world was progressing—always riding the power seesaw of oppression and fear. I thought about my Templar knight and how he showed me, at least symbolically, how to lead a life dedicated to hidden truths, a life sacrificed for secret commerce with the divine. I was comfortable sitting in the light of a place built for that express purpose, knowing that the time was drawing nigh for greater consciousness.

---

4. Louis Charpentier, *The Mysteries of Chartres Cathedral* (Haverhill, UK: Research into Lost Knowledge Organization, 1966), p. 167.

ENDINGS

Though we spent a few more days walking through museums, climbing Montmartre, and dining in the Latin Quarter, our trip to Chartres marked the end of our journey through the spiritual world we had entered and explored for three weeks. On the day before we left France, Deborah Rose (dear friend, I still marvel at her very name!) and I sat in a café on Montmartre overlooking the huge picturesque city. We discussed the beautiful, contemplative, and joyful journey we had taken. The sun was dropping ever so slowly and the few clouds in the sky lingered like lavender fingerpaint, rosey-rimmed. Even the surly waiter couldn't dampen our spirits as we ordered our favorite Rhone wine.

Because Paris is so expensive, I shared a room with Joan at the Golden Tulip Cayre Hotel on the left bank. Joan has a Masters in Library Science, but was earning another degree in Feminist Spirituality. She had led several goddess trips to the island of Crete, where she spends her summers with her Greek husband. She impressed me throughout the trip with her lovely and gentle appearance, her store of knowledge, and her unassuming way of sharing it. Dressed in her long skirts and flowing jackets, she lent a dimension of goddess beauty to our group. We had eaten a number of dinners alone together, sharing our personal histories, and I was sorry to say goodbye to her. The rest of us lived in New England and knew we could be in touch easily, but Joan lived in Chicago.

On our final night, I had a very vivid, if simple, dream in which, as I said goodbye to Joan, she stood up and executed a beautiful swan dive into the Earth. The emotional tone and affect of the dream were ecstatic, and I shared it with her for that reason, ignoring any interpretation that her plane home might be in jeopardy. We pondered the dream as we packed. I kept emphasizing the Earth and the goddess power that dwelt there, and the deep wells where the Black Madonnas were buried and found along the sacred meridians. In the dream, Joan is, of course, an aspect of me—perhaps my scholarly aspect, digging deeper for information. Katie, Deborah, and I hugged Joan at the airport as she boarded her plane for Chicago and then headed toward our own flight to Boston.

On the long flight home, I checked to see if my Templar knight was still in touch with me, but when I closed my eyes and focused in on my third eye, I was back in the aristocratic ballrooms and sculpted gardens and he was gone. I was grateful that I had been given more pieces of my mystery and

I vowed to remain more consciously in touch with the powers around me, even as I knew I would inevitably be pulled back into that world that we collectively, and perhaps mistakenly, refer to as "real."

I vowed to stand more firmly in the two worlds, trying to keep balance between my temporal ego and my eternal soul. The trip allowed me to understand myself more deeply than I had through any therapy. My visions were as powerful, but distinctly different from the altered state I entered when I worked actively and imaginatively with dreams.

It's hard to believe that, six years later, Deborah would be gone from this Earth. Shortly after we returned to Boston, she found a lump in her breast. She underwent surgery, radiation, and chemotherapy several times over the next six years before she surrendered to metastasizing cancer. Deborah introduced hundreds of people to the power of the Black Madonnas and I suspect she'd completed her mission and had more to do on the other side. The last time I saw her, she was extremely weak and thin. I picked her up from a chemo treatment and we went to a little restaurant on Mass Ave in Cambridge, not far from the teahouse where we'd met six years ago. It was late December and Christmas was in the air. Her spirits were up despite her very apparent fatigue. I spoke to her several times after that—once in a phone session where we worked her dream of a beautiful gypsy and a dark, threatening lady, no doubt a projection of her cancer.

Deborah went about her passage with great courage. She sought as much healing as she could, both traditional and untraditional. She died with an intimate circle of friends gathered around her bedside two days after she made up her mind not to seek more treatment. Deborah is survived by a sister and her longtime group of close women friends who made the arrangements. I was unable to attend her service, as I was with my mother in Florida, who had had a stroke. Joanie, however, e-mailed me about the memorial:

A pictorial slideshow set to thoughtful music, brought us both back to memories of Deborah and forth to sides of her showing so many facets of her marvelous personality: Deborah the beekeeper; Deborah the healer; Deborah in outrageously hilarious Halloween getups; an artistically-posed Deborah, her flesh bared to the world; Deborah with her black Labrador and Deborah, inwardly reflective by the sea. Those from the audience were invited to share as well and many anecdotes were told—of her teaching brilliance, her humorous spirit, her healing ways, and how in light of our human limitations, she would simply sigh in knowing, sympathetic comfort "O these bodies."

In addition to giving many lectures illustrated by her wonderful photographs, Deborah founded a Web site, (magdalineage.com) made a CD, and took a half dozen trips all over the world, introducing women to the Magdalen's heritage and the secrets of the Black Madonnas long before Mary Magdalen became a "household wife of Christ." In June of 2007, in a reading with a psychic medium, Deborah's spirit came through to Katy, who had traveled with us in France. Katy wrote me about the experience:

> Her initial message was about my sister who had just been diagnosed with breast cancer. Deborah wanted me to know that the greatest gift you can give another is to pray for his or her highest good. When she was sick there were many who understood this, but there were others who prayed only for her recovery which sent her into a confusing pattern for a time. She also wanted me to know that she was grateful for her life, for the opportunities to serve and to reach many people with her work.

It seems an important message for those of us who are confronted with the illnesses of loved ones. We all have contracts we've made before incarnating and these often include exit options. The photo on Deborah's memorial program shows her with her long wild curls, wrapped in a red shawl against blue sky, similar to my images of her that last day in Montmartre when I felt so much a part of her life.

BEGINNINGS

In the previous lives I'd been shown, the timing apparently was not right for spreading the sacred knowledge. Perhaps the Lords of Karma were still owed their due. A multitude of apocryphal writings, however, mark the 21st century as the end of time. Most of us didn't notice much difference as the centuries changed on New Year's Eve 1999, a night that I spent with Jean Houston and her Mystery School at a wonderful dinner and evening of ritual. No. No tidal waves or earthquakes occurred, but time was ending, nonetheless, in another way. It was ceasing to exist *in the way that we have known it*. The consciousness movement has expanded greatly, even since the turn of the millennium. On the winter solstice in the year 2012, when the Mayan calendar ends, there will be celebrations all over the Earth marking a new confidence that we can create a peaceful, abundant, and tolerant world.

All the enlightenment teachings speak of the *now* and favor a life in the moment. It is only in the now that we can manifest the changes we wish for. If you only look at the surface, humanity does not seem to be evolving past war and hatred. Indeed, the first years of the 21st century have created a polarized war of light and dark forces. Still, the number of those who believe in peace is greater than ever before. Anyone over thirty can see that interest in the esoteric arts has been on the rise for the last thirty years. The number of people with psychic experiences has exploded. And, although the media either scorn or ignore the idea (admittedly there are many bogus rumors, and misinformation abounds), if we look hard beneath the great shadows that are now cast across the globe, behind the violence and threats of destruction, the quest for wholeness on this Earth is much more apparent in the world at large.

Chapter 28

HANDJTAND

As God consciousness, we cannot create a learning experience that we do not need, and we cannot create these learning experiences before or after we need them. So where did we not do it right? How could we possibly be not good enough?
VAISHALI, *YOU ARE WHAT YOU LOVE*

As for the French aristocratic scene I continually saw through my third eye even after returning to Boston, a connection developed several months later with a man (I'll call him P) to whom I was strongly drawn. I was giving a poetry reading with two other writers, one of whom was P. This man is a poet and a psychologist, two professions high on my list of interests. As we got to know one another over the next four years, I had this uncanny notion that we'd met before, that he was the other half of the couple in the ballroom, the gardens, the bedroom. And it turned out that he also had an obsession with covering his neck! Later, I told him about my intuitive feeling in an amused tone, suggesting that perhaps we were both guillotined along with hundreds of aristocrats during the French Revolution. The notion may seem silly or just too simplistic, yet I've found that Spirit speaks in many obvious symbols that our rational intellects feel are too precious to be relevant. I became close with this man and, to this day, as far as I know, we both are still obsessive about exposing our necks. Strangely, he has a name that is etymologically associated with the French nobility.

Years before I met P, David had given me this man's initials, which is why I felt certain the relationship was karmic. I felt an uncanny charge in the air from the moment I met him; I could not *not* fall in love with him. But the relationship pulled me off the course I had set at the center of Chartres' labyrinth. Although I thought I could never again suffer the sense of loss I had suffered with C, I was wrong. The neural pathways we dig with our emotional thoughts are deep and we fall into their ditches unless we change our unconscious thoughts. I was unprepared for the emotional explosion that overtook me when I repeated the devastating experience of a faltering relationship. I now take responsibility for the unconscious nudge that began this relationship and for the consequences of my poor choice.

The loss of C so many years ago made me suspicious of men in general. In this new relationship, I chose to doubt rather than trust—and rightfully so, since P was just contemplating leaving his marriage when we first met. Still, C was always honest and forthcoming. My more desperate entanglement with P unleashed a rage of frustration that grew out of control. P was much more evasive and equivocating, and, although he did stress his ambivalence upfront, he was also persistent, implying a genuine interest in long-term commitment. He convinced me in an eight-month Email correspondence, before we were sexually intimate, that we held similar ideals and that we wanted the same kind of relationship. Admittedly, I was ambivalent about relationships. In the recent past, I had accumulated doubts about "available" men over forty. Time after time, in my social circles, I saw that most men don't leave a relationship unless they have another one waiting in the wings. But this man had been married for twenty years, so I felt he must be pretty solid. I was naive. It turned out that he was armed with passive aggressive strategies from his marriage and oddly enough, (I thought because I told him my "story") uneasy about me because I had been single for so long!

Still, we did have great fun together—much humor and laughter—so that, after ten years, I felt youthful and alive again. I was in love. We enjoyed so many dinners and conversations about literature and psychology. We enjoyed the same activities. I was a muse for him and he inspired me, lightened me up.

One summer, we went to a tiny Island in Maine to an inn I remembered from years before—a stately old wooden hotel, like the 1920s hotels built in Atlantic City. When we arrived there, however, it felt more like the Bates Motel from *Psycho*. Athough the view was magnificent, we were the only ones on our floor. Indeed, for midsummer the hotel was practically empty and clearly it had been allowed to become rundown. We discovered it was changing hands soon and the current owner did not want to spend another penny on it. P was accustomed to a higher lifestyle and I was afraid his mood would sour. But we made the most of our weekend there. We read on the beach all day and began laughing at everything—from the little stone he named after the Sun god, Ra, to the hour-long walk to a country store under brilliant sunshine. I got sick on the lobster one night and we stole towels from the rooms across the hall, but we kept laughing. Nothing spectacular or horrible occurred and I loved being with him, even if I didn't always feel secure.

There were times he helped me with my car problems, times he talked me down from anxiety, times he drove out of his way to see me. As long as the conversation didn't have to do with our future, he was available. Moreover, he never judged me as crazy when I spoke about the spirits and my psychic claire-sentience. Actually, I thought he was fully supportive of my spiritual views and even shared some of them.

But he kept a lot of his judgments from me. Here's one of the more enchanted poems I wrote while under his spell.

I Was Looking into Your Eye

The tight skein of skin, the folds, a flake
a freckle, that fiftyish shift in the crows' feet,
expanding bends and dents and shadowed
gutters—then back to the rich copper,
denuded eye, without the frame of its usual lens.
how vulnerable it is, more so than from a distance
when you are handsome and pensive, a bit out of focus.
In the loft of your cheekbone, the mottled sun-
spanked skin, pulled to intersections of pigment
and damage. And your blink, the animal caged
under scope, shrunken pupil, widened iris,
that driven quest up a mountain top or
God—I loved it! That will to keep looking,
to keep looking for—.

In the end, after all our writing and talking, I can't say I know for sure what he thought at any time. And I guess he kept looking too —because, in no time, he found someone new.

PUER AETERNUS

It wasn't until my relationship with P ended that I consciously realized I was always drawn to the same kind of man—the *Puer Aeternus*, as Jung named him. These men are exciting, charming, and flirtatious, often talented and artistic. They are the men about whom so many flattered women think: *When he's met the right woman, he will change.* But these men don't often change, because they don't have to. They are so charming, creative, and clever that they continue to find women who will accept them without knowing who they really are.

I thought that by laying open my past and my intentions, I would not be subject to confusion, but prepared for intimacy. But P was a dance-away lover, a trickster mix of saint and sinner, highly skilled at keeping his options open. As for myself, I allowed too many transgressions against good faith to diminish me over the four-year period, and I was sent back to the root of my father's abandonment once again. It amazed me that, after all my hard work, I had fallen again into the abyss of unconsciousness, seduced by my own vanity. My lover may have kept his cards close to the vest, but I had only my denial to blame. I hadn't been in a relationship for ten years, but I wasn't even aware of my loneliness for intimacy until I met him. Something in me was absolutely certain I had known him before.

He certainly pulled the rug out from under me. He had parties to which I wasn't invited. He asked me to look at a house he wanted to rent with me and, the next day, told me he had not slept all night and felt sick at the thought. As time went on, he hinted that he would need ten years alone. I slowly realized I was a closed compartment in his life. He said his body couldn't metabolize his divorce, but I suspected it was due more to financial fears. He left me the day after my only son's wedding to go to a barbecue his wife was having, because, as he said quite frankly, he hadn't seen the neighbors in a while and his son and friends would be there. I realized that I had opened my life and family to him, but he had kept his life with me secret, even when it wasn't necessary.

And there were also a few outright lies. He dropped little bombs on me as if they were nothing. It all chipped away at me, piece by piece. I was as angry about the casual last-minute way he delivered information as I was about the way he withheld it. I kept thinking he needed time and I put up with these intolerable situations because I truly thought we loved each other. Indeed, I think he loved me as much as he had ever loved any woman—which is to say, incompletely. And I loved him as best I could, until his repeated carelessness wounded my self-esteem so badly that I began hating myself, who I had become with him through my own victimized, reactive behavior.

I do know that his guilt about leaving his long marriage continued for four years after his separation. That, for me, was too long. The guilt seemed to spill onto me. He couldn't move on. I felt tainted. I tried to understand what he was going through, but I know now that I should have waited until he was fully divorced to become involved with him. But then, of course, the whole relationship would never have happened. The fact that he did not divorce until I left him sadly enlightened me further. But to tell me of his love for me right up until the week we parted hurt me more than anything. He was just waiting for my time to run out.

Throughout our years together, I held nothing back. I made it clear that I did not want to have an "affair." I believed, because he was a psychologist, that he wanted to grow, and he told me he wanted more emotional intimacy than he had found in his marriage. But intimacy demands risk, and I was the one taking the risks. I believe now that he saw what a romantic I was and pursued me, knowing full well that he would not make a commitment to me. I was furious and shocked to discover that he consciously took advantage of me. I discovered too late that I did not fit his needs as an ideal partner on several accounts. I was angry at him, angry at myself, and angry that I had to feel anger. And I felt obsessed by it and "possessed" by the terrible toll it took on my self-esteem. I spoke to him a week after I arrived in Florida and when I accused him of manipulating me, his answer was, "Well, you always knew I was married." But he never went back to his wife. And he'd been proclaiming his love and admiration for me for years!

Looking back at the unconscious warning signs evident from day one, I see that I allowed my own emotional destruction. His flirtatious Emails were provocative, but enigmatic. We were both wordsmiths and I enjoyed our playful parley. Even in the first dream I had of him, I should have seen the danger. I dreamt that he entered the foyer of the house I lived in as an adolescent when my father had died. He crossed the threshold into the house. That was the entire dream. For years I had dreamt of that foyer, which was the site of a terrible memory regarding my father. It was an entryway into my unconscious terror.

But I let P step into the foyer, into my cleft heart. Denial is strong and a sense of fate combined with new pheromones is stronger still. I willingly believed his repeated declarations of love for me; I counted on them, even as I suffered from a terrible insecurity due to his mixed messages. He spun me around and around. I broke up with him several times, but he was outwardly so sweet, so essentially a poetic soul—if also an opportunist lost in his choices—and he was always willing to take me back. So I went back to him several times as well.

As an adolescent, I had no choice but to accept my father's erratic and contradictory behavior. It had been my model. But as an adult, in this romantic relationship, I was living a deeply entrenched cliché. Only in retrospect do I realize my pattern of rescuing and being rescued, of persevering in relationships that hurt. Apparently I needed to go this far in the Romantic School of Hard Knocks to understand, finally, that my suffering was my own fault, because I only listened to P's words and never learned from his actions. He professed his love even as he let me down, even as he set up a new relationship.

In one dream, he is breaking everything in my house. In another, I am trapped in a burning parking lot with bleeding bodies and awake crying, "I have to get out!" And synchronicities abounded. On a slippery snowy morning while driving behind him into town from his suburban apartment, I lost control of my car and rear-ended his. The entire hood of my car was dented up and his car got but a scratch. I had already repressed enough anger to have it appear outside me as fate!

On a trip by taxi to the airport after an argumentative telephone call to P, I developed a blinding headache. The taxi lurched this way and that over the bumpy tarmac of a construction zone—part of the endless project of Boston's Big Dig. As I covered my eyes with my hand to soothe the pain in my head, I looked up to see us heading up a side street to the access road, catching the street sign out of the corner of my eye. It read: "Maria's Way." Maria is the name of P's wife. "Ha!" I said sarcastically to my miserable self, "the universe has a warped sense of humor." But that was only half of it. When I looked up a few minutes later, my eyes caught the license plate of the car in front of us, which read: "It's Tuff." How could I miss the message? *Maria's way. It's tuff!* I didn't miss it. I just unconsciously denied it, and denial is a death knell in an imbalanced relationship.

Yet I was the one, this time, who did make the ending final. Although I never issued any ultimatum, I did express it in a poem. After things had gone as badly as they could possibly go, the collection of poems I had written throughout the relationship won the Riverstone Chapbook Competition. The book was published in December 2005, the same month I left Boston. For me, this marked as good a place as any for significant closure. At the center of the book lay this poem:

Final Longitude

There are broken rosaries in my dreams.
We are up to our knees in murky water and the rain
has been poisoned, sallowing our skin with pesticides.
All your life you've been immunized from risk, waiting
for the roof to fall. Listen, the past will always carry its cross

uphill and the future is just a phantom
in an evening dress seen through stained glass.
No doorbell, no mail slot will let her in. The truth is
you have only these small moments fallen in your lap,
swarms of fireflies you've brushed aside without notice.

It is time to take the measure of their wings. We are blessed
with an aria only the two of us can sing—I want us to call
each other's names in the wind that never stops
messing up our hair, our clothes. Let's remember flesh

coming together, what it is that humans do mixing their limbs,
how a man dips into a woman in a room lit by touch, and sunlight
shifts through curtains where the pattern is latticed so even
the shadows on the ceiling climb out of their bodies,
above gravity and time. You can feel the fear again tonight

on the evening news, warning us not to trust the streets,
not to knead the lotion of another's arms
without some notarized adherence to rules. Fine print
is full of bars in the jails we are taught to believe in.
I am weary of elusive words and wary
of a world that doesn't want my miracles.

There is a border to the territory
of you, a final longitude
and I am headed there.

P's reaction to the poem was professionally objective, complimentary, as if it had nothing to do with him. I had to move away geographically to tear myself from this man, who would have continued to call and confuse me. Though I still loved him and loved Boston, I needed a radical change. My teaching jobs were more and more draining, and I felt more and more worthless, as he caused me to realized that my status as an adjunct professor did not provide a sufficiently secure income. That was also one of the grave doubts that he harbored about me. My reactions to his off-and-on cold behavior were full of blame, so perhaps we were equally horrid.

MOVING ON

Meanwhile, my mother, who lived alone in Florida, was developing dementia and I was the only sibling in a position to go and help her. Unfortunately, when we move, we have to take ourselves with us, and it took a great deal of energy to lift my own baggage, even as I stored some of it back in Boston. All my losses came up again: my father, my ex-husband, C, and P. I moved with a heavy heart.

Coming into my mother's life after thirty years of living 1500 miles away brought up all sorts of eerie shadows. In some ways, I found myself back in adolescence, with parental limitations. In some ways, I saw her in her long widowhood as a woman whose resentment had gotten the best of her. "There but for *the grace, the grace, the grace* of the spirits, the angels, the guides, the workshops, the $10,000 of analysis," I thought, "go I." And so the broken heart comes round again, a mirrored reflection, a theme amidst themes. It is something I have had to go through again and again, in order to grow beyond the original loss of my father. To stop my panic and hysteria when treated badly. To stop trying to rescue troubled men who, despite what they provoke, don't really want to be rescued. To know the past is always gone. To choose joy in the present moment in order to manifest a joyful future.

Ironically, I realized my mother's own heart had been broken so many years ago when my father broke down and died suddenly, and that she had never allowed herself time to grieve. Perhaps the dementia is what allowed that grief finally to surface. Several months after my arrival, she suffered a stroke and her condition worsened. Depression and sadness are typical in my mother's aging generation. But the sense of loss she verbalized in an emotional manner that she had never displayed as an adult and as a parent leaves me curious, as well as painfully touched. For eighteen months, I accepted my role as her caretaker with my own open, if broken, heart.

It took me over a year after leaving Boston, but ultimately I forgave P and asked his forgiveness. It was the only way to transcend his power over me. He was in another relationship and refused to discuss what had happened between us. After initial anger and humiliaton that I'd been replaced within a month, I worked hard at forgiving, if not forgetting. Alhough there is still pain, I surrendered to what I think is a karmic debt. I've seen him a few times since—once at a conference and at poetry readings—and we Emailed a few polite, if strained, little pieces of news to one another. But I expressed my initial, unconscious closure on my own in another poem from my Chapbook collection. For me, self-forgiveness is the most difficult business of all

Last Words

> There is no more to be taught.
> No more to be taken
> away. Less is the same
> as loss. A small idea
>
> of the mind in a polarized universe.
> I can be naked in rage or naked in
> knowledge. Though my pajamas
> are torn, I can still sleep.
>
> Despair is a deadly sin
> but not surrender.
> Though you may think
> you're no longer protected,
> you can hold more
> if you open your arms.

Two months before I left Boston, I attended a dream seminar at Harvard Divinity School led my dream mentor, the globe-trotting RB. Each participant had time to present a dream. I had this one on the third night the group met.

I AM AT AN AIRPORT with my carry-on luggage, packed to the maximum capacity, even its expander space, overly stuffed. My back aches from lugging the baggage. There are delays. Then I am sitting in bleachers with my cousins looking down at the airport. Suddenly my cousin Christina does a perfect handstand in the center of the airport. As she does, I meld with her. Now it is me in the handstand and I feel tremendous strength move through the core of my body as I attain perfect balance. Then I am talking with my high school boyfriend, M. He tells me not to worry, he will carry my luggage anywhere I want to go.

I have thought a lot about this dream in recent months. In many ways, it was prescient. In the work on this dream, I noticed that RB's way of working had evolved. Rather than focusing on the two opposing poles of feeling, he layered each emotion, stacking one on top of the other—no matter how many there were—so that all the feelings brought forth a body of energy. When we felt the handstand in comparison to the weight of the luggage and my aching back, the empowering strength gave me a new energy body to remember and hold. I could feel the spirits moving the chi in my body in synch with the quiet, intense work on the dream.

The most physical aspect of the dream is the life-force flooding my core, transmitted through my cousin Christina's hands. On one level, there is the heavy inertia of my rolling suitcase, the overstuffed baggage of my relationships with men that I lugged around behind me. And at the other extreme is the strength in my arms ascending up from the floor. As I merge with Christina, I feel the flow of that power wave up through my hands, wrists, arms, and elbows, then further up my stomach and thighs. In the dream, the handstand is easy and effortless, and I feel pride in my body's ability. I have been doing handstands since I was a kid, so the movement and the unconscious access to the image were familiar.

In the movement, I feel the Earth's power, its unconditional love, as if I am tapping an energy source that comes from the land—like that of the ley lines where the crypts that hold the Black Madonnas reside, where wells spring, where the great cathedrals are built. I feel the tensile vibrations lifting through layers of magma, the geological strata. I feel this raised energy literally, and it opposes the downward pull of the first scene with my carry-on bag. Since I am planning a move, the airport setting is significant.

I had traveled a great deal for my teaching job with Lesley University and I believe my unconscious selected an airport as the location of the dream because it was familiar as well as symbolic. I wanted to hold the grid of the handstand's energy points of which RB helped me make conscious, so I would remember them when the journey got rough. I would need to extend that moment to help me when I was inundated with a sense of inadequacy and sorrow—when I discovered later, for instance, that P had replaced me almost immediately with someone else.

As for my high school sweetheart, M, we had been out of touch for a number of years, but had reconnected when he was doing business in Boston around 1999. We had dinner together a few times. I knew he had a fulfilling marriage and a lovely family, and had survived recurring bouts with cancer. In my dream, M is a positive animus figure, willing to carry my baggage anywhere and make it easier for me to move on. My inner M has given me courage and determination and resilience. He has become an inspiration for faith, someone I truly admire and respect. In many areas, this dream is not about leaving Boston, but about healing my mind and body, and about the future strength and happiness I can find in accepting myself. I wrote a poem after my first heartbreak experience and it seemed to apply again:

Sell-Portrait With Phoenix

You see I've come back to you,
she said. And I knew the blue ashes

as roses from my own throat,
to chamber her, inhale those ashes
there, petals, blue smoke.

SOLSTICE

When I first got to Florida, run-down physically and emotionally, I discovered a Neuro-Integrated Action dance class (NIA)—a program that strengthens core muscles. The hours I spent in the class became the most pleasurable part of my week. Gradually, I became stronger and more balanced. My chronically sore back bothered me less and less and I found the endorphic zone in that class, lost in the movements and music. My first new friends came from the class as well. I don't know how I would have healed without it.

On the night of the Full Moon, the winter solstice 2007, I joined two of my NIA dance friends at a drumming ceremony presided over by a Peruviantrained shaman. We came to Spanish River Beach in Boca Raton with candles and rattles. The night was gorgeous and warm, the sky clear, and the moon brightening a path over the water, only occasionally pouring its light through a gauzy cloud. Stars and constellations were visible. Some thirty people sat in a circle as first we saluted the four directions and elements, then sang, then toned. During the toning, I felt the spirits zinging meridians inside my buzzing body. Then, as we were instructed, we went, one at a time, through a ritual of release.

The shaman asked us to think of something we wanted to leave behind in the old year that was passing. I weighed several options in my mind. For the last year, I had had a contract with my siblings to be paid to live with and take care of my mother. Her progressive dementia made it difficult and was, in many ways, depressing and restrictive. Still, there were many moments of humor and love between us. I also had time to finish my book, which compensated somewhat for my sense of inactivity in the world. In the meantime, I had published another Chapbook containing several of my goddess poems. I had given some dream workshops, freelanced book reviews, taught some poetry courses, read and edited part time. But, as usual, none of this was lucrative. Nor did I have a man in my life. I tossd my issues around in my mind: "Do I give up my money complex or my relationship complex?" I 'd taken several workshops in Theta Healing, which uses muscle-testing for unconscious beliefs to help clear the way for healing. Repeatedly, the belief of my own unworthiness was shown to be deeply embedded. I decided I would release my money complex that night at the ceremony, on the eve of Christmas, my birthday, and a new year.

We each approached the first shaman, who lit our candles. Then we blew them out, waving the smoke above our heads into the beautiful night. Then he and his three trainees slammed their medicine bags into our foreheads (or minds), our chests (or hearts), our stomachs (or emotions). Each shaman hollered three corresponding Indian words and blew rose water at us for cleansing. My experience was powerful. I felt almost knocked off my feet, which were dug into the sand hip-distance apart. At the end of the ceremony, we sang again in the native language; we drummed and rattled again. As we strolled away, we remarked to each other that we felt lighter. And I was struck with an urge to turn myself upside down. I told my friends, and athletic Jody dove into a cartwheel. My handstand was awkward, but adequate. The three of us laughed as we crossed the Christmas-lit highway and headed for Jody's car.

The next day, the *very next day*, I received a birthday package from my Rosemont college group of friends, those with whom I've remained close now for forty years. They sent me a pillow embroidered with the message "Celebrate Everything until Further Notice," and a beautifully framed, funny, and touching poem—a clever takeoff on A. A. Milne's "When We Were Six." I loved it and can imagine the fun they had writing it. I can almost identify who wrote each line. As I put the box on the dining room table, I noticed a folded check in the bottom. I quickly peeked at it and saw it was for $600. Of course, my first thought was that it was an outrageous gift! But, although my friends lifestyles are out of my price range, they are generous and love me. I like to think that I am their token New Age scout and moreover, they have always been supportive of my poetry. Although they lead lives a good deal more affluent than mine, I am often included in their generous ventures and I don't believe I am their charity case.

All day, as I went about chores and errands, I thought how wonderful these friends were, how grateful I was. And I made a perfectly beautiful connection to last night's ceremony: *I am worthy.* I can accept this gift. I have learned money is energy; it must flow and we must give to receive. If I have received it, I must be worthy. And to those who have given it to me, more abundance will come. I expressed gratitude to them, to my guides, to the shaman. I thanked the universe and vowed to love myself as I am.

At the end of the day, I went to the ATM to deposit the check. As I was putting in my PIN and the amount of the check, I looked at it again and blinked. I had misread it. The check was for *$6000!* Tears began to fall as I chanted to myself: *I am worthy! I am worthy! I am worthy!*

Epilogue:

REALITY SHOW

Just your change from the known to the unknown, your readiness to move from the known to the unknown, is what matters. It is immensely valuable. And in all kinds of experiences, go on doing that . . . What matters is your choice: your choice to learn, your choice to experience, your choice to go into the dark. Slowly, slowly your courage will start functioning.
OSHO, COURAGE: THE JOY OF LIVING DANGEROUSLY

I was listening to a tape by social activist and astrologer Caroline Casey quoting a lovely verse by Rumi as she spoke of a kind of mass hypnosis that seems to have befallen our country. I expected a reaction of protest on the level of the Sixties when the war began in Iraq. Yet even a huge protest in New York City (over 100,000 people) was largely ignored by the media, which seems more and more compromised. Even as the Earth clamors through her laborious birth pains, it takes more than a group of powerful, wealthy rock stars to change legislation. We appear to be fiddling while our planet burns. It all comes down to deprogramming fear. The Indian poet, Rabindranath Tagore, says it very well in his poem:

Where the Mind Is without Fear

Where the mind is without fear and the head is held high;
Where knowledge is free;
Where the world has not been broken up into fragments by
    narrow domestic walls;
Where words come out from the depth of truth;
Where tireless striving stretches its arms toward perfection;
Where the clear stream of reason has not lost its way into the
    dreary desert sand of dead habit;
Where the mind is led forward by thee into ever-widening
    thought and action—
Into that heaven of freedom, My Father, let my country awake.[1]

---

1. Intrator. Sam & Megan Scribner, eds. *Teaching with Fire; Poetry that Sustains the Courage to Teach.* (San Francisco: Jossey-Bass, 2003), p. 169. © Swapan Majumdar.

Perhaps it is too difficult a concept for the government to grasp, but none of us are victims. It certainly took me long enough to "get it." And the more sensitive we consider ourselves, the more our egos become highly involved. I have often felt victimized and meek, hoping to inherit, not the Earth, but one small piece of security in a crazy world.

The laws of karma have brought the causes and boomeranging effects of our individual and collective actions into our own backyards. Time is shrinking between the imbalances, now that the doors between worlds are more open. We no longer need to wait lifetimes for adjustment. I can accept that aspects of my soul may have made heartless, selfish decisions out of their own fear, and I have more forgiveness for those misled, powerful figures who have made heartless, selfish decisions in our own politics. But when the horrible cycle of aggression and retaliation occurs, too many of us either agree with the wrong actions, or are lulled into tranquilizers and antidepressants, consumerism and the illusions of comfort and resignation, rather than motivating ourselves to rethink what's occurring. All negative energy between countries will attract more fear and anger. Nationalism itself is a huge problem. Our flag-waving pride is divisive. Maybe we need a World flag, a flag for humanity. We must take down the barriers to have a planetary evolution.

I've hypothesized that one aspect of my soul may have chosen, or chooses now, to live in the opulent world of a French aristocrat before and during the madness of that era—perhaps entangled emotionally with some aspect of P's incarnations. During meditation, I vividly see this woman in her layered satins and white wig, a coquette with her lover on a settee in a luxurious castle bedroom. I don't know if I am, in a parallel universe, or was, in a past life, that woman. Or perhaps I was the man seduced by the lady on the stone bench between the high sculpted hedges at Versailles. And I wonder if I am, or was, the knight chained to starve in that medieval dungeon. Another aspect of my monad or "soul group" may choose to play the role of a male initiate drawn to the mysterious cult of the Templar knights. And still another may seek to join the Essene community, withdrawing from the dangerous world dominated by the Roman Empire during its occupation of Israel. I think of these figures as functioning simultaneously in their time and age while I operate in my own dimension. This multiplicity helps explain certain contradictory aspects of my current personality. To speculate that I had an incarnation as a knight who was burned at the stake, or one who helped build a cathedral, or one who smuggled a Black Madonna from the Holy Land to Europe, provides me with more insight into myself, particularly my search for truth. It also demands self-forgiveness and, with that, the forgiveness of others. As I continue to merge and own all sides of myself, I must include the marauding, self-righteous masculine, along with the exiled, sexual, dark feminine who became the deranged hag. She is my inner Black Madonna—the one I began excavating in RB's dream group after my heartbreak with C. I must summon her into power now. She has been buried too long and she is the agent of change, the miracle-maker. As Mary Magdalen, she has undergone a transformation in history:

> Jesus said, "Show me the stone which the builders have rejected. That one is the 'cornerstone.'"[2]

I realize that I can effect only small changes from the position I'm in, but there are thousands more working in alignment with me. There will be no security during the huge transition humanity is undertaking. The more we cling to the old ways, the more we will find ourselves hanging on in fear and tested by circumstances. Vaishali, a powerful New Age teacher I met in Florida, insists that, whatever is disturbing you in your current lifetime, you are here to get over it. On the collective level, the huge movement of fundamentalist religions worldwide is the shadow cast by the light flooding the planet. This is *not* the time to be conservative. The Age of Aquarius is all about the *new*. New and different ideas, new and different ways of relating to each other, new and different ways of setting systems in place or, in the words of a popular phrase, "thinking outside the box." Invention and new technology are inherent in Aquarian thinking. Consensus is preferable to hierarchy, and equality is the first and foremost Aquarian value. Uranus, the planet associated with the sign of Aquarius, was discovered at the time of the American and French revolutions. When life feels bad, change is good. Where there has been no precedent, there can be one choice only—that of faith in true democratic living and compassion for the estranged parts of ourselves—compassion for *everyone*.

Offering unconditional love and forgiveness to ourselves and others is the one thing we, as a species, haven't tried. *It is already done*, our present-day prophets have said of humanity's ascension. In John's healing group, he shouted at us in his raucous voice: "You've already made it!" Still, we have to go through it according to our own illusion of a linear timeline and in the unreliable vehicle of a material body. I want to be there when we reach

---

2. James Robinson, *The Nag Hammadi Library* (San Francisco: HarperCollins 1981), p. 66.

the critical mass and awaken together in understanding—with many of us working at once for everyone's liberation.

I have been told by the oracles that I have lived many lives in desolation. I have been told that, prior to these lives, I was on top, but that I misused my gifts. Power corrupts. We become sensitive by losing it. Perhaps this is what many of us old souls are here to acknowledge now. *We must stop reacting, stop judging.* We must teach others by our example to stop this cycle of victim and victimizer. The Course in Miracles tells us our own judgments of both ourselves and others have created the illusion. As Osho says "God has already judged. It is not something that is going to happen in the future, it has already happened ." [3]

Perhaps when we make our last judgment about ourselves or others, the end can come to a world that reverberates its negativity. No more wars, no more vindication. A poem in my recent collection speaks of this:

Last Judgment

:after Rilke

In togas, in rags, in gowns of falling flesh, disorderly
they kneel, they supplicate, they squat. Gathered in plazas,
on playgrounds, on the commons, not to be distracted
from their prayer, which they have found themselves
like a lake of loons and pines, inside of.
Then angels come, begin their renovation,
magnetic plasma honing throats that speak belief—
dispatching the actual gods of themselves toward wish,
toward trust—those reliquaries deep in the solar plexus,
dousing the fiery fields where fear is eaten whole by risk.
And the only judgment comes when fear looks back
on the world it made, appalled—as wild roses rise
from the parking lots. As if to say *We grow*—
That's what we do. We've been here all along.

---

3. Osho. *Courage, The Joy of Living Dangerously: Insights for a New Way of Living.* New York: St. Martin's Griffin, 1999, p. 116

Justice is mine sayeth the Lord. Not ours. It is time to accept (not approve) those lost in darkness. Time to forgive, acknowledge, and heal the wounded. Killing terrorists is only treating the symptoms. It is time to look deeper at how the world's resources are shared. Time to be grateful for what is ours and time to initiate a dialogue with those disturbing the peace. In an era of fundamentalist revival worldwide, isn't it time to see what the "laws" of religion have created?

In the Gospel of Philip, which is especially philosophical, there is an enigmatic verse that may, in some indirect manner, explain the emphasis put on virginity in Christian fundamentalist misinterpretations.

> Adam came into being from two virgins, from the Spirit and from
> the virgin earth. Christ therefore, was born from a virgin to rectify
> the fall which occurred in the beginning.[4]

Humanity will be rebirthed from its present denigrated body, its own rejected Black Madonna. Sexual expression can no longer be twisted and violent and abused, as it has been in the pornography of a woman-fearing society. And with healing, the guilt of the Fall will dissolve and render shame in the pleasures of the physical body meaningless. Like the Earth, women's bodies are to be honored, respected, celebrated, and protected from violation. Ancient indigenous cultures spoke to the Earth and listened for her response. And she told them how to find sustenance—food upon her surface and water within her.

But the Petrine Church is the one that survived the march of history. Early Christian sects were stamped out and, with them, other practices and truths. It seems logical that this institution, like other literal-minded religious lawmakers, misinterpreted some very basic teachings that are found universally in all the mystical branches of religion. The Roman fathers misunderstood and mythologized the symbolism of Mother Mary's virginity. And Mary Magdalen, the apostle whom Jesus loved more than the others, was written into history as a prostitute.

> "Why do you love her more than all of us?" (say the male disciples)
> The Savior answered . . . "Why do I not love you like her?"[5]

Is it not timely that the Magdalen's message of withholding judgment and transcending her own shadow has waited two centuries to surface at the

---

4. Robinson, *Nag Hammadi Library*, p. 143.
5. Robinson, *Nag Hammadi Library*, p. 138.

very moment that we shift into the Aquarian Age? As the Goddess' followers increase, may all nations and businesses around the globe try a "kinder, gentler" way to share Earth and her resources. May they understand the basic esoteric teaching: *There is enough for everyone.*

> His disciples said to Him, "When will the repose of the dead come about and when will the new world come?" He said to them "What you look forward to has already come, but you do not recognize it."[6]

Paradise is available here and now, although most of us do not see it. Indeed, Adam sleeps. However, the lost feminine way of knowing can awaken him. And we are arriving, on schedule, in the 21st century, as predicted. Humanity is laboring for its own delivery from the pain of a punishing, exclusive, lawmaking Patriarchy.

> A great portent appeared in heaven: a woman clothed by the sun, with the moon under her feet, and on her head a crown of twelve stars. She was pregnant and was crying out in birth pangs in the agony of giving birth. (Revelation 12:1–3)

The Age of Patriarchy and its scientific twin, the rational mind, was an important stage in our evolution, but it has left us unbalanced, living more in fear than trust. With physicists expanding ideas of unified fields and string theory, predictions that science and spirituality will coincide seem highly probable. Mysticism will be demystified, the hidden made visible. "The woman clothed with the Sun" is giving birth. In Saint John's Revelation, he sees a pregnant woman whose newborn child is endangered by a dragon, or the tyranny of the personal ego—the imprisoned mind whose fearful and hateful thoughts have hardened into our three-dimensional world. The coming birth of a new world will herald humanity's freedom from the imagined original sin. That freedom consists of forgiveness, self-forgiveness, self-acceptance, tolerance, and acceptance of others.

The poet W. B. Yeats speaks of another world that is already within this one. The poet Rumi tells us that the world is inside us. Buddha tells us we are more than our minds. Rumi says that, to change our beliefs, we must change our minds. Like Eckhart Tolle, Osho, the Indian Guru, says we must live in the *now*, not in the past or the future: "Time is where it is; it is not passing. Watches and clocks are man's creation to measure the passing time, which is

---

6. Robinson, *Nag Hammadi Library*, p. 51.

not passing at all."[7] And the contemporary best-selling author of *Loving What Is* reminds of our oneness: "Everyone is a mirror image of yourself—your own thinking coming back at you."[8] Magnify this image by families, ethnic groups, and nations and you have the world we live in. But we can only recreate the world in the now. And it is *now* right now.

Meanwhile there is everyday living—a neighbor stealing my parking place, a friend on the phone pushing my buttons, an elderly mother needing my presence and comfort, a half-written poem consoling my personal sorrows. Even in the pit of my self-pitying complaints and my temptation to despair, I can express gratitude each day for the life I have and, by doing so, create the space for something new, for change. Meditation is an emptying, an undoing of habitual thought. How difficult it is to fix one's thinking. And still, such a simple solution: *Change your mind!*

Yet, because of our history, so many have so little faith to persist in that effort. To those who say that this is the way of the world, that war will always be with us, that we cannot escape disaster, crisis, poverty, and death, I can only say: If you believe that, simply choose *not* to believe that. Be discriminating about what you let into your reality. But be sure to find a balance between discrimination and denial. Accept what is here without judgment, but focus your attention on what new and improved reality you can imagine.

And yes, I suppose I'll continue to fantasize about some blissful life in the lavender fields of Provence with my non-abandoning, ever-devoted partner. But how else can he manifest? How can I have such a partner this late in life if I don't believe I can? And on this morning, in the midst of southern Florida's August temperatures, I slide behind the wheel of my ten-year-old car and affirm that the air conditioner, which has been on the fritz, will immediately flow cool through the ducts. That I won't have a hot flash until it kicks in. That I will one day exhibit the strength, calm, and confidence of the two wonderful Jamaican women, Black Madonnas themselves, who have taken over the care of my ninety-two-year-old mother. That the car ahead of me just might, out of random kindness, pay a dollar toward my toll, as I spring for the car behind me. That the traffic on the turnpike will be lighter than usual.

---

7. Osho, *Courage, The Joy of Living,* p. 143.
8. Byron Katie, *Loving What Is: Four Questions that Can Change Your Life* (New York: Harmony Books, 2002), p. 22.

BIBLIOGRAPHY

Addison, Charles Greenstreet. *The History of the Knights Templar, The Temple Church and the Temple.* London: Longman & Company, 1842.

Arrien, Angeles. *Tarot Handbook; Practical Applications of Ancient Visual Symbols.* New York: Jeremy P. Tarcher, 1997.

Bachelard, Gaston. *Water and Dreams: An Essay on the Imagination of Matter.* Dallas: The Dallas Institute Publications, 1983.

Baigent, Michael, Richard Leigh and Henry Lincoln. *The Holy Blood and the Holy Grail.* London: Jonathan Cape, 1982; revised edition London: 1996.

Barber, Malcolm. *The Trial of the Templars.* Cambridge: Cambridge University Press, Cambridge, 1978.

Begg, Ean. *The Cult of the Black Virgin.* Herndon, VT: Lindisfarne Books, 2006.

Begg, Ean and Deike. *In Search of the Holy Grail and the Precious Blood.* London: Thorsons, 1995.

Berman, Morris. *Coming to Our Senses.* New York: Bantam Books 1990.

Birks, Walter and R. A. Gilbert. *The Treasure of Montsegur.* London: Crucible, 1987.

Black, Matthew. *The Scrolls and Christian Origins: Studies in the Jewish Background of the New Testament.* London: Thomas Nelson and Sons, 1961.

Bolen, Jean. *Crossing to Avalon.* San Francisco: Harper Collins, 1994.

Bosnak, Robert. *Tracks in the Wilderness of Dreaming: Exploring Interior Landscape through Practical Dreamwork.* New York: Delacorte Press, 1996.

————. *A Little Course in Dreams.* Boston: Shambhala, 1973.

Braden, Gregg. *The Isaiah Effect: Decoding the Lost Science of Prayer and Prophecy.* New York, Three Rivers Press, 2000.

Charpentier, Louis. *The Mysteries of Chartres Cathedral.* Haverhill, UK: Research into Lost Knowledge Orgnization, 1966.

Churton, Tobias. *The Gnostics.* New York: Barnes and Nobles/Curtis Brown Ltd., 1987.

Cirlot, J. E. *A Dictionary of Symbols, Second Edition.* New York: The Philosophical Library, 1971.

A Course in Miracles. New York: Foundations for Inner Peace, second edition, Viking/Penguin, 1975.

Crossan, John Dominic. *Who Killed Jesus.* New York: HarperCollins, 1995.

————. *Jesus: A Revolutionary Biography.* San Francisco: HarperCollins, 1995.

Cooper. *An Illustrated Encyclopaedia of Traditional Symbols.* London: Thames and Hudson, Ltd., 1978

Cunneen, Sally. *In Search of Mary: The Woman and the Symbol.* New York: Ballantine, 1996.

The Dalai Lama's Book of Transformaton. London: Thorsons, 2000.

DeBoer, Ester. *Mary Magdalene: Beyond the Myth.* Harrisburg, PA: Trinity Press International, 1996.

Deming, Alison. *The Edges of the Civilized World.* New York: Picador, 1998.

DeNicola, Deborah. *Where Divinity Begins.* Cambridge: Alice James Books, 1994.

————. *Inside Light.* Georgetown: Finishing Line Press. 2007.

————. *The Harmony of the Next.* Carefree, AZ: Riverstone Press, 2005

Dodd, C. H. *The Interpretation of the Fourth Gospel.* Cambridge: Cambridge University Press, 1953.

Doresse, Jean. *The Secret Books of the Egyptian Gnostics.* London: Hollis and Carter, 1960.

Findel, J. G. *The History of Freemasonry from its Origins Down to the Present Day.* London: George Kenning, 1869.

Fontana, David. *The Secret Language of Symbols: A Visual Key to Symbols and Their Meanings.* San Francisco: Chronicle Books, 1993.

Fox, Matthew & Rupert Sheldrake. *The Physics of Angels: Where Science and Spirit Meet.* San Francisco: HarperCollins, 1996.

Gamalinda, Eric. *Zero Gravity.* Farmington, ME: Alice James Books, 1998.

Goodchild, Veronica. *Eros and Chaos: The Sacred Mysteries and Dark Shadows of Love.* York Beach, ME: Nicolas-Hays, 2001.

Graves, Robert. *Mammon and the Black Goddess.* Garden City: Doubleday and Company, 1965.

Greer, Mary K. *Women of the Golden Dawn: Rebels and Priestesses.* Rochester, VT: Park Street Press, 1995.

Grof, Stanislav. *The Cosmic Game: Explorations of the Frontiers of Human Consciousness.* Albany: State University of New York Press, 1998.

Haich, Elisabeth. *Initiation.* New York: Seed Center, 1974.

Harvey, Andrew. *Son of Man: The Mystical Path to Christ.* New York: Tarcher/Putnam, 1998.

Harvey, Andrew and Mark Matousek. *Dialogues with a Modern Mystic.* Wheaton, IL: Quest, 1994.

Harvey, Andrew. *The Way of Passion: A Celebration of Rumi.* New York: Tarcher/Putnam, 1994.

Haskins, Susan. *Mary Magdalen.* London: HarperCollins, 1993

Helminsky, Kabir. *An Anthology of Translations of Mevlana Jalaluddin Rumi.* Boston: Shambhala Books, 1998

The Herder Symbol Dictionary. Wilmette, IL: Chiron Publications, 1986.

Hillman, James "Athene, Ananke, and Abnormal Psychology," in *Mythic Figures,* Uniform Edition of the Writings of James Hillman, Vol. 6.1 (Putnam, Conn.: Spring Publications, 2007), pp. 52–53

Kubler-Ross, Elisabeth. *The Wheel of Life.* New York: Touchstone/Simon and Schuster, 1997.

Intrator, Sam & Megan Scribner, eds. *Teaching with Fire: Poetry that Sustains the Courage to Teach.* San Francisco: Jossey-Bass, 2003.

Irwin, Mark. *White City.* Rochester, VT: BOA Editions Ltd., 1999.

Javane, Faith and Dusty Bunker. *Numerology and the Divine Triangle.* Gloucester, MA: Para Research, 1979.

Johnson, H. Thomas, ed. Emily Dickinson, *The Complete Poems.* New York: Little Brown and Company., 1960.

Jung, Carl. *Man and His Symbols.* New York: Dell, 1968.

———. *The Undiscovered Self.* New York: Signet, 1957.

Katie, Byron. *Loving What Is: Four Questions that Can Change Your Life.* New York: Harmony Books, 2002.

King, Karen. *The Gospel of Mary of Magdala: Jesus and the First Woman Apostle.* Santa Rosa, CA: Polebridge Press, 2003.

Ladurie, Le Roy Emmanuel. *Montaillou: The Promised Land of Error.* New York: Vintage, 1979.

LeLoup, Jean-Yves. *The Gospel of Mary Magdalene.* Rochester, VT: Inner Traditions, 2002.

Leach, Maria, ed. *Standard Dictionary of Folklore, Mythology and Legend.* New York: Harper and Row, 1972.

Malvern, Marjorie. *Venus in Sackcloth: The Magdalen's Origins and Metamorphoses.* Carbondale IL: Southern Illinois University Press, 1975.

Mack, Burton L. *The Book of Q and Christian Origins.* Shaftesbury: Element Books, 1994.

Martin, Calvin Luther. *The Way of the Human Being.* New Haven and London: Yale University Press, 1999.

Markale, Jean. *The Great Goddess.* Rochester, VT: Inner Traditions, 1997.

Mascetti, Manuela Dunn. *The Song of Eve: Mythology and Symbols of the Goddess.* London: Aquarium Press, 1994.

Matoon, Mary Ann. *Understanding Dreams.* Dallas: Spring Publications, Inc., 1984.

Meurois-Givaudan, Anne and Daniel. *The Way of the Essenes: Christ's Hidden Life Remembered.* Rochester, VT: Destiny Books, 1993.

Myss, Caroline. *Anatomy of the Spirit: The Seven Stages of Power and Healing.* New York: Three Rivers Press, 1996.

Naydler, Jeremy. *Temple of the Cosmos: The Ancient Egyptian Experience of the Sacred.* Rochester, VT: Inner Traditions, 1996.

O'Murchu, Diarmuid. *Quantum Theology: Spiritual Implications of the New Physics.* New York: The Crossroad Publishing Company, 1997.

Osho. *Courage, The Joy of Living Dangerously: Insights for a New Way of Living.* New York: St. Martin's Griffin, 1999.

Pagels, Elaine. *Beyond Belief: The Secret Gospel of Thomas.* New York: Random House, 2003.

———. *The Gnostic Gospels.* New York: Vintage Books, 1981.

Partner, Peter. *The Murdered Magicians: The Templars and their Myth.* Oxford: Oxford University Press, 1981.

Pickett, Lynn and Clive Prince. *The Templar Revelation: Secret Guardians of the True Identity of Christ.* New York: Simon & Schuster, 1997.

Phipps, William E. *Was Jesus Married?* New York: Harper and Row, 1970.

Pomeroy, Sarah B. *Goddesses, Whores, Wives and Slaves, Women in Classical Antiquity.* New York: Schocken Books, 1975.

Qualls-Corbett, Nancy. *The Sacred Prostitute: Eternal Aspect of the Feminine.* Toronto: Inner City Books, 1975.

Rasha, *Oneness: The Teachings.* San Diego: Jodere Group, 2003.

Robinson, James M. ed. *The Nag Hammadi Library in English.* San Francisco: Harper and Row, 1978.

Ruiz, Don Miguel. *The Four Agreements: A Toltec Wisdom Book.* San Rafael, CA: Amber-Allen Publishing, 1997.

———. *The Mastery of Love.* San Rafael, CA: Amber-Allen Publishing, 1999.

Rumi, and Coleman Barks, trans. *Birdsong: Rumi, Fifty-three Short Poems.* Athens, GA: Maypop Publishers 1993.

———. Barks, trans. *The Essential Rumi.* San Francisco: Harper and Row, 1995.

Rumi, John Moyne and Coleman Barks, trans. *Open Secret: Versions of Rumi.* Boston: Shambhala Books, 1984.

———. Moyne & Barks, trans. *Unseen Rain: Quatrains of Rumi.* Boston: Shambhala Books, 1986.

Russell, Peter. *Waking Up in Time: Finding Inner Peace in Times of Accelerating Change.* Novato, CA: Origin Press, 1992.

Sagan, Samuel. *Awakening the Third Eye.* Sydney: Clairvision, 1997.

Schoenfield, Hugh J. *The Essene Odyssey.* Shaftesbury, UK: Element Books, 1984.

Sheldrake, Rupert. *A New Science of Life.* Rochester: Inner Traditions, 1981.

———. *The Presence of the Past.* Rochester, VT: Park Street Press, 1995

Shelley, Percy Bysshe. *The Complete Poems.* New York: Modern Library 1994.

Singer, Michael A. *The Untethered Soul: The Journey Beyond Yourself.* Oakland, CA: New Harbinger and Noetic Books, 2007.

Starbird, Margaret. *The Woman with the Alabaster Jar.* Santa Fe: Bear & Company, 1993.

———. *The Goddess in the Gospels: Reclaiming the Sacred Feminine.* Rochester, VT: Inner Traditions, 1998.

———. *Magdalene's Lost Legacy: Symbolic Numbers and the Sacred Union in Christianity.* Rochester, VT: Bear & Company, 2003.

Stone, Merlin. *When God Was a Woman.* New York: Harcourt Brace and Company, 1976.

"String's the Thing." *Nova.* Host, Brian Greene. National Public Television, 9 March 2004.

Tolle, Eckhardt. *The Power of Now.* Novato, CA: New World Library, 1999.

Torjeson, Karen Jo. *When Women Were Priests.* San Francisco: HarperCollins, 1993.

Vaishali. *You Are What You Love.* Naples. FL: Purple Haze Press, 2006.

Walker, Barbara G. *The Woman's Encyclopedia of Myths and Secrets.* New York: Harper and Row, 1983.

Warner, Marina. *Alone of All Her Sex: The Myth and Cult of the Virgin Mary.* New York: Vintage Books, 1976.

Walsch, Neale Donald. *Conversations with God: An Uncommon Dialog.* New York: G. P. Putnam's Sons, 1996.

————. *The New Revelations: A Conversation with God.* New York: Atria Books, 2002.

Wasserman, James. *The Templars and the Assassins: The Militia of Heaven.* Rochester, VT: Inner Traditions, 2001.

West, Morris. *In the Shoes of the Fisherman.* London: Heinemann, 1963.

Ziegler, Gerd. *Tarot: Mirror of the Soul.* York Beach, ME: Samuel Weiser, 1988.

Zukov, Gary. *The Seat of the Soul.* New York: Fireside, 1990.

POETRY BY DEBORAH DeNICOLA

PERMIJJIONJ

Grateful acknowledgment is made to the following publishers and copyright holders for permission to reprint selected poems and excerpts:

Poem #298, "Alone I Cannot Be" by Emily Dickinson, reprinted by permission of the publishers and the Trustees of Amherst College from *The Poems of Emily Dickinson*, Thomas H. Johnson, ed., Cambridge, MA: The Belknap Press of Harvard University Press, © 1951, 1955, 1979, 1983 by the President and Fellows of Harvard College.

"Love's Fire" and "Define and narrow me . . ." from *The Way of Passion: A Celebration of Rumi*, by Andrew Harvey. © 1994 by Andrew Harvey. Used by permission of Jeremy P. Tarcher, an imprint of Penguin Group (USA) Inc.

Excerpt from *Birdsong: Rumi, Fifty-three Short Poems*, translated by Coleman Barks (Athens, GA: Maypop Publishers) © Coleman Barks, 1993. Used by permission of the author.

Excerpt from "The Perfect Thunder, Perfect Mind" from *The Nag Hammadi Library in English, 3rd, Completely Revised Edition*, by James M. Robinson, general ed © 1978, 1988 by E.J. Brill, Leiden, The Netherlands. Reprinted by permission of HarperCollins Publishers.

Excerpts from *Magdalene's Lost Legacy*, by Margaret Starbird © 2003 Inner Traditions/Bear & Co., and *The Goddess in the Gospels*, by Margaret Starbird © 1998 Inner Traditions/Bear & Co., reprinted by permission of the publisher (Rochester, VT 05767). www.BearandCompanyBooks.com

Excerpts from *Open Secret: Versions of Rumi*, by John Moyne and Coleman Barks, ©1984 by John Moyne and Coleman Barks. Reprinted by arrangement with Shambhala Publications Inc., Boston, MA. www.shambhala.com.

Excerpts from *Unseen Rain: Quatrains of Rumi*, translated by John Moyne and Coleman Barks, ©1986 by Coleman Barks. Reprinted by arrangement with Shambhala Publications Inc., Boston, MA. www.shambhala.com.

Excerpt from *The Rumi Collection*, edited by Kabir Helminski, ©1998 by Kabir Helminski. Reprinted by arrangement with Shambhala Publications Inc., Boston, MA. www.shambhala.com.

Poems previously published by Deborah DeNicola:

"The Day The World Froze," from the journal *Cadence*.

"The Day of His Passing," from the journal *Prairie Schooner* (University of Nebraska Press, Lincoln, NE).

"Death's Dreams: In The Beginning," "Death's Dreams: The Clearing, and "After," from the journal *Salamander* (Suffolk University, Boston).

"The Future That Brought Her Here" originally published in *Where Divinity Begins*, © Deborah DeNicola (Cambridge, MA: Alice James Books, 1994).

"The Gospel of Mary," "Magdalen," "Transfiguration on Mount Tabor," "The Shadow of the

T H   E R E

Valley," "Bronze Goddess Speaks," "Last Judgment," and "Down to Zero," originally published
in *Inside Light,* © Deborah DeNicola (Georgetown, KY: Finishing Line Press, 2007).
"I was Looking into Your Eye," "Final Longitude," and "Last Words," originally published in
Harmony of the Next, © Deborah DeNicola (Carefree, AZ: Riverstone: A Press for Poetry,
2005):
Chapter II, "Intersecting Worlds," first appeared online in *Entelechy Journal.*

DATE DUE